CONCEPTUALISING ARBITRARY DETENTION

Power, Punishment and Control

Carla Ferstman

First published in Great Britain in 2024 by

Bristol University Press
University of Bristol
1-9 Old Park Hill
Bristol
BS2 8BB
UK
t: +44 (0)117 374 6645
e: bup-info@bristol.ac.uk

Details of international sales and distribution partners are available at bristoluniversitypress.co.uk

© Carla Ferstman 2024

This publication was supported by the University of Essex's open access fund.

The digital PDF and EPUB versions of this title are available open access and distributed under the terms of the Creative Commons Attribution-NonCommercial-NoDerivatives 4.0 International licence (https://creativecommons.org/licenses/by-nc-nd/4.0/) which permits reproduction and distribution for noncommercial use without further permission provided the original work is attributed.

British Library Cataloguing in Publication Data
A catalogue record for this book is available from the British Library

ISBN 978-1-5292-2249-4 paperback
ISBN 978-1-5292-2250-0 ePub
ISBN 978-1-5292-2251-7 ePdf

The right of Carla Ferstman to be identified as author of this work has been asserted by her in accordance with the Copyright, Designs and Patents Act 1988.

The print version of this title is available under all rights reserved: no part of this publication may be reproduced, stored in a retrieval system, or transmitted in any form or by any means, electronic, mechanical, photocopying, recording, or otherwise without the prior permission of Bristol University Press.

Every reasonable effort has been made to obtain permission to reproduce copyrighted material. If, however, anyone knows of an oversight, please contact the publisher.

The statements and opinions contained within this publication are solely those of the author and not of the University of Bristol or Bristol University Press. The University of Bristol and Bristol University Press disclaim responsibility for any injury to persons or property resulting from any material published in this publication.

Bristol University Press works to counter discrimination on grounds of gender, race, disability, age and sexuality.

Cover design: Andrew Corbett
Front cover image: © Ricky Romain. All rights reserved, DACS 2023.
Bristol University Press uses environmentally responsible print partners.
Printed and bound in Great Britain by CPI Group (UK) Ltd, Croydon, CR0 4YY

Contents

List of Abbreviations		viii
About the Author		xii
Acknowledgements		xiii
Foreword by Priya Gopalan and Matthew Gillett		xvi
1	Introduction	1

PART I Theorising and Conceptualising "Arbitrariness"

2	Notions of the "Arbitrary"	9
3	"Arbitrariness" as an Indication of Harm	51

PART II The Law and Practice of Arbitrary Detention in Context

4	Enforcing Hostility and Social Control	85
5	Deterring Dissent	137
6	The Securitisation of Detention: Exceptional Regimes, Security Frameworks and Counter-Terrorism Measures	173
7	Detention of Dual and Foreign Nationals for Leverage	212
8	Detention and Pandemic Exceptionality	245
9	Conclusions	277
Index		281

Detailed Contents

List of Abbreviations	viii
About the Author	xii
Acknowledgements	xiii
Foreword by Priya Gopalan and Matthew Gillett	xvi

1	**Introduction**	**1**
	1.1 The impetus for the book	1
	1.2 Some of the themes explored in the book	2
	1.3 The trajectory	4

PART I Theorising and Conceptualising "Arbitrariness"

2	**Notions of the "Arbitrary"**	**9**
	2.1 Introduction	9
	2.2 Multiple meanings	10
	2.3 Theorising "arbitrariness"	12
	2.4 "Arbitrariness" in human rights law	17
	2.4.1 "Arbitrariness" and the social conception of rights	19
	2.4.2 "Arbitrary interference" and human rights decision-making	25
	(i) Qualified rights	26
	(ii) Limited rights: the arbitrary deprivation of the right to life	29
	2.4.3 "Arbitrariness" and positive obligations	32
	2.5 The "arbitrariness" in arbitrary detention	34
	2.5.1 The history and meaning of "arbitrary" in arbitrary detention	35
	2.5.2 Arbitrary detention: both qualified and limited	40
	2.5.3 States' positive obligations to ensure that detention is non-arbitrary	42
	2.5.4 Relationship with other rights	44
	2.6 The grey zones of "detention" and their impact on arbitrariness	45
	2.7 Conclusions	49

3		**"Arbitrariness" as an Indication of Harm**	51
	3.1	Introduction	51
	3.2	The harms of arbitrary detention	55
	3.3	Connection to torture and other cruel, inhuman, or degrading treatment or punishment	62
		3.3.1 The torture definition and its component parts	64
		(i) Severity	64
		(ii) For such purposes as	69
		(iii) The involvement of the state	74
		(iv) Does not constitute lawful sanctions	77
		3.3.2 Other forms of cruel, inhuman, or degrading treatment or punishment	78
	3.4	Conclusions	80
PART II		**The Law and Practice of Arbitrary Detention in Context**	
4		**Enforcing Hostility and Social Control**	85
	4.1	Introduction	85
	4.2	Agamben and the theorisation of containment	86
	4.3	Methods of containment	88
		4.3.1 Detention as criminalisation	88
		4.3.2 Detention as pathologisation	93
		4.3.3 Detention as deterrence	95
	4.4	The arbitrary detention of socially excluded and marginalised groups	99
		4.4.1 The "unseen": economic and social "degenerates"	101
		(i) Detention of persons who are homeless	102
		(ii) Detention on mental health grounds	105
		(iii) Detention of people who use drugs	111
		4.4.2 The "reviled and resented": racism, xenophobia, and other discriminatory treatment	113
		(i) Groups discriminated against based on race, ethnicity or religious identity	114
		(ii) Indigenous peoples	119
		(iii) Discrimination based on gender or gendered roles	123
		4.4.3 The "undeserving": refugees and other migrants	126
	4.5	Conclusions	135

5	**Deterring Dissent**		**137**
	5.1 Introduction		137
	5.2 How arbitrary detention is used to deter dissent		141
		5.2.1 Criminalisation	142
		(i) Securitising dissent	142
		(ii) Criminally defamatory speech acts	148
		5.2.2 Pathologising dissent	151
		5.2.3 Isolating dissenters and using other non-traditional forms of detention	154
	5.3 The dissenters		155
		5.3.1 Opposition politicians	155
		5.3.2 Environmental activists	159
		5.3.3 Mass protest movements	163
	5.4 Ulterior or pretextual motives		167
	5.5 Interpol and the cross-border persecution of dissenters		170
	5.6 Conclusions		171
6	**The Securitisation of Detention: Exceptional Regimes, Security Frameworks and Counter-Terrorism Measures**		**173**
	6.1 Introduction		173
	6.2 The power of the exception and the shunning of the everyday		175
		6.2.1 The exigent exception: emergencies, exceptions and derogations	175
		6.2.2 The exception of place: denial of extraterritoriality	179
		6.2.3 The person as exception: "terrorists", "non-combatants" and other rhetorical labels	182
		6.2.4 The exception of law: lawfare and other narrative devices	184
	6.3 Detention during armed conflicts		186
		6.3.1 Detention by multinational forces	189
		6.3.2 "Extraterritorial NIACs", UN Security Council resolutions and the power to detain	197
		6.3.3 Challenges with the transfer of detainees	200
	6.4 National security, counter-terrorism and indefinite detention		203
		6.4.1 Counter-terrorism and forever prisoners	204
		6.4.2 Da'esh and quasi-carceral zones of exclusion	207
	6.5 Conclusions		210

DETAILED CONTENTS

7	**Detention of Dual and Foreign Nationals for Leverage**	212
	7.1 Introduction	212
	7.2 Arbitrary detentions and state-to-state leverage: the practice	215
	7.3 The salience of labels: arbitrary detention, hostage-taking and unlawful coercion	222
	7.3.1 The human rights violation of arbitrary detention	224
	7.3.2 The crime of hostage-taking	226
	(i) 'Any person'	227
	(ii) 'In order to compel'	230
	(iii) Application to dual nationals detained in one of their states of nationality	231
	7.3.3 Violating the principle of non-intervention	233
	7.4 Negotiating release	236
	7.5 Conclusions: the importance of multilateral approaches	241
8	**Detention and Pandemic Exceptionality**	245
	8.1 Introduction	245
	8.2 Human rights, infectious diseases and the positive obligation of non-discrimination	246
	8.3 The proportionality of anti-COVID measures that deprive persons of their liberty	251
	8.4 Quarantines, lockdowns and other pandemic-related restrictions on liberty	254
	8.5 Confinement: positive obligations in a state of hyper-engagement	258
	8.5.1 Reconciling the equivalence of care principle in a pandemic	259
	8.5.2 Anti-COVID measures in detention centres	262
	8.5.3 Access to vaccines and treatment for detainees	265
	8.5.4 COVID-19 and justifications for early release	268
	8.6 Conclusions: the transformative potential of positive obligations	274
9	**Conclusions**	277
Index		281

List of Abbreviations

ACHPR	African Charter on Human and Peoples' Rights (adopted 27 June 1981, entered into force 21 October 1986)
ACHR	American Convention on Human Rights (adopted 22 November 1969, entered into force 18 July 1978)
ACommHPR	African Commission on Human and Peoples' Rights
ACtHPR	African Court on Human and Peoples' Rights
AP1	Additional Protocol 1 to the Geneva Conventions of 12 August 1949, and relating to the Protection of Victims of International Armed Conflicts (adopted 8 June 1977, entered into force 7 December 1978) 1125 UNTS 3
AP2	Additional Protocol 2 to the Geneva Conventions of 12 August 1949, and relating to the Protection of Victims of Non-International Armed Conflicts (adopted 8 June 1977, entered into force 7 December 1978) 1125 UNTS 609
Arab Charter	Arab Charter on Human Rights (adopted 15 September 1994, League of Arab States)
ARS	Articles on the Responsibility of States for Internationally Wrongful Acts, Report of the International Law Commission on the Work of Its 53rd Session (23 April–1 June and 2 July–10 August 2001) UN Doc A/CN.4/SER.A/2001/Add.1
ASEAN Human Rights Declaration	ASEAN Human Rights Declaration (adopted 18 November 2012, Heads of State/Government of ASEAN Member States)
CAT	United Nations Committee against Torture
CERD Committee	United Nations Committee on the Elimination of Racial Discrimination
CESCR	United Nations Committee on Economic, Social and Cultural Rights
CIA	Central Intelligence Agency

LIST OF ABBREVIATIONS

CoE	Council of Europe
Convention of Belem do Para	Inter-American Convention on the Prevention, Punishment and Eradication of Violence against Women (adopted 9 June 1994, entered into force 5 March 1995)
CPRMW	Convention on the Protection of the Rights of All Migrant Workers and Members of Their Families (adopted 18 December 1990, entered into force 1 July 2003)
CRC	Convention on the Rights of the Child (adopted 20 November 1989, entered into force 2 September 1990)
CRPD	Convention on the Rights of Persons with Disabilities (adopted on 13 December 2006, entered into force on 3 May 2008)
CRPD Committee	United Nations Committee on the Rights of Persons with Disabilities
Declaration on Friendly Relations	'Declaration on Principles of International Law, Friendly Relations and Co-Operation among States in Accordance with the Charter of the United Nations', UN Doc A/RES/2625(XXV) (24 October 1970)
DRC	Democratic Republic of the Congo
ECHR	European Convention for the Protection of Human Rights and Fundamental Freedoms (adopted 4 November 1950, entered into force 3 September 1953)
ECOWAS	Economic Community of West African States
ECtHR	European Court of Human Rights
EMRIP	United Nations Expert Mechanism on the Rights of Indigenous Peoples
GC1	Geneva Convention (I) for the Amelioration of the Condition of the Wounded and Sick in Armed Forces in the Field (adopted 12 August 1949, entered into force 21 October 1950) 75 UNTS 31
GC2	Geneva Convention (II) for the Amelioration of the Condition of Wounded, Sick and Shipwrecked Members of Armed Forces at Sea (adopted 12 August 1949, entered into force 21 October 1950) 75 UNTS 85
GC3	Geneva Convention (III) relative to the Treatment of Prisoners of War (adopted 12 August 1949, entered into force 21 October 1950) 75 UNTS 135

GC4	Geneva Convention (IV) relative to the Protection of Civilian Persons in Time of War (adopted 12 August 1949, entered into force 21 October 1950) 75 UNTS 287
Hostages Convention	International Convention against the Taking of Hostages (adopted 19 December 1979, entered into force 3 June 1983) 1316 UNTS 205
HRC	Human Rights Council
HRDDP	Human Rights Due Diligence Policy
HRW	Human Rights Watch
IAC	international armed conflict
IACommHR	Inter-American Commission on Human Rights
IACPPT	Inter-American Convention to Prevent and Punish Torture (adopted 9 December 1985, entered into force 28 February 1987)
IACtHR	Inter-American Court of Human Rights
IASC	Inter-Agency Standing Committee
ICCPR	International Covenant on Civil and Political Rights (adopted 16 December 1966, entered into force 23 March 1976)
ICESCR	International Covenant on Economic, Social and Cultural Rights (adopted 16 December 1966, entered into force 3 January 1976)
ICRC	International Committee of the Red Cross
ICJ	International Court of Justice
ICTY	International Criminal Tribunal for the former Yugoslavia
IHL	international humanitarian law
ISAF	International Security Assistance Force
M23	Mouvement du 23 mars
MINUSMA	United Nations Multidimensional Integrated Stabilization Mission in Mali
MONUSCO	Mission de l'Organisation des Nations Unies pour la stabilisation en République démocratique du Congo [UN Stabilization Mission in the Democratic Republic of the Congo]
NATO	North Atlantic Treaty Organization
NGO	nongovernmental organisation
NIAC	non-international armed conflict
OHCHR	Office of the United Nations High Commissioner for Human Rights
OMCT	Organisation Mondiale Contre la Torture [World Organisation against Torture]

PACE	Parliamentary Assembly of the Council of Europe
PTSD	post-traumatic stress disorder
Refugee Convention	Convention Relating to the Status of Refugees (adopted 28 July 1951, entered into force 22 April 1954)
Rome Statute	Rome Statute of the International Criminal Court) (adopted 17 July 1998, entered into force 7 July 2002) UN Doc A/CONF.183/9
SDF	Syrian Defence Forces
SLAPPs	strategic lawsuits against public participation
SPEHA	Special Envoy for Hostage Affairs
UDHR	Universal Declaration of Human Rights, General Assembly Resolution 217 A (10 December 1948)
UK	United Kingdom
UN	United Nations
UNCAT	United Nations Convention against Torture and Other Cruel, Inhuman or Degrading Treatment or Punishment (adopted 10 December 1984, entered into force 26 June 1987)
UNGA	United Nations General Assembly
UNHCR	United Nations High Commissioner for Refugees
UNMIK	United Nations Interim Administration Mission in Kosovo
UNODC	United Nations Office on Drugs and Crime
UNSC	United Nations Security Council
US	United States of America
VCCR	Vienna Convention on Consular Relations (adopted 24 April 1963, entered into force 19 March 1967)
WGAD	Working Group on Arbitrary Detention
WHO	World Health Organization
YPG	Yekîneyên Parastina Gel [Kurdish People's Protection Units]

About the Author

Carla Ferstman is Professor of Law at Essex Law School, United Kingdom. Her research focuses on the intersections between public international law, human rights law and international criminal law. She is a qualified barrister and solicitor (British Columbia, 1994). She has worked in private practice, and has advised governments, intergovernmental and nongovernmental organisations. Since 2018 she has been a member of the Council of Europe's Expert Council on NGO Law and was a judge on the Aban Tribunal, a People's Tribunal established to investigate atrocities during the November 2019 protests in Iran. She served as Legal Director (2001–2004) then Director (2004–2018) of the nongovernmental human rights organisation REDRESS, and as Executive Legal Advisor (1999–2001) of the Commission for Real Property Claims in Bosnia and Herzegovina. She holds a DPhil (Public International Law) (Oxon); LLM (NYU); LLB (UBC); BA (Philosophy) (Western).

Acknowledgements

I am so grateful to Ricky Romain for allowing me to feature his painting 'One of the Musicians Who Only Play for the Drowning,' on the cover of this book. He has written that the title of this series of his work, 'The Musicians Who Only Play and Sing for the Drowning,' 'is drawn from the pain [he feels] as a visual artist, and musician about the migration of peoples, the loss of life and of dreams which have been sacrificed on route to a sometimes hostile destination.'[1] Ricky's work resonates with me, as it captures so well the sense of isolation and trauma that is a constant feature of human rights violations and, in this series, he contrasts that with the consoling and regenerative power of music.

Thank you to the University of Essex for funding the open access version of this publication. I am also grateful to the European University Institute for awarding me the Fernand Braudel fellowship in 2022, which afforded me a period of respite in Fiesole which was the perfect place to bring together the different strands of my thinking on the book.

Thank you to all the brave individuals I have had the privilege to know and to work with who experienced arbitrary detention or whose loved ones underwent arbitrary detention. It is impossible to mention all, but among those who were and are key inspirations for me (perhaps more than they know) are Keith Carmichael, the founder of the nongovernmental organisation REDRESS and survivor of years of arbitrary detention and brutal torture in Saudi Arabia, with whom I collaborated over many years; Şebnem Korur Fincancı, President of the Turkish Medical Association and a life-long human rights advocate who I have had the honour to work with and who was arbitrarily detained in Turkey on false terrorism-related charges for parts of the time in which this book was written; Richard Ratcliffe, husband of Nazanin Zaghari-Ratcliffe who was arbitrarily detained in the context of state hostage-taking perpetrated by Iran;

---

[1] Ricky Romain, 'The Musicians Who Only Play and Sing for the Drowning' (3 December 2019) <www.rickyromain.com/portfolio/the-musicians-who-only-play-and-sing-for-the-drowning/> accessed 7 July 2023.

Yemsrach (Yemi) Hailemariam, whose then partner Andargachew Tsege was kidnapped, illegally rendered to Ethiopia where he was under sentence of death following an *in absentia* trial; Olivier Acuña Barba, a journalist falsely arrested, arbitrarily detained, tortured and subject to an unfair trial in Mexico; Suny Wilson, a former death row detainee in The Philippines who had been accused and then maintained in detention as a result of a plot of corruption and whose experience of arbitrary detention led him to call himself 'Dead Man Alive'; Bill Sampson, a British/Canadian expatriate who was arbitrarily detained and tortured in Saudi Arabia. My hypothesis that arbitrary detention can amount to torture stems in large part from my glimpsing into the realities of their suffering, still reverberating years, decades and even lifetimes after the respective releases. My interest in detention stems too from my work in the prisons and *cachots* of Rwanda in the aftermath of the 1994 genocide.

I am thankful to my friends, colleagues and former colleagues (over time, all these labels blur) with whom I collaborated, shared ideas and drew inspiration, particularly to Sabina Garahan and Lutz Oette who graciously provided me comments and insights on the full draft of the manuscript and to Julie Hannah, Timo Jütten, Noam Lubell, Steven Malby, Jude Bueno de Mesquita and Marina Sharpe for providing helpful feedback on various parts, and to Frances D'Souza, Alice Edwards, Faten Ghosn, Emily Jones, Kai Yin Low, Shadi Sadr, Elham Saudi, Jürgen Schurr, Christoph Sperfelt and Patricia Palacios Zuloaga for encouraging me in other ways. I am also grateful to Priya Gopalan and Matthew Gillett of the Working Group on Arbitrary Detention, and to the psychologists, traumatologists and clinicians who helped me fathom the unfathomable and shaped my understanding of trauma and the psychological sequelae of torture, and particularly to the indomitable Yael Danieli. Thank you too to four of my doctoral (and former) doctoral students who inspired in different ways parts of this research: particularly Sabina Garahan's study of the European Court of Human Rights' treatment of the right to liberty and the practice of arbitrary detention; Sarah Zarmsky's consideration of the different ways to conceive of harm and, particularly, psychological harm; Ronit Matar's analysis of the law's tendencies to exclude non-hegemonic human legal subjects and the role of boundaries, and Matteo Bassetti's consideration of how the law pathologises marginalised groups. I am also grateful for the feedback from colleagues in response to my presentation of parts of this monograph at the Human Rights Centre at the University of Essex. All errors and omissions are my responsibility alone.

I also want to thank Helen Davis, the Senior Commissioning Editor, Law at Bristol University Press, as well as the editorial team and peer reviewers at Bristol University Press for their faith in this project and their insightful comments.

ACKNOWLEDGEMENTS

Parts of this book were written in my place of freedom, Salt Spring Island, my somewhat retreat that has in recent years served as a kind of respite and a place of quiet. Thanks to Lisa, Melody, Andrew and others I have reconnected with on the West Coast who have made it a joyous homecoming of sorts.

Foreword

*Priya Gopalan and Matthew Gillett,
Chair and Vice-Chair of the UN Working
Group on Arbitrary Detention*

Arbitrary detention is sadly ubiquitous around the world. However, it varies greatly in its form and impact. Because of this variation, practitioners seeking to prevent and redress arbitrary detention have an acute need for scholarly works focused on concepts and principles underlying this scourge. At the same time, human rights specialists appreciate works that match the theoretical analyses with practical contextualisation and specific examples. In Professor Carla Ferstman, readers are fortunate to have a scholarly author who is also steeped in human rights practice. Of particular significance, she has extensive experience on the precise issue of arbitrary detention. Her work lives up to the promise of her illustrious career, with insightful theoretical discussions interspersed with real-world cases and considerations. It promises to be a leading book, which will influence scholarship and practice for years to come.

To establish a conceptual foundation for her work, Professor Ferstman explores the notion of arbitrariness. Drawing on a rich and fascinating tour of past and present commentators, her exegesis of the concept of arbitrary detention spans a broad range of authorities from Dicey to Locke, and authoritative institutions such as the International Court of Justice. This inter-institutional perspective is particularly helpful when addressing the issue of arbitrary detention, as it arises in a wide variety of contexts, from human rights allegations, to international criminal law cases, to inter-state disputes.

Based on her survey of the theoretical underpinnings of arbitrary detention, she notes that it is a malleable concept. She observes that, while this malleability is necessary to a certain extent to avoid states and others operating outside the law and creating zones of exception, the flexibility leads to a greater risk of the arbitrary application of the law, to suit political and factional ends. Such arbitrariness frequently manifests itself in the deprivation of liberty, as a means to effectively remove opposition public figures and to target minority groups that protest against incumbent authorities. The use of legal procedures to detain those who speak against power structures all too often leads to arbitrary detention. Notable detainee, Nelson Mandela, aptly observed in this respect that "I was made, by the law, a criminal, not because of what I had done, but because of what I stood for, because of what I thought, because of my conscience" (spoken in court when Mandela was on trial on charges of incitement and illegally leaving the country, November 1962).

Professor Ferstman's reference to zones of exception and her situating of this within the context of arbitrary detention also recalls Giorgio Agamben's description of how 'the state of exception is neither external nor internal to the juridical order, and the problem of defining it concerns precisely a threshold, or a zone of indifference, where inside and outside do not exclude each other but rather blur with each other'.[1] It is particularly apposite in areas where arbitrary detention is used repeatedly and for groups who are repeatedly subjected to arbitrary detention. Ferstman surveys both – geographic areas of concern and groups with particular vulnerabilities. In the latter respect, she notes that human rights law has become progressively less revolutionary and is increasingly used to legitimise the status quo, which is especially evident 'in areas involving non-citizens, racialised communities and minority groups, and responses to security threats.' This dedication to highlighting the plight of vulnerable communities is admirable and well-justified; experience shows that arbitrary detention is a commonly used tool against groups who fall outside the main power structures and majority population. Exploring the common denominators among targeted groups allows for human rights advocates to identify cross-cutting challenges and governmental techniques to focus on in their advocacy work.

Professor Ferstman's work is wide-ranging. She looks at both the substantive matters – why the decision was imposed, and the procedural – how the detention was implemented. Specific topics addressed include the linkage between arbitrary detention and torture, cruel, inhuman, and degrading treatment; detention of marginalised and socially excluded groups; and the use of detention to deter dissent and free expression. Importantly, she applies the thorough research of the underlying conceptual framework to contemporary manifestations of arbitrary detention, including the security complex use of detention; and the detention of dual and foreign nationals for the purposes of leverage and bargaining at the inter-state level.

Notably, she dedicates Chapter 8 to arbitrary detention and a state of exceptionality during pandemics. One of the unfortunate collateral effects of the COVID-19 pandemic was the instrumentalisation of this state of

---

[1] Giorgio Agamben, *State of Exception* (trans. Kevin Attell) (University of Chicago Press 2005) 23.

emergency to impose excessive restrictions on various features of open and fair trials. Another effect was the justification of detention per se on the basis of the threat presented by the pandemic. In its 'Deliberation No. 11 on prevention of arbitrary deprivation of liberty in the context of public health emergencies' the Working Group on Arbitrary Detention surveyed the range of impacts presented by pandemics in relation to detention. The Working Group also introduced language into many of its opinions noting that '[i]n the current context of the global coronavirus disease (COVID-19) pandemic and the threat that it poses in places of detention, the Working Group calls upon the Government to take urgent action to ensure the immediate release of [the detainee].' Given the heightened threat of contracting respiratory diseases in crowded and confined spaces such as prisons and other detention centres, the restriction of people's liberty in the context of such emergencies must meet an elevated standard of justification and, where it is strictly necessary and proportionate, should be accompanied by appropriate adjustments to ensure that the detained person is not exposed to an overly heightened risk of contracting the disease by virtue of their incarceration.

As a human rights violation, arbitrary detention has been widely recognised to constitute a jus cogens prohibition under international law. As such, it is a bedrock principle, which undergirds the possibility to enjoy many other human rights. Equally, the violation of this prohibition can rapidly lead to a plethora of serious human rights abuses, including torture, enforced disappearance and even the deprivation of life. Professor Ferstman's commitment to redressing and removing the spectre of arbitrary detention is evident from her years of academic and professional work on the subject. This monograph stands as a testament to the conceptual coherence and intellectual acuity that underlies her work to combat arbitrary detention. From this robust scholarly foundation, Professor Ferstman draws in the reader with the depth and diversity of her materials – whether Behrouz Boochani's image of "people sitting, being tortured by time", or Maya Angelou's "caged bird". This book also showcases her willingness to stand up for communities and individuals who are all too often targeted for their innate characteristics or their legitimate political, social, or religious activities. It raises complex questions that require contemplation and action to consolidate the presumption of liberty enshrined in international human rights law. As members of the human rights community, we commend her in the strongest terms for this excellent and impactful work of legal scholarship.

1

Introduction

1.1 The impetus for the book

My motivations to write this book stem in part from my having left in 2018 my work at the nongovernmental organisation REDRESS after what then felt like a lifetime of 17 years. I was trying to unpack and process what I learnt from all those I worked with – my colleagues, our partners and, of course, our clients – all of them survivors of torture, and the bulk of them having been arbitrarily detained, many for extended periods of time. The subject matter shaped my work over many years representing and advocating on behalf of persons detained in different parts of the world for reasons including their human rights advocacy, connections to certain political or other movements, the persecution they faced in their home countries, and the policies of deterrence put in place by countries attempting to stem the flow of migrants or respond to the threats of terrorism. The trauma of arbitrary detention and torture, and the heavy emotions associated with pursuing remedies, was at the heart of what we did, why we did it, who we did it with, and what it meant to survivors. It framed why we kept going, how we approached the barriers we faced and the motivation we brought to the advocacy work and the litigation. My decision to concentrate on arbitrary detention in this book is because it was at the heart of so many of the cases I encountered and was so central to the intense and continuing suffering of former detainees. Added to this was my belief from the world around me that the scourge of detention, including arbitrary detention, was being normalised by a growing number of governments for increasingly nefarious reasons.

The other impetus stems from my experience of the COVID-19 lockdowns. Early in the pandemic, I co-edited a collection of reflections on COVID in which I began to think through the relationship between pandemics and detention.[1] These early reflections helped to hone my

---

[1] Carla Ferstman, 'Detention and Pandemic Exceptionality', in Carla Ferstman and Andrew Fagan (eds), *COVID-19, Law and Human Rights: Essex Dialogues* (Essex Law School and Human Rights Centre 2020).

thinking on exceptionalities, arbitrariness, vulnerabilities and the placement of law, which have become crucial themes explored in the book.

1.2 Some of the themes explored in the book

We live in a world where there is pressure to conform to the will of the ordinary and the constraints of the powerful. And we are conditioned to understand that we will avoid complication when we manage to align our thinking and our conduct in such ways. For many people, however, conformity is impossible, even nonsensical; the difference that they embody means they are not even permitted to align with the narrative of the powerful. For others, conformity is simply not desirable. As I explore in this book, arbitrary detention becomes a tool of the powerful to exert social control on those who do not conform to the rules of the imagined society. It is the ultimate abuse of power and denial of humanity to constrain personal liberty, to enclose or encage as a form of domination, to discriminate against or to force people to conform to imagined standards. This abuse of power is explored in this book, conceptually, psychologically and legally.

The book examines how decisions to detain or to maintain in detention are taken, what motivates those decisions, and the relative weight of the laws and associated principles that can be used to advocate for release. As such, the book is less focused on the conditions of detention or with the scenario of criminal sentencing, though both subject areas are touched upon to the extent that they are relevant to analyses of arbitrary detention. The focus of the book is on the role of the state and its officials – those who have the responsibility to protect individuals from the arbitrary exercise of power, in overseeing and implementing a system in which arbitrary detention is not only tolerated but at times pursued as part of state policy.

I argue that forms of marginalisation and other arbitrary factors influence which individuals will be detained, when, for how long and in what conditions. Policies of securitisation, regimes of exception, and criminalisation have exacerbated these arbitrary distinctions given their propensity to target "otherness", even though there is nothing exceptional about "otherness". How these policies are applied, and their impact on individuals and communities, depends on the underlying political values and goals at stake, which differ between countries and over time.

The book also explores how arbitrary detention has become normalised. I demonstrate that arbitrary detention is not ultimately or mainly about occasional departures from lawful detention affecting random persons in random places. Arbitrary detention has become an insidious policy tool used purposely by governments to foster divisions and to enforce hostility against socially marginalised groups who I classify in this book as: the "unseen" (those marginalised on account of their destitution and/or extreme social needs); the "reviled and resented" (the recipients of racist, xenophobic and discriminatory attacks); and the "undeserving" (refugees and other migrants).[2] Arbitrary detention is also employed to secure international relations advantages; to quash dissent or stifle pluralist debates within society; and to pursue other policy objectives. What we see progressively is the application of entire systems of arbitrary detention, countenanced by laws and promoted by states and institutions.

Arbitrary detention is a malleable concept. To a certain extent malleability is needed. If concepts are too fixed, states and others would work around that fixity and operate within the zones of exception. But the elasticity means that the concept is shaped to suit political objectives, and those objectives have the tendency to change with time. In the legal sense I am looking at the arbitrary application of law but also law that is inherently arbitrary. The imperative to "conceptualise" arbitrary detention stems from the need to know what the concept means to the extent that it is clear enough to know. It also serves to clarify how the concept is being construed, applied and, at times, manipulated, and the consequences of such manipulations.

Human rights law is the principal lens through which many of the problems and potential solutions in this book are presented. But admittedly it is an uneasy and often unhelpful lens. International human rights courts and treaty bodies have had only minimal success in clawing back against the tendencies of securitisation and criminalisation that often foster arbitrary detention, particularly in those areas of detention perceived to raise the greatest concerns about sovereignty, national identity and national security. And, instead of reversing the processes of social exclusion, human rights law has become progressively less revolutionary and more inclined to legitimise and reinforce the status quo. This is particularly evident in areas involving non-citizens, racialised communities and minority groups, and responses to security threats. Human rights bodies have been robust in withstanding the direct pressure from states to change major course by watering down human rights standards in areas states perceive to be fundamental to their national interests. Yet, these bodies have been less adept at resisting (and they have not always resisted) the more subtle pressures to widen flexibilities and contextualisation into their decision-making processes, or in some cases to fill in what are porous, nuanced standards with state-friendly moderations, in some cases leading to the same result of lowered standards. Thus, for the most contentious issues, human rights law risks becoming the apologist, the language and procedure of denial. The challenge of human rights law to address arbitrary detention thus serves as a mirror through which we can see these wider tendencies.

---

[2] See Chapter 4.

1.3 The trajectory

The book has two parts. Part I – Theorising and Conceptualising "Arbitrariness" – provides the theoretical framework for the book. Chapter 2 interrogates the multiple meanings of "arbitrariness" and considers how these meanings engage with the definition of arbitrary detention. Chapter 3 then reviews and analyses the linkages between arbitrary detention and notions of harm and the severity of harm. It posits that the "arbitrariness" in arbitrary detention, because of the feelings of helplessness it engenders, is itself capable of producing harm that attains the seriousness of torture and other forms of cruel, inhuman, or degrading treatment.

Part II – The Law and Practice of Arbitrary Detention in Context – explores scenarios of arbitrary detention that are particularly pervasive and problematic. Chapter 4 focuses on enforcing hostility and social control. It analyses how discrimination, xenophobia and marginalisation fuel detention policies and contribute to arbitrary detention. It explores how detention is used to deter or suppress segments of society and fuels and is fuelled by discrimination, poverty and social exclusion. Sometimes, detention stems from policies of over-criminalisation; in other cases, non-criminal confinement is used to remove individuals from circulating in privileged spaces as a form of social cleansing. Chapter 5 considers the detention of political opponents, human rights activists and members of social movements. It explores the methods of criminalisation of defenders and their organisations and associated judicial harassment that lead to arbitrary detention and the untenable linkages often made by governments between legitimate expressions of dissent, resisting authority and attacks against the security of the state. Chapter 6 considers how states of emergency and other regimes of exception contribute to arbitrary detention on an individual and mass scale. It analyses the law on emergencies and tensions with the right to liberty and security of the person. The chapter explores how emergency legislation put in place in different countries has led to arbitrary and often indefinite detention, through vague or overly broadly worded provisions, or simply the misuse of law for ulterior purposes. Chapter 7 considers the detentions of dual and foreign nationals as a form of state hostage-taking and interrogates the (often limited) role of states of nationality in responding to such scenarios. Chapter 8 explores the circumstances of persons deprived of their liberty in the context of pandemics, and of COVID-19 in particular. The chapter considers the extent to which pandemics impact upon the exceptional character of detention. It also evaluates how governments, specialist agencies and courts have grappled with the legal, ethical and public health issues relevant to considerations about how pandemics impact upon the law on detention.

The book concludes with an analysis of the challenges of the law, and human rights law in particular, to address the phenomenon of arbitrary detention. It identifies areas where the law is inadequate or unclear to effectively regulate the use of detention and to avoid its use as an arbitrary tool to abuse power. There is a need to recognise the factors contributing to these trends, but also to acknowledge the importance of finding ways in which to address the lacunae. The book therefore aims to encourage reflection about the best ways to address the gaps with the law and the practice. At its heart, the book is not just a cogent call for greater respect for the rule of law, but a detailed explanation as to why the law itself must sometimes be challenged.

PART I

Theorising and Conceptualising "Arbitrariness"

2

Notions of the "Arbitrary"

2.1 Introduction

One tends to have a clear image of detention – what confinement looks like, what restriction to liberty must feel like, and the contexts that may give rise to such situations. Detention seems straightforward. However, the outer edges are less obvious, and these borders continue to widen. Whether someone is deprived of liberty requires spatial and temporal analyses and depends on both factual and legal assessments involving objective and subjective factors. On the peripheries, we might ask: What distinguishes a violation of freedom of movement from that of liberty and security of the person? Does the place of confinement – what it is labelled, who is held inside, its size, level of comfort or access to amenities, or the nature of supervision – say anything about whether it constitutes detention? Must the confinement be overseen by state authorities? What amount of time must a person be held before the treatment is considered a form of detention? Can a person be detained emotionally or psychologically as opposed to physically? If there are no physical barriers preventing a person from leaving but if they leave, they or others are very likely to be subjected to significant harms, does it constitute detention?

Detention is not an obvious label. And adding "arbitrariness" to this complex picture further blurs the subject.

This chapter unpacks the "arbitrary" in arbitrary detention and explains the philosophical, sociological and legal underpinnings of the concept. First, it considers the etymology of the term "arbitrary" and its theoretical foundations. It studies the multiple meanings of "arbitrary", also having regard to the many disciplines employing the term, the political contexts in which the theories have arisen and the evolution of these contexts over time, as well as the persons and groups to whom it is applied. These various meanings are not inherently contradictory; they emphasise different facets of a concept that has been applied from diverse vantage points.[1]

The chapter continues by exploring how the concept of "arbitrary" has been co-opted by the law, the many usages of "arbitrary" in law, the principles of the rule of law and procedural fairness. This is then followed by an examination of "arbitrariness" in international human rights law, considering the ways in which "arbitrary" is used and applied in legal texts, treaties, case law and scholarly writings. This sets the stage for the analysis of the human rights prohibition of "arbitrary detention".

2.2 Multiple meanings

The word "arbitrary" derives from the Latin *arbī^trārĭus*, '*motus in arteriā naturalis, non arbitrarius*' – 'depending upon the will, arbitrary'[2]; voluntary, or at the discretion of the arbiter or decision-maker. The *Oxford English Dictionary* defines "arbitrary" as '[t]o be decided by one's liking; dependent upon will or pleasure; at the discretion or option of anyone'.[3] This is consistent with the standard legal definition, which centres on 'conduct or acts based alone upon one's will, and not upon any course of reasoning and exercise of judgment'.[4] This focus on decisions taken by discretion as opposed to logic or reason is consistent with Diderot and Le Rond d'Alembert's definition, which explains "arbitrary" as 'that which is not defined or limited by any express law or constitution, but is left solely to the judgment and discretion of individuals'.[5] The adjective "arbitrary" can be applied to both the decision-making process and the outcome of that process.

The term "arbitrary" often has negative connotations: '[d]erived from mere opinion or preference; not based on the nature of things; *hence*, capricious, uncertain, varying'; 'Unrestrained in the exercise of will; of uncontrolled

---

[1] However, Wright argues in relation to its usage in administrative law that 'the meaning of "arbitrary" will change significantly as context and the underlying, possibly conflicting, purposes, interests, and stakes vary. The significance, degree, and frequency of the changes of meaning of arbitrary lead to the conclusion that it is more misleading than helpful to imagine that arbitrary has a standard, convenient, legal definition, even in particular legal contexts, such as judicial review of administrative actions': R George Wright, 'Arbitrariness: Why the Most Important Idea in Administrative Law Can't Be Defined, and What This means for the Law in General' (2010) 44(2) *U Rich L Rev* 839, 846.

[2] Charlton Lewis and Charles Short, *A Latin Dictionary* (Clarendon Press 1879).

[3] 'arbitrary, adj. and n.', *OED Online* (OUP June 2022) <www.oed.com/view/Entry/10180?redirectedFrom=arbitrary&> accessed 26 July 2022.

[4] 'arbitrariness', *Black's Law Dictionary* 104 (11th edn, Thomson Reuters 2019).

[5] '*arbitraire*', unofficial translation, *Encyclopédie, ou Dictionnaire raisonné des sciences, des arts et des métiers*, vol. 1 (1st edn, Denis Diderot and Jean Le Rond d'Alembert 1751) 578.

power or authority, absolute; *hence*, despotic, tyrannical'.[6] In this sense, to describe an action, rule or decision as "arbitrary" implies unpredictability or capriciousness and the failure of the decision-maker to exercise power or authority with restraint. Vague rules afford much space for 'corrupt, arbitrary, or idiosyncratic decision-making or decision-executing'[7] and appear unfair for this reason. However, inflexible rules that result in mechanistic application, without consideration of the underlying policies behind the rule, can also appear unfair.[8]

The emphasis on unpredictability or idiosyncratic decision-making belies an often-present facet of the arbitrary exercise of power: that it is 'neither random nor accidental'; it is most readily exercised 'against certain categories of [marginalised] subjects who cannot rely on the self-restraint that the social order imposes on officials and on society at large. Seen from this point of view, arbitrariness seems rather to blur the already slippery boundaries that differentiate it from the notion of discrimination.'[9] In this sense, "arbitrariness" is connected to unfair decision-making though the reason for the unfairness or bias may have little to do with the arbitrariness of the process.[10] Here, the unfairness is substantive. True, an excess of discretion in how a decision to detain is imposed lends to arbitrary decision-making, which is likely to disadvantage marginalised groups, but the arbitrary exercise of power that is 'neither random nor accidental' is a different kind of phenomenon. The focus is on why the decision to detain was imposed (a substantive matter) as opposed to how the decision to detain was arrived at (a procedural matter).

"Arbitrariness" is also associated with randomness. It is used in statistical sampling to foster equality of opportunities and, in this sense, improve fairness.[11] But here randomness is pursued in furtherance of a higher goal (and in that teleological sense the strategy is purposive and not fully arbitrary) and it overcomes the negative characteristics associated with arbitrariness on that basis. As Schmidtz says, 'when "arbitrary" means random, […] there is no connection between being arbitrary and being improper'.[12] For example, the randomness of lotteries suggests that each ticket holder or potential beneficiary of a scarce resource has an equal

---

[6] *OED Online* (n 3).
[7] Thomas Franck, *Fairness in International Law and Institutions* (OUP 1995) 7.
[8] Joseph William Singer, 'The Player and the Cards: Nihilism and Legal Theory' (1984) 94(1) *Yale LJ* 1, 12.
[9] Enrica Rigo, 'Arbitrary Law Making and Unorderable Subjectivities in Legal Theoretical Approaches to Migration' (2020) 14(2) *Etikk I Praksis – Nordic J Applied Eth* 71, 79.
[10] Wright (n 1) 841.
[11] Lincoln Moses, *Think and Explain with Statistics* (Addison-Wesley 1986).
[12] David Schmidtz, *The Elements of Justice* (CUP 2006) 218.

chance of being rewarded.[13] However, the more important the task, or the more serious the consequences, the less one may want to rely on randomness to determine outcomes. This is because decisions that are made without a transparent decision-making logic can be unfair or lead to mistakes if the outcomes were supposed to be anything other than arbitrary. But this proposition requires confidence in the fairness of the rules-based system that is capable to cut across culture-specific values, and therefore it depends on one's vantage point. The degree to which one wants to rely upon random decision-making depends upon how one perceives relative privilege vis-à-vis the rules. Individuals from marginalised groups who are 'excluded by the procedures which establish the rules that affect them'[14] may believe they will fare better with random processes rather than rules-based systems, even more so if those processes are weighted to address disadvantage.[15] This is particularly the case if rules-based systems adopt fallible measurement criteria that unjustly privilege the already privileged or unfairly discriminate against, exclude or further marginalise already marginalised groups.[16]

2.3 Theorising "arbitrariness"

"Arbitrariness" is a key lens through which theories about morality, ethics, politics, social relations and justice are explained. For social theorists Bourdieu and Passeron, arbitrariness is a way to explain the contingency of values and meanings that have no absolute or eternal justification. They describe how dominant groups within society co-opt educational structures to legitimise certain interpretations of value and meaning. This reinforces pre-existing power relations that contribute to the status quo of their continued dominance.[17] Here, "arbitrariness" is understood as the contingency or fluidity of meaning and it is the targeted appropriation of that contingency that reinforces domination, oppression and violence. Bourdieu's passage from *doxa* to discourse is only possible when common sense propositions of culture begin to lose their naturalised character, revealing the underlying arbitrariness of the given social order.[18]

---

[13] Ben Saunders, 'The Equality of Lotteries' (2008) 83(3) *Philosophy* 359, 363.
[14] Seyla Benhabib, *The Rights of Others: Aliens, Residents, and Citizens* (CUP 2004) 15.
[15] Lynn Jansen and Steven Wall, 'Weighted Lotteries and the Allocation of Scarce Medications for Covid-19' (2021) 51(1) *Hastings Center Report* 39.
[16] Oliver Dowlen, *The Political Potential of Sortition* (Imprint Academic 2008) 15–16.
[17] Pierre Bourdieu and Jean-Claude Passeron, *Reproduction in Education, Society, and Culture* (Sage 1977) 5.
[18] Pierre Bourdieu, *Outline of a Theory of Practice* (CUP 1977) 165–166.

The understanding of the arbitrary exercise of power as a condition for domination is developed by Locke.[19] For him, arbitrary power involves being at the mercy of another's arbitrary will and consequently being dominated by that other person. Decisions taken on this basis would risk being inconsistent, uncertain and unknowable.

Republican theorist Pettit[20] also considered the role of domination in the exercise of power. Pettit's conception of freedom as non-domination requires that no one has the capacity to interfere on an arbitrary basis in another's choices.[21] Arbitrariness depends on the arbitrary will of the person or body exercising power or causing the interference. The only exceptions to this (non-arbitrariness) according to Pettit would be where the interference is the result of rule-governed procedures that minimise or exclude the influence of the arbitrary will of others. Further, this interference should track the qualified interests and opinions of those affected, and the claim that it does this must be controllable and contestable by those affected, if there is appropriate protection against arbitrary interference: 'The parliament or the police officer, then, the judge or the prison warden, may practise non-dominating interference, provided – and it is a big proviso – that a suitably constraining, constitutional arrangement works effectively.'[22] In a similar sense, Lovett explains that "arbitrariness" is not simply an excessive form of discretion, it is a condition for domination.[23] He argues that 'the degree to which social power is arbitrary is captured by the ratio, so to speak, of its potential uses that are unconstrained to those that are constrained (by rules, procedures, or goals)'.[24]

Non-"arbitrariness" is equally a critical component of conceptions of law, the rule of law and procedural fairness.[25] In Dicey's formulation, the rule of law stands against 'the exercise by persons in authority of wide, arbitrary, or discretionary powers of constraint'.[26] For Dicey, the rule of law requires that persons are only punished on the basis of law properly established.[27]

---

[19] John Locke, *The Second Treatise of Civil Government*, ed. John W Gough (Basil Blackwell 1946) 'On the Extent of Legislative Power'.

[20] Phillip Pettit, *Republicanism: a Theory of Freedom and Government* (Clarendon Press 1997).

[21] Pettit (n 20) 67. For an extrapolation of the analysis on freedom as non-domination to international institutions, see Carmen Pavel, 'The International Rule of Law' (2020) 23(3) *Crit Rev Intl Soc & Pol Phil* 332, 334.

[22] Pettit (n 20) 65. These ideas are further explored in Phillip Pettit, 'The Common Good', in Keith Dowding et al, *Justice and Democracy: Essays for Brian Barry* (CUP 2004) 150, 151–158.

[23] Frank Lovett, *A General Theory of Domination and Justice* (OUP 2010) 96.

[24] Lovett (n 23) 96.

[25] Phillip Pettit, 'Keeping Republican Freedom Simple' (2002) 30 *Political Theory* 339.

[26] AV Dicey, *Introduction to the Study of the Law of the Constitution* (10th edn, Macmillan 1964) 188.

[27] Dicey (n 26).

This core principle of legality is designed to outlaw the exercise of arbitrary power or the unreasonable interference by governments with persons' life, liberty, and property. Governments should only exercise authority that is clear, certain, predictable and accords with laws promulgated in advance and properly enforced by independent and impartial courts. Thus, arbitrary power is power that is exercised against individuals or groups *without* having been derived from laws properly enacted (though the blind adherence to laws is not favoured either,[28] and some discretion is necessary for decision-making in complex societies), or conversely, as Lovett has argued, 'the power exercised by political and legal authorities over citizens counts as non-arbitrary, [...], to the extent that those authorities observe the rule of law'.[29]

Waldron gives "arbitrary" three main meanings: unpredictable, unreasoned, and without authority or legitimacy.[30] Law that is overly broad or vague can lead to unpredictable results, though according to Endicott this does not necessarily make it arbitrary; indeed, increasing precision can have the opposite effect and increase arbitrariness.[31] Thus, beyond formal conceptions of the rule of law, the concept has also been understood by Endicott and some other legal scholars as having a substantive value, a reason of the law, the need for judgment, as a means to sift through the sense of contingency.[32] The International Court of Justice has construed this substantive notion of "arbitrariness" as 'not so much something opposed to a rule of law, as something opposed to the rule of law [...]. It is wilful disregard of due process of law, an act which shocks, or at least surprises a sense of judicial propriety.'[33]

---

[28] Judith Shklar, 'Political Theory and the Rule of Law', in Allan Hutchinson and Patrick Monahan (eds), *The Rule of Law: Ideal or Ideology* (Carswell 1987) 13–14; Ernst Fraenkel and Jens Meierhenrich, *The Dual State: a Contribution to the Theory of Dictatorship* (Oxford 2017).

[29] Lovett (n 23) 99.

[30] Jeremy Waldron, *Law and Disagreement* (OUP 1999) 167–168.

[31] Timothy Endicott, 'The Impossibility of the Rule of Law', in Endicott, *Vagueness in Law* (OUP 2000) 188, 192.

[32] Endicott (n 31) 187, 203; Martin Loughlin, '*Rechtsstaat*, Rule of Law, *l'Etat de droit*', in Loughlin, *Foundations of Public Law* (OUP 2010) 312. See, also, Mary Liston, 'Governments in Miniature: the Rule of Law in the Administrative State', in Lorne Sossin and Colleen Flood (eds), *Administrative Law in Context* (Emond Montgomery 2013) 39, who argues that '[t]he principle of the rule of law is animated by the need to prevent and constrain arbitrariness within the exercise of public authority by political and legal officials in terms of process, jurisdiction, and substance' (41).

[33] *Elettronica Sicula S.p.A.* (*ELSI*) (*USA v Italy*) [1989] ICJ Rep 15, [128]. For further discussion of this standard under international investment law, see Jacob Stone, 'Arbitrariness, the Fair and Equitable Treatment Standard, and the International Law of Investment' (2012) 25(1) *Leiden J Intl L* 77, 85–105; Veijo Heiskanen, 'Arbitrary and Unreasonable Measures', in August Reinisch (ed), *Standards of Investment Protection* (OUP 2008) 87–110; Kurt Hamrock, 'The ELSI Case: Toward an International Definition of Arbitrary Conduct' (1992) 27 *Texas Intl LJ* 837; August Reinisch and Christoph Schreuer,

Rawls' theory of justice as fairness[34] recognises that one's conception of justice should seek to nullify the effects of both the privileges and disadvantages that arise by accidental circumstance and are thus arbitrary. He posits a form of egalitarianism that goes significantly beyond the equality of opportunity, to require one to interrogate the influence of what he sees as equally arbitrary factors – unequal initial social positions and natural endowments.[35] Thus, here, arbitrariness is likened to the (undeserved) status or positions over which individuals have no control. While Rawls does not see those initial positions as fundamentally just or unjust from an ethical standpoint, he holds that the fact that they exist because of happenstance and are undeserved requires, as a condition for fairness, that institutions within societies counter their influence through distributive justice by way of a system of social cooperation or similar policies.[36] Rawls contends that the only inequalities that should be tolerated in society are those that ultimately benefit the least favoured. For Rawls, "arbitrariness" serves as an antithesis to a conception of justice[37] that accepts 'social contingencies that lead to social subordination and domination'.[38] Thus, "arbitrariness" is a given, and its consequences can be justified by social institutions governed by his principles of justice. "Arbitrariness" here is a property of the distribution of natural assets.

This Rawlsian difference principle remains seminal in advancing theoretical understandings of social justice,[39] and builds upon key social justice precursors, such as Virchow who, when reporting on the catastrophic impacts of the typhus epidemic in Upper Silesia, sought to encourage the state to recognise its moral responsibility to do more to mitigate deadly social conditions that had an unequal impact on the poor and most marginalised in society. In a foreshadowing to Rawls' theory of moral arbitrariness, Virchow wrote of the importance of the 'great struggle of critical thinking against authoritarian rule, of natural history against dogma, of eternal human

---

'Protection against Arbitrary or Discriminatory Measures', in *International Protection of Investments: the Substantive Standards* (CUP 2020).

[34] John Rawls, 'Justice as Fairness: Political not Metaphysical' (1985) 14 *Philosophy and Public Affairs* 223; *Justice as Fairness: a Restatement* (Belknap Press 2001); *A Theory of Justice* (revised edn, Harvard University Press 1999).

[35] Rawls, *A Theory of Justice* (n 34) 64–65.

[36] Rawls, *A Theory of Justice* (n 34) 86, 87.

[37] Rawls, *A Theory of Justice* (n 34) 5

[38] Rainer Forst, 'The Point of Justice: On the Paradigmatic Incompatibility between Rawlsian "Justice as Fairness" and Luck Egalitarianism', in Jon Mandle and Sarah Roberts-Cady (eds), *John Rawls: Debating the Major Questions* (OUP 2020) 157.

[39] Note however, that in Rawls' theory, equal liberties and equal opportunities have lexical priority to the difference principle, which should prevent arbitrary factors from being decisive. See, John Rawls, 'Justice as Fairness: Political not Metaphysical' (n 34) 227–228.

rights against human arbitrariness'.[40] Nevertheless, the Rawlsian difference principle has been variously critiqued by libertarian scholars,[41] luck egalitarians[42] and civic republicans.[43] The principle has also been critiqued by some theorists for its ambiguity, impracticality and inability to solve or radically transform real-time problems of injustice and inequality[44] and, indeed, for its failure to identify the pluralistic and intersectional character, persistence and impact of the many different forms and layers of injustice based, for instance, on race, class or gender.[45] Mouffe, who criticises Rawls' methods, considers that Rawls:

> is so confident that [...] rational persons deliberating within the constraints of the reasonable and moved only by their rational advantage will choose his principles of justice that he considers it would be enough for one man to calculate the rational self-interest of all. In that case the process of deliberation is supererogatory. [...] As current controversies about abortion clearly show, pluralism does not mean that all those conflicting conceptions of the good will coexist peacefully without trying to intervene in the public sphere and the frontier between public and private is not given once and for all but constructed and constantly shifting. Moreover at any moment "private" affairs can witness the emergence of antagonisms and thereby become politicized. Therefore Rawls's "well-ordered society" rests on the elimination of the very idea of the political.[46]

---

[40] Rudolf Virchow, 'The Ministry of Health', in LJ Rather (ed), *Collected Essays on Public Health and Epidemiology, vol. 1* (Amerind Publishing 1985) 6–13, referred to in Steven Jensen, 'Human Rights against Human Arbitrariness: Pandemics in a human rights historical perspective', in Morten Kjaerum, Martha Davis and Amanda Lyons (eds), *COVID-19 and Human Rights* (Routledge 2021) 6.

[41] See, for example, Robert Nozick, *Anarchy, State and Utopia* (Basic 1974) 213–227; Robert Nozick, 'Distributive Justice' (1973) 3(1) *Philosophy & Public Affairs* 45; Friedrich Hayek, *Social Justice, Socialism, and Democracy* (Centre for Independent Studies 1979) 39.

[42] Gerald Cohen, 'On the Currency of Egalitarian Justice' (1989) 99(4) *Ethics* 906.

[43] Lovett (n 23); Phillip Pettit (n 25).

[44] See, for example, Amartya Sen, *The Idea of Justice* (Harvard University Press, 2009) 52–74; Susan Moller Okin, *Justice, Gender and the Family* (Basic Books 1989); Nancy Fraser, *Scales of Justice: Reimagining Political Space in a Globalizing World* (Columbia University Press 2009).

[45] Katrina Forrester, *In the Shadow of Justice: Post War Liberalism and the Remaking of Political Philosophy* (Princeton University Press 2019); Iris Marion Young, *Justice and the Politics of Difference* (Princeton University Press 1990).

[46] Chantal Mouffe, 'Rawls: Political Philosophy Without Politics' (1987) 13(2) *Philosophy & Social Criticism* 105, 114–115.

2.4 "Arbitrariness" in human rights law

"Arbitrariness" is used in public international law to determine whether a state acted in bad faith when encroaching on the rights of another state. Here, conduct that 'is unreasonable, and pursued in an arbitrary manner, without due consideration of the legitimate expectations of the other State',[47] is considered wrongful. Similarly, if a state's exercise of discretion is arbitrary and unreasonable, this would be an abuse of rights for which a state could be held internationally responsible.[48] Also, "arbitrariness" is a frequently appearing descriptor in domestic legal frameworks, particularly regarding the exercise of discretion, including in the law of contracts.[49] It is also used as a means to protect against interferences by public authorities in public or administrative law,[50] criminal law[51] and constitutional law.[52]

Many of the public international law, administrative and criminal law references to "arbitrariness" frame how the term has come to be used in human rights law. Human rights law uses "arbitrariness" to explain the extent to which measures taken by a state which restrict or deprive access to certain rights are a legitimate exercise of executive power. The term "arbitrary" is used in treaties to frame certain human rights, including:

- arbitrary deprivation of life[53];
- arbitrary arrest or detention[54];

---

[47] Hersch Lauterpacht, *Oppenheim's International Law* (8th edn, Longmans 1955) 345.
[48] *Trail Smelter Arbitration (USA v Canada)* (1938/1941) III RIAA 1904, 1965.
[49] *Braganza v BP Shipping Ltd* [2015] UKSC 17.
[50] See, for example, *Abu Dhabi National Tanker Co v Product Star Shipping Ltd (The Product Star) (No. 2)* [1993] 1 Lloyd's Rep 397 (CA), 404 (Leggatt LJ); *Yam Seng Pte Ltd v International Trade Corpn* [2013] EWHC 111 (QB); *Wastech Services Ltd v Greater Vancouver*, 2021 SCC 7. See, also, Rigo (n 9) 74; Jacob Gersen and Adrian Vermeule, 'Thin Rationality Review' (2016) 114 *Mich L Rev* 1355; Lisa Bressman, 'Beyond Accountability: Arbitrariness and Legitimacy in the Administrative State' (2003) 78 *NYU L Rev* 461, 496.
[51] Offences and penalties must be both accessible and foreseeable to prevent arbitrariness by domestic courts. See Peter Westen, 'Two Rules of Legality in Criminal Law' (2007) 26(3) *Law and Philosophy* 229.
[52] For example, Shankar Narayanan, 'Rethinking Non-Arbitrariness' (2017) 4 *NLUD Student Law Journal* 133; Marc Ribiero, *Limiting Arbitrary Power: the Vagueness Doctrine in Canadian Constitutional Law* (UBC Press 2004).
[53] Art 6(1) International Covenant on Civil and Political Rights (ICCPR) (adopted 16 December 1966, entered into force 23 March 1976): 'No one shall be arbitrarily deprived of his life'; Art 4(1) American Convention on Human Rights (ACHR) (adopted 22 November 1969, entered into force 18 July 1978); Art 4 African Charter on Human and Peoples' Rights (ACHPR) (adopted 27 June 1981, entered into force 21 October 1986); Art 5(2) Arab Charter on Human Rights (Arab Charter) (adopted 15 September 1994, League of Arab States).
[54] Art 9(1) ICCPR: 'No one shall be subjected to arbitrary arrest or detention'; Art 37(b) Convention on the Rights of the Child (CRC) (adopted 20 November 1989, entered into

- arbitrary deprivation of the right to enter one's own country[55];
- arbitrary deprivation of the right to one's nationality or the right to change it[56];
- arbitrary deprivation of the right to leave a country, including one's own[57];
- arbitrary interference with privacy, family, home or correspondence, or unlawful attacks on honour and reputation[58];
- arbitrary deprivation of property.[59]

"Arbitrariness" features in both social conceptions of human rights and as a tool to demarcate what are the acceptable limits on access to certain rights. When considering the practice of human rights, one can observe two main tensions:

(1) The control over the meaning and scope of human rights to limit how broadly social conceptions of human rights are construed; those doing the reigning in see themselves as an anti-expansionist lobby, but they can equally be understood as reductionist – they see the need to restrain the arbitrary power of courts and international institutions. There is a constant push–pull between the readily apparent needs of marginalised

---

force 2 September 1990): 'No child shall be deprived of his or her liberty unlawfully or arbitrarily'; Art 14(1)(b) Convention on the Rights of Persons with Disabilities (CRPD) (adopted on 13 December 2006, entered into force on 3 May 2008): 'are not deprived of their liberty unlawfully or arbitrarily'; Art 16(4) Convention on the Protection of the Rights of All Migrant Workers and Members of Their Families (CPRMW) (adopted 18 December 1990, entered into force 1 July 2003): 'Migrant workers and members of their families shall not be subjected individually or collectively to arbitrary arrest or detention'; Art 7(3) ACHR; Art 6 ACHPR; Art 14(1) Arab Charter; Art 12 ASEAN Human Rights Declaration (adopted 18 November 2012, Heads of State/Government of ASEAN Member States).

[55] Art 12(4) ICCPR: 'No one shall be arbitrarily deprived of the right to enter his own country'; Art 18(1)(d) CRPD.
[56] Art 20(3) ACHR; Art 29(1) Arab Charter; Art 18 ASEAN Human Rights Declaration.
[57] Art 27(1) Arab Charter: 'No one may be arbitrarily or unlawfully prevented from leaving any country, including his own, nor prohibited from residing, or compelled to reside, in any part of that country.'
[58] Art 17(1) ICCPR: 'No one shall be subjected to arbitrary or unlawful interference with his privacy, family, home or correspondence, nor to unlawful attacks on his honour and reputation'; Art 16(1) CRC; Art 22(1) CRPD; Art 14 CPRMW; Art 11(2) ACHR; Art 21(1) Arab Charter; Art 21 ASEAN Human Rights Declaration.
[59] Art 12(5) CRPD; Art 15 CPRMW; Art 31 Arab Charter; Art 17 ASEAN Human Rights Declaration.

and excluded individuals and groups and certain governments' and others' efforts to entrench narratives of exclusion in order to negate or limit state obligations to such groups. For instance, neoliberal economic policies tend to create a disabling environment for the enjoyment of human rights by socially excluded or marginalised groups. There is the push–pull between nationalism, universalism and extraterritoriality, between human rights minimalist prohibitions and more maximalist positive obligations, and about the recognition and justiciability of economic, social and cultural rights.

(2) The pressure to widen exceptions to human rights to prevent categories of persons from benefiting from protections because of who they are or what they allegedly did. Under this rubric, there is also pressure to exempt categories of persons from having to comply with human rights, whether because of their formal role or status or the context in which they operate. Such exceptionalist framings see just about everything as contingent. Even rights recognised as absolute are sought to be made contingent by way of domestic reinterpretations and rationalisations of their scope and reach. This is the tension between the inclusion/exclusion parameters of the "us" and the "them", between those that are (or are permitted to be) associated with the common narrative of privilege and the morally dubious misfits, degenerates and dissenters who remain outsiders. It is between security or stability and terror and fear. The arbitrary power being exerted by states and their officials is justified in the name of a public good that is narrowly construed, appropriated and naturalised[60]; a necessary evil to promote "core" values. The 'safety valve' of ostracism ensures 'a smoother, more peaceful, and less tumultuous running of the state'.[61]

Both these tensions reveal different conceptions of the placement of human rights and what human rights are meant to do. And there is a relationship between these two tensions. Groups that tend to be excluded in (2) are often those that most need the wider social protections of (1).

2.4.1 *"Arbitrariness" and the social conception of rights*

"Arbitrariness" is a lens through which to evaluate whether the specific interests of individuals or groups, often the most vulnerable, have been met. The classification helps to frame contingencies in subjecthood, identity and

---

[60] Bourdieu (n 18) 165–156.
[61] Donald Kagan, 'The Origin and Purposes of Ostracism' (1961) 30(4) *Hesperia* 393.

representation that in turn help structure human rights arguments about equality and non-discrimination and how different rights relate to each other.

Rawls' understanding of moral arbitrariness has been used by some scholars and social justice advocates to question government policies that fail to adequately account for morally arbitrary factors, such as race, gender and class, or which have the effect of restricting or denying access to rights based on these or other characteristics over which the targeted group has no control. This is the claim made by Jensen about Virchow's call for the German government to address health inequalities in Upper Silesia.[62] It is also part of what is behind Pogge's claim, who, when considering the impact of arbitrarily acquired privilege, 'find[s] it morally troubling, at least, that a world heavily dominated by us [the privileged] burdens so many people with such deficient and inferior starting positions'.[63] It is also asserted by Cole, who widens Rawlsian moral arbitrariness beyond borders when terming the liberal realist justifications of the UK government policy to exclude certain groups of migrants from free treatment under the National Health Service as 'shallow brutality'.[64] Cole posits that borders:

> might be the result of war, geography or discovery; but from a liberal point of view national borders cannot bear much, if any, moral weight. What is of interest to moral theory is not the processes through which territorial boundaries become fixed in particular places, but how the distinction between insiders and outsiders is established, the boundaries of membership.[65]

In many ways, human rights have become the battleground between the excluded seeking both literal and conceptual entry to privileged domains, and the privileged, recognising that a condition for their continued privilege is the maintenance of exclusions. This collision underpins the tensioned reasoning of all human rights legal and political institutions, and it is why the human rights project is destined to be fundamentally political.

---

[62] Jensen (n 40), referring to Virchow.
[63] Thomas Pogge, *World Poverty and Human Rights: Cosmopolitan Responsibilities and Reforms* (2nd edn, Polity 2008) 3.
[64] Phillip Cole, 'Human Rights and the National Interest: Migrants, Healthcare and Social Justice' (2007) *J Med Ethics* 269, 272.
[65] Cole (n 64) 270. Cole's argument is further developed in Philip Cole, 'Taking Moral Equality Seriously: Egalitarianism and Immigration Controls' (2012) 8(1–2) *J Intl Political Theory* 121. See, also, Geert Demuijnck, 'Poverty as a Human Rights Violation and the Limits of Nationalism', in Andreas Follesdal and Thomas Pogge (eds), *Real World Justice* (Springer 2006) 65–83; Seyla Benhabib, 'The Law of Peoples, Distributive Justice and Migrations' (2004) 72 *Fordham L Rev* 1761.

A social conception of human rights would see value in understanding how the presence or absence of morally arbitrary factors impact on rights access and enforcement. Thus, it is not only important to eradicate arbitrary detentions and killings and the arbitrary procedures that may have led to them, but to understand and address specifically how factors such as race, gender and class impact upon who is unlawfully detained or killed. One must understand and address what makes it possible for 'the systematic relegation of an entire group of people to a condition of inferiority', which then goes on to markedly increase their susceptibility to human rights violations.[66] The United Nations (UN) Human Rights Committee, in its consideration of the arbitrary deprivation of life, noted that '[d]ata suggesting that members of religious, racial, or ethnic minorities, indigent persons or foreign nationals are disproportionately likely to face the death penalty may indicate an unequal application of the death penalty. [...] Any deprivation of life based on discrimination in law or fact is *ipso facto* arbitrary in nature.'[67] The US Supreme Court recognised in *Furman v Georgia*[68] that the death penalty would be unconstitutional under the Eighth Amendment prohibition against cruel and unusual punishment when imposed in an arbitrary and capricious manner (disproportionately against certain classes of defendants, most often African Americans and the poor) and leading to discriminatory results. The absence of clear guidelines on how the death penalty or indeed any harsh penalty is applied can lead to racial and other discrimination: prejudice can lead to harsher penalties for disfavoured minorities. The Supreme Court held:

> The high service rendered by the "cruel and unusual" punishment clause of the Eighth Amendment is to require legislatures to write penal laws that are even handed, nonselective, and nonarbitrary, and to require judges to see to it that general laws are not applied sparsely, selectively, and spottily to unpopular groups.[69]

Nevertheless, and underscoring the power of the push–pull, the death penalty was reinstated in many American states despite the continuing spectre of its discriminatory (and hence, arbitrary) application.[70] The position continues to fluctuate.

---

[66] Catharine McKinnon, *Feminism Unmodified* (Harvard University Press 1987) 41.
[67] Human Rights Committee, 'General Comment No 36 (2018) on Article 6 of the ICCPR, on the Right to Life' (30 October 2018) UN Doc CCPR/C/GC/36, paras 44, 61.
[68] *Furman v Georgia*, 408 US 238 (1972).
[69] Ibid, 408.
[70] David Baldus et al, 'Racial Discrimination and the Death Penalty in the Post-Furman era: an Empirical and Legal Overview with Recent Findings from Philadelphia' (1997) 83 *Cornell L Rev* 1638.

Any discrimination between groups must serve a rational purpose, but what counts as such involves a value judgment about a society's legal and political culture. As the South African Constitutional Court recognised in a case involving the differentiation between citizens and non-citizens for the purpose of social assistance benefits, to comply with the Constitution, 'that differentiation, if it is to pass constitutional muster, must not be arbitrary or irrational nor must it manifest a naked preference. There must be a rational connection between that differentiating law and the legitimate government purpose it is designed to achieve.'[71]

Rawlsian distributive ethics might tolerate those distinctions that ultimately benefit the least favoured in society, but again exhibiting the push–pull not all societies will be structured in such a way. For instance, to avoid arbitrariness in guaranteeing access to health, the social determinants of ill-health (including food and nutrition, housing, access to safe and potable water and adequate sanitation, safe and healthy working conditions, and a healthy environment) must be studied, challenged, and addressed.[72] The failure to address such particularities for all persons and groups contributes to morally arbitrary and discriminatory effects. Nevertheless, states continue to deny basic healthcare to migrants or persons with undocumented status, despite human rights pronouncements.[73] And, as Yamin explains, '[i]t is far from clear that we have a consensus in the human rights community about which inequalities in health constitute inequities or how egalitarian a society must be before all human rights, including health, can be realized'.[74]

Such arbitrary and discriminatory effects are only partially addressed by courts and institutions given that the laws they apply tend to underpin the naturalised narratives of privilege that they notionally are supposed to combat. Many courts give lip-service to wider or more differentiated social conceptions of rights but, foundationally, exhibit a deference to the status

---

[71] *Khosa v Minister of Social Development* 2004(6) BCLR 569 (CC), para 53. See, also, for landmark Indian constitutional court jurisprudence, *Maneka Gandhi v Union of India* AIR 1978 SC 597.

[72] UN Committee on Economic, Social and Cultural Rights (CESCR), 'General Comment No 14: the Right to the Highest Attainable Standard of Health (Art 12 of the Covenant)' (11 August 2000) UN Doc E/C.12/2000/4, para 4; World Health Organization/ Commission on the Social Determinants of Health, *Closing the Gap in a Generation. Health Equity through Action on the Social Determinants of Health* (2008). See, generally, Brigit Toebes and Karien Stronks, 'Closing the Gap: a Human Rights Approach towards Social Determinants of Health' (2016) 23(5) *Eur J Health L* 510.

[73] Toebes and Stronks (n 72).

[74] Alicia Ely Yamin, 'Shades of Dignity: Exploring the Demands of Equality in Applying Human Rights Frameworks to Health' (2009) 11 *Health & Hum Rts* 1, 2.

quo ladened with 'subjective values'.[75] When they stray from such deference, the "anarchist" judges are themselves attacked for their arbitrariness.[76]

A social conception of human rights would also see value in giving space and agency to those who have ostensibly been the objects of human rights protection but rarely the protagonists in framing their experiences of violations (if indeed that is a frame they wish to adopt) and identifying what would be required to rectify the breaches. It is progressively recognised that narratives that exclude rights holders from actively contributing to solutions or indeed maintaining their silence should they wish[77] end up legitimising certain interpretations of value and meaning and reinforcing Bourdieu and Passeron's sense of 'domination, oppression and violence'.[78] Individuals and groups that have been victimised hold the key to interpreting the impact of their experiences of victimisation (if this is how they wish to characterise those experiences) and determining how their situations can be improved on their terms. The growing recognition of the procedural rights of victims of crime,[79] and of the need for reparations to empower victims both procedurally and substantively by helping to transform the social contexts that contributed to the violations,[80] attest to this shift. But this 'juridified victimhood'[81] and the 'juridification' of their transformation through reparations[82] is arguably too the product of an arbitrary legal process that identifies who fits within the narrowed category of victimhood and who is excluded. And it also determines how transformation through reparations is to be achieved, with perfunctory opportunities for victims to participate in the self-flagellatory process of submission to the established, pious and self-congratulatory narratives of redemption and restoration. To call the process

---

[75] Alana Klein, 'The Arbitrariness in "Arbitrariness" (And Overbreadth and Gross Disproportionality): Principle and Democracy in Section 7 of the Charter' (2013) 63 *Supreme Ct L Rev*: Osgoode's Annual Constitutional Cases Conference 377, 384.

[76] Timothy Endicott, 'The Coxford Lecture: Arbitrariness' (2014) 27(1) *Can J Law & Jur* 49.

[77] Michelle Brear, 'Silence and Voice in Participatory Processes – Causes, Meanings and Implications for Empowerment' (2020) 55(2) *Comm Dev J* 349.

[78] Bourdieu and Passeron (n 17) 5.

[79] See, for example, Jonathan Doak, *Victims' Rights, Human Rights and Criminal Justice: Reconceiving the Role of Third Parties* (Bloomsbury 2008).

[80] Rashida Manjoo, 'Introduction: Reflections on the Concept and Implementation of Transformative Reparations' (2017) 21(9) *Intl J Hum Rts* 1193.

[81] Sara Kendall and Sarah Nouwen, 'Representational Practices at the International Criminal Court: the Gap Between Juridified and Abstract Victimhood' (2014) 76 *Law & Contemp Prob* 235, 241.

[82] On the arbitrariness of certain reparations processes, see Carla Ferstman, 'Reparations at the ICC: the Need for a Human Rights Based Approach to Effectiveness', in Carla Ferstman and Mariana Goetz (eds), *Reparations for Victims of Genocide, War Crimes and Crimes against Humanity: Systems in Place and Systems in the Making. Second Revised Edition* (Brill 2020) 446, 477.

reparative remains aspirational if not ideational. As Kendall notes, '[f]rom the standpoint of conflict-affected communities, the use of legal categories to determine qualification as a victim may seem arbitrary at best, in the sense that they are completely disconnected from their lived realities'.[83]

The shift in voice is also evident in the recognition of the need for prior consultation and consent of affected indigenous peoples and communities about development projects affecting land use and access to resources.[84] The African Court on Human and Peoples' Rights recognised, in its consideration of the claim brought by the Ogiek community against Kenya, that 'it is a basic requirement of international human rights law that indigenous peoples, like the Ogiek, be consulted in all decisions and actions that affect their lives. […] in an active and informed manner, in accordance with their customs and traditions, […] in good faith and using culturally-appropriate procedures'.[85] The Inter-American Court of Human Rights has found similarly.[86] For environmental matters, public participation has been recognised as essential to integrate public concerns and knowledge into policy decisions affecting the environment.[87] The transformation to victim-centred, public or people-centred procedures is intended, at least in principle, to rebalance the subjectivities of human rights, but it also risks reifying narratives of hierarchy and neo-colonial charity. Here still, while there has been significant progress, engagement risks being tokenistic or being part of a process leading towards broad, symbolic pronouncements without the practical impetus to ground a veritable enforcement of rights.

---

[83] Sara Kendall, 'Juridified Victimhood at the ICC', in Rudina Jasini and Gregory Townsend (eds), *Advancing the Impact of Victim Participation at the International Criminal Court: Bridging the Gap Between Research and Practice* (30 November 2020) <www.law.ox.ac.uk/sites/files/oxlaw/iccba_-_oxford_publication_30_november_2020_.pdf> 137, 142 accessed 10 July 2023.

[84] See, for example, UNCERD, General Recommendation No 23, Rights of Indigenous Peoples (Fifty-First Session, 1997) (18 August 1997) UN Doc A/52/18, annex V, para 4 (calling upon states to take certain measures to recognise and ensure the rights of indigenous peoples); Lorenzo Cotula, 'Between Hope and Critique: Human Rights, Social Justice and Re-Imagining International Law from the Bottom up' (2020) 48 *Ga J Intl & Comp L* 473; UN, *Guiding Principles on Business and Human Rights: Implementing the UN Protect, Respect and Remedy Framework* (2011) UN Doc HR/PUB/11/04.

[85] *African Commission on Human and Peoples' Rights v Republic of Kenya* (Reparations) (ACommHPR, 23 June 2022) App No 006/2012, para 142.

[86] *Saramaka People v Suriname* (Preliminary Objections, Merits, Reparations, and Costs) Series C No 172 (IACtHR 28 November 2007) paras 133–137.

[87] Economic Commission for Latin America and the Caribbean (ECLAC), 'Access to Information, Participation, and Justice in Environmental Matters in Latin America and the Caribbean: towards Achievement of the 2030 Agenda for Sustainable Development' (October 2018) LC/TS.2017/83, 13.

2.4.2 *"Arbitrary interference" and human rights decision-making*

The avoidance of arbitrary state power is a key function of human rights[88] and why the bar on arbitrary interference is a core principle underlying most rights protections: one cannot interfere with rights unless there is a legitimate reason to do so. Many, though not all[89] human rights prohibitions are relative in how they are applied. Whether a restriction, limitation or deprivation is justifiable will depend on the treaty framework and the right or freedom at issue.

"Arbitrariness" helps to clarify what is meant by the relative access to rights. A deprivation of a right would only be permissible on non-arbitrary grounds – on such grounds and in accordance with such procedures as are established by law,[90] or based on specific enumerated grounds.[91] Courts and treaty bodies routinely recognise that "arbitrary" interferences violate the underlying human rights obligation. But when is an interference considered "arbitrary"? How do courts assess "arbitrariness" in the context of relative rights, and what conclusions can be drawn from the practice?

Many human rights treaties and declarative texts recognise the overarching principles of legality, necessity and proportionality when determining whether an interference with rights is arbitrary. For example, Article 29 of the Universal Declaration of Human Rights provides: 'everyone shall be subject only to such limitations as are determined by law solely for the purpose of securing due recognition and respect for the rights and freedoms of others and of meeting the just requirements of morality, public order and the general welfare in a democratic society'.[92] For some other treaties without an explicit or overarching limitations clause, one has been derived through interpretation. For instance, the UN Human Rights Committee has interpreted "arbitrary interference" in Article 17(2) of the International Covenant on Civil and Political Rights (ICCPR), as a concept that:

> can also extend to interference provided for under the law. The introduction of the concept of arbitrariness is intended to guarantee that even interference provided for by law should be in accordance

---

[88] *Taxquet v Belgium* (Grand Chamber) App No 926/05 (ECtHR, 16 November 2010).

[89] There are some rights such as the prohibition of torture which are recognised as absolute – there can never be a legitimate justification to perpetrate torture.

[90] For example, Arts 6(1), 9(1) ICCPR.

[91] For example, Art 5(1) European Convention for the Protection of Human Rights and Fundamental Freedoms (ECHR) (adopted 4 November 1950, entered into force 3 September 1953).

[92] Universal Declaration of Human Rights (UDHR), General Assembly Resolution 217 A (10 December 1948) Art 29.

with the provisions, aims and objectives of the Covenant and should be, in any event, reasonable in the circumstances.[93]

This is similar to the approach taken in the International Covenant on Economic, Social and Cultural Rights (ICESCR) (though it does not use the term "arbitrary"). The Covenant delineates when rights can be limited and concludes that, among other factors, such limitations cannot be arbitrary. It provides that 'the State may subject such rights only to such limitations as are determined by law only in so far as this may be compatible with the nature of these rights and solely for the purpose of promoting the general welfare in a democratic society'.[94] By introducing a requirement that the limitation must be undertaken to promote general welfare in a democratic society, the ICESCR introduces a social conception of rights into its understanding of the purpose and weight to be given to relative rights and the circumstances in which such rights might be restricted. The UN Committee on Economic, Social and Cultural Rights, which has interpreted Article 4, has explained that the provision was intended to be protective of the rights of individuals and was not designed to introduce limitations on rights affecting the subsistence or survival of the individual or the integrity of the person.[95]

Some treaties also address the limitation of rights within the substantive provisions dealing with enumerated rights. Each treaty will have a slightly differently formulated limitation clause, for various rights within a treaty, and as between the treaties for same or similar rights. Several examples follow.

(i) Qualified rights

Qualified rights, such as the right to privacy, freedom of thought and religion, freedom of expression, assembly, or association, are those rights that are naturally subject to a range of competing interests. Human rights decision-making bodies regularly apply proportionality balancing to assess whether these rights can be legitimately restricted. This is the case though the rights and values at stake are rarely commensurate[96] and the task is not

---

[93] Human Rights Committee, General Comment No 16: Article 17 (Right to Privacy) Compilation of General Comments and General Recommendations, UN Doc HRI/GEN/1/Rev.1, 21 (1994).

[94] Art 4 International Covenant on Economic, Social and Cultural Rights (ICESCR) (adopted 16 December 1966, entered into force 3 January 1976).

[95] Committee on Economic, Social and Cultural Rights, Fact Sheet No.16 (Rev.1) (May 1996).

[96] Timothy Endicott, 'Proportionality and Incommensurability', in Grant Huscroft, Bradley Miller and Grégoire Webber (eds), *Proportionality and the Rule of Law: Rights, Justification, Reasoning* (CUP 2014) 311. Scholars such as Habermas have argued that the balancing of

really one of balancing, as how the rights are weighed against other interests is not a simple task of determining which weighs more.[97]

The weighing of interests occurs in stages. First, there is a determination of whether the infringement is provided for by law. This criterion requires that there is a law, legitimately enacted, on which the interference with the right is based and in which the authorities are authorised to limit the right in question. The law must be clear, sufficiently precise and accessible to enable persons to reasonably foresee the consequences.[98] For example, the Inter-American Commission on Human Rights has clarified in relation to freedom of expression that 'vague or ambiguous legal provisions that grant [...] very broad discretionary powers to the authorities, are incompatible with the American Convention, because they can support potential arbitrary acts that are tantamount to prior censorship or that establish disproportionate liabilities for the expression of protected speech'.[99]

Second, the restriction should pursue a legitimate aim.[100] What might constitute a legitimate aim or purpose would depend on the right being restricted and the rationale given for the restriction. The rationales considered in the case law include the need to protect the rights of others, the protection of the reputation or rights of others, or the need to fulfil a particular public interest such as national security, the prevention of crime or maintenance of public order, the protection of public health, morals, the economic well-being, or territorial integrity of the country. The basic understandings of these conditions may be obvious societal aims, but the outer edges much less so. Many are laden with moralistic visions that lend a form of arbitrariness to the weighing up of seemingly competing rights and the results of that process.[101] As Çali argues: 'Communal interests that are bundled under public morality and general economic welfare of the country are particularly

---

rights and interests is essentially a policy exercise void of objectivity in which judges base their decisions on excessive discretion. See Juergen Habermas, *Between Facts and Norms* (trans. W Rehg) (Cambridge 1996) 256–259.

[97] As Çali notes: '[A]ny exercise of balancing implies an image of weights assigned to values and a head to head comparison of these weights. In order for a balancing exercise to work, the differences between important interests have to be differences in degree. In the field of human rights protection, this view assumes that human rights are in constant competition with communal aims. Therefore, it overlooks that differences in kind between interests and values are not susceptible to weighing on a single scale': Başak Çali, 'Balancing Human Rights? Methodological Problems with Weights, Scales and Proportions' (2007) 29(1) *Hum Rts Q* 251, 256–257.

[98] *The Sunday Times v United Kingdom* App No 6538/74 (ECtHR, 26 April 1979) para 49.

[99] IACommHR, Office of the Special Rapporteur for Freedom of Expression, *The Inter-American Legal Framework regarding the Right to Freedom of Expression* (2010) para 70.

[100] For example, Art 19(3) ICCPR.

[101] *S.A.S. v France (Grand Chamber)* App No 43835/11 (ECtHR, 1 July 2014) paras 141–159.

suspect as challenges to the recognition and accommodation of diversity by human rights protections.'[102]

Third, the interference with the right should be necessary in a democratic society. This requires a showing of a "pressing social need" for the interference and that it is rationally connected with and proportionate to the aim pursued, in the sense that the restriction impaired the right in the least obstructive way. This condition affords significant contingency in how it is applied, though states must still show that the measure taken to limit the right in question is the least restrictive as possible. The European Court of Human Rights (ECtHR) has generally conceded a wide margin of appreciation to national authorities to determine what is 'necessary in a democratic society'.[103] What constitutes "democratic values" is subject to differing viewpoints, and there is a tendency to valorise majoritarian interpretations; in the sense of Bourdieu this contributes to the reinforcement of the status quo.[104] What constitutes a "pressing social need" is equally value laden. Every limitation will additionally be subject to the principle of non-discrimination; measures that limit rights in a discriminatory way will fail the test of proportionality. Nevertheless, it is not always apparent how discrimination enters into the evaluation of the different rights at stake.

The example of the qualified right to privacy and family life[105] follows (more or less) the patterns described. Any interference with the right must be proportional to the end sought and be necessary in the circumstances of any given case.[106] In *Toonen v Australia*,[107] which concerned the prohibition of homosexual sex as a violation of the right to privacy, the UN Human Rights Committee determined that, to avoid arbitrariness, interference with rights must be reasonable and proportional to the end sought and be necessary in the circumstances of the case. The Committee further clarified that 'the introduction of the concept of arbitrariness is intended to guarantee that even interference provided for by law should be in accordance with the provisions, aims and objective of the Covenant and should be, in any

---

[102] Çali (n 97) 263.
[103] *Handyside v United Kingdom* App No 5493/72 (ECtHR, 7 December 1976) para 48.
[104] Bourdieu and Passeron (n 17) 5. See, also, Louis Althusser, *On the Reproduction of Capitalism: Ideology and Ideological State Apparatuses* (Verso 2014).
[105] Art 17 ICCPR; Art 11(2) ACHR; Art 8 ECHR; Art 16(3) UDHR.
[106] Human Rights Council (HRC), 'The Right to Privacy in the Digital Age', Report of the Office of the UN High Commissioner for Human Rights (30 June 2014) UN Doc A/HRC/27/37, para 21.
[107] *Toonen v Australia*, Comm No 488/1992, UN Doc CCPR/C/50/D/488/1992 (31 March 1994) para 8.3. See, also, *Van Hulst v The Netherlands*, Comm No 903/1999, UN Doc CCPR/C/82/D/903/1999 (1 November 2004) para 7.3 (regarding unlawful interference with the right to privacy).

event, reasonable in the particular circumstances'.[108] Thus, public authorities can only legitimately interfere with the right where it can be demonstrated that doing so is lawful, necessary and proportionate and, in respect of the European Convention on Human Rights (ECHR) framing of the right,[109] when it is done to protect one of a list of enumerated rights: national security; public safety; the economy; health or morals; the rights and freedoms of other people; or to prevent disorder or crime.[110]

The ECtHR has taken a similar approach, recognising that the purpose of the right to respect for privacy and family life is 'essentially that of protecting the individual against arbitrary interference by the public authorities'.[111] In the *Christine Goodwin* case, which involved the legal acknowledgment of the post-transition gender of a transsexual person, the ECtHR recognised that in the absence of any 'concrete or substantial hardship or detriment to the public interest', 'society may reasonably be expected to tolerate a certain inconvenience to enable individuals to live in dignity and worth in accordance with the sexual identity chosen by them at great personal cost'.[112]

(ii) Limited rights: the arbitrary deprivation of the right to life

With the qualified rights described earlier, upon the determination that there is an interference, there will be a secondary assessment using proportionality criteria to decide whether that interference is legitimate. Limited rights operate differently. Such rights are limited only in specific and narrow ways and are not subject to the same sort of balancing exercise as qualified rights. The determination as to whether the treatment resulting in the act in question was legitimate is mainly incorporated directly into the definition of the right. There will only be a violation of the right if the acts in question do not fulfil the non-arbitrariness clauses already situated within the definition. This single-stage approach is evident in respect of the arbitrary deprivation of the right to life, which is discussed in this section, and with respect to the arbitrary deprivation of liberty and security of the person, canvassed in section 2.5 of this chapter.

The distinction between qualified and limited rights is explained by Verdirame, who indicates:

---

[108] Human Rights Committee, 'General Comment No 16: Article 17 (Right to Privacy)' (n 93).
[109] Neither the ICCPR nor the ACHR sets out a list of permissible limitations.
[110] Art 8(2) ECHR.
[111] *Airey* v *Ireland* App No 6289/73 (ECtHR, 9 October 1979).
[112] *Christine Goodwin v United Kingdom* (Grand Chamber) App No 28957/95 (ECtHR, 11 July 2002) para 91.

> [T]he exercise of limited rights is not subject to a general principle of balancing. To say that my right is limited is to say that it does not extend beyond a specified area: no question of balancing arises if I stay within the limits of the right. The areas excluded from the scope of the right may be defined teleologically, in which case a means-end review will be called for.[113]

However, even under this view this should not mean that there is no balancing exercise at all. In *McCann*, a right to life case that involved the killing by members of the security forces of three members of the Irish Republican Army, the ECtHR determined that, in considering the meaning of the use of lethal force that is no more than absolutely necessary, the use of the term "absolutely necessary" 'indicates that a stricter and more compelling test of necessity must be employed from that normally applicable when determining whether State action is necessary in a democratic society'; the provisions must be 'strictly construed' and are limited only by the 'exhaustive and narrowly interpreted' objectives listed.[114] Thus, even when those listed scenarios of non-arbitrariness are present, the use of lethal force must be essential and strictly proportionate to be considered non-arbitrary. Force is proportionate when it is appropriate and no more than necessary to address the problem concerned. Consequently, there may be aspects of the definitions that require contextual proportionality analysis, even though this is a more focused review than what is envisioned for qualified rights.

Most relevant human rights treaties recognise the prohibition on the arbitrary deprivation of life.[115] Some of the articles setting out this prohibition list specifically the conduct that would qualify as non-arbitrary. For example, Article 2 of the ECHR (which does not refer explicitly to the prohibition of the arbitrary deprivation of life) identifies the scenario of when the death penalty is applied in the execution of a sentence of a court following a conviction of a crime for which this penalty is provided by law

---

[113] Guglielmo Verdirame, 'Rescuing Human Rights from Proportionality', in Rowan Cruft et al, *Philosophical Foundations of Human Rights* (OUP 2015), 341, 348.

[114] *McCann, Farrell, and Savage v United Kingdom* (Grand Chamber) App No 18984/91 (ECtHR, 27 September 1995) paras 147–150.

[115] Art 6(1) ICCPR; Art 4(1) ACHR; Art 4 ACHPR; Art 5(2) Arab Charter all refer to the prohibition of the "arbitrary" deprivation of life. Art 2(1) ECHR; Art 6 CRC; Art 10 CPRMW; Art 11 ASEAN Human Rights Declaration; Art 4(a) Inter-American Convention on the Prevention, Punishment and Eradication of Violence against Women ('Convention of Belem do Para') (adopted 9 June 1994, entered into force 5 March 1995); and Art 10 CRPD do not use the word "arbitrary" in the respective provisions on the right to life though the prohibition of arbitrary interferences with the right to life can be gleaned from the texts and their interpretations.

(in countries where the death penalty remains permissible and is itself not arbitrarily applied). It also lists the scenarios in which the deprivation of life would be permissible so long as the use of force was no more than absolutely necessary.[116] In interpreting these provisions, the ECtHR focuses on ensuring that states have in place an adequate legal framework to regulate the use of firearms and effective safeguards against arbitrariness and abuse of force.[117] Also, the ECtHR has held that states must have in place a system to review the lawfulness of the use of lethal force.[118]

The UN Human Rights Committee has clarified the meaning of "arbitrary deprivation" in the context of the right to life and the ICCPR treaty framework,[119] giving scenarios of non-arbitrary conduct: the use of lethal force in self-defence or to protect life from an imminent threat, and in pursuit of exceptional measures established by law and accompanied by effective institutional safeguards designed to prevent arbitrary deprivations of life.[120] Human Rights Committee General Comment 36 on the right to life makes clear that the requirement that the prohibition is 'protected by law' and the prohibition against "arbitrary" deprivation of life, though independent, are overlapping in that 'a deprivation of life that lacks a legal basis or is otherwise inconsistent with life-protecting laws and procedures is, as a rule, arbitrary in nature'.[121] Furthermore, even if a deprivation of life is authorised by domestic law, it may still be arbitrary to the extent that it demonstrates features such as 'inappropriateness, injustice, lack of predictability and due process of law, as well as elements of reasonableness, necessity and proportionality'.[122]

The American Convention on Human Rights and African Charter on Human and Peoples' Rights both prohibit the arbitrary deprivation of life, though provide no definition of "arbitrariness".[123] In the context of an armed conflict, determinations as to whether there has been an arbitrary deprivation of life in the sense of Article 6 ICCPR would need to take into account the standards of arbitrariness under international humanitarian law

---

[116] Art 2(1) and (2) ECHR.

[117] *Giuliani and Gaggio v Italy (Grand Chamber)* App No 23458/02 (ECtHR, 24 March 2011) para 209; *Nachova v Bulgaria (Grand Chamber)* App Nos 43577/98, 43579/98 (ECtHR, 6 July 2005) paras 99–102.

[118] *McCann v United Kingdom* (n 114) para 161.

[119] Human Rights Committee, General Comment No 36 (n 67) paras 10–12.

[120] Ibid. See, also, Human Rights Committee, *Suárez de Guerrero v Colombia*, Comm No R.11/45, UN Doc Supp. No 40 (A/37/40) (31 March 1982) para 13.2.

[121] Human Rights Committee, General Comment No 36 (n 67) para 11.

[122] Ibid para 12. See, also, UNGA, 'Report of the Special Rapporteur on Extrajudicial, Summary or Arbitrary Executions', UN Doc A/73/314 (7 August 2018) para 15.

[123] Art 4 ACHPR; Art 4(1) ACHR.

(IHL).[124] Thus, the interpretation of arbitrariness within a treaty may also vary if the context brings to the fore another branch of law.

2.4.3 "Arbitrariness" and positive obligations

Human rights obligations encompass the obligation to respect, protect and fulfil the rights in question. While the nature of the obligations will depend upon the right in question, they invariably include both negative obligations (what a state must refrain from doing) and positive obligations (what a state must do to secure to individuals and groups within its jurisdiction access to the rights in question).

As set out in section 2.4.2, a deprivation or limitation of a right would only be permissible on non-arbitrary grounds. The state's failure to meet its positive obligations to ensure the realisation of rights in practice (whether these stemmed from the failure to meet a general duty to adopt new laws or procedures; the duty to investigate certain human rights abuses; or the duty to take operational measures to protect persons at real and immediate risk to life or bodily or mental integrity, where the authorities know or ought to know of the risk)[125] would also constitute a deprivation of a human right and violate the state's human rights obligations. A proportionality analysis is relevant to interpret or determine the scope of states' positive obligations as there must be a rational assessment of competing interests and objectives to ensure that decisions about the actions to take to meet the positive obligations were not arbitrary. However, the proportionality analysis may look slightly different given the emphasis of positive obligations on requiring states to exercise due diligence to ensure that human rights can be realised.[126]

Still, assessing whether states have met their positive obligations in respect of qualified rights such as the right to privacy, the freedom of thought and religion, freedom of expression, assembly, or association has been

---

[124] *Legality of the Threat or Use of Nuclear Weapons* (Advisory Opinion) [1996] ICJ Rep 226, para 25. Exactly how much consideration should be given to IHL is subject to debate. See, for example, Marko Milanović, 'Norm Conflicts, International Humanitarian Law, and Human Rights Law', in Orna Ben-Naftali (ed), *International Humanitarian Law and International Human Rights Law*, Collected Courses of the Academy of European Law (OUP 2011) 95, 99–101.

[125] *Volodina v Russia* App No 41261/17 (ECtHR, 9 July 2019) para 77 (referring to positive obligations under Art 3 ECHR).

[126] This is the argument put forward by Matthias Klatt in 'Positive Obligations under the European Convention on Human Rights' (2011) 71 *Heidelberg J Intl L* 691, 695, where he argues that for positive obligations, the proportionality test 'necessarily contains two lines of values: Both the intensity of interference by non-protection and the degree of protection are required in order to assess whether the prohibition of insufficient means has been violated' (718).

challenging. As Stoyanova has argued regarding the ECtHR, while states are required when restricting qualified rights to do so in a way that restricts the right in the most limited way possible, there is not a comparable test for positive obligations in which the state is required 'to undertake the most protective measures to ensure the rights. The starting point is rather that States can choose the measures and their failure to choose the best measure for protecting a person (arguably in fulfilment of a positive obligation) does not necessary lead to a breach.'[127]

In regards to the right to privacy and family life, the ECtHR has considered *inter alia* the importance of the interest at stake and whether 'fundamental values' or 'essential aspects' of the right are at issue as well as the impact of the positive obligation at stake on the state concerned.[128] While the ECtHR has recognised that in cases raising 'particularly important facet[s] of an individual's existence or identity, the margin of appreciation that states enjoy will be restricted, this will nevertheless become more expansive if there is no European consensus, and particularly where the case raises sensitive moral or ethical issues, the margin will be wider'.[129] Arguably, however, the rationale for affording greater flexibility to states when sensitive moral or ethical issues are engaged is questionable, as this is when vulnerable or marginalised persons may be at greatest risk of violations. This approach risks diluting the protection of the Convention as opposed to ensuring adequate protection when it is needed most. In some other cases involving qualified rights, the ECtHR has recognised the existence of positive obligations. For instance, it recognised that the right to peaceful assembly encompasses both negative obligations (to abstain from interfering with the right to protest) and positive obligations (to protect a lawful demonstration against counter-demonstrations).[130]

---

[127] Vladislava Stoyanova, 'Framing Positive Obligations under the European Convention on Human Rights Law: Mediating between the Abstract and the Concrete' (2023) 23 *Hum Rts L Rev* 1, 10.

[128] *Hämäläinen v Finland* (Grand Chamber) App No 37359/09 (ECtHR, 16 July 2014) para 66. In denying the existence of a violation, the Grand Chamber held that given the sensitive moral and ethical issues raised by the case and the absence of a European consensus, Art 8 did not require states to provide for non-heterosexual marriages nor to accord the right of a transgender person to preserve their marriage. See, the joint dissenting opinion of Judges Sajó, Keller and Lemmens in the *Hämäläinen* case (ibid) in which it is argued that the interference is not necessary in a democratic society (para 14). A similar approach to the majority in *Hämäläinen* is *Johnston et al v Ireland* App No 9697/82 (ECtHR, 18 December 1986) where the Court held that Art 8 cannot be regarded as extending to an obligation to introduce measures permitting divorce and re-marriage (para 57; see, also, para 55(c)).

[129] *Hämäläinen v Finland* (Grand Chamber) App No 37359/09 (ECtHR, 16 July 2014) para 67.

[130] *Öllinger v Austria* App No 76900/01 (ECtHR, 29 June 2006).

With respect to the arbitrary deprivation of the right to life, the UN Human Rights Committee confirmed states' 'due diligence obligation to take reasonable, positive measures that do not impose disproportionate burdens on them in response to reasonably foreseeable threats to life'.[131] It also requires states to *inter alia* 'take special measures of protection towards persons in vulnerable situations whose lives have been placed at particular risk because of specific threats or pre-existing patterns of violence',[132] and to take 'appropriate measures to address the general conditions in society that may give rise to direct threats to life or prevent individuals from enjoying their right to life with dignity'.[133] Of course, what will constitute 'appropriate measures' will depend on the circumstances, but it is argued here that, in order to meet the requirement of non-arbitrariness, there is a need to adopt some form of proportionality analysis to assess the measures taken against the known risks.

2.5 The "arbitrariness" in arbitrary detention

In this book, I argue that forms of privilege and other morally arbitrary factors influence which individuals are detained, when, for how long and in what conditions. Policies of securitisation and criminalisation have exacerbated these arbitrary distinctions given their propensity to reify "otherness". How these policies are applied and their impact on individuals and communities depends on the underlying political values and goals at stake, which differ between countries and over time. The security posited by these policies has little to do with the liberty and security of the person that the prohibition of arbitrary detention is supposed to foster. It is the contingency of this double meaning of security – "who's security?" – which makes the prohibition of arbitrary detention so rudderless. And it is this rudderless prohibition of arbitrary detention that infuses the prohibition itself with an excess of arbitrariness.

International human rights courts and treaty bodies have had only minimal success in clawing back against these tendencies of securitisation and criminalisation, particularly in those areas of detention perceived to raise the greatest concerns about sovereignty, national identity and national security. The tension is particularly evident in areas involving non-citizens, racialised communities and minority groups, and responses to internal or international security threats. Human rights bodies have been relatively robust in withstanding the direct pressure from states to change major

---

[131] Human Rights Committee, General Comment No 36 (n 67) para 21.
[132] Human Rights Committee, General Comment No 36 (n 67) para 23.
[133] Human Rights Committee, General Comment No 36 (n 67) para 26.

course by watering down human rights standards in areas states perceive to be fundamental to their national interests. Yet, these bodies have arguably been less adept at resisting (and they have not always resisted) the more subtle pressures to widen flexibilities and contextualisation into their decision-making processes, or in some cases to fill in what are mainly porous, nuanced standards with state-friendly moderations, in some cases leading to the same result of lowered standards.

2.5.1 *The history and meaning of "arbitrary" in arbitrary detention*

The right to liberty and security of the person is a fundamental human right recognised by most relevant international human rights treaties and declarative texts.[134] It is intrinsically connected to human dignity and is the ultimate expression of the minimum protections individuals (should) have against the coercive power of the state. The right to liberty and security of the person also constitutes an essential component of many countries' constitutional systems.[135]

Following on from the adoption in 1956 of the Universal Declaration of Human Rights (UDHR) and its Article 9, the (then) UN Commission on Human Rights established a committee to study the right of everyone to be free from arbitrary arrest, detention and exile.[136] Attesting to the importance the Commission placed on the issue, it was the first-ever subject it selected for special study.[137] In defining "arbitrary", the Commission had regard to the *travaux préparatoires* on Article 9 UDHR, as well as Article 9 of the (then) draft Covenant on Civil and Political Rights.[138] It understood that 'an arrest or detention is arbitrary if it is (a) on grounds or in accordance with procedures other than those established by law, or (b) under the provisions of a law the purpose of which is incompatible with respect for the right to liberty and security of person'.[139] Thus, there was a clear concern about laws that were properly enacted but nevertheless unnecessarily oppressive or unfair. The Commission set out fundamental guarantees against arbitrary arrest

---

[134] Art 9 UDHR; Art 9(1) ICCPR; Art 7 ACHR; Art 6 ACHPR; Art 5 ECHR; Art 14 Arab Charter; Art 12 ASEAN Human Rights Declaration; Art 14(1) CRPD; Art 37(b) CRC; Art 16 CPRMW.

[135] UN Commission on Human Rights, 'Study of the right of everyone to be free from arbitrary arrest, detention, and exile' (1964) UN Doc E/CN.4/826/Rev.1, para 54.

[136] Ibid.

[137] Ibid para 1. See, also, UN Commission on Human Rights, Report of the 12th session (5–29 March 1956) UN Doc E/CN.4/731, particularly paras 72–83.

[138] Study of the right of everyone to be free from arbitrary arrest, detention, and exile (n 135) paras 24–27.

[139] Ibid para 27.

and detention, including an independent judiciary,[140] procedural safeguards against arbitrary arrest and detention[141] including restrictions on pre-trial detention.[142] Its focuses in the report foreshadow many of the areas in which arbitrary detention remains most problematic. In addition to criminal law detentions, the Commission also considered the potential for arbitrariness with respect to the detention of persons with reduced mental capacities,[143] with infectious diseases,[144] drug addictions,[145] unauthorised aliens,[146] and the use of detention for minor offences or debt.[147] It also addressed the powers of arrest in emergency or exceptional situations.[148]

The work of the Commission contributed substantially to the development of the definition of arbitrary detention in Article 9 ICCPR, and influenced later texts and procedures, such as the UN Body of Principles for the Protection of All Persons under Any Form of Detention or Imprisonment.[149] It also contributed to the impetus to create the UN Working Group on Arbitrary Detention (WGAD), which was established in 1991 by the former Commission on Human Rights.[150] According to the WGAD, 'the prohibition of all forms of arbitrary deprivation of liberty forms a part of international customary law and constitutes a peremptory or jus cogens norm'.[151] The peremptory status of the prohibition of arbitrary detention has also been affirmed by the Human Rights Committee in its General Comment No. 29 on states of emergency,[152] the Committee on the Protection of the Rights of All Migrant Workers and Members of Their Families[153] and, as the International Court of Justice (ICJ) made clear in

---

[140] Ibid paras 58–68.
[141] Ibid paras 72–74.
[142] Ibid paras 211–223.
[143] Ibid paras 731–736.
[144] Ibid para 737.
[145] Ibid paras 738–740.
[146] Ibid paras 741–742.
[147] Ibid paras 743–744.
[148] Ibid paras 753–787.
[149] General Assembly Resolution 43/173 (9 December 1998).
[150] UN Commission on Human Rights, Resolution 1991/42 (5 March 1991) UN Doc E/CN.4/RES/1991/42.
[151] WGAD, 'Deliberation No 9 concerning the definition and scope of arbitrary deprivation of liberty under customary international law', UN Doc A/HRC/22/44 (24 December 2012) para 75.
[152] Human Rights Committee, 'General Comment No 29: States of Emergency (Article 4)', UN Doc CCPR/C/21/Rev.1/Add.11 (31 August 2001) para 11.
[153] Committee on the Protection of the Rights of All Migrant Workers and Members of Their Families, 'General Comment No 5 (2021) on Migrants' Rights to Liberty and Freedom from Arbitrary Detention and their Connection with Other Human Rights', (21 July 2022) UN Doc CMW/C/GC/5 para 16: 'The prohibition of arbitrary detention is

the *Hostages* case, '[w]rongfully to deprive human beings of their freedom and to subject them to physical constraint in conditions of hardship is in itself manifestly incompatible with the principles of the Charter of the United Nations, as well as with the fundamental principles enunciated in the Universal Declaration of Human Rights'.[154] The prohibition has also been recognised as a peremptory norm applicable in both international and non-international armed conflicts.[155]

The meaning of "arbitrary" in arbitrary detention derives from the framing of the concept under human rights law. The right to detain in certain circumstances is well-recognised; detention is only illegitimate when it meets the conditions for arbitrariness. This has been taken to include elements of inappropriateness, injustice, lack of predictability or due process of law, unreasonableness, or is otherwise unnecessary or disproportionate.[156] In *A v United Kingdom* the ECtHR indicated:

> to avoid being branded as arbitrary, detention [...] must be carried out in good faith; it must be closely connected to the ground of detention relied on by the Government; the place and conditions of detention should be appropriate; and the length of detention should not exceed that reasonably required for the purpose pursued.[157]

The Human Rights Committee has indicated that even 'remand in custody pursuant to lawful arrest must not only be lawful but reasonable in all the circumstances'.[158] It had also made clear already from 1982 that preventive

---

absolute; it is a non-derogable rule of customary international law, or a jus cogens norm. The prohibition of arbitrary deprivation of liberty also protects migrants…'.

[154] *Case Concerning United States Diplomatic and Consular Staff in Tehran (United States of America v Iran)* [1980] ICJ Rep 3, para 91.

[155] ICRC, 'Customary International Law Database' (undated) <www.icrc.org/customary-ihl/eng/docs/home> accessed 11 July 2023, Rule 99: Arbitrary deprivation of liberty is prohibited.

[156] *Mukong v Cameroon*, Comm No 458/1991, UN Doc CCPR/C/51/D/458/1991 (21 July 1994) para 9.8. See, also, UN Human Rights Committee, General Comment No 35, Article 9 (Liberty and Security of Person) (16 December 2014) UN Doc CCPR/C/GC/35 para 12; Committee on the Protection of the Rights of All Migrant Workers and Members of Their Families, General Comment No 5 (n 153) para 19: arbitrary detention is 'any deprivation of liberty that exceeds the limits of reasonableness. It is not sufficient for the detention to pursue a legitimate purpose and be permitted by law, rather, it must meet the criteria of necessity and proportionality, be based on an individualized assessment and be periodically reassessed to ensure that it continues to meet those criteria.'

[157] *A v United Kingdom (Grand Chamber)* App No 3455/05 (ECtHR, 19 February 2009) para 164.

[158] *Van Alphen v The Netherlands*, Comm No 305/1988, UN Doc A/45/40 (15 August 1990) para 5.8.

detention on security grounds must satisfy those same conditions of non-arbitrariness.[159] Detention that is initially considered lawful may become "arbitrary" if it is unduly prolonged or not subject to periodic review.[160]

The Committee on the Protection of the Rights of All Migrant Workers has explained that, as a function of the rule against arbitrariness:

> [a]ny use of detention in the context of migration must [...] be based on a legitimate State objective, provided for in national law, employed always as an exceptional measure of last resort compatible with the criteria of necessity and proportionality, limited in scope and duration, imposed only where less restrictive alternatives have been considered and found inadequate to meet legitimate purposes, and subject to periodic re-evaluation and judicial review. In addition, the conditions of detention must be proportionate to the legitimate aim sought and must always meet minimum international standards. [...] Any compulsory, automatic, systematic or widespread detention of migrant workers and members of their families is arbitrary. In addition, the Committee considers that the prohibition of arbitrary detention also extends to the use of detention as a deterrent or as a general migration management tool to contain immigration.[161]

The prohibition of arbitrary detention has also been affirmed in judgments of the Inter-American Court of Human Rights[162] and reports of the Inter-American Commission on Human Rights,[163] as it has by the African Commission on Human and Peoples' Rights.[164]

---

[159] Human Rights Committee, 'General Comment No 8: Article 9 (Right to Liberty and Security of Persons)' (30 June 1982) para 4, in Compilation of General Comments and General Recommendations Adopted by Human Rights Treaty Bodies, UN Doc HRI/GEN/1/Rev.1 at 8 (1994). This (and other contexts of detention which may give rise to arbitrariness) are expanded upon in General Comment No 35 (n 156).

[160] Human Rights Committee, General Comment No 35 (n 156) para 12.

[161] Committee on the Protection of the Rights of All Migrant Workers and Members of Their Families, General Comment No 5 (n 153) paras 16, 17.

[162] See, for example, *Tibi v Ecuador* (Preliminary Objections, Merits, Reparations and Costs) Series C No 114 (7 September 2004) paras 94–98; *Case of Gangaram Panday v Surinam* (Merits, Reparations and Costs) Series C No 16 (21 January 1994) para 47; *Vélez Loor v Panama* (Preliminary Objections, Merits, Reparations and Costs) Series C No 218 (23 November 2010) para 139.

[163] See, for example, IACommHR, *Toward the Closure of Guantánamo* (3 June 2015) OAS/Ser.L/V/II. Doc 20/15.

[164] *Jean-Marie Atangana Mebara v Cameroon*, Comm No 416/12 (ACommHPR, 8 August 2015); *Amnesty International v Sudan*, Comm Nos 48/90, 50/91, 52/91, and 89/93 (ACommHPR, 15 November 1999).

The WGAD has brought further clarity to the definition of "arbitrariness", noting:

> [It] can arise from the law itself or from the particular conduct of Government officials. A detention, even if it is authorized by law, may still be considered arbitrary if it is premised upon an arbitrary piece of legislation or is inherently unjust, relying for instance on discriminatory grounds. An overly broad statute authorizing automatic and indefinite detention without any standards or review is by implication arbitrary.[165]

As part of its working methods, the WGAD identifies five categories of scenarios that would amount to arbitrary detention:

> Category I: When it is clearly impossible to invoke any legal basis justifying the deprivation of liberty (as when a person is kept in detention after the completion of their sentence or despite an amnesty law applicable to them);
>
> Category II: When the deprivation of liberty results from the exercise of the rights or freedoms guaranteed by articles 7, 13, 14, 18, 19, 20 and 21 of the Universal Declaration of Human Rights and, insofar as states parties are concerned, by articles 12, 18, 19, 21, 22, 25, 26 and 27 of the International Covenant on Civil and Political Rights;
>
> Category III: When the total or partial non-observance of the international norms relating to the right to a fair trial, spelled out in the Universal Declaration of Human Rights and in the relevant international instruments accepted by the states concerned, is of such gravity as to give the deprivation of liberty an arbitrary character;
>
> Category IV: When asylum seekers, immigrants or refugees are subjected to prolonged administrative custody without the possibility of administrative or judicial review or remedy; and
>
> Category V: When the deprivation of liberty constitutes a violation of international law for reasons of discrimination based on birth; national, ethnic, or social origin; language; religion; economic condition; political or other opinion; gender; sexual orientation; or disability or other status, and which aims towards or can result in ignoring the equality of human rights.[166]

---

[165] WGAD, 'Deliberation No 9 Concerning the Definition and Scope of Arbitrary Deprivation of Liberty under Customary International Law', UN Doc A/HRC/22/44 (24 December 2012) para 63.

[166] Ibid para 38.

2.5.2 Arbitrary detention: both qualified and limited

The ICCPR sets out a general prohibition against arbitrary detention and refrains from enumerating what may constitute legitimate reasons to detain, though it recognises the possibility for individuals to be detained on criminal charges (without specifying the circumstances in which such detentions might be arbitrary).[167] When interpreting the ICCPR, the Human Rights Committee has applied a proportionality analysis to assess whether a given detention is justifiable in the circumstances of the case.[168] In *A v Australia*, the Committee made clear its view that the detention of migrants is not per se arbitrary,[169] though it could be considered arbitrary 'if it is not necessary in all circumstances of the case, for example to prevent flight or interference with evidence'.[170] It also held that it was necessary to review periodically the grounds for justifying the detention and to ensure that detention did not continue beyond the period in which the state could provide appropriate justification.[171] The Committee has further clarified that detention will be arbitrary when a detainee is not accorded adequate procedural safeguards.[172] Thus, for detention to be non-arbitrary, it would need to be used as a last resort – when there are no other available options.

While ultimately the Human Rights Committee determined in *A v Australia* that the detention was arbitrary, its framing of the issues represents a subtle shift away from the recognition of a natural state of liberty and security of the person. It indicates that detention *could* be considered arbitrary if the requirement for necessity was not made out. However, the Human Rights Committee should have contended that it *would* be considered arbitrary if the grounds for necessity were not present. If necessity is a required criterion, then the absence of the criterion would surely lead to a finding of arbitrariness. Is this simply a question of semantics? The Committee on the Protection of the Rights of All Migrant Workers and Their Families has seen the need to underscore this point: '*Any* compulsory, automatic, systematic or widespread detention of migrant workers and members of their families *is* arbitrary'[173] [emphases added].

Certainly detentions should comply with the requirements of legality, necessity and proportionality, indeed, they must do. The issue is how these

---

[167] Arts 9(2) and 9(3) ICCPR.
[168] *A v Australia*, Comm No 560/1993 UN Doc CCPR/C/59/D/560/93 (30 April 1997).
[169] Ibid para 9.3.
[170] Ibid para 9.2.
[171] Ibid para 9.4.
[172] *Campbell v Jamaica*, Comm No 618/1995, UN Doc CCPR/C/64/D/618/1995 (3 November 1998) para 6.3.
[173] Committee on the Protection of the Rights of All Migrant Workers and Members of Their Families, General Comment No 5 (n 153) para 17 (emphasis added).

various requirements interact. As the Special Rapporteur on the Human Rights of Migrants has indicated, the obligation to always consider alternatives to detention (non-custodial measures) before resorting to detention should be established by law, and detailed guidelines and proper training should be developed for judges and other state officials, such as police, border and immigration officers, in order to ensure a systematic application of non-custodial measures instead of detention.[174] Any decision to detain must consider all relevant factors, including the availability of less invasive options to achieve ends that are determined to be legitimate on a case-by-case basis and not be based on a mandatory rule for a broad category of persons. This approach is like that of most other human rights treaties and their interpretive bodies, including the American Convention[175] and the African Charter on Human and Peoples' Rights.[176]

As already explored in sub-section 2.4.2(ii) of this chapter: 'Limited rights: the arbitrary deprivation of the right to life', at least in respect of the ECtHR, a heightened test of necessity – 'no more than absolutely necessary' – is employed for violations involving the use of lethal force.[177] But what test is used for arbitrary detention?

The ECtHR recognises that detention will only be lawful in accordance with the various sub-sections of Article 5 when it is both in accordance with a 'procedure prescribed by law' and where the deprivation of liberty is in keeping with the purpose of Article 5, namely to protect the individual from arbitrariness.[178] The case law makes clear that what will be considered arbitrary shifts depending on the type of detention involved. In some cases, detention will only need to satisfy a lesser test of necessity, where it is 'reasonably considered necessary to prevent his committing an offence or fleeing after having done so'.[179] This lowered standard of necessity, which has been applied by the ECtHR to preventive detention cases involving allegations of involvement in organised crime and terrorism, has not been taken on board by other bodies. Indeed, the WGAD has set out that '[r]esort

---

[174] HRC, 'Report of the Special Rapporteur on the Human Rights of Migrants, François Crépeau to the UN Human Rights Council (20th session)' UN Doc A/HRC/20/24 (2 April 2012) para 53.
[175] See, for example, *Chaparro Alvarez and Lapo Iniguez v Ecuador* (Preliminary Objections, Merits, Reparations, and Costs) Series C No 170 (21 November 2007) para 93.
[176] *Mebara v Cameroon* (n 164) paras 125–131.
[177] *McCann, Farrell, and Savage v United Kingdom* (n 114).
[178] *Amuur v France* App No 19776/92 (ECtHR, 25 June 1996) para 50. However, see *Saadi v UK* App No 13229/03 (ECtHR, 29 January 2008) paras 67–74, discussed in more detail in Chapter 4 of this book.
[179] Article 5(1)(c) ECHR.

to administrative detention against suspects of such [terrorist] criminal activities is inadmissible',[180] whereas the Inter-American Court has indicated:

> [P]reventive detention is the most serious measure that can be applied to someone accused of a crime, wherefore its application must be exceptional, as it is limited by the principles of *nullum crimen nulla poena sine lege praevia*, presumption of innocence, need, and proportionality, which are essential in a democratic society.[181]

In other cases involving immigration detention, detention will not need to satisfy at all the requirement of being necessary in a democratic society.[182] Ignoring altogether the principle of necessity for some categories of detention is a significant departure from even the Human Rights Committee's less than watertight commitment to the principle of necessity in *A v Australia*.[183] Thus, at least for the ECtHR, it is easier to violate the liberty and security of the person than it is to violate freedom of expression, association or the right to privacy.[184]

2.5.3 States' positive obligations to ensure that detention is non-arbitrary

The right to liberty and security of the person gives rise to states' positive due diligence obligations to prevent and respond to both individual instances and wider patterns or phenomena of arbitrary detention.

Concretely, to meet their positive obligations, states must ensure that persons detained within their jurisdiction are informed of the reasons for their detention and not only entitled but also enabled to have the lawfulness of their detention reviewed promptly by a court.[185] States are obligated to

---

[180] WGAD, 'Report of the Working Group on Arbitrary Detention' UN Doc A/HRC/10/21 (10 February 2009) para 54(b).

[181] *García Asto and Ramírez Rojas v Peru, García Tuesta (on behalf of García Asto and Ramírez Rojas) v Peru* (Preliminary Objection, Merits, Reparations, and Costs) Series C No 137 (25 November 2005) para 106.

[182] *Saadi v UK* (n 178) paras 67–74.

[183] *A v Australia* (n 168) para 9.2. See, for example, Helen O'Nions, 'No Right to Liberty: the Detention of Asylum Seekers for Administrative Convenience' (2008) 10(148) *Eur J Mig & L* 149; Cathryn Costello, 'Human Rights and the Elusive Universal Subject: Immigration Detention Under International Human Rights and EU Law' (2012) 19(1) *Indiana J Global L Stud* 257; Violeta Moreno-Lax, 'Beyond Saadi v UK: Why the Unnecessary Detention of Asylum Seekers is Inadmissible under EU Law' (2011) 5(2) *Hum Rts & Intl Leg Disc* 166.

[184] All "qualified" rights subject to classic proportionality analyses to determine whether infringements may be lawful. See sub-section 2.4.2(i) of this chapter.

[185] *London Borough of Hillingdon v Neary* [2011] EWCOP 1377 (9 June 2011) para 202.

actively consider the imposition of alternatives to detention.[186] This is an obvious requirement if detention is going to meet the requirement of being "exceptional". This principle has been applied in cases of detention on grounds related to psychiatric treatment,[187] recognising that authorities must:

> strike a fair balance between the competing interests emanating, on the one hand, from society's responsibility to secure the best possible health care for those with diminished faculties [...] and, on the other hand, from the individual's inalienable right to self-determination. In other words, it is imperative to apply the principle of proportionality inherent in the structure of the provisions enshrining those Convention rights that are susceptible to restrictions.[188]

It has also been applied to cases involving pre-trial detention,[189] and to asylum seekers.[190]

States must also take appropriate steps to protect vulnerable persons from arbitrary detention, including persons at particular risk of arbitrary detention, such as those in need of psychiatric treatment or social care.[191] Courts have equally recognised that a state's responsibility will be engaged if it acquiesces in a person's loss of liberty by private individuals or fails to put an end to the situation.[192] Consistent with this special emphasis on protecting vulnerable persons, it follows that states have a positive obligation to prevent and respond to the increased risk of arbitrary detention faced by particularly marginalised groups. This point was underscored by the Inter-American Commission on Human Rights in respect of the heightened risks of being subjected to

---

[186] Durban Declaration against Racism, Racial Discrimination, Xenophobia and Related Intolerance (8 September 2001) para 25.

[187] *Plesó v Hungary* App No 41242/08 (ECtHR, 2 October 2012) paras 62, 65, 68.

[188] Ibid para 65.

[189] *Litwa v Poland* App No 26629/95 (ECtHR, 4 April 2000) para 78; *Idalov v Russia* (Grand Chamber) App No 5826/03 (ECtHR, 22 May 2012) paras 139, 148. For the application of the principle in relation to children, see IACommHR, *Juvenile Justice and Human Rights in the Americas* (13 July 2011) OEA/Ser.L/V/II Doc 78 paras 267–288; 'Committee on the Rights of the Child, General Comment No 10: the Rights of the Child in Juvenile Justice' (25 April 2007) UN Doc CRC/C/GC/10 paras 79–81.

[190] UNHCR, *Guidelines on the Applicable Criteria and Standards relating to the Detention of Asylum Seekers and Alternatives to Detention* (2012), Guideline 4.3; *Rahimi v Greece* App No 8687/08 (ECtHR, 5 April 2011) para 109 (regarding the detention of an unaccompanied child asylum seeker).

[191] *Storck v Germany* App No 61603/00 (ECtHR, 16 June 2005) paras 100–108; *Stanev v Bulgaria* (Grand Chamber) App No 36760/06 (ECtHR, 17 January 2012) para 120.

[192] *Riera Blume v Spain* App No 37680/97 (ECtHR, 14 October 1999) paras 31–35; *Rantsev v Cyprus and Russia* App No 25965/04 (ECtHR, 8 January 2010) paras 323–324.

pre-trial detention faced by 'persons of African descent, indigenous persons, LGBTI and older persons, and persons with disabilities', and the need to adopt special measures that consider:

> particular conditions of vulnerability and the factors that may increase the risk of exposure to acts of violence and discrimination in contexts of pretrial detention, such as sex, race, ethnicity age, sexual orientation, gender identity and expression, and disability. It is also important to consider the frequent intersectionality of the factors mentioned, which may accentuate the situation of risk of persons held in pretrial detention.[193]

Certainly, the heightened risk is not limited to these groups only or to pre-trial detention.

2.5.4 Relationship with other rights

Arbitrary detention increases the risk of additional human rights violations, including: fair trial violations; torture and other cruel, inhuman, or degrading treatment; involuntary and enforced disappearances; and extrajudicial executions. The same is also true in reverse: torture and other forms of prohibited ill-treatment and many other human rights violations are also just as likely to lead to prolonged arbitrary detention, particularly after the conclusion of unfair trials. As will be discussed in the next chapter, arbitrary detention may in and of itself, under certain circumstances, amount to torture and other forms of cruel, inhuman, or degrading treatment or punishment given the extreme helplessness it can engender in persons subjected to the practice.

Arbitrary detention can violate the principles of IHL. Rules on the reasons for which persons may be deprived of their liberty by a party to an international armed conflict are to be found in all four of the 1949 Geneva Conventions.[194] Arbitrary detention may also violate international refugee law. Article 31 of the 1951 Refugee Convention provides that contracting states shall not penalise refugees who enter or are present in a country without permission, provided they present themselves without delay to the authorities and show good cause for their illegal entry or presence. This provision has been interpreted to protect refugees from arbitrary detention. The United Nations High Commissioner for Refugees

---

[193] IACommHR, *Measures Aimed at Reducing the Use of Pretrial Detention in the Americas* (3 July 2017) OAS/Ser.L/V/II 163 Doc 105, para 17.

[194] ICRC, Customary International Law Database (n 155) Rule 99.

(UNHCR) detention guidelines make clear that 'the right to seek asylum, the non-penalisation for irregular entry or stay and the rights to liberty and security of person and freedom of movement – mean that the detention of asylum-seekers should be a measure of last resort, with liberty being the default position'.[195]

Arbitrary detention may also constitute a form of hostage-taking, whether perpetrated by non-state or state actors.[196] International criminal law definitions recognise that, when the underlying criteria for the crimes are present, arbitrary detention may constitute a war crime,[197] and a crime against humanity.[198]

2.6 The grey zones of "detention" and their impact on arbitrariness

We all know what "detention" is, so we say. But on the outer edges, the grey zones, particularly where people are being held in *de facto* locations or zones that are not normally labelled or perceived as "detention centres", the distinction between a "detention" and a "restriction on movement" is nuanced and depends on how facts and circumstances are analysed by those with the power to decide. The ECtHR has held that whether someone has been deprived of their liberty within the meaning of the ECHR will depend on the concrete situation, and account must be taken of the range of criteria such as the type, duration, effects and manner of implementation of the measure in question.[199] The WGAD has similarly taken into account contextual factors when making this determination. It considers whether there are limitations on the person's physical movements, on receiving visits from others and on means of communication, as well as the level

---

[195] UNHCR, Detention Guidelines (n 190) para 14.

[196] See, Art 1 International Convention against the Taking of Hostages (adopted 19 December 1979, entered into force 3 June 1983) 1316 UNTS 205 (emphasis added) (hereinafter Hostages Convention). This is discussed in more detail in Chapter 7.

[197] 'Unlawful confinement' of a protected person is a war crime under Article 8(2)(a)(vii) of the ICC Statute and features as a crime in the statutes of other international criminal law tribunals (Rome Statute of the International Criminal Court) (adopted 17 July 1998, entered into force 7 July 2002) UN Doc A/CONF.183/9.

[198] Imprisonment or other severe deprivation of physical liberty is recognised as one of the possible underlying offences of crimes against humanity in accordance with Article 7(1)(e) of the ICC Statute, and is reflected in the other statutes and principles setting out crimes against humanity.

[199] *Guzzardi v Italy* App No 7367/76 (ECtHR, 6 November 1980) paras 92–93 (finding a detention); see, also, *De Tommaso v Italy (Grand Chamber)* App No 43395/09 (ECtHR, 23 February 2017) para 80 (finding that the facts did not give rise to detention).

of security around the place where the person is confined,[200] and, in so doing, has determined that 'placing individuals in temporary custody in stations, ports and airports or any other facilities where they remain under constant surveillance',[201] or situations of house arrest that are 'carried out in closed premises which the person is not allowed to leave',[202] may amount to detention. Thus, the underlying circumstances of the confinement are considered when determining whether there is a deprivation of liberty, or whether the facts reveal a lesser or different restriction of liberty or movement.

The consequences of labelling a situation as one or the other can be significant from a human rights perspective. Under the ECHR, only certain reasons for detention are lawful, so anything falling outside those reasons will *ipso facto* be unlawful and arbitrary.[203] Thus, there is a strong incentive to label contexts of containment that fall outside the permissible reasons to detain as restrictions on movement, as this would still make them at least potentially lawful. As a second stage, any rights restriction would only be justifiable if it was deemed as reasonable, necessary and proportionate in the light of the circumstances. This is a test that is applied by many human rights systems to all forms of detention.[204] Because detention is perceived as a more significant limitation of rights than a restriction on movement, at this second level of analysis too there is incentive in the grey zones to label acts as restrictions on movement as they are more likely to be adjudged as proportional responses. For instance, in its proportionality analyses pertaining to freedom of movement, the ECtHR has recognised that 'situations commonly occur in modern society where the public may be called upon to endure restrictions on freedom of movement or liberty in the interests of the common good',[205] 'so long as they are rendered unavoidable as a result

---

[200] WGAD, *Opinion No 16/2011 Concerning Liu Xia (China)*, UN Doc A/HRC/WGAD/2011/16 (5 May 2011) para 7: *Opinion No 50/2021 Concerning Raman Pratasevich (Belarus)* UN Doc A/HRC/WGAD/2021/50 (7 December 2021) paras 60, 61.

[201] WGAD, 'Report of the WGAD, Deliberation No 9', UN Doc A/HRC/22/44 (24 December 2012) para 59.

[202] WGAD, *Opinion No 2/2002 Concerning Aung San Suu Kyi (Myanmar)*, UN Doc E/CN.4/2003/8/Add.1 (19 June 2002) para 13; *Opinion No 8/1992 Concerning Aung San Suu Kyi (Myanmar)*, UN Doc E/CN.4/1993/24 (12 January 1993) para 15. See, also, WGAD, Deliberation 01: 'House Arrest', UN Doc E/CN.4/1993/24 (12 January 1993) 9.

[203] Art 5(1)(a)–(e) ECHR. Though note *Hassan v United Kingdom*, App No 29750/09 (16 September 2004) discussed further in Chapter 6 (where the ECtHR interpreted Art 5(1)(a)–(f) as allowing exceptionally for additional bases to detain when those bases stem from other applicable legal regimes).

[204] Human Rights Committee, General Comment No 35 (n 156) paras 12, 18, 19, 20, 66.

[205] *Austin v United Kingdom (Grand Chamber)* App Nos 39692/09, 40713/09 and 41008/09 (ECtHR, 15 March 2012) paras 58–59; *De Tommaso v Italy (Grand Chamber)* App No 43395/09 (ECtHR, 23 February 2017) para 81.

of circumstances beyond the control of the authorities, are necessary to avert a real risk of serious injury or damage, and are kept to the minimum required for that purpose'.[206]

Human rights courts have some room to manoeuvre in how they label these grey zones because, after all, they are assessing facts and contexts, and some contingency is simply inherent. But there should be limits to the manoeuverability. However, as is explained in several forthcoming chapters, avoiding the label of "detention" has become yet a further tool to avoid upending governmental programmes of confinement. For example, the ECtHR has held that refugees and migrants exercised their free will to enter the transit zone and were therefore consenting to their confinement, and thus they could not be considered as being subjected to "detention".[207] When up to 2,000 people were contained within a police cordon (a measure known as "kettling") at Oxford Circus in London without access to food, water or toilets, the ECtHR Grand Chamber held that this did not amount to "detention".[208] Persons are frequently subjected to confinement in the private sphere for reasons linked to gender, such as persons subjected to forced marriages, women confined to the home unless they have a male chaperone, LGBTI+ persons forcibly confined by family or community members to undergo "rehabilitation" or other coercive rituals and persons confined for the purpose of sexual slavery.[209] For the most part these contexts have not been considered under the lens of arbitrary detention, though arguably they could be.[210]

At the other end of the spectrum there is the WGAD's opinion on Julian Assange.[211] Assange remained in his place of confinement (the Ecuadorian embassy) because he had reason to believe that he would suffer significant injustice, including persecution, inhuman treatment and physical harm, if he were to leave and, as the WGAD found, his autonomy to leave the embassy was thereby compromised. Consequently, he argued, and the WGAD found, his confinement in the embassy was not "self-imposed". This is a reasonable

---

[206] *Austin v United Kingdom* (n 205) para 59.

[207] *Ilias and Ahmed v Hungary (Grand Chamber)* App No 47287/15 (ECtHR, 21 November 2019), discussed in Chapter 4 (paras 220–223).

[208] *Austin* (n 205).

[209] Mathuri Thamilmaran, 'Sri Lanka: Stop Unnecessary "Psychiatric Evaluations" Based on Sexual Orientation', International Commission of Jurists (1 December 2022) <www.icj.org/sri-lanka-stop-unnecessary-psychiatric-evaluations-based-on-sexual-orientation/> accessed 26 July 2023.

[210] Sara Malkani, 'When Women Can't Escape: a Gender-Sensitive Approach to Arbitrary Detention' (2015) 30 *Wis J L Gender & Soc'y* 1, 20.

[211] WGAD, *Opinion No 54/2015 Concerning Julian Assange (Sweden and the UK)*, UN Doc A/HRC/WGAD/2015 (22 January 2016) para 10.

proposition in light of the principles espoused in *Guzzardi*, though the position, and the WGAD Opinion that resulted, have not been free from criticism.[212] At the heart of the criticism of the WGAD opinion is whether Assange could use the arguments about mistrust of the legal system forcing him to stay confined to avoid the implementation of an arrest warrant that had been validly issued by a court of law known for its judicial independence.[213] But what leeway if any should decision-makers be giving to courts "known for" anything at all? Does this not strike as Çali's concerns about the deference shown by judges or courts towards the 'good faith interpreters' that they trust?[214] Is there not too great a risk of arbitrariness when judges choose deference instead of the facts they find before them?

We could add another permutation to the Assange "self-imposed" (according to some) detention and arrive at the perplexing situation of the eight Rwandan nationals acquitted by the International Criminal Tribunal for Rwanda or whose sentences issued by that Tribunal had been served. Given their well-founded fears of persecution, these persons ostensibly at liberty could not be transferred to Rwanda. Ultimately, they voluntarily agreed to be transferred to Niger on the undertaking that they would be provided with residency permits, be allowed to work and travel,[215] and pursuant to a Relocation Agreement agreed on 15 November 2021 by Niger and the Registrar of the International Residual Mechanism for Criminal Tribunals on behalf of the United Nations. Instead, on 27 December 2021 the Nigerien authorities issued an order requiring the eight individuals to leave Nigerien territory within seven days, confiscated their identity documents, and placed them under house arrest under armed guard where, at the time of writing in August 2023, they remained. Surely, the house arrest they currently experience was not "self imposed" given that what

---

[212] 'Julian Assange decision by UN panel ridiculous, says Hammond', *BBC News* (5 February 2016); Joshua Rozenberg, 'How Did the UN Get It So Wrong on Julian Assange?', *The Guardian* (5 February 2016); Philipp Janig, 'Julian's Golden Cage: Julian Assange, the UN Working Group on Arbitrary Detention and the Quest for Scholarly Diligence – A Case Study' (2016) 18 *Austrian Rev Intl & Eur L* 1. See, in contrast, Binoy Kampmark, 'Julian Assange, the UN and the Limits of Detention' (2018) 11(1) *Theory in Action* 57; Liora Lazarus, 'Is the United Nations Working Group on Arbitrary Detention Decision on Assange "So Wrong"?' (2016) *UK Const L Blog*.

[213] WGAD Member Vladimir Tochilovsky's dissent in the Assange WGAD Opinion (n 211) para 3.

[214] Başak Çali, 'Coping with Crisis: Whither the Variable Geometry in the Jurisprudence of the European Court of Human Rights' (2018) 35(2) *Wisc Intl LJ* 237, 261.

[215] Asymmetrical Haircuts, Podcast Episode 75: 'Failures of Justice with Kate Gibson and Barbora Hola' (17 February 2023) <https://www.asymmetricalhaircuts.com/episodes/episode-75-failures-of-justice-with-kate-gibson-and-barbora-hola/> accessed 13 August 2023.

they had previously agreed to had not materialised, and they are not free to leave, as no other state has offered protection, and the Residual Mechanism has thus far refused to approve their relocation to The Hague.[216] Clearly Niger is responsible for their arbitrary detention, but what of the parallel responsibility of the Residual Mechanism operating under the auspices of the United Nations, and the states parties to the United Nations, all required pursuant to Security Council Resolution 955(1994) to cooperate with the Rwanda Tribunal, and the Residual Mechanism that followed (not excluding those aspects of cooperation which pertain to relocations)?[217] While the responsibility of international organisations is a vast topic outside the scope of this book,[218] certainly the Residual Mechanism has a continuing duty of care to the eight men to ensure enforcement of the Relocation Agreement that it brokered, failing which to secure another solution. Who is responsible for these failed efforts?

While there are good reasons not to blur the distinctions between the denial of freedom of movement and arbitrary detention, or indeed to subsume inappropriately any number of problematic situations within the frame of arbitrary detention, there is sense in continually evaluating whether current descriptions, focuses and lenses are sufficiently encompassing of all persons and contexts. But too much room to manoeuvre makes the arbiters of the facts no better, no more fair or consistent, than the arbitrary rule of the sovereigns – the application of blind power on the basis of pure will, which gave rise to the earliest conceptions of arbitrariness introduced at the outset of this chapter. So, we risk ending this chapter where we started.

2.7 Conclusions

Theories about "arbitrariness" are useful lenses through which to observe and comment upon power relations whether in governance, social relations or the rule of law. Many of these theories were conceived in different times, though the concerns they raise about how best to restrain arbitrary state power and promote equality still resonate today. Today's highly contested political landscape must also tackle the added concerns of political disenfranchisement, widening power imbalances and inequalities, private actors supplanting weak

---

[216] 'Decision on Nzuwonemeye Request for Transfer', MICT-22-124 1356 D1356–D1354 (25 July 2023); motion for judicial review pending at the time of writing ('Ntagerura Motion for Judicial Review of Relocation Agreement', MICT-22-124 1367 D1367–D1363 (10 August 2023)).

[217] UNSC, Resolution 1966 (2010) UN Doc S/RES/1966 (2010) (22 December 2010).

[218] See, Carla Ferstman, *International Organizations and the Fight for Accountability: the Remedies and Reparations Gap* (OUP 2017).

public authority, and growing mistrust of facts and truths. Conceptions of "arbitrariness" must therefore evolve to remain relevant.

Arbitrary detention is outlawed by international law in all circumstances without exception. What constitutes arbitrary detention is reasonably clear. It includes both the requirement that a particular form of deprivation of liberty is taken in accordance with the applicable law and procedure and that it is proportional to the aim sought, reasonable and necessary. This framing of arbitrary detention is meant to ensure that detention remains exceptional and any decision to detain is subject to law, reasoned, necessary, proportionate and non-discriminatory. But, as with any definition that refrains from providing an enumerated list of instances of detention that would be recognised as arbitrary, there is debate about which factual scenarios would qualify as permissible grounds to detain or, conversely, which scenarios are inherently arbitrary, and what steps are required to determine the permissibility of detention in individual cases.

The absence of an enumerated list is meant to ensure that conceptions of arbitrariness can evolve to account for modern-day concerns. After all, a certain amount of vagueness is needed to be capable of 'coping appropriately with the complexity of public disorder'.[219] However, there is a countervailing tendency for policy and decision-makers to use the malleability of the concept and shape it to suit short-term goals. This is perhaps most evident in how proportionality analyses have broached both qualified and limited rights. These analyses set us on a path of contingency in which the "arbitrariness" of arbitrary detention may result in inconsistent or diverging interpretations (impeding the overall coherence of the case law). It also has the potential to become a shape-shifting void of nothing but pernicious manipulations or, as Bourdieu and Passeron might posit,[220] a targeted appropriation of the contingency that reinforces domination, oppression and violence, or an empty receptable in which to fill the violence and domination of the status quo. In such scenarios the well-meaning advocates tend to wish for more concrete understandings to foster greater certainty, transparency and accountability in how decisions to detain are taken. But this too is part of the inevitable push–pull, and we must be conscious of our placement in the status quo. What escapes us still is a framework for analysis and accountability as to why the decision to detain particular individuals and groups was taken, and why the decision was normalised.

---

[219] Endicott, 'The Impossibility of the Rule of Law' (n 31).
[220] Bourdieu and Passeron (n 17) 5.

3

"Arbitrariness" as an Indication of Harm

3.1 Introduction

The ability to detain is strictly limited: it must be subject to law, used only to pursue a legitimate aim, and it must reflect a proportionate response to that aim understood as strictly necessary in the circumstances.[1] As is described later in this chapter, individuals who have been subjected to detention that falls outside those boundaries, and is arbitrary, speak about hopelessness, despair and the impact the denial of freedom has on their sense of self. Former Special Rapporteur on Torture Nils Melzer has indicated that to purposefully engender this hopelessness is a common feature in virtually all situations of torture: 'A psychological method applied in virtually all situations of torture is to purposefully deprive victims of their control over as many aspects of their lives as possible, to demonstrate complete dominance over them, and to instil a profound sense of helplessness, hopelessness and total dependency on the torturer.'[2] He has explained that 'sustained institutional arbitrariness fundamentally betrays the human need for communal trust and, depending on the circumstances, can cause severe mental suffering, profound emotional destabilization and lasting individual and collective trauma'.[3]

For many this hopelessness is about the uncertainty of time and space, about the loss of meaning. The "arbitrary" is central to this despair because it reflects the absence of autonomy that is crucial to human dignity and the lack of predictability. The individuals subjected to arbitrary detention could

---

[1] The test related to the permissibility of detention is canvassed in Chapter 2.
[2] Human Rights Council, *Torture and Other Cruel, Inhuman, or Degrading Treatment or Punishment: Report of the Special Rapporteur*, Mr Nils Melzer, UN Doc A/HRC/43/49 (20 March 2020) para 49.
[3] Ibid para 63.

not have truly taken steps to avoid being deprived of their liberty. With arbitrary detention, there is no possibility to rationalise the denial of freedom as a punishment for doing something wrong, as a legitimate cause and effect. It happens despite the detainee's inherent dignity and autonomy as a human being. It is Behrouz Boochani's image of 'people sitting, being tortured by time',[4] or Maya Angelou's 'caged bird'[5] struggling to sing. Freedom and subjectivity are absent and will only be restored upon the arbitrary will of the powerful. As one of the 76 detained migrant women Gerlach spoke to explained, 'they kill us from inside. If you could [kill] you by any way this be easier, easier, cause they kill you from inside. So they are criminal, more than they kill me by knife or gun.'[6]

This chapter analyses this connection between arbitrariness and harm. It considers the extent to which the "arbitrariness" of arbitrary detention is in and of itself a form of torture or other cruel, inhuman, or degrading treatment or punishment, having regard to the legal connotations of those terms. Certainly, there is a connection between arbitrary detention and torture. Arbitrary detention is 'a terrain in which torture thrives'.[7] Such detention is often accompanied by specific acts of torture and other prohibited ill-treatment, particularly prolonged solitary confinement and threats of, or actual, physical violence. It can also lead to torture and other prohibited ill-treatment because of the lack of procedural safeguards associated with arbitrary detention, which leaves the detainee in a situation of special vulnerability. Similarly, torture can lead to arbitrary detention when the torture results in coerced confessions and the admission of torture evidence, resulting in unfair convictions and wrongful imprisonment.[8] In this chapter I consider a slightly different question: can the "arbitrariness" of arbitrary detention constitute a form of torture *in and of itself* and, if so, in what circumstances?

To an extent, the question is theoretical because arbitrary detention rarely occurs without additional indicia of torture or other ill-treatment. It can therefore be difficult to isolate the harm caused by the arbitrariness of detention from the wider harms the detainee experiences, such as

---

[4] André Dao and Behrouz Boochani, 'Interview: André Dao and Behrouz Boochani' (2020) 24 *Law Text Culture* 50, 53.
[5] Maya Angelou, *I Know Why the Caged Bird Sings* (2nd edn, Random House 2002).
[6] Alice Gerlach, 'Women's Experiences of Indignity in Immigration Detention and Beyond' (2022) 3(2) *Incarceration* 1, 12.
[7] Nigel Rodley and Matt Pollard, *The Treatment of Prisoners under International Law* (3rd edn, OUP 2011) 43.
[8] See Category III of the WGAD's classifications of arbitrary detention, which focuses on arbitrary detentions stemming from unfair trials. WGAD, 'Deliberation No 9 Concerning the Definition and Scope of Arbitrary Deprivation of Liberty under Customary International Law', UN Doc A/HRC/22/44 (24 December 2012) para 38.

inhuman detention conditions, beatings within detention facilities, solitary confinement or *incommunicado* detention, or the refusal to provide medical care.[9] Nevertheless, understanding that the arbitrariness of a deprivation of liberty can *itself* produce harm that is significant and may amount to torture is an important realisation that is ammunition against the growing number of instances in which states are authorising detention that would qualify as arbitrary in order to deter certain people or behaviours. The ammunition that this kind of recognition provides is all the more potent for the prohibition against torture's absolute, non-derogable and unqualified status.

Melzer has recognised that:

> when institutional arbitrariness or persecution intentionally and purposefully inflicts severe mental pain or suffering on powerless persons, it can constitute or contribute to psychological torture. In practice, this question is of particular, but not exclusive, relevance in relation to the deliberate instrumentalization of arbitrary detention and related judicial or administrative arbitrariness.[10]

The Inter-American Commission on Human Rights has likewise recognised this connection between arbitrary detention and torture or other cruel, inhuman, or degrading treatment or punishment in relation to the continued detention of persons at Guantánamo Bay, Cuba. It determined that 'even in extraordinary circumstances, the indefinite detention of individuals, most of whom have not been charged, constitutes a flagrant violation of international human rights law and in itself constitutes a form of cruel, inhuman, and degrading treatment'.[11] So has former UN Special Rapporteur on Torture, Juan Méndez, who determined that Australian legislation on the detention of migrants 'violates the [Convention Against Torture] because it allows for the arbitrary detention and refugee determination at sea, without access to lawyers'.[12] He made a similar statement regarding detention at Guantánamo

---

[9] See, for example, R Douglas Bruce and Rebecca Schleifer, 'Ethical and Human Rights Imperatives to Ensure Medication-assisted Treatment for Opioid Dependence in Prisons and pre-trial Detention' (2008) 19 *Intl J Drug Policy* 17, 20. They argue: 'The failure to provide access to MAT – an effective medical treatment for opioid dependence, as well as critical to preventing HIV – may result in violations of basic obligations to protect prisoners from exposure to inhuman or degrading treatment' (20).

[10] Melzer (n 2) para 63.

[11] Inter-American Commission on Human Rights (IACommHR), *Toward the Closure of Guantánamo* OAS/Ser.L/V/II. Doc 20/15 (3 June 2015) para 134.

[12] Human Rights Council, 'Report of the Special Rapporteur on Torture and Other Cruel, Inhuman, or Degrading Treatment or Punishment, Juan E Méndez', Observations on communications transmitted to Governments and replies received, UN Doc A/HRC/28/68/Add.1 (5 March 2015) paras 30, 31.

Bay.[13] Researchers[14] and advocacy organisations[15] have expressed similar perspectives. The International Criminal Tribunal for the former Yugoslavia has also held that: 'to the extent that the confinement of the victim can be shown to pursue one of the prohibited purposes of torture and to have caused the victim severe pain or suffering, the act of putting or keeping someone in solitary confinement may amount to torture'.[16] And, also recognising that certain situations of detention can amount to torture, the WGAD has determined that 'prolonged detention for counter-terrorism purposes increases the likelihood that individuals will be subjected to solitary confinement and/or situations of detention that are contrary to the prohibitions of torture and other forms of ill-treatment'.[17] Thus, as a matter of principle, the presence of a prohibited purpose together with the conditions of severe pain or suffering relate not just to solitary confinement but to any situation of detention. Nevertheless, this kind of explicit recognition of the alignment between arbitrary detention and torture remains rare amongst international bodies and mandate holders, as well as courts.

This chapter reviews the findings of scientific studies of harms experienced by current and former detainees in arbitrary situations of detention undertaken by psychologists and others. This produces a nuanced picture because individuals experience harms personally and subjectively. The

---

[13] Juan Méndez, 'Statement of the UN Special Rapporteur on Torture at the Expert Meeting on the Situation of Detainees Held at the US Naval Base at Guantánamo Bay' (IACommHR, 3 October 2013): 'at Guantánamo, the indefinite detention of individuals, most of whom have not been charged, goes far beyond a minimally reasonable period of time and causes a state of suffering, stress, fear and anxiety, which in itself constitutes a form of cruel, inhuman, and degrading treatment'.

[14] See, for example, David Isaacs, 'Are Healthcare Professionals Working in Australia's Immigration Detention Centres Condoning Torture?' (2016) 42 *J Med Ethics* 413, 413–414, in which he argues: 'There is a case that prolonged immigration detention itself constitutes torture.'

[15] See, for example, Amnesty International, *Island of Despair: Australia's 'Processing' of Refugees on Nauru*, AI Index: ASA 12/4934/2016 (17 October 2016), strongly condemning Australian immigration policies and indicating: 'the Government of Australia has made a calculation in which intolerable cruelty and the destruction of the physical and mental integrity of hundreds of children, men, and women, have been chosen as a tool of government policy. In doing so the Government of Australia is in breach of international human rights law and international refugee law. The conditions on Nauru – refugees' severe mental anguish, the intentional nature of the system, and the fact that the goal of offshore processing is to intimidate or coerce people to achieve a specific outcome – amounts to torture' (7).

[16] *Prosecutor v Milorad Krnojelac* Trial Judgment (ICTY, 15 March 2002) IT-97-25-T para 183.

[17] WGAD, 'Report of the Working Group on Arbitrary Detention', UN Doc A/HRC/22/44 (24 December 2012) para 73.

nature of those experiences depends on individuals' histories and unique perspectives. The chapter also considers the case law.

This chapter finds that arbitrariness causes its own harms, which can produce significant, often long-lasting, suffering capable of amounting to torture. This is an important finding because it recognises that all kinds of psychological suffering if sufficiently severe and when produced intentionally or with reckless disregard for the consequences[18] can amount to torture when perpetrated for a prohibited purpose.[19] It attaches arbitrary detention to the torture taboo, the violation of which has been understood as having 'a contagion effect that harms social institutions and dehumanises and stigmatises the torturer as "uncivilised" or "barbaric"'.[20] In this way it associates the stigma of torture – a privileged form of suffering and cruelty, with 'immense ethical, political, and cultural power [...] the worst thing that can happen to someone or that one person can do to another',[21] however problematic that rhetoric on stigma may be[22] – with what is the mundane or innocuous practice of detention. In this sense it undermines the argument that the industrial-scale arbitrary detentions that have become commonplace in the name of controlling borders and strengthening national security are somehow justifiable, because some of these detentions may constitute torture and torture is never justifiable. At least notionally, it also gives rise to a remedy and reparation that, unlike the usual, limited compensation payments for wrongful detention,[23] recognises the heinousness of torture and the need to prevent recurrence.

3.2 The harms of arbitrary detention

Much empirical research has been undertaken with detainees and former detainees about the impacts of detention on their health and well-being. Further accounts of detainee suffering have been made public as part of court judgments, in accounts by caregivers, and as narrated in memoirs

---

[18] On the different ways to frame intentionality, see the former Special Rapporteur on Torture, Mr Nils Melzer's thematic report on psychological torture (n 2) para 34.
[19] The extent to which these harms meet the definition of torture is considered in section 3.3 of this chapter.
[20] Jamal Barnes, 'The "War on Terror" and the Battle for the Definition of Torture' (2016) 30(1) *Intl Relations* 102, 104.
[21] Tobias Kelly, *This Side of Silence: Human Rights, Torture, and the Recognition of Cruelty* (University of Pennsylvania Press 2011) 3.
[22] Michelle Farrell, 'The Marks of Civilisation: the Special Stigma of Torture' (2022) 22 *Hum Rts L Rev* 2022.
[23] George Zdenkowski, 'Remedies for Miscarriage of Justice: Wrongful Imprisonment' (1993) 5(1) *Current Issues in Criminal Justice* 105.

by detainees themselves.[24] Butler alludes to the harms caused by arbitrary detention, noting: 'It is, however, a most intensified form of injustice not to know what the allegation is, what is being said, yet to feel indefinitely its punishing effects.'[25] Many of such studies and accounts concern contexts of detention that can readily amount to arbitrary detention, such as immigration detention, prolonged preventive or security-related detention, and detention on mental health grounds. These contexts of detention are notorious for their industrial scales.

Këllezi and others surmise: 'For many detainees, the distress of detention is imbedded in the socio-political inequality and injustice they are experiencing as [a] social group.'[26] In this sense, it is the detention itself, a form of "structural violence",[27] that is the cause of, or at least a large contributor to, the distress. This aligns with the many studies that have been undertaken with detainee and former detainee populations. Psychological studies have found growing evidence that the prolonged confinement of asylum seekers in detention centres results in adverse mental health outcomes, including contributing significantly to post-traumatic stress, depression and anxiety symptoms. For example, Cleveland and others concluded that 'after a median imprisonment of only 18 days detained asylum seekers were almost twice as likely as their non-detained peers to experience clinical levels of PTSD symptoms [...] and 50% more likely to have clinical levels of depression'.[28]

Silove and others, who studied the impact of mandatory, indefinite detention on asylum seekers in Australia, determined that prolonged detention has adverse mental health and psychosocial impacts on adults,

---

[24] See, for example, Behrouz Boochani, *No Friend but the Mountains: Writing from Manus Prison* (House of Anansi Press 2019); Nelson Mandela et al, *The Prison Letters of Nelson Mandela* (WW Norton 2018); Gulbahar Haitiwaji, *How I Survived a Chinese 'Re-education' Camp: a Uyghur Woman's Story* (Canbury Press 2022); Ngiigi wa Thiong'o, *Detained: a Writer's Prison Diary* (Heinemann 1981); Hwang Sok-yong, *The Prisoner: a Memoir* (Verso 2021); Jason Rezaian, *Prisoner: My 544 Days in an Iranian Prison – Solitary Confinement, a Sham Trial, High-Stakes Diplomacy, and the Extraordinary Efforts It Took to Get Me Out* (ABEcco 2019); William Sampson, *Confessions of an Innocent Man: Torture and Survival in a Saudi Prison* (McClelland & Stewart 2006); Mohamedou Ould Slahi, *Guantánamo Diary* (Canongate Books 2015).

[25] Judith Butler, 'Indefinite Detention' (2020) 29(1) *qui parle* 15, 19.

[26] Blerina Këllezi et al, 'Healthcare Provision Inside Immigration Removal Centres: a Social Identity Analysis of Trust, Legitimacy and Disengagement' (2021) 13(3) *Applied Psychology: Health and Well-being* 578, 584.

[27] Janet Cleveland and others, 'Symbolic Violence and Disempowerment as Factors in the Adverse Impact of Immigration Detention on Adult Asylum Seekers' Mental Health' (2018) 63 *Intl J Pub H* 1001, 1002.

[28] Cleveland (n 27) 1005.

families and children.[29] Gerlach, who conducted 76 qualitative interviews with women immigration detainees and former detainees in the UK, concluded that part of the harm stemmed from the indignity associated with 'the disconnect between their own perceived sense of being a "good" person, and their treatment at the hands of the Home Office'.[30] This was also concluded by Rivas and Bull, who examined the experiences of women held in long-term immigration detention in Australia.[31] They also found that women detainees 'experience this detention differently than their male counterparts'. Other research 'found that 60 per cent of the general long-term detainee population experienced mental health problems, alarmingly for the women described in the reports we analysed this figure rose to 90 per cent'.[32] One of Coffey and others' interviewees explained:

> It is like you are a big criminal, you are there even though you never did any crime, or you never did anything wrong. but they are watching you. every step you take from outside your room. Wherever you go they are watching. That started a negative effect on my mind.[33]

An interviewee who had been detained in a Canadian immigration detention facility similarly explained: 'I am thinking it is like I am not a human being. I am trying to tell the truth and he treats you like you are lying.'[34] This sense of vilification is a common feeling for victims of arbitrary detention, as their detention is out of sync with their moral sense of justice and right versus wrong, as Gerlach notes, 'to be treated as though they were criminal was hurtful, because it was in direct opposition to their sense of self as an upstanding moral citizen'.[35]

---

[29] Derrick Silove, Patricia Austin and Zachary Steel, 'No Refuge from Terror: the Impact of Detention on the Mental Health of Trauma-affected Refugees Seeking Asylum in Australia' (2007) 44(3) *Transcultural Psychiatry* 359, 362. See, also, Sol Pía Juárez et al, 'Effects of Non-Health-Targeted Policies on Migrant Health: a Systematic Review and Meta-Analysis' (2019) 7 *Lancet Glob Health* e420–435; Guy Coffey et al, 'The Meaning and Mental Health Consequences of Long-Term Immigration Detention for People Seeking Asylum' (2010) 70 *Social Science & Medicine* 2070–2079; Zachary Steel et al, 'Psychiatric Status of Asylum Seeker Families Held for a Protracted Period in a Remote Detention Centre in Australia' (2004) 28(6) *Aus & NZ J Pub H* 527.

[30] Gerlach (n 6) 8.

[31] Lorena Rivas and Melissa Bull, 'Gender and Risk: an Empirical Examination of the Experiences of Women Held in Long-Term Immigration Detention in Australia' (2018) 37 *Refugee Survey Quarterly* 307, 311.

[32] Rivas and Bull (n 31) 326.

[33] Coffey et al (n 29) 2073.

[34] Cleveland et al (27) 1004.

[35] Gerlach (n 6) 8. See, also, Sandra Passardi et al, 'Moral Injury Related to Immigration Detention on Nauru: a Qualitative Study' (2022) 13(1) *Eur J Psychotraumatology* 1, 9 (finding

The indefinite nature of the detention produces further harm, in that it 'inherently stops an individual from the ability to plan for their future, in the event of either outcome of release or removal'.[36] The distress stems from the denial of autonomy, '[b]eing subjected to a coercive authority and deprived of basic human rights tends to jeopardize people's sense of safety, especially as they can neither flee nor fight back'.[37] The "mental defeat" produced by the threat to one's psychological autonomy can serve as a predictor of PTSD (post-traumatic stress disorder) symptom severity.[38] Because the detainees have committed no crime, 'their sense of grievance at injustice will likely increase the harm. In addition, the uncertainty of their future and loss of control compound the suffering.'[39]

Uncertainty about the future, including lack of information about when or whether they would be released, was one of the factors that produced the greatest ongoing stress for security detainees detained as part of counter-terrorism operations.[40] This 'continuing state of suffering and uncertainty creates grave consequences such as stress, fear, depression, and anxiety, and affects the central nervous system as well as the cardiovascular and immunological systems'.[41] Similarly, Sultan, an Iraqi medical practitioner who was himself detained in Australian immigration detention, explained that what was most psychologically destabilising was the detainees' eventual loss of faith that Australian authorities would accept the veracity of their legitimate applications for protection.[42]

---

that negative changes in core beliefs and feelings of humiliation and disempowerment may be attributable to moral injury appraisals regarding dehumanisation by a trusted institution (the Australian government)).

[36] Gerlach (n 6) 10.

[37] Cleveland et al (n 27) 1005.

[38] Anke Ehlers et al, 'Posttraumatic Stress Disorder Following Political Imprisonment: the Role of Mental Defeat, Alienation and Perceived Permanent Change' (2000) 109(1) *J Abnormal Psych* 45.

[39] Isaacs (n 14) 414.

[40] Physicians for Human Rights, *Broken Laws, Broken Lives: Medical Evidence of Torture by US Personnel and Its Impact* (2008) 75. See, also, IACommHR, *Toward the Closure of Guantánamo* (n 11) para 134 (citing Press Release 29/13: IACommHR et al Reiterate Need to End the Indefinite Detention of Individuals at Guantánamo Naval Base in Light of Current Human Rights Crisis, 1 May 2013): 'the severe and lasting physiological and psychological damage caused by Guantánamo detainees' high degree of uncertainty over basic aspects of their lives, including whether or when they will be tried; whether or when they will be released; and whether they will see their family members again. This continuing state of suffering and uncertainty causes stress, fear, depression, and anxiety, and affects the central nervous system and the cardiovascular and immune systems.'

[41] IACommHR, *Toward the Closure of Guantánamo* (n 11) para 134.

[42] Aamer Sultan and Kevin O'Sullivan, 'Psychological Disturbances in Asylum Seekers Held in Long Term Detention: a Participant-Observer Account' (2001) 175 3(17) *Med J Aus* 593.

A psychiatrist reflecting on her work with detainees in an offshore Nauru detention facility spoke of:

> the psychological damage inflicted on them by not knowing their future or feeling like they had any freedom or agency. […] We found that having a lack of control over their life was associated with patients experiencing PTSD, depression, anxiety, suicidal thoughts, and suicide attempts. I saw how people's functioning steadily deteriorated, including their ability to care for themselves.[43]

These observations aligned with studies on self-harm in Nauru immigration detention facilities, where researchers highlighted 'the extraordinarily high rates of self-harm among detained asylum seekers compared to rates observed in the general Australian population, and among asylum seekers in community-based settings. This almost certainly reflects the deleterious effects of immigration detention, and warrants urgent investigation.'[44] They were also confirmed by Cleveland and others: detention 'contributes to a loss of sense of self as a competent, autonomous adult'; 'feeling powerless was found to be the detention condition most strongly correlated with PTSD, depression, and anxiety symptoms'.[45]

The impact on children can be particularly acute. O'Connor describes how 'a cluster of children developed a rare life-threatening psychiatric condition known as resignation syndrome. Ten children presented to us with symptoms of depression and social withdrawal, before progressing to refusing food and fluids, becoming bed bound, mute, and unresponsive.'[46] This is consistent with other findings pertaining to Australian immigration detention:

> Children in immigration detention for long periods of time are at high risk of serious mental harm. The Commonwealth's failure to implement the repeated recommendations by mental health professionals that certain children be removed from the detention environment with their parents amounted to cruel, inhumane, and degrading treatment of those children in detention.[47]

---

[43] Beth O'Connor, 'I Witnessed the Horrors of Offshore Detention and Am Appalled by the UK's Rwanda Plans' (2022) *Brit Med J* 377:o1502.
[44] Kyli Hedrick et al, 'Self-harm in the Australian Asylum Seeker Population: a National Records-Based Study' (2009) 8 *SSM – Population Health* 100452, 8.
[45] Cleveland et al (n 27) 1005.
[46] O'Connor (n 43) 1.
[47] Australian Human Rights and Equal Opportunity Commission, *A Last Resort? National Inquiry into Children in Immigration Detention* (April 2004) 850.

Coffey and others describe that interviewees spoke about mounting fatigue, loss of vitality, accompanied by a reduced ability to act purposefully, as well as cognitive impairment over time with respect to memory and concentration.[48] They also explain that former detainees experienced pervasive difficulties to rebuild their lives:

> [They] suffered an ongoing sense of insecurity and injustice, difficulties with relationships, profound changes to view of self and poor mental health. Depression and demoralisation, concentration and memory disturbances, and persistent anxiety were very commonly reported. Standardised measures found high rates of depression, anxiety, PTSD and low quality of life scores.[49]

They find that the nature of this harm compromises the capacity of refugees to benefit from permanent protection or the opportunities ultimately afforded by permanent protection and may well be irrevocable.[50] These findings are consistent with research undertaken by von Werthern and others. They reviewed 26 relevant studies reporting on a total of 2099 participants in Australia, Canada, Israel, Japan, Sweden, Switzerland, the UK and the US and found that detention plays an independent role in contributing to poor mental health outcomes among asylum seekers.

von Werthern and others also found that prior exposure to trauma before the detention exacerbates rates of anxiety, depression and PTSD in the context of detention: '[t]he experience of detention may act as a new stressor, which adds to the cumulative effect of exposure to trauma, leading to an increased likelihood of developing mental health difficulties'.[51] Also, they found a significant relationship between detention duration and mental health deterioration.[52] In contrast, one analysis has presented more cautious

---

[48] Coffey et al (n 29) 2074.
[49] Coffey et al (n 29) 2070.
[50] Coffey et al (n 29) 2078.
[51] Martha von Werthern et al, 'The Impact of Immigration Detention on Mental Health: a Systematic Review' (2018) 18(1) *BMC Psychiatry* 1, 14: 'having greater trauma exposure of any kind (whether torture or other exposure) prior to detention seems to be associated with higher rates of anxiety, depression and PTSD in the context of such detention' (14).
[52] von Werthern et al (n 51) 14. This is similar to the findings of the study conducted by the Bellevue/NYU Program for Survivors of Torture together with Physicians for Human Rights. They found that 'the level of symptom distress worsened the longer individuals were held in detention': Physicians for Human Rights and the Bellevue/NYU Program for Survivors of Torture, *From Persecution to Prison: the Health Consequences of Detention for Asylum Seekers* (Author 2003) 55, also 58. See, also, Steel et al, who notes that their study 'suggests that prolonged detention exerts a long-term impact on the psychological well-being of refugees. Refugees recording adverse conditions in detention centres also reported persistent sadness, hopelessness, intrusive memories, attacks of anger and physiological

findings; while there is evidence to suggest an independent adverse effect of detention on the mental health of asylum seekers, more research is needed in order to fully investigate the effect of detention on mental health.[53]

The literature on the effects of prolonged immigration detention accords with detainees' experiences of other contexts of arbitrary detention, including security-related preventive detention,[54] false arrest and imprisonment,[55] and hostage-taking.[56] Snell, commenting on the prolonged arbitrary detention of Nazanin Zaghari-Ratcliffe in Iran as a form of torture, notes: 'Years of detention for no reason is an act intended to humiliate and hurt. It means suffering. And with each iteration in what Zaghari-Ratcliffe has suffered, each new return to prison after a mirage of freedom or relaxation, the torturer emerges from the judge, the jailor, and the bureaucrat.'[57]

According to Grounds, who studied 18 men who had been released after their convictions had been quashed for miscarriages of justice following long-term imprisonment, 'the assessments revealed a pattern of disabling symptoms and psychological problems that were severe, unfamiliar to me at that stage and similar in all the cases'.[58] Features he described included enduring personality change, acute psychological trauma as a result of the miscarriage of justice, chronic psychological trauma, PTSD, other psychiatric disorders such as depression, and problems adjusting on release.[59] Bauer and others conducted a study with 55 psychiatric patients who had previously been detained for political reasons in East Germany for a minimum duration of six weeks. They determined that the psychiatric disorders they diagnosed, 'mental sequelae that lasted for several years and will probably persist for the rest of their lives in some cases',[60] were 'due

---

reactivity, which were related to the length of detention': Zachary Steel et al, 'Impact of Immigration Detention and Temporary Protection on the Mental Health and Temporary Protection on the Mental Health of Refugees' (2006) 188 *Brit J Psychiatry* 58, 63).

[53] Trine Filges, Edith Montgomery and Marianne Kastrup, 'The Impact of Detention on the Health of Asylum Seekers: a Systematic Review' (2018) 28(4) *Research on Social Work Practice* 399–414.

[54] Adrian Grounds, 'Psychological Consequences of Wrongful Conviction and Imprisonment' (2004) 46(2) *Cdn J Criminology & Crim J* 165.

[55] Robert Simon, 'The Psychological and Legal Aftermath of False Arrest and Imprisonment' (1993) 21(4) *Bull Am Acad Psychiatry Law* 523.

[56] Terry Waite, *Taken on Trust* (Harcourt 1993); David Alexander and Susan Klein, 'Kidnapping and Hostage-Taking: a Review of Effects, Coping and Resilience' (2009) 102(1) *J Royal Soc Medicine* 16; Robert Hillman, 'The Psychopathology of Being Held Hostage' (1981) 138(9) *Am J Psychiatry* 1193.

[57] James Snell, 'Iran's Hostage Diplomacy', Artillery Row, *The Critic* (6 May 2021).

[58] Grounds (n 54) 167.

[59] Grounds (n 54).

[60] Michael Bauer et al, 'Long-Term Mental Health Sequelae of Political Imprisonment in East Germany' (1993) 181 *J Nervous & Mental Disease* 257, 262.

mainly to long-term stress and particularly to imprisonment in the GDR [East Germany], and not caused by any adjustment problems that may have occurred afterward'.[61] Willis and others' review of studies concerning the impact of detention on political prisoners find long-lasting psychological effects of political imprisonment, which include PTSD, depression, anxiety, substance misuse, somatic complaints and dissociative disorders.[62] They concluded that the prevalence rates of post-traumatic stress ranged from 30.1% to 50% in former political prisoner populations, and from 0% to 2.6% in control group populations.[63] Similar patterns and psychological sequelae exist with former prisoners of war.[64]

3.3 Connection to torture and other cruel, inhuman, or degrading treatment or punishment

My understanding of arbitrary detention as torture takes much from Pérez-Sales' notion of 'torturing environments',[65] which 'challenge the perception of torture as directed foremost against physical integrity. Instead, it might not leave physical marks but has a severe impact on the detainees' mental health and social relations.'[66] Thus, the landscape of torture is not simply one of understanding and assessing methods or techniques of ill-treatment, but centres on the intention to destroy the victim, to break their will and diminish their sense of who they are. Pérez Sales explains that there is a need to:

> (a) break the myth of wrecked bodies as the defining nucleus of torture and (b) focus our reflection on the psychological processes associated with the breaking of will that torture implies. Physical

---

[61] Bauer et al (n 60) 261.

[62] Stacey Willis et al, 'A Systematic Review on the Effect of Political Imprisonment on Mental Health' (2015) 25(A) *Aggression & Violent Behavior* 173, 181.

[63] Willis et al (n 62) 179.

[64] See, for example, Harry Klonoff et al, 'The Neuropsychological, Psychiatric, and Physical Effects of Prolonged and Severe Stress: 30 Years Later' (1976) 163 *J Nervous & Mental Disease* 246; Thomas Miller et al, 'Traumatic Stress Disorder: Diagnostic and Clinical Issues in Former Prisoners of War' (1989) 30 *Comprehensive Psychiatry* 139; Basem Saab et al, 'Predictors of Psychological Distress in Lebanese Hostages of War' (2003) 57 *Social Science & Medicine* 1249; Robert Ursano, 'Prisoners of War: Long-Term Health Outcomes' (2003) 362 *The Lancet Extreme Medicine* S22.

[65] Pau Pérez-Sales, *Psychological Torture: Definition, Evaluation, and Measurement* (Routledge 2017).

[66] Julia Manek, Andrea Galán-Santamarina and Pau Pérez-Sales, 'Torturing Environments and Multiple Injuries in Mexican Migration Detention' (2022) 9(263) *Humanities and Social Sciences Communications* 1, 3.

pain and broken bodies are usually the main source of suffering in the short term. But, in the long term, torture is about submission, dignity and will, and this is what, in most cases, defines damage and healing.[67]

The "arbitrariness" of arbitrary detention, through the uncertainty, disorientation, helplessness and denial of autonomy and control over one's time and place that it engenders, arguably has the capacity to produce the cognitive and emotional suffering that may lead to threats and fear. And the dismantling of the detainee's sense of values over right and wrong and their understanding of their identity and placement in that order, may contribute to their questioning of the core self through emotions (humiliation, shame and guilt).[68]

The definition of torture as set out in the United Nations Convention against Torture (UNCAT) invites one to consider the severe physical and/or psychological pain and suffering experienced by survivors rather than solely or mainly the nature of the different acts that can inflict such suffering. Thus, it is focused on the impact of the acts on survivors as opposed to simply the methods instituted by perpetrators that are designed to achieve those impacts. This is important as it recognises that there is no need for an especially gruesome, sadistic or extraordinary technique to be used to produce a result that can be characterised as torture. Torture exists just as easily in the mundane and the ordinary, as it does in the extraordinary. And the mundane does not necessarily equate with moderate or lukewarm pain or suffering. Mundanity can produce the entire constellation of pain or suffering, both physical and psychological sequelae and usually some non-binary combination of the two. Also, the notion of 'torturing environments' recognises that torture depends, at least in part, on how victims experience pain and suffering. There is therefore a subjective component to the definition.

The definition of torture also places great emphasis on the reason the treatment is inflicted. There can be a direct purpose to torture, but often the purpose is diffuse or not obvious in an individual or narrow or direct sense. The acts are often intended to break the will of the group of which the individual victim(s) may form a part,[69] and there may be more targeted motivations for breaking the person's will, or for what should or could be done with the person once their will is broken.

---

[67] Pau Pérez-Sales, 'Psychological Torture', in Malcolm Evans and Jens Modvig (eds), *Research Handbook on Torture* (Elgar 2020) 432, 435.
[68] Pérez-Sales (n 67) 434.
[69] Pérez-Sales (n 67) 434.

Whether the harms caused by arbitrary detention will constitute torture or other prohibited forms of cruel, inhuman, or degrading treatment or punishment will depend on whether, in a given case, the circumstances of arbitrary detention meet the legal definition of torture, or of other prohibited ill-treatment. The distinction between these two classifications is not straightforward given the absence of an accepted, clear definition of cruel, inhuman, or degrading treatment or punishment, and the different perspectives on what are the most essential characteristics of torture. The ambiguity also stems from challenges identified within the scientific community to apply (and indeed to make sense of) the legal definition of torture.[70] These issues have themselves been the subject of academic debate, as will be described. In this section I consider the different elements of the definitions to assess whether, and in what circumstances, arbitrary detention may satisfy the requirements of the torture definition.

3.3.1 The torture definition and its component parts
(i) Severity

"Severity" is the threshold of the intensity of pain or suffering required for an act to constitute torture, as referred to in the UNCAT definition of torture and several other treaty texts.[71] However, its meaning is ambiguous and value-laden, and subject to myriad interpretations. Psychologists have differed in their approaches to the assessment of the severity of victims' sequelae.[72]

---

[70] See, for example, Pérez-Sales, *Psychological Torture* (n 65) 3; Debbie Green, Andrew Rasmussen and Barry Rosenfeld, 'Defining Torture: a Review of 40 Years of Health Science Research' (2010) 23(4) *J Traumatic Stress* 528; Loran Nordgren, Mary-Hunter Morris McDonnell and George Loewenstein, 'What Constitutes Torture? Psychological Impediments to an Objective Evaluation of Enhanced Interrogation Tactics' (2011) 22(5) *Psychological Science* 689. For instance, research undertaken by Nordgren and others, ibid, demonstrates 'empathy gaps for physical and psychological pain undermine people's ability to objectively evaluate interrogation practices' (693).

[71] Art 1(1) Convention against Torture and Other Cruel, Inhuman or Degrading Treatment or Punishment (adopted 10 December 1984, entered into force 26 June 1987) 1465 UNTS 85 (UNCAT): 'the term "torture" means any act by which *severe pain or suffering, whether physical or mental*, is intentionally inflicted on a person' (emphasis added). "Severity" is also referred to in the definition of torture in the UN Declaration against Torture (Art 1(1)) and the Rome Statute of the International Criminal Court (adopted 17 July 1998, entered into force 7 July 2002) (Art 7(2)(e)). It is absent from the definition in Art 2 of the Inter-American Convention to Prevent and Punish Torture (adopted 9 December 1985, entered into force 28 February 1987) (IACPPT).

[72] Pérez-Sales, *Psychological Torture* (n 65) 3; Green, Rasmussen and Rosenfeld (n 70); Metin Başoğlu, 'A Multivariate Contextual Analysis of Torture and Cruel, Inhuman, and Degrading Treatments: Implications for an Evidence-Based Definition of Torture' (2009) 79(2) *Am J Orthopsychiatry* 135.

The interpretation of "severity" in the legal definition of torture has been somewhat inconsistent in the case law.[73] There is also debate whether the assessment is purely subjective or should include also objective elements that reflect what would ordinarily be understood as causing, or being capable of causing, severe pain or suffering.[74]

Whether conduct will amount to torture has been understood to depend 'on all the circumstances of the case, such as the nature and context of the treatment, its duration, its physical or mental effects and, in some instances, the sex, age, state of health or other status of the victim'.[75] There is debate about the relative weight that should be placed on the severity of the pain or suffering when considering whether a finding of torture is made out.[76] The case law is variable on this point. There is a distinct and continuing thread in the case law on the need for the pain and suffering to reach a level of intensity that is clearly severe,[77] and in some, though much less frequent, rulings a recognition that the special stigma of torture requires that the pain and suffering goes well above and beyond what might be required to demonstrate cruel, inhuman, or degrading treatment or punishment – a sort of aggravated form of prohibited ill-treatment.[78] Evans emphasises that severity is 'only one element of an increasingly complex matrix',[79] and this appears to be a fair assessment of the state of the jurisprudence. Some judgments rely much more, some exclusively so, on the purpose of the ill-treatment to determine whether particular conduct amounts to torture.[80] Severity is an appropriate factor to consider in the overall mix of factors, but it is not a higher-value condition precedent in torture cases, or what necessarily differentiates torture from other prohibited ill-treatment (which also requires severe pain or suffering).

---

[73] See, Nigel Rodley, 'The Definition(s) of Torture in International Law' (2002) 55 *Current Legal Problems* 467.

[74] Hernán Reyes, 'The Worst Scars Are in the Mind: Psychological Torture' (2007) 89(867) *Intl Rev Red Cross* 591, 595–598.

[75] *Brough v Australia* UN Doc CCPR/C/86/D/1184/2003 (17 March 2006) para 9.2. See, similarly, *Huri-Laws v Nigeria* Comm No 225/1998 (ACommHPR, 6 November 2000) para 41.

[76] Rodley (n 73).

[77] *Selmouni v France* (Grand Chamber) App No 25803/94 (ECtHR, 28 July 1999) para 160. For instance, In *Aksoy v Turkey*, the ECtHR determined that 'Palestinian hanging' (tying a person's hands behind the back and stringing them up by the arms) and other ill-treatment was 'of such a serious and cruel nature that it can only be described as torture' (App No 21987/93 (18 December 1996) para 64).

[78] *Ireland v United Kingdom* App No 5310/71 (ECtHR, 18 January 1978) para 167; *Prosecutor v Delalic*, Trial Judgment IT-96-21-T (ICTY, 16 November 1998) paras 462–468.

[79] Malcolm Evans, 'Getting to Grips with Torture' (2002) 51 *ICLQ* 365, 372–373.

[80] *Keenan v United Kingdom* App No 27229/95 (ECtHR, 3 April 2001) para 113.

Traditionally, treatment was only understood to be sufficiently severe to constitute torture if the methods employed were, in the minds of decision-makers, unquestionably severe. Of course, what is meant by unquestionably severe is not only subjective, but it naturally reveals the personal ethics, biases and limitations of decision-makers, as the research of Nordgren and others reveals.[81] At the height of the US "war on terror" in August 2002, American legal bureaucrats wrongly and narrowly interpreted the "severity" test in the ban on torture to require the degree of pain to be 'equivalent in intensity to the pain accompanying organ failure, impairment of bodily function, or even death', and required mental harm to be 'prolonged', which it interpreted as requiring proof of harm lasting 'months or years'.[82] Total sensory deprivation or prolonged or indefinite solitary confinement are often characterised as not meeting the threshold of severity for torture precisely because these methods do not attract the kind of moral opprobrium that other methods do, though this too is in flux.[83] With respect to rape, the International Criminal Tribunal for the former Yugoslavia (ICTY) recognised that *obviously* all acts of rape will satisfy the severity requirement for torture.[84] This approach takes note of rape victims' undeniably severe pain and suffering; however its focus on the form or method of the conduct to determine severity as opposed to the actual pain and suffering of specific victims could lead to situations where victims' actual severe pain and suffering is undervalued because, in the minds of decision-makers, it is not undeniably severe.[85] What is undeniably or unquestionably severe, or clearly insufficiently severe, as already stated, is something that lies in the eyes of the beholder. It is preferable to focus on the impact the conduct has on victims; the actual pain and suffering they experience.

If "severity" is concerned primarily with the impact on the victim, as opposed to the egregiousness or inherent gravity of the methods deployed and how those methods are perceived by judges, this avoids the arguable over-emphasis on the supposed stigma associated with discrete methods of

---

[81] Nordgren and others (n 70).
[82] Discussed in David Cole (ed), *The Torture Memos: Rationalizing the Unthinkable* (New Press 2009).
[83] See *Selmouni v France* (n 77), in which it was recognised that the Convention was a living instrument, treatment which had in the past been considered as "inhuman and degrading treatment" as opposed to "torture" could be classified differently in future. It noted that an 'increasingly high standard' in the protection of human rights inevitably required 'greater firmness in assessing breaches of the fundamental values of democratic societies' (101).
[84] *Prosecutor v Kunarac*, Appeals Judgment, IT-96-23&23/1 (ICTY, 20 June 2002) paras 150, 151.
[85] *Prosecutor v Jean-Pierre Bemba Gombo*, Decision on Warrant of Arrest, ICC-01/05-01/08 (ICC, 10 June 2008) paras 39, 40.

torture. It also aligns more effortlessly with the significant harms experienced by victims because of what some may understand as the more banal acts of arbitrary detention,[86] as was set out in section 3.2. There is some evidence of this approach already with the former European Commission on Human Rights findings in the *Greek Case*, where it held (though primarily on the basis of its understanding that torture had to be severe, but what distinguished it from other forms of prohibited ill-treatment was the prohibited purpose) that 'the failure of the Government of Greece to provide food, water, heating in winter, proper washing facilities, clothing, medical and dental care to prisoners constitutes an "act" of torture in violation of article 3 of the ECHR'.[87] The European Commission found similarly in *Ireland v UK* that the five combined stress techniques that had been used by British security forces against suspected terrorists in Northern Ireland amounted to torture.[88] Finding the mundanity of prison conditions and the rather ordinary sounding five stress positions to meet the definition of torture was significant and in many ways ground-breaking, even though the ECtHR ultimately overruled the Commission in its *Ireland v UK* judgment and underscored the need for torture to have that extra-special something else.[89]

This area of the jurisprudence remains tentative. There is a need to employ more empirical and scientific evidence in pleadings to underpin both the contexts that may give rise to sufficient severity and victims' individualised

---

[86] The notion of banal acts stems from Hannah Arendt's seminal text – *Eichmann in Jerusalem: Report on the Banality of Evil* (Penguin 2006) and has been taken up in Ioannis Kalpouzos and Itamar Mann, 'Banal Crimes against Humanity: the Case of Asylum Seekers in Greece' (2015) 16 *Melb J Intl L* 1. They argue that it would be wrong to focus only on 'radically evil acts'; banal acts, which they see as 'those whose gravity emanates precisely from the fact that they normally cannot be seen from the perspective of their victims. They are grave because the current world order somehow conceals their adverse consequences on the populations they target', are not necessarily less grave (4).

[87] *Opinion of the Commission of 5 November 1969 in the Greek Case* (1969) XII Yearbook, 461.

[88] *Ireland v UK*, Report of the Commission of 25 January 1976, ECHR Ser B, No, 23–1, 410. See, similarly, the UN Committee against Torture's conclusions that Israel's use of stress techniques in interrogations pursuant to the "Landau rules" constitute torture particularly when used in combination. See UN Committee against Torture (CAT), 'Report of the Committee against Torture' UN Doc A/52/44 (10 September 1997) para 257 and also the Committee's conclusion's regarding the use by the US of "enhanced interrogation techniques" as part of its "high value" detainee programme: CAT, 'Concluding Observations: USA' (2006) UN Doc CAT/C/USA/CO/2, para 24, in which it recommended: 'The State party should rescind any interrogation technique, including methods involving sexual humiliation, "waterboarding", "short shackling" and using dogs to induce fear, that constitutes torture or cruel, inhuman or degrading treatment or punishment, in all places of detention under its de facto effective control, in order to comply with its obligations under the Convention.'

[89] *Ireland v United Kingdom* (n 78) para 167.

experiences of pain and suffering, and for judges to give this expert evidence due weight.[90] If this approach were taken, arbitrary detention would certainly be capable of meeting the threshold for the intensity of the pain or suffering required for an act to constitute torture.

Also, there is the understanding that a defining feature of torture is the infliction of pain or suffering on a victim that is powerless. Manfred Nowak, in his former role as UN Special Rapporteur on Torture, noted:

> a thorough analysis of the *travaux préparatoires* of articles 1 and 16 of the Convention as well as a systematic interpretation of both provisions in light of the practice of the Committee against Torture leads one to conclude that the decisive criteria for distinguishing torture from cruel, inhuman and degrading treatment may best be understood to be the purpose of the conduct and the powerlessness of the victim, rather than the intensity of the pain or suffering inflicted.[91]

Thus, from this perspective, ill-treatment applied in a context giving rise to powerlessness (which could include arbitrary detention) would be more likely to result in a finding of torture. One can recall the research findings of Cleveland and others: 'feeling powerless was found to be the detention condition most strongly correlated with PTSD, depression, and anxiety symptoms'.[92] Nowak notes that '[t]orture is predominantly inflicted on persons deprived of their liberty in any context'[93]; however, he does not specify whether this situation of powerlessness (the arbitrary detention) would itself be sufficient to give rise to torture in particular circumstances.

Mavronicola, in her analysis of the ECtHR's jurisprudence on the meaning of "severity" in the context of the minimum level of severity required by Article 3 (torture and other prohibited ill-treatment), argues that 'the Court is grappling with a qualitative, morally loaded concept of "severity" through which inhumanity and degradation are understood. Severity, on this account, goes beyond the degree of pain, suffering, humiliation or anguish inflicted'. 'Severity, rather, is tied to the wrong in inhuman and in degrading treatment

---

[90] David Rhys Jones and Sally Verity Smith, 'Medical Evidence in Asylum and Human Rights Appeals' (2004) 16 *Intl J Refugee L* 381; Helen Baillot, Sharon Cowan and Vanessa Munro, 'Reason to Disbelieve: Evaluating the Rape Claims of Women Seeking Asylum in the UK' (2014) 10(1) *Intl J Law in Context* 105.
[91] HRC, 'Report of the Special Rapporteur on Torture and Other Cruel, Inhuman or Degrading Treatment or Punishment, Manfred Nowak', UN Doc A/HRC/13/39 (9 February 2010) paras 44, 60.
[92] Cleveland et al (n 27) 1005. See, also, Ehlers et al (n 38) 45.
[93] Nowak (n 91) para 44.

or punishment.'[94] She refers to the case of *Bouyid v Belgium*, where police officers slapped a child who was in their custody, where the majority held that 'even one unpremeditated slap devoid of any serious or long-term effect on the person receiving it may be perceived as humiliating by that person' because 'it highlights the superiority and inferiority which by definition characterise the relationship between the former and the latter in such circumstances and may arouse in the person(s) on whom it is inflicted "a feeling of arbitrary treatment, injustice and powerlessness"'.[95] Thus she argues: '"severity" does not stem straightforwardly from the degree of harm or suffering inflicted, but relates rather to the character of the treatment at issue'. It 'ultimately involves grappling with the wrongs themselves, and takes place in a context-sensitive way, where power asymmetry and the vulnerability it creates may play an important role in shaping the character of the treatment'.[96]

In many ways, Mavronicola's arguments about the minimum level of severity align with Nowak's understanding of the relevance of powerlessness to the definition of torture. The powerlessness of the victim should help to determine qualitatively the barometer of acceptable behaviour, not simply because the victim is vulnerable and needs to be protected (though this too is important), but because the perpetrator is comparably powerful, and this power differential amplifies the inhumanity and degradation associated with the perpetrator's offensive conduct. Thus, the abuse of power and the denial of autonomy it engenders plays an important role in determining the nature and the severity of the pain and suffering. This is familiar to victims of arbitrary detention, who have been arbitrarily deprived of their liberty, their autonomy and have no control over their situation and how or when it will be resolved.[97]

(ii) For such purposes as

The requirement that the act be carried out for a specific purpose is central to the UNCAT torture definition and, for some authors, it is the key ingredient to distinguish torture from other prohibited forms of ill-treatment.[98] Burgers

---

[94] Natasa Mavronicola, *Torture, Inhumanity and Degradation under Article 3 of the ECHR: Absolute Rights and Absolute Wrongs* (Bloomsbury 2021) section 5.2.2.
[95] *Bouyid v Belgium (Grand Chamber)* App No 23380/09 (ECtHR, 28 September 2015) paras 105, 106.
[96] Mavronicola (n 94) section 5.2.2.
[97] Gerlach (n 6) 10; Cleveland et al (n 27) 1005.
[98] Rodley and Pollard (n 7) 117–121. See, also, Rodley, 'The Definition(s) of Torture in International Law' (n 73) 489; Manfred Nowak and Elizabeth MacArthur, *The United Nations Convention against Torture: a Commentary* (2nd edn, OUP 2008) 54.

and Danelius[99] specify that the purpose of torture does not need to be an illegitimate one and, according to Zach, the torture definition 'does not necessarily depend on a subjectively verified purpose or intensity of the inflicted pain or suffering, but on the intentionality and purposefulness of that infliction in combination with the powerlessness of the victim'.[100]

The purposive requirement has been interpreted broadly and non-exhaustively though, at least for UNCAT, the inclusion of the words 'such as' implies that purposes other than those listed must bear some similarity to the purposes enumerated in the text explicitly.[101] This is different to the formulation in the Inter-American Convention to Prevent and Punish Torture, which adds to the list of enumerated purposes the phrase 'or for any other purpose'.[102] International jurisprudence has recognised extracting a confession or obtaining from the victim or other person information,[103] intimidating the victim or the wider population,[104] causing humiliation,[105] discrimination[106] and punishment[107] as among the relevant qualifying purposes.

To determine whether the purposive requirement is met for acts of arbitrary detention, in each situation one must first consider what the specific purpose of arbitrary detention is or could be and assess the extent to which it complies with the purposive requirement of the torture definition. Second, given that decisions about arbitrary detention often (but not always) derive from policies targeting entire communities or groups, there is a need to consider whether the purposive requirement must be specific to the individual detainee or whether it is sufficient that the individual was detained for a purpose applying more diffusely to an entire category of persons. Third

---

[99] Herman Burgers and Hans Danelius, *The United Nations Convention against Torture: Handbook on the Convention against Torture and Other Cruel, Inhuman or Degrading Treatment or Punishment* (Nijhoff 1988) 119.

[100] Gerrit Zach, 'Convention against Torture and Other Cruel, Inhuman or Degrading Treatment or Punishment, Part I Substantive Articles, Art 1 Definition of Torture', in Manfred Nowak et al, *The United Nations Convention against Torture and its Optional Protocol: a Commentary* (2nd edn, OUP 2019) 56.

[101] Burgers and Danelius (n 99) 118.

[102] Art 2 IACPPT.

[103] *Cantoral Benavides v Peru* (Merits) Series C No 67 (IACtHR, 18 August 2000) para 104; *Tibi v Ecuador* (Preliminary Objections, Merits, Reparations and Costs) Series C No 114 (IACtHR, 7 September 2004) para 148.

[104] *Gomez-Paquiyauri Brothers v Peru* (Merits, Reparations and Costs) Series C No 110 (IACtHR, 8 July 2004) para 116.

[105] *Prosecutor v Kvočka et al*, Trial Judgment, IT-98-30/1-T (2 November 2001) para 152.

[106] *Prosecutor v Kunarac et al*, Trial Judgment, IT-96-23 and IT-23/1-T (22 February 2001) para 654.

[107] *Opinion of the Commission of 5 November 1969 in the Greek Case* (1969) XII Yearbook, 461.

is how the purposive requirement applies to situations that stem from states' failure to act. Each of these scenarios is analysed in turn.

Whether the act of subjecting someone to arbitrary detention falls within the purposive requirement for torture will depend on the context. This book describes a variety of contexts in which arbitrary detention has been deployed. There is, firstly, the general resort to arbitrary detention as a result of poor law enforcement practices, where police or other detaining authorities are depriving someone of their liberty without following relevant standards of only detaining in accordance with a law that is legitimate and properly enacted, in a situation where detention is an appropriate and proportionate response to address a legitimate concern and strictly necessary in the circumstances. This scenario can stem from the actions of an ill-informed or incompetent arresting officer, in which case, assuming that the error is quickly identified and rectified, the purposive requirement for torture is unlikely to have been met. Law enforcement error or incompetence would not, in the ordinary course of events, give rise to the necessary intent and purpose for torture regardless of the severity of pain or suffering caused. However, if arbitrary detention results from a discriminatory stop and search or other arrest process,[108] and the unlawful arrest was not immediately rescinded by the competent authorities, leaving aside the question of severity, this could already enter into the realm of a prohibited purpose, of course depending on the circumstances, via the route of discrimination. Even if there is not a particular policy of profiling, such profiling arises out of the prejudice of the individuals who set the policies, or that which is present in the neighbourhoods where they work. Similarly, the frequent resort to arbitrary detention to instil fear in or punish political activists and human rights defenders would fall squarely within the prohibited purposes of intimidation and punishment.[109]

In other circumstances, states enact laws and policies in accordance with legitimate, democratic processes, however, these laws and policies may be enacted as tools of structural violence or destructive social control and may themselves be discriminatory. Key examples here are the detention of

---

[108] UN Committee on the Elimination of Racial Discrimination (CERD Committee), 'General Recommendation No 36 on Racial profiling', UN Doc CERD/C/GC/32 (24 November 2020).

[109] See, for example, *Kavala v Turkey* App No 28749/18 (ECtHR, 10 December 2019) where the ECtHR found a violation not only of Art 5(1) (right to liberty) but also Art 18 (restrictions applied for any purpose other than those for which they have been prescribed), insofar as 'in the Court's opinion, the various points examined above, taken together with the speeches by the country's highest-ranking official (quoted above), could corroborate the applicant's argument that his initial and continued detention pursued an ulterior purpose, namely to reduce him to silence as a human-rights defender' (para 230).

entire classes of persons such as people who use drugs, people with mental health challenges, persons who are homeless, or asylum seekers. In each of these cases, the policies are intentional and directed, the opposite to what one might immediately perceive to be "arbitrary". However, as already canvassed in Chapter 2, what is arbitrary in law is not simply those acts that can be classified as 'random or accidental'[110]; arbitrariness is the 'product of compromises between divergent national interests and idealistic arguments'.[111] Thus, the colloquial randomness of arbitrariness does not detract from the legal definition of arbitrary detention, which also encompasses detentions that may be authorised by domestic law but are nonetheless arbitrary, because the authorising law is inappropriate, unjust, discriminatory, insufficiently predictable or unreasonable.[112] Two examples explored next are the targeting of people who use drugs and migrants.

First, the WGAD's seminal report on the arbitrary detention of people who use drugs notes the increasing frequency of the resort to arbitrary detention as a consequence of implementing drug control laws and policies, including when people who use or are suspected of using drugs are confined against their will in compulsory drug detention centres run by the state or privately.[113] The typical rationale for such detentions is to protect such persons from themselves or others, or to pursue health objectives, though the WGAD has also linked the detentions to discrimination, as has the UN Committee on the Rights of Persons with Disabilities.[114] The WGAD has held:

> The war on drugs may be understood to a significant extent as a war on people. Its impact is often greatest on those who are poor, but also frequently overlaps with discrimination in law enforcement directed

---

[110] Enrica Rigo, 'Arbitrary Law Making and Unorderable Subjectivities in Legal Theoretical Approaches to Migration' (2020) 14(2) *Etikk I Praksis – Nordic J Applied Eth* 71, 79.

[111] Benoît Mayer, 'The Arbitrary Project of Protecting Environmental Migrants', in Robert McLeman, Jeanette Schade and Thomas Faist (eds), *Environmental Migration and Social Inequality* (Springer 2016) 189, 195. See, also, Marks, who asks 'does it remind us that arbitrary detention, while reprehensible, is often rational, in the sense that it has a purpose within a contested political order?': Susan Marks, 'Human Rights and Root Causes' (2011) 74 *Modern L Rev* 57, 64.

[112] Human Rights Committee, General Comment No 35, Article 9 (Liberty and Security of Person) (16 December 2014) UN Doc CCPR/C/GC/35 para 12.

[113] WGAD, 'Arbitrary Detention Relating to Drug Policies: Study of the Working Group on Arbitrary Detention', UN Doc A/HRC/47/40 (18 May 2021) paras 3, 84, 92.

[114] CRPD Committee, 'Guidelines on Article 14 of the Convention on the Rights of Persons with Disabilities: the Right to Liberty and Security of Persons with Disabilities' (September 2015) paras 6, 10 <www.ohchr.org/Documents/HRBodies/CRPD/14th session/GuidelinesOnArticle14.doc> accessed 22 July 2023.

at vulnerable groups. This has been referred to as the intersectionality of different forms of discrimination, which reinforces disadvantage.[115]

Second, there is a proliferation of immigration detention regimes in destination countries, which detain asylum seekers and others as a matter of routine. UN treaty bodies have regularly found such detentions to be arbitrary where they do not take account of the particular circumstances and vulnerabilities of individuals, or where they are time unlimited in law or in practice. On one level, the detention regimes have been put in place to allow authorities to prevent unauthorised entry,[116] to determine claimants' identities and to process them upon arrival, to ensure the claimants show up for legal hearings, or, in the case of persons whose claims have been rejected, to ensure the persons concerned can be deported.[117] With some variability, these detention rationales have been upheld by courts as valid and lawful reasons to detain. In contrast, findings of arbitrariness have been made where there has been no legal basis to detain[118] or, but only very infrequently, where these lawful rationales have been shown to be smokescreens, part of a hostile environment and xenophobic responses to migrants in order to coerce them into voluntarily returning to their own or another country, to punish persons for deigning to seek asylum and/or to deter others from seeking asylum.[119] The prohibited purposes of punishment, instilling fear or intimidation, or discrimination, when coupled with instances in which the detention caused severe pain or suffering, could bring this phenomenon of immigration detention within the realm of torture.

---

[115] WGAD, 'Arbitrary Detention Relating to Drug Policies' (n 113) para 51.

[116] Note, however, that Art 31 of the Refugee Convention specifically provides for the non-penalisation of refugees (and asylum-seekers) having entered or stayed irregularly if they present themselves without delay and show good cause for their illegal entry or stay: Convention Relating to the Status of Refugees (adopted 28 July 1951, entered into force 22 April 1954).

[117] *Saadi v United Kingdom (Grand Chamber)* App No 13229/03 (ECtHR, 29 January 2008) para 74: 'To avoid being branded as arbitrary, therefore, such detention must be carried out in good faith; it must be closely connected to the purpose of preventing unauthorised entry of the person to the country; the place and conditions of detention should be appropriate, bearing in mind that "the measure is applicable not to those who have committed criminal offences but to aliens who, often fearing for their lives, have fled from their own country" and the length of the detention should not exceed that reasonably required for the purpose pursued.'

[118] *Khlaifia v Italy* (Grand Chamber) App No 16483/12 (15 December 2016).

[119] Stefanie Grant, 'Immigration Detention: Some Issues of Inequality' (2011) 7 *Equal Rts Rev* 69.

(iii) The involvement of the state

The UNCAT definition of torture provides that for an act to constitute torture, it must be inflicted 'by or at the instigation of or with the consent or acquiescence of a public official or other person acting in an official capacity'.[120] The *travaux préparatoires* explain:

> The problem with which the Convention was meant to deal was that of torture in which the authorities of a country were themselves involved and in respect of which the machinery of investigation and prosecution might therefore not function normally. In a typical case torture is inflicted by a policeman or an officer of the investigating authority.[121]

Rodley and Pollard make clear that 'the prohibition is not concerned with private acts of cruelty: international concern arises only where cruelty has official sanction'. They argue that this focus on public officials aligns with international law's focus on state responsibility: 'It is no accident that the purposive element of torture reflects precisely state purposes or, at any rate, the purposes of an organised political entity exercising effective power.'[122] However, this emphasis on state instigation, consent or acquiescence has been criticised by some scholars and practitioners,[123] and it is not a requirement that exists in all legal frameworks.[124]

---

[120] UNCAT Art 1(1).

[121] Burgers and Danelius (n 99) 119–120.

[122] Rodley and Pollard (n 7) 88–89.

[123] Rhonda Copelon, 'Recognizing the Egregious in the Everyday: Domestic Violence as Torture' (1994) 25 *Colum Hum Rts L Rev* 291, 297; Hilary Charlesworth and Christine Chinkin, 'The Gender of Jus Cogens' (1993) 15 *Hum Rts Q* 63, 69, 72; Alice Edwards, *Violence against Women Under International Human Rights Law* (CUP 2011) 198; Robert McCorquodale and Rebecca La Forgia, 'Taking Off the Blindfolds: Torture by Non-State Actors' (2001) 1 *Hum Rts Law Rev* 189, 217–218.

[124] For instance, the IACPPT in its Art 2: 'or purposes of criminal investigation, as a means of intimidation, as personal punishment, as a preventive measure, as a penalty, or for any other purpose'. Similarly, Art 2(b) of the Inter-American Convention on Violence against Women (Convention of Belém do Pará) (adopted 9 June 1994, entered into force 3 February 1995), establishes state responsibility for violence against women including torture perpetrated by private actors. Also, international criminal law does not limit acts of torture to conduct perpetrated by, at the instigation of, or with the consent or acquiescence of public officials. When torture operates as an underlying act for genocide or is committed as a war crime or crime against humanity, the definition diverges from the one applicable to torture as a discrete crime under international human rights law, in that there is no requirement for the involvement of a public official. See, for example, Arts 7(2)(e), 8(2)(a)(ii), 8(2)(c)(i) Rome Statute of the International Criminal Court 2187 UNTS 90, UN Doc A/CONF.183/9. See, also, *Prosecutor v Kunarac, et al,* Trial Judgment, IT-96-23 & 23/1-A-T (22 February 2001) affirmed on appeal.

Over time, more nuance has entered into the interpretation of the requirement. Certain domestic judgments have begun to find routes to interpret the public official requirement more broadly or flexibly; for example, while it may exclude purely private acts, it should not exclude acts perpetrated by quasi-governmental entities or private contractors performing governmental functions or acts of persons or bodies clearly exuding and abusing power[125] such as armed opposition or militia groups.[126] Furthermore, state responsibility has been imputed for acts causing severe pain or suffering that are understood ostensibly as private acts through states' due diligence obligations to prevent, investigate, prosecute and punish such acts. In its General Comment 2, the UN Committee against Torture has interpreted 'with the consent or acquiescence of a public official or other person acting in an official capacity' to mean that privately inflicted harm against women, children or groups may be covered under the definition of torture if severe pain or suffering is caused and if the state fails to act with due diligence to prevent or protect individuals, since it would be committed for a discriminatory purpose.[127]

It is sometimes misunderstood that acts amounting to torture require that there is a specific person (a public official or a person acting with the consent or acquiescence of the state) who has taken it upon him or herself to commit the acts (for instance to apply the blows or administer the electric shocks) that then results in the severe pain or suffering. Yet the public official requirement, however narrowly or broadly it is construed, is about conduct (whether acts or omissions) that can be attributable or imputable to the state, quasi-state or state-like structures or institutions. As Cakal argues: '[T]orture is often systemically produced and inflicted slowly, routinely, and undramatically. This production implicates, instrumentalizes, and entangles both individual and institutional agents, and must be viewed as emerging from a complex apparatus responsible for torture's instigation and infliction.'[128] Institutional policies or practices that do not consist in a specific, dramatic or 'radically evil'[129] act and/or are not implemented by or directed at any particular individual may nevertheless cause severe pain or suffering when those policies or practices, sometimes authorised or justified by the highest echelons of government, are made applicable to particular

---

[125] See discussion about the role of abuse of power and powerlessness under sub-section 3.3.1(i): Severity.
[126] See, for example, *R v Reeves Taylor* [2019] UKSC 51.
[127] CAT, General Comment No 2: Implementation of Article 2 by States Parties, UN Doc CAT/C/GC/2 (24 January 2008) para 18.
[128] Ergün Cakal, 'Entangling Intentionality: Reflections on Torture and Structure' (2023) 48(3) *Social Justice* 1.
[129] Kalpouzos and Mann (n 86).

individuals. Depending upon the context, these policies or practices, such as regimes of solitary confinement, severe prison overcrowding, inhuman conditions of detention, *incommunicado* detention, routine body searches or use of restraints, denial of medical treatment and force-feeding, may amount to or result in acts of torture.[130] For example, in the *Greek Case*, the European Commission on Human Rights had held that 'the failure of the Government of Greece to provide food, water, heating in winter, proper washing facilities, clothing, medical and dental care to prisoners constitutes an "act" of torture in violation of article 3 of the ECHR'.[131] In this same sense, regimes of arbitrary detention that are set up as part of a specific institutional policy and for a prohibited purpose, established by or with the consent or acquiescence of states, and which cause severe pain or suffering, may also give rise to torture.[132] The Inter-American Commission on Human Rights underscored this point in Djamel Ameziane's case, whose prolonged detention at Guantánamo Bay it found to be cruel and inhuman, because:

> [it] deliberately cause[d] severe mental or psychological suffering, which, given the particular situation, is unjustifiable. […] Mr. Ameziane's continued detention after 2009 is apparently attributable not to a particular, deliberate cruelty directed against him by a particular judge or jailer, but the deliberate cruelty of a legislature that did everything in its power to halt efforts to close Guantánamo and, within the Executive, a (deliberate) bureaucratic indifference to the existence and well-being of Mr. Ameziane and his fellow detainees, and an institutional inertia that, according to the information before the Commission, resulted in a failure to make even one 'phone call, email, meeting, or other discussion' in furtherance of his release from Guantánamo at any time from 2009 to August 2013. Under these circumstances, of course, any suffering caused to Mr. Ameziane following his clearance for transfer is flatly unjustifiable, because he should not have been detained, and the U.S. had no basis to continue treating him as a suspected terrorist housed with and subject to the same regime as detainees who have been charged; rather, he should have been 'treated as [a] person […] who ha[s] never been charged – which is what [he is] – whom the authorities have no legitimate interest in detaining'.[133]

---

[130] See, for example, *Ilaşcu v Moldova and Russia* (Grand Chamber) App No 48787/99 (ECtHR, 8 July 2004) para 440.

[131] *Opinion of the Commission of 5 November 1969 in the Greek Case* (1969) XII Yearbook, 461.

[132] See, also, discussions earlier in this chapter in sub-section 3.3.1(ii): 'For such purposes as […]'.

[133] IACommHR, *Toward the Closure of Guantánamo* (n 11) para 288.

(iv) Does not constitute lawful sanctions

Article 1(1) UNCAT specifies that the definition of torture 'does not include pain or suffering arising only from, inherent in or incidental to lawful sanctions'. This clause derives from the 1975 Torture Declaration, which excluded from the definition of torture 'pain or suffering arising only from, inherent in or incidental to, lawful sanctions to the extent consistent with the Standard Minimum Rules for the Treatment of Prisoners'.[134] The reference to the Standard Minimum Rules was omitted from UNCAT, as the drafters did not wish the Convention to reference rules that were non-binding, though the meaning of the clause as ultimately adopted is somewhat opaque.[135]

Much of the discussion in this area focuses on corporal punishment applied as a form of discipline to children, and specific forms of punishment such as caning, mutilation, stoning and immolation that are practised in some parts of the world, as well as certain practices associated with the imposition of the death penalty. The UN Committee against Torture and successive UN Special Rapporteurs on Torture have given their interpretation that the exclusionary clause in Article 1(1) UNCAT does not allow for corporal or other punishments that would otherwise fall foul of Article 1(1) or other provisions in international law, regardless of their compliance with domestic law.[136]

The lawful sanctions exception is particularly important for those instances in which regimes of detention are imposed in accordance with domestic laws, but which cause or result in severe pain or suffering. Indeed, the former UN Special Rapporteur on Torture, Sir Nigel Rodley explained that the regime of 'lawful sanctions' was in many ways intended for instances of lawfully imposed imprisonment. He has argued:

> The 'lawful sanctions' exclusion must necessarily refer to those sanctions that constitute practices widely accepted as legitimate by the international community, such as deprivation of liberty through

---

[134] Art 1(1), UN Declaration on the Protection of All Persons from Being Subjected to Torture and Other Cruel, Inhuman or Degrading Treatment or Punishment, UNGA Res 3452 (XXX) (9 December 1975).

[135] Burgers and Danelius (n 99) 122; Chris Ingelse, *The UN Committee against Torture: an Assessment* (Kluwer 2001) 231–236.

[136] See, for example, CAT, 'Concluding Observations: Saudi Arabia' (2016) UN Doc CAT/C/SAU/CO/2, para 1; UN Committee against Torture, 'Concluding Observations: Qatar' (2006) UN Doc CAT/C/QAT/CO/1, para 12; Commission on Human Rights, *Report of the Special Rapporteur, Mr P. Kooijmans*, UN Doc E/CN.4/1988/17 (12 January 1988) para 42; *Report of the UN Special Rapporteur on Torture, Mr Nigel S. Rodley*, UN Doc E/CN.4/1997/7 (10 January 1997) paras 7–8; Melzer (n 2) para 42.

imprisonment, which is common to almost all penal systems. Deprivation of liberty, however unpleasant, as long as it comports with basic internationally accepted standards [...] is no doubt a lawful sanction.[137]

Nevertheless, lawfully imposed imprisonment or detention is diametrically opposed to regimes or one-off instances of arbitrary detention. This is so, even though a good part of the practice of arbitrary detention has been normalised by governments. However, when detention is arbitrary this invariably means the detention is unlawful. The WGAD has affirmed this, when it clarified that, for a deprivation of liberty not to be arbitrary, it must result from a final decision taken by a domestic judicial instance and that is (a) in accordance with domestic law; and (b) in accordance with other relevant international standards set forth in the UDHR and the relevant international instruments accepted by the states concerned.[138] Consequently, the imposition of arbitrary detention can never be a justifiable punishment or 'lawful sanction' under Article 1(1) UNCAT.

3.3.2 Other forms of cruel, inhuman, or degrading treatment or punishment

Unlike many other anti-torture and human rights treaties, UNCAT distinguishes between torture and other forms of cruel, inhuman, or degrading treatment or punishment.[139] Unhelpfully, the Convention does not provide a clear definition for these other forms of prohibited ill-treatment. To constitute cruel, inhuman, or degrading treatment, the ill-treatment must (like torture) reach a minimum level of severity or intensity, though there is no need for such acts to be committed for a prohibited purpose.

The debate about what factors distinguish torture from other acts of cruel, inhuman, or degrading treatment or punishment[140] is not a moot issue. In addition to the special stigma often attached to torture[141] canvassed earlier in

---

[137] *Report of the UN Special Rapporteur on Torture, Mr Nigel S. Rodley* (n 136) para 8.
[138] WGAD, Revised Fact Sheet No 26 (8 February 2019), 5.
[139] Art 16 UNCAT.
[140] This is set out earlier in this sub-section 3.3.1(i): Severity.
[141] See, generally, Farrell (n 22), who discusses the role of 'special stigma' in the ECtHR's judgment in *Ireland v United Kingdom*. Farrell's analysis suggests that this language of stigma was used somewhat conspiratorially to classify torture as something reserved for despots; to distinguish it from the banal acts of otherwise civilised governments: 'the Court underlined the seriousness of torture by setting a particularly brutal bar for what constitutes torture, allowing it to deny the applicants their recognition as torture victims, whilst sending "a subliminal message to the UK government that it could continue to tolerate heavy-handed interrogation tactics without having to worry too much about

this chapter, the classification of acts causing severe pain or suffering as torture (as opposed to cruel, inhuman, or degrading treatment or punishment) ensures they receive the full disapprobation of UNCAT. Several UNCAT obligations applicable to torture do not apply seamlessly to other forms of ill-treatment (for example, the prohibition of refoulement, the obligation to criminalise acts amounting to cruel, inhuman, or degrading treatment or punishment, or disallow evidence procured by such treatment),[142] and these distinctions have formed the basis of certain states' policies to permit ill-treatment.[143] The UN Committee against Torture has recognised that both torture and other forms of prohibited ill-treatment form part of a continuum of ill-treatment that states are obligated to prevent, prohibit and repair[144]; however the distinctions remain relevant at the level of state policy development and compliance.

For the most part, courts have refrained from using the torture label outside a very narrow set of circumstances involving the physical ill-treatment of persons deprived of their liberty. Often, judges simply categorise acts as cruel, inhuman, or degrading treatment or punishment in lieu of torture, or where the two categories appear as part of the same prohibition, the decision-makers refrain from distinguishing between the two categories. This is particularly the case for acts constituting mainly psychological forms of violence,[145] such as solitary confinement and prolonged *incommunicado* detention,[146] poor prison conditions and humiliation of prisoners,[147] including when the ill-treatment stems from detention in refugee and migrant detention facilities.[148]

Consequently, the easier argument to make is that arbitrary detention that itself causes severe pain or suffering would amount to cruel, inhuman, or

---

international opprobrium'": Farrell (n 22) 4–5, citing Brice Dickson, *The European Convention on Human Rights and the Conflict in Northern Ireland* (OUP 2010) 167.

[142] UNCAT Art 16.

[143] The example of the US justification of acts characterised as ill-treatment in the context of counter-terrorism, is set out in Carla Ferstman, 'The Human Security Framework and Counterterrorism: Examining the Rhetoric Relating to "Extraordinary Renditions"', in Alice Edwards and Carla Ferstman (eds), *Human Security and Non-Citizens: Law, Policy and International Affairs* (CUP 2010) 532, 541–547.

[144] CAT, General Comment No 2 (n 127) para 3; General Comment No 3, UN Doc CAT/C/GC/3 (13 December 2012) para 1.

[145] See, Ergun Cakal, 'Debility, Dependency and Dread: On the Conceptual and Evidentiary Dimensions of Psychological Torture' (2018) 28(2) *Torture Journal* 15.

[146] *El-Megreisi v Libya* UN Doc CCPR/C/46/D/440/1990 (23 March 1994) para 5.4; *Aber v Algeria* UN Doc CCPR/C/90/D/1439/2005 (16 August 2007) para 7.3; *Suárez-Rosero v Ecuador* (Merits) Series C No 35 (IACtHR, 12 November 1997) paras 90–91.

[147] *Womah Mukong v Cameroon* UN Doc CCPR/C/51/D/458/1991 (10 August 1994) para 9.4; *Hénaf v France* App No 65436/01 (ECtHR, 27 February 2004) paras 55–60; *Loayza-Tamayo v Peru* (Merits) Series C No 33 (IACtHR, 17 September 1997) paras 46(d), 58.

[148] *MSS v Belgium and Greece* App No 30696/09 (21 January 2011) paras 233, 263.

degrading treatment or punishment (as opposed to torture). This we know for sure, and this would be most consistent with the practice of understanding torture through a highly restricted, "othered", and arguably distorted, lens of egregiousness. But doing so contributes to the trivialisation of acts we see as banal,[149] even though the acts may be 'an expression of structurally unjust policies, ... and the harm caused [...] is due to the structure of the system itself, not the result of "a few bad apples"'[150]; it underscores that it is only the electric shocks, the falanga, the hanging of prisoners by their limbs or similar that will amount to torture. This is helpful, and unnecessarily and even gratuitously so, to the governments whose highly educated politicians and advisors will have sat down in their drawing rooms and mapped out, with cold detachment, a plan of arbitrary detention. Is this clean, intellectual ill-treatment not as severe as the dirty, rough stuff that happens in distant gaols? Allowing for such distinctions to be made has a prophecy-fulfilling effect – it ultimately contributes to the maintenance of the narrow understanding of the crime of torture. This is unfortunate, as the prohibition of torture should apply to all relevant acts of severe pain or suffering, whether physical or mental, regardless of whether they shock our sensibilities or align with what we imagine to be egregious or gruesome, wherever these acts happen and whoever decides to authorise them.

3.4 Conclusions

In addition to violating individuals' right to liberty, this chapter has demonstrated that arbitrary detention can cause severe pain or suffering in its own right that is capable of amounting to torture or other cruel, inhuman, or degrading treatment or punishment. This is because of the hopelessness, helplessness, disorientation and despair the arbitrariness produces and the impact the denial of freedom without lawful justification and often for indefinite periods has on the sense of self, sense of justice and vision for the future. It also stems from an understanding of torture that is centred on the intention to break the will of the victim and does not necessarily require especially gruesome, sadistic or extraordinary techniques. These can be acts undertaken simply by individuals acting in some official capacity targeting particular persons or they can result from institutional policies or practices targeting entire communities.

---

[149] Kalpouzos and Mann (n 86).

[150] Theodore Baird, 'Who Is Responsible for Harm in Immigration Detention? Models of Accountability for Private Corporations', Global Detention Project Working Paper No 11 (February 2016) 14.

Recognising that the arbitrariness of a deprivation of liberty can *itself* produce harm that is significant and may amount to torture attaches arbitrary detention to the torture taboo, and is an important ammunition against the growing resort by states to regimes of arbitrary detention to deter certain people or behaviours.

PART II

The Law and Practice of Arbitrary Detention in Context

4

Enforcing Hostility and Social Control

4.1 Introduction

This chapter explores the role of detention as a method to enforce hostility and social control. It focuses on three methods of containment or routes to detention: criminalisation, pathologisation and deterrence. These methods are probed in relation to how they impact on typologies of marginalisation: (1) the "unseen" (those marginalised in neoliberal societies on account of their destitution and/or extreme social needs); (2) the "reviled and resented" (those subjected to racist, xenophobic, and/or discriminatory attacks); and (3) the "undeserving" (refugees and other migrants).

These typologies, which are fluid and often overlapping, may appear provocative to the reader, unhelpful or indeed overly blunt descriptors. However, I use them to underscore the role of labels in the process of "othering" the individuals and groups concerned. The labels also set the stage for what Foucault refers to as an understanding of punishment as political tactic, as a mode to change behaviour or 'technology of power',[1] all of which is a study in the promotion of conformity. This technology as discipline is applied to privilege certain behaviours and to make others more marginal.

Who does the labelling, who falls within the classifications and the classifications themselves, depend on the social context in a given place and time. Which groups are subjected to arbitrary treatment may also change over time depending on class mobility, shifting social attitudes and governments' wavering commitment to eradicating discrimination.

The chapter considers the efficacy of the legal strategies adopted to combat the arbitrary detention these groups experience and identifies the need for

---

[1] Michel Foucault, *Discipline and Punish: the Birth of the Prison* (trans. Alan Sheridan) (Penguin 2020) 194.

more systemic approaches. There is a constant tension in the chapter about the role and placement of the law and its relationship to broader notions of justice. We can see how the law is being used, and even co-opted, to justify the state of exception, to give credence to it, and underpin what is being excepted. As will be explored, theorists continue to debate to what extent the exception is in the service of the law, regulated, framed and tempered by the law, or whether it is the law itself that serves the exception, paving the way for the exception to ultimately overtake the law. Some might posit that this overtaking has already happened, and we are simply in a phase of damage control.

4.2 Agamben and the theorisation of containment

The marginalised and excluded groups in this chapter's "othering" remind of Agamben's *homo sacer*. They are prevented from benefiting from the protection of the law, but at the same time the state retains biopolitical control over them.[2] They are 'stripped of political and legal attributes, whose very existence is a sign of, and countersign to, the sovereign's bloating potency'.[3] Agamben's use of the *homo sacer* and 'biopolitics' in rooted in his sense of the state of exception which, he claims, has become 'the dominant paradigm of government in contemporary politics'.[4]

Agamben's theories are helpful when exploring and problematising what happens in zones of exception or exclusion. His framing of the banning by the sovereign of subjects within its jurisdiction but outside its protection or sense of political obligation, an act that rises in importance during a state of exception, serves the purpose of labelling, signalling and constructing – as enemy, degenerate, criminal and outsider. It is analogous to the enactment of Butler's sinister vision of 'the monopoly of the state on power and violence', which afford security 'to those defending national and ethnic purity, those who oppose Muslims and migrants from North Africa and the Middle East on the basis of their faith (which constitutes discrimination) or a toxic image that constitutes them as pure menace, threatening violence to institutions of white dominance'.[5] It is also symptomatic of Butler's notion of the denial

---

[2] Giorgio Agamben, *Homo Sacer: Sovereign Power and Bare Life* (trans. Daniel Heller-Roazen) (Stanford University Press 1998) 28–29, 126.

[3] Stephen Humphreys, 'Legalizing Lawlessness: on Giorgio Agamben's State of Exception' (2006) 17(3) *Eur J Intl L* 677, 687.

[4] Giorgio Agamben, *State of Exception* (trans. Kevin Attell) (University of Chicago Press 2005) 2. See, also, Claudio Minca, 'Giorgio Agamben and the New Biopolitical *Nomos*' (2006) 88(4) *Geografiska Annaler. Series B, Human Geography* 387–403.

[5] Judith Butler, 'Indefinite Detention' (2020) 29(1) *qui parle* 15, 16.

of 'grievability' for certain marginalised groups,[6] and those who, according to Arendt, do not possess the 'right to have rights'.[7]

This tactic of labelling and excluding is also for Foucault, 'a racism that society will direct against itself, against its own elements and its own products [...] the internal racism of permanent purification, and it will become one of the basic dimensions of social normalization'.[8] It legitimises the exclusion of these groups and foreshadows the violence meted out against them while serving to fuel the false binary, the fantasy of security and privilege that such exclusion brings for the fortunate groups that remain in the zone of inclusion. It is necessarily a top-down analysis because it operates by denying subjectivity to the "degenerates" below. And the act of categorisation meted out by those with power against the powerless or the less powerful is itself a form of violence for its capacity to co-opt the autonomy and agency of the subject.

The sites and spaces of detention have an important role in framing how confinement is perceived and experienced. The concentration camp is central to Agamben's space of exception or zone of lawlessness. It is 'the very paradigm of political space at the point at which politics becomes biopolitics and *homo sacer* is virtually confused with the citizen'.[9] It is the site that allows for 'juridical procedures and deployments of power by which human beings [were] completely deprived of their rights and prerogatives that no act committed against them could appear any longer as a crime'.[10] The physical infrastructure and spatial conceptualisations of the "camp" have been considered widely[11] and have been invoked in theoretical analyses related to the securitisation of detention,[12] borders and border control.[13]

---

[6] Judith Butler, *Precarious Life: the Powers of Mourning and Violence* (Verso 2004).

[7] Arendt refers to this right as 'the right of every individual to belong to humanity': Hannah Arendt, *The Origins of Totalitarianism* (Penguin 2017 [1951]) 390.

[8] Michel Foucault, *Society Must be Defended, Lecture Series at the Collège de France, 1975–76* (trans. D Macey) (Picador 2003) 62.

[9] Agamben, *Homo Sacer* (n 2) 171.

[10] Ibid. See, also, Giorgio Agamben, *Remnants of Auschwitz: the Witness and the Archive* (Zone Books 1999).

[11] Minca (n 4). See, also, Richard Ek, 'Giorgio Agamben and the Spatialities of the Camp: an Introduction' (2006) 88(4) *Geografiska Annaler. Series B, Human Geography* 363; Nick Vaughan-Williams, 'Borders, Territory, Law' (2008) 2 *Intl Political Sociology* 322.

[12] Agamben, *State of Exception* (n 4); Derek Gregory, 'The Black Flag: Guantánamo Bay and the Space of Exception' (2006) 88(4) *Geografiska Annaler. Series B, Human Geography* 405–427; Claudia Aradau, 'Law Transformed: Guantanamo and the "Other" Exception' (2007) 28(3) *Third World Quarterly* 489–501.

[13] Didier Bigo, 'Detention of Foreigners, States of Exception, and the Social Practices of Control of the Banopticon', in PK Rajaram and C Grundy-Warr (eds), *Borderscapes: Hidden Geographies and Politics at Territory's Edge* (University of Minnesota Press 2007) 57; Suvendrini Perera, 'What is a Camp?' (2002) 1(1) *Borderlands e-journal* 1; Joseph Pugliese, 'The Tutelary Architecture of Immigration Detention Prisons and the Spectacle of "Necessary Suffering"' (2008) 13(2) *Architectural Theory Review* 206.

4.3 Methods of containment

There are at least three cross-cutting methods by which detention enforces hostility and social control.

4.3.1 Detention as criminalisation

Criminalisation is the process by which decisions are taken as to what acts and omissions to prohibit and sanction, which persons are charged and ultimately convicted of having contravened those prohibitions, and what sentences are applied from a range of permissible sanctions.[14] I am here mainly concerned with the first aspect about what to prohibit and sanction. There are theories about what factors should underpin decisions about whether particular conduct should be made criminal or whether another type of sanction would be more appropriate or effective as a strategy to deter that conduct, discipline and/or rehabilitate the perpetrator(s), protect victims and would-be victims, and/or show societal contempt for the behaviour.[15] These decisions involve considerations about what harm the conduct is causing and to whom, how serious the harm is (and what "seriousness" means in context), whether the public needs to be protected from the conduct and, if so, how best to ensure such protection, and whether there is a less restrictive means to deter the conduct and ensure public protection.[16] They also involve conceptions about the relative "wrongfulness" of different acts, which injects a sense of morality or values into decision-making,[17] which is unsurprising though highly subjective.

The decision to criminalise certain behaviours and not others involves inherent biases and subjective considerations that have differential impacts on individuals and groups depending upon socio-economic status, race, religion, national origin, citizenship status, gender and age, among other factors.[18] These biases involve perspectives about what behaviours are most dangerous, who the society is and from whom it needs to be protected, and what degree of risk is acceptable within the society. Most societies recognise that criminalisation will not be an effective response to complex

---

[14] Andrew Simester and Andreas von Hirsch, *Crimes, Harms, and Wrongs: On the Principles of Criminalisation* (Hart 2011) 3.
[15] See, generally, David Garland, *The Culture of Control: Crime and Social Order in Contemporary Society* (University of Chicago Press 2001).
[16] Douglas Husak, *Overcriminalization: the Limits of the Criminal Law* (OUP 2008) 122–132.
[17] Simester and von Hirsch (n 14) 19–32.
[18] Elizabeth Kiely and Katharina Swirak, *The Criminalisation of Social Policy in Neoliberal Societies* (Bristol University Press 2022).

social problems and alternatives to criminalisation should be considered and discounted before deciding to make an act criminal – it is a last resort.[19] However, seeing issues through the lens of social problems brings them to the fore of the society; solutions necessarily involve the community, and the social problems are part of the community. At least at a theoretical level, criminalisation justifies putting barriers between the community and the "criminals". Thus, decisions about what responses should be taken do not only involve considerations of "effectiveness", and what constitutes effectiveness is equally contingent on who one is and how one is situated in relation to the "imagined" society.

Criminalisation occurs when a government decides to enact criminal laws outlawing certain behaviours and to impose a sanction or penalty to address the violation of the laws enacted. At times, governments will criminalise behaviours that are not commonly associated with crimes, to register their disapproval of and to distance themselves from those behaviours. An example of this is the criminalisation of homelessness, loitering, trespassing and vagrancy, and/or other daily survival activities associated with living on the streets and other extreme forms of poverty. This neoliberal response to poverty includes the use of 'ordinances relating to civic or anti-social behaviour, which regulate activities in public spaces and restrict options when it comes to sleeping, eating, drinking or washing oneself on the street',[20] and fosters 'situations of absolute poverty that the system no longer seeks to solve, but rather just attempts to conceal, move, incarcerate or expel'.[21] As Blagg and Anthony have noted in relation to the criminalisation of poverty-stricken indigenous populations, it 'problematises the notion of deterrence because it assumes that there are ways that Indigenous people can avoid crimes when often they are criminalised for being themselves'.[22]

Criminalisation of "antisocial" conduct also results in reduced access to support, treatment and care, ultimately increasing vulnerabilities and harms.[23]

---

[19] Joel Feinberg, *The Moral Limits of the Criminal Law*, vol. 1 (OUP 1987), 'General Introduction' 22–25.

[20] Guillem Fernàndez Evangelista, 'Penalising Homelessness in Europe', in Helmut Gaisbauer, Gottfried Schweiger and Clemens Sedmak (eds) *Absolute Poverty in Europe: Interdisciplinary Perspectives on a Hidden Phenomenon* (Policy Press 2019) 315–334, 320.

[21] Evangelista (n 20) 329.

[22] Harry Blagg and Thalia Anthony, *Decolonising Criminology: Imagining Justice in a Postcolonial World* (Palgrave Macmillan 2019) 188.

[23] UNGA, 'Report of the Special Rapporteur on the Right of Everyone to the Enjoyment of the Highest Attainable Standard of Physical and Mental Health', UN Doc A/65/255 (6 August 2010) para 62. See, also, International Commission of Jurists, 'The 8 March Principles for a Human Rights-Based Approach to Criminal Law: Proscribing Conduct Associated with Sex, Reproduction, Drug Use, HIV, Homelessness and Poverty' (March 2023).

The same could be said for the criminalisation of conduct on religious or "moral" grounds, such as sex work and the procurement of abortions,[24] or the possession or consumption of drugs for personal use,[25] where the impact is to drive such conduct underground and make it more difficult for affected persons to seek help. Similarly, the criminalisation of migration and migrants exacerbates their vulnerability and makes them more likely to become victims of crime. The former UN Special Rapporteur on Migrants has noted in this respect:

> [C]riminalizing irregular migrants for the offence of being in a country without adequate documentation makes all migrants, regardless of immigration status, vulnerable to potential racist or xenophobic acts. Societies quickly distort the particular situations of migrants, and associate them with criminality, including organized crime, drug trafficking, robbery or even terrorism.[26]

Criminalisation can also occur indirectly, when government policy impacts certain segments of society in such a way that they are more prone to commit certain crimes. An example of this is the removal of social safety nets and services to the point that persons and communities living precariously feel compelled to commit crimes to meet basic needs. Another example of indirect criminalisation is the removal of safe routes to enter a country so that desperate refugees and other migrants are compelled to seek entry through irregular and typically unauthorised means.

Also relevant to criminalisation is the way in which policing measures are applied that impacts differentially upon the susceptibility of marginalised

---

[24] Dipika Jain, 'Time to Rethink Criminalisation of Abortion? Towards a Gender Justice Approach' (2019) 12(1) *NUJS L Rev* 21–42; Michael Rekart, 'Sex-Work Harm Reduction' (2005) 366 *Lancet* 2123–2134; Pippa Grenfell et al, 'Policing and Public Health Interventions into Sex Workers' Lives: Necropolitical Assemblages and Alternative Visions of Social Justice' (2022) *Critical Public Health* 1; Human Rights Watch (HRW), 'Off the Streets: Arbitrary Detention and Other Abuses against Sex Workers in Cambodia' (19 July 2010).

[25] UNGA, 'Report of the Special Rapporteur on the Right of Everyone to the Enjoyment of the Highest Attainable Standard of Physical and Mental Health' (n 23) paras 19–29. See, also, Rick Lines, '"Deliver us from evil" – the Single Convention on Narcotic Drugs, 50 Years on' (2010) 1 *Intl J Hum Rts & Drug Policy* 3.

[26] UNGA, 'Report of the Special Rapporteur on the Human Rights of Migrants' (the impact of the criminalization of migration on the protection and enjoyment of human rights) UN Doc A/65/222 (3 August 2010) para 16.

groups to be charged with criminal offences, and how offences are pursued through the criminal justice system.[27] In many countries, discriminatory practices mean that certain communities are more likely to be suspected of criminal behaviour, whether because they are profiled by the police or by the application of automated systems using biased data.[28] In the UK, the Stephen Lawrence Inquiry report described the policing of the murder of Black teenager Stephen Lawrence as a systematic and 'collective failure of the organisation to provide an appropriate and professional service to people because of their colour, culture or ethnic origin'.[29] In many countries, ethnic, racial and religious minorities, and indigenous peoples are significantly over-represented as defendants and detainees in criminal justice systems.[30] Persons with disabilities, particularly those with intellectual or psychosocial disabilities, are overrepresented among homeless populations and also over-represented in the criminal justice system.[31]

Detention can be both a precursor to and an outcome of criminalisation. As a precursor, individuals and groups who experience marginalisation are more likely to be denied bail in the lead up to criminal trials. This is certainly the case with non-nationals, particularly those who are charged with offences related to their efforts to gain access. Winkler and Mayr in their 2023 study for Borderline Europe about the pre-trial detention of persons accused of people smuggling in Greece (which the Greek

---

[27] *The Lammy Review: an Independent Review into the Treatment of, and Outcomes for, Black, Asian, and Minority Ethnic Individuals in the Criminal Justice System* (8 September 2017) <www.gov.uk/government/publications/lammy-review-final-report> accessed 22 July 2023.

[28] Fair Trials, *Automating Injustice: the Use of Artificial Intelligence and Automated Decision-Making Systems in Criminal Justice in Europe* (2021) <www.fairtrials.org/app/uploads/2021/11/Automating_Injustice.pdf> accessed 22 July 2023; Osonde Osoba and William Welser IV, *An Intelligence in Our Image: the Risks of Bias and Errors in Artificial Intelligence* (Rand Corp 2017) <www.rand.org/pubs/research_reports/RR1744.html> accessed 22 July 2023.

[29] Sir William Macpherson, *The Stephen Lawrence Inquiry: Report of an Inquiry* (Home Office 1999) para 6.34.

[30] Lammy Review (n 27); Marianne Nielsen and Linda Robyn, 'Colonialism and Criminal Justice for Indigenous Peoples in Australia, Canada, New Zealand and the United States of America' (2003) 4(1) *Indigenous Nations Studies J* 29.

[31] UNGA, 'Report of the Special Rapporteur on the Rights of Persons with Disabilities' (thematic study on disability-specific forms of deprivation of liberty) UN Doc A/HRC/40/54 (11 January 2019) paras 33, 45; Royal Commission into Violence, Abuse, Neglect and Exploitation of People with Disability, *Criminal Justice System: Issues Paper* (January 2020) <https://disability.royalcommission.gov.au/system/files/2022–03/Issues%20paper%20-%20Criminal%20justice%20system.pdf> accessed 22 July 2023.

Ministry of Citizenship indicated involved 634 detainees as of February 2023), indicated:

> According to the interviewed lawyers, pre-trial detention orders are routinely issued for third country nationals accused of smuggling, with little consideration for the specific circumstances of the case. This is consistent with other reports, which indicate that the mere lack of a fixed residence is often considered a decisive factor for ordering pre-trial detention – a characteristic that applies to everyone who is arrested upon arrival. Additionally, this research suggests that pretrial detention orders rarely include references to specific evidence or arguments presented by the defence.[32]

Money bail systems have a discriminatory effect on the poor,[33] and on minority ethnic and racialised groups.[34] The WGAD has found as much in the case of Marcos Antonio Aguilar-Rodríguez, a national from El Salvador who had relocated to the US where he started a family and claimed asylum. He was detained by immigration authorities for almost six years, because the "bail" was set so high that he was unable to pay it. According to the WGAD, 'requiring the posting of excessively large bonds does not provide an alternative to detention to those who are detained. Moreover, the practice is discriminatory, as it disproportionately affects those of humble economic backgrounds.'[35]

Pre-trial detainees also have an increased incentive to quickly plead guilty to be released.[36] This has a follow-on impact on the direction of trials and sentencing and compounds the impact of any further discrimination to be faced during the trial, judgment, and sentencing phases.[37]

Criminalisation policies that result in deprivations of liberty that do not serve a pressing social need are disproportionate to the societal benefits they are intended to engender, or that are selectively enforced in a discriminatory

---

[32] Julia Winkler and Lotta Mayr, 'A Legal Vacuum: the Systematic Criminalisation of Migrants for Driving a Boat or Car to Greece' (Borderline Europe July 2023) 25.

[33] Michael Gottfredson, 'An Empirical Analysis of Pre-Trial Release Decisions' (1974) 2 *J Crim Justice* 287, 288.

[34] Brandon Martinez, Nick Petersen and Marisa Omori, 'Time, Money, and Punishment: Institutional Racial-Ethnic Inequalities in Pretrial Detention and Case Outcomes' (2019) 66 (6–7) *Crime & Delinquency* 837.

[35] WGAD, *Opinion No 72/2017 Concerning Marcos Antonio Aguilar-Rodríguez (United States of America)* UN Doc A/HRC/WGAD/2017/72 (28 December 2017) para 67.

[36] Martin Schönteich, *Presumption of Guilt: the Global Overuse of Pretrial Detention* (Open Society Justice Initiative 2014) 33.

[37] Michael Klarman, 'The Racial Origins of Modern Criminal Procedure' (2000) 99(1) *Michigan L Rev* 48; Sonja Starr, 'Evidence-Based Sentencing and the Scientific Rationalization of Discrimination' (2014) 66(4) *Stanford Law Rev* 803.

manner against marginalised persons or groups are arbitrary and will result in arbitrary detention.

4.3.2 Detention as pathologisation

Pathologisation is the process by which human traits are conceptualised as disorders that can be diagnosed and treated medically and therapeutically.[38] Pathologisation is connected to what Brinkmann refers to as the 'logics of diagnostic cultures'[39] where the diagnosis serves to ensure that certain forms of suffering are followed up in a particular way. Yet, diagnoses, particularly those that involve mental health, are 'invented modes of reasoning'[40] that necessarily involve value judgments about the placement of the boundaries of "normality" and "disorder". Diagnoses can move quickly from an analysis of discrete traits to the medicalisation of social norms and identities resulting in individuals, groups and/or entire communities being illegitimately pathologised as deviant or morally unacceptable.[41] It has a more sinister, stigmatising and constraining impact. As Moncrieff explains, referring to the research of Coulter,[42] 'someone is said to be mad or mentally ill when their behaviour infringes social norms of intelligibility. What counts as intelligible, reasonable, or rational is determined by unwritten rules of conduct that are constituted by social groups.'[43]

Detention as pathologisation is thus the process by which certain persons or groups are diagnosed as unwell or unsound and in need of treatment, discipline, rehabilitation, or some other form of therapeutic intervention; and the subsequent decision to require those persons to have those needs met in a closed facility. Indeed, it is both the result of failed community inclusion and a justification of that failure by way of the diagnosis that serves as the tool to banish and exclude. The classic example of this is the compulsory detention of persons said to be of 'unsound mind',[44] where a person's mental disability is used to "protect" them from criminal proceedings, but, in the process,

---

[38] Svend Brinkmann, 'The Pathologization of Morality', in Kieran Keohane and Anders Petersen (eds), *The Social Pathologies of Contemporary Civilization* (Ashgate 2013) 103, 107.

[39] Svend Brinkmann, *Diagnostic Cultures: a Cultural Approach to the Pathologization of Modern Life* (Routledge 2016) 13–14, 23–25.

[40] Alison Howell, 'Victims or Madmen? The Diagnostic Competition over "Terrorist" Detainees at Guantánamo Bay' (2007) 1 *Intl Political Sociology* 29, 31.

[41] Sander Gilman, *Difference and Pathology: Stereotypes of Sexuality, Race, and Madness* (Cornell University Press 1985) 233.

[42] Jeff Coulter, *The Social Construction of Mind* (Macmillan 1979) 149.

[43] Joanna Moncrieff, 'Psychiatric Diagnosis as a Political Device' (2010) 8 *Soc Theory Health* 370, 373.

[44] *Winterwerp v Netherlands* App No 6301/73 (ECtHR, 24 October 1979) para 39. See Art 14(1)(b) Convention on the Rights of Persons with Disabilities (CRPD) (adopted 13 December 2006, entered into force 3 May 2008); CRPD Committee, 'Guidelines on Article 14 of the CRPD', in Report of the CRPD Committee, UN Doc A/72/55 (2016) Annex.

denies them agency and sometimes results in far more punitive outcomes.[45] Regardless of whether this medical containment or treatment imperative is understood factually or metaphorically, it introduces a new hierarchy and is an important part of the legitimisation of the logic of detention, with the clinicians using the nomenclature of care to decide not only upon the boundaries of sickness and health, but also on the imposition of the cure, which can be highly problematic and put extremely vulnerable people at risk.

The pathologisation has extended to persons who are deemed to fall outside societal morals and standards of acceptable conduct. An example of this is the detention of ostracised women and girls in "social rehabilitation" centres for the apparent transgression of moral codes.[46] In Ireland for instance, women and girls were involuntarily confined (detained) in the Magdalene laundries, children's institutions, and mother and baby homes, including unmarried mothers who were regarded as deviant for having engaged in, or having been susceptible to, inappropriate sexual behaviour. These convents and homes were stigmatising and cruel places of detention designed to discipline women for subverting gender norms and to encourage them to conform.[47] Another example is the compulsory detention of persons with drug addictions (largely perceived as a moral failing[48]) to serve the purported aims of treatment or rehabilitation.[49] The WGAD has explained that the threat of imprisonment should never be used to coerce people into drug treatment.[50] It has recommended that 'States should make available voluntary, evidence-informed and rights-based health and social services in the community' as an alternative to compulsory drug detention centres.[51]

Once detained, the continued pathologisation of detainees can serve an added purpose. By focusing on detainees' "disorders" the authorities and institutions responsible for the detention emphasise a narrative about what is "wrong" or deviant with the detainees and what must be cured or fixed. This can serve to mask any institutional causes for the symptoms observed

---

[45] Piers Gooding et al, 'Unfitness to Stand Trial and the Indefinite Detention of Persons with Cognitive Disabilities in Australia: Human Rights Challenges and Proposals for Change' (2017) 40 *Melb Univ Law Rev* 816.

[46] HRW, 'Libya: a Threat to Society? The Arbitrary Detention of Women and Girls for "Social Rehabilitation"' (February 2006).

[47] Christina Quinlan, 'Women, Imprisonment and Social Control', in Deirdre Healy (ed), *The Routledge Handbook of Irish Criminology* (Routledge 2015) 500–521. See, also, Frances Finnegan, *Do Penance or Perish: Magdalen Asylums in Ireland* (OUP 2004).

[48] HRC, *Arbitrary Detention Relating to Drug Policies* UN Doc A/HRC/47/40 (18 May 2021) para 87.

[49] Rick Lines, Julie Hannah and Giada Girelli, '"Treatment in Liberty" Human Rights and Compulsory Detention for Drug Use' (2022) 22 *Hum Rts L Rev* 1.

[50] HRC, *Arbitrary Detention Relating to Drug Policies* (n 48) para 83.

[51] HRC, *Arbitrary Detention Relating to Drug Policies* (n 48) para 88.

(which, given the conclusions from the analysis of the harms of arbitrary detention in Chapter 3, may be connected back to the detention itself or detention-related ill-treatment).[52] Howell canvasses this phenomenon in relation to the US response to detainee suicidality at Guantánamo Bay: 'the U.S. military, and [by] the Bush administration, told the story of irrational, uncivilized, crazed killers – terrorist madmen ...'[53] who they portrayed as 'incurable, irredeemable, as suicidal (and homicidal), and manipulative'; the suicides were constructed as 'manipulative self-injurious behavior'.[54]

The use of detention to "cure" people because they do not fit within the "imagined" society is the epitome of hostility and social control, in that it deems the way these individuals or groups "are" – their inherent nature and characteristics – as needing to be fixed or cured. Mandating, and indeed requiring, that fixing constitutes a further act of violence. These decisions impact upon the liberty and security, autonomy and privacy of the individuals and groups affected. Often, they will result in cruel, inhuman, or degrading treatment or punishment, if not torture.[55]

4.3.3 Detention as deterrence

Deterrence theory is a theory of punishment by which the goal is the reduction of offending (and future offending) by both the individual offender and any future would-be offenders through the sanction or threat of sanction. It plays an important role in criminal law detention, both pre-trial detention (some of the rationales being to prevent reoffending or protect the public order, though these rationales have been subject to criticism[56]) and post-conviction sentencing to a term of imprisonment (where specific and general deterrence are part of the sentencing objectives).[57] Detention

---

[52] Though in this respect Howell finds the alternative narrative put forward by human rights and humanitarian organisations of the traumatised victims driven to suicide equally pathologising. See Howell (n 40) 38–41.

[53] Howell (n 40) 30.

[54] Howell (n 40) 35, 37.

[55] See, for example, *Gorobet v Moldova* App No 30951/10 (ECtHR, 11 October 2011) para 52 (finding a violation of Art 3 and holding that there was 'no medical necessity to subject the applicant to psychiatric treatment' and noting the considerable duration of the medical treatment, that the applicant was denied contact with the outside world during his confinement, and finding that 'such unlawful and arbitrary treatment was at the very least capable to arouse in the applicant feelings of fear, anguish and inferiority').

[56] Antony Duff, 'Pre-Trial Detention and the Presumption of Innocence', in Andrew Ashworth, Lucia Zedner and Patrick Tomlin (eds), *Prevention and the Limits of Criminal Law* (OUP 2013) 128–131.

[57] Jeremy Bentham, *The Principles of Morals and Legislation* (Prometheus Books 1988 [1789]) 1; Johs Andenaes, 'General Prevention-Illusion or Reality?' (1952) 43 *J Crim L, Criminology*

is often justified as a form of criminal deterrence though there is limited empirical evidence of its effectiveness,[58] particularly for 'non-deterrable' criminal offending linked to social issues,[59] such as offending in the context of alcohol intoxication or drug use. Clearly, deterrence plays no role in detentions fuelled by discrimination. As was discussed earlier (and is further developed later) in this chapter, deterrence is also a rationale for detention on mental health grounds (where detention is justified as being required to protect the health or safety of the individual to be detained or where it is believed that the detainee poses a significant risk to other people).

Deterrence has also become a political rationale to detain refugees and other migrants. It does not deter those that have already arrived, but detention has been justified by governments on the basis that it serves as a form of general deterrence (though with little evidence of its effectiveness[60]) to disincentivise other would-be refugees and other migrants from choosing to seek entry to the country of destination. This policy of deterrence is pursued even though many refugees and other migrants, including victims of serious human rights violations in their home states, children, victims of trafficking and stateless persons are recognised as vulnerable groups entitled to special protection, and detention would likely exacerbate those vulnerabilities.

The externalisation of border control involves the outsourced detention of would-be migrants in transit countries, contiguous border zones and international waters to deter them from reaching destination countries. It has fuelled the detention crises in Libya,[61] the zones of exclusion in the Spanish enclaves of Ceuta and Melilla,[62]

& *Police Sci* 176; Jack Gibbs, 'Crime, Punishment and Deterrence' (1968) 48 *Southwestern Soc Sci Q* 515, 515–516.

[58] See, for example, Emily Ryo, 'Detention as Deterrence' (2019) 71 *Stanford L Rev* 237; Athula Pathinayake, 'Contextualizing Specific Deterrence in an Era of Mass Incarceration' (2019) 18(2) *Conn Public Interest LJ* 359; Aaron Chalfin and Justin McCrary, 'Criminal Deterrence: a Review of the Literature' (2017) 55(1) *J Economic Literature* 5.

[59] Donald Ritchie, 'Sentencing Matters Does Imprisonment Deter? A Review of the Evidence' (Victoria Sentencing Advisory Council April 2011) 17.

[60] Robyn Sampson, 'Does Detention Deter? Reframing Immigration Detention in Response to Irregular Migration' (April 2015) *International Detention Coalition Briefing Paper* 1; Ryo (n 58).

[61] Ian Urbina, 'The Secretive Prisons That Keep Migrants Out of Europe', *The New Yorker* (6 December 2021); HRC, 'Report of the Independent Fact-Finding Mission on Libya', UN Doc A/HRC/52/83 (3 March 2023) paras 40–53.

[62] Luca Queirolo Palmas, '*Frontera Sur*: Behind and Beyond the Fences of Ceuta and Melilla' (2021) 22(4) *Ethnography* 451; *ND and NT v Spain* (Grand Chamber) App Nos 8675/15, 8697/15 (ECtHR, 13 February 2020), effectively holding that Spain was justified in pushing back refugees and migrants at the Spanish–Moroccan border.

the long-standing offshore processing of migrants seeking to enter Australia,[63] among other places.

Regardless of its administrative basis, the detention of refugees and other migrants has the character of, and is experienced by those subjected to the practice as, a punitive form of criminalisation.[64] As Fekete has explained in relation to the adoption of the philosophy of deterrence by European states:

> [T]he idea is to create a system so harsh and unwelcoming as to deter all but the most desperate. The result beggars belief for a continent that prides itself on superior Enlightenment values. Seas that have turned into vast graveyards. A welcome that resembles the concentration camp. A process of removal that is not only cruel and arbitrary, but a destroyer of human dignity. An archipelago of battlements and internment centres across Europe and North Africa that generates huge profits for private security companies whose executives daily dine out on the fare of human misery.[65]

Deterrence has also been used in Australia to justify the introduction of mandatory detention for those that arrive without a valid visa and claim asylum, and later as part of the justification for the resort to offshore detention centres (focusing on the need to remove the incentives to pay people smugglers).[66] However, there is no evidence to suggest that detaining refugees and other migrants has any impact on the disincentivisation of people smugglers. According to the United Nations Office on Drugs and Crime (UNODC), 'increased border enforcement efforts [which would include criminalisation measures] in geographically limited areas often result in displacement of smuggling routes to different borders, smuggling methods or to other routes. If applied in isolation these measures do not reduce the number of smuggled migrants or the size of the smuggling problem'.[67] The UNODC has called for a comprehensive, multipronged approach, which

---

[63] Madeline Gleeson and Natasha Yacoub, 'Cruel, Costly and Ineffective: the Failure of Offshore Processing in Australia', Kaldor Centre for International Refugee Law (August 2021) <www.kaldorcentre.unsw.edu.au/sites/kaldorcentre.unsw.edu.au/files/Policy_B rief_11_Offshore_Processing.pdf> accessed 30 July 2023.

[64] Sharon Pickering and Leanne Weber, 'New Deterrence Scripts in Australia's Rejuvenated Offshore Detention Regime for Asylum Seekers' (2014) 39(4) *Law & Social Inquiry* 1006, 1006.

[65] Liz Fekete, 'The Globalisation of Indifference', Institute of Race Relations (20 March 2014) <https://irr.org.uk/article/the-globalisation-of-indifference/> accessed 22 July 2023.

[66] Pickering and Weber (n 64) 1016.

[67] UNODC, 'Global Study on Smuggling of Migrants' (2018) 12.

should include, among the measures, limiting the demand for smugglers. In this regard, it has indicated that:

> Limiting the demand for migrant smuggling can be achieved by broadening the possibilities for regular migration and increasing the accessibility of regular travel documents and procedures. Making regular migration opportunities more accessible in origin countries and refugee camps, including the expansion of migration and asylum bureaux in origin areas, would reduce opportunities for smugglers.[68]

According to Pickering and Lambert, who have studied Australian government usages of deterrence to justify increasingly oppressive policies pertaining to refugees and migrants, including detention:

> Deterrence was never meant to be measurable or justifiable in its own terms, not least because of the difficulties involved of proving its effectiveness or otherwise. Rather, deterrence is about a strategy of control that only those apart from the experiences of persecution and forced migration could contemplate, only an internal audience would consider.[69]

Even if there was evidence of effectiveness, deterrence would not constitute a lawful rationale to detain all migrants entering a country,[70] nor would it be a lawful basis to interdict persons at sea and direct them to other countries where they would face almost certain arbitrary detention. Nevertheless, this illegality has not stemmed the practice. Systematically resorting to the detention of irregular migrants, regardless of their individual personal circumstances, contradicts the right to liberty and security of the person and constitutes arbitrary detention. Despite this, and as is further explained later in this chapter,[71] some human rights courts have given an increasingly

---

[68] Ibid.

[69] Sharon Pickering and Christine Lambert, 'Deterrence: Australia's Refugee Policy' (2002) 14(1) *Current Issues in Criminal Justice* 65.

[70] As there are no crimes involved, there are only limited recognised rationales to detain refugees or other migrants: to establish the migrant's identity, where a specific migrant is believed to present a risk to public security, poses a risk of absconding or detention is needed to ensure the presence of the migrant at hearings, or to comply deportation or expulsion orders. See, for example, Human Rights Committee, 'General Comment No 35: Article 9: Liberty and Security of Person', UN Doc CCPR/C/GC/35 (16 December 2014) para 18.

[71] See section 4.4.3.

wide berth to states to implement such actions, which has simply fuelled more repressive policies.

4.4 The arbitrary detention of socially excluded and marginalised groups

This section reviews how the law has responded to arbitrary detention falling within three typologies of marginalisation: the "unseen"; the "reviled and resented"; and the "undeserving". There are important social drivers to the deprivations the individuals and groups reflected in these typologies experience, which increase their susceptibility to arbitrary detention. As will be explained, human rights law has not succeeded to adequately address either the causes or consequences.

The typologies are interlinked in three important ways:

(1) the groups of persons fitting within the typologies are fluid, with some observations applicable to more than one group, and with the groups themselves often reflecting more than one typology;
(2) the typologies share a commonality wherein the transactional justifications given by state authorities to authorise the detention of individuals appear fabricated, more of an excuse that masks the "real" reasons for detention, which are more totemic; and
(3) the identities and groups referred to in the typologies are not oppressed to the same extent or in the same ways. It is the essentialised "other" that, as Iris Marion Young explains, undergoes 'a paradoxical oppression, in that they are both marked out by stereotypes and at the same time rendered invisible'.[72] However, there are many "others", and arbitrary treatment may result from more than one dimension of persons' identities. A person may face multiple disadvantages or advantages because of the coincidence of two or more of their characteristics, their relationality, the social context and the operation of power relations.[73]

Both socially generated inequalities, such as those attributable to differences in wealth inheritance, family station, and upbringing and inequalities generated by racism, xenophobia and other forms of discrimination are morally arbitrary in the Rawlsian sense.[74] These inequalities also lead to a higher likelihood of being subjected to violence and abuse, including

---

[72] Iris Marion Young, *Justice and the Politics of Difference* (Princeton University Press 2011) 59.
[73] Peter Hopkins, 'Social Geography I: Intersectionality' (2019) 43(5) *Progress in Human Geography* 937–947.
[74] Discussed in Chapter 2.

of being subjected to arbitrary detention. This stems principally from the discrimination they experience both procedurally and substantively.

The WGAD considers claims related to arbitrary detention stemming from discriminatory grounds in its Category V, focusing on 'discrimination based on birth, national, ethnic or social origin, language, religion, economic condition, political or other opinion, gender, sexual orientation, disability, or any other status, that aims towards or can result in ignoring the equality of human beings'.[75] This list is different and arguably broader than the protected grounds stipulated in Article 26 ICCPR[76] in that it refers specifically to disability; replaces sex with gender and sexual orientation, race and colour with ethnic origin, and property with economic condition; and includes a catch-all 'or any other status, that aims towards or can result in ignoring the equality of human beings'. In determining whether persons have been subjected to arbitrary detention on the discriminatory grounds set out in Category V, the WGAD has paid special attention to the existence of patterns of persecution against the detained person or other persons with similar distinguishing characteristics, situation in which the authorities have made statements or conducted themselves towards the detained person in a manner that indicates a discriminatory attitude, the context suggests discriminatory grounds for the detention, or the conduct for which the person is detained is only an offence for members of their group(s).[77]

Discrimination increases the susceptibility of certain groups to be subjected to arbitrary detention, because, in the criminal justice system: (1) authorities single out certain ethnic, racial or religious minority persons for heightened suspicion or detention; (2) such persons are more likely to be subject to pre-trial detention, which then has a knock-on effect on convictions and sentencing. Members of these groups may also face disproportionate prosecutions, unfair trials and disproportionately severe punishments on conviction. Outside the criminal justice system, certain persons from marginalised or minority backgrounds are more susceptible to homelessness, displacement and addiction, and migrants are more likely to face discrimination based on their status of non-citizens, even more so when they exhibit additional features of difference. These characteristics are thus intersectional factors that must be accounted for in the analysis of the role of arbitrary detention in the enforcement of hostility and social control.

---

[75] HRC, 'Methods of Work of the WGAD', UN Doc A/HRC/36/38 (13 July 2017); Leigh Toomey, 'Detention on Discriminatory Grounds: an Analysis of the Jurisprudence of the United Nations WGAD' (2018) 50(1) *Columbia Hum Rts L Rev* 185.

[76] International Covenant on Civil and Political Rights (adopted 16 December 1966, entered into force 23 March 1976).

[77] HRC, 'Report of the WGAD', UN Doc A/HRC/36/37 (19 July 2017) para 48.

4.4.1 The "unseen": economic and social "degenerates"

The first typology has to do with the criminalisation of poverty, a phenomenon linked to the neoliberal state's emphasis on punitive containment, though not exclusively so.[78] It concerns the reduced toleration and progressive erosion of social protections for persons who are situated at the fringes of society, such as persons who are homeless, persons with mental health challenges, disabilities, drug dependencies and the increased resort to criminalisation to punish such persons for deigning to exist in accepted society as well as the use of administrative (rehabilitative) detention to separate such persons from society. These groups are in plain sight, but social protection structures conspire to aid in the process of "unseeing" them. Thus the "solution" is to hide what has become, in the eyes of the privileged society, too visible. Detention here is used as a method of socio-economic control, to censure and punish "degenerate" behaviour.

Much of the practice of "unseeing" concerns the refusal to recognise the autonomy of these marginalised groups because of who they are perceived to be and what role they are allowed to have in the society, as opposed to anything they may have done individually or collectively. Detention masquerades as care for those who are pathologised and as moralistic re-education and rehabilitation.

The right to liberty case law pertaining to the "unseen" focuses predominantly on the adequacy of the rationale for detention. Courts will consider whether detention was lawful,[79] and whether the justification for detention met the conditions of necessity and proportionality. Human dignity is an overarching principle related to evolving human rights and social justice standards, including in respect to decisions about who, whether, and in what circumstances to detain. Those being considered for detention are not "rogue", "vagabond", "idle" or "disorderly" as these terms reflect 'an outdated and largely colonial perception of individuals without any rights' and violate human dignity because 'their use dehumanizes and degrades individuals with a perceived lower status'.[80] The application of vagrancy laws 'often deprives the underprivileged and

---

[78] See, for example, Garland (n 15); Bronislaw Geremek, *Poverty: a History* (English trans Agniezska Kolakowska, Wiley-Blackwell 1994); Loïc Wacquant, *Punishing the Poor: the Neoliberal Government of Social Insecurity* (Duke University Press 2009).

[79] *Purohit and Moore v Gambia*, Comm No 241/2001 (ACommHPR, 16th Activity Report 2002–2003 Annex VII) para 64.

[80] African Court on Human and Peoples' Rights (ACtHPR), 'The Compatibility of Vagrancy Laws with the African Charter on Human and Peoples' Rights and Other Human Rights Instruments Applicable in Africa', Advisory Opinion No 001/2018 (4 December 2020) para 79.

marginalized of their dignity by unlawfully interfering with their efforts to maintain or build a decent life or to enjoy a lifestyle they pursue'.[81] In *Purohit and Moore,* the African Commission on Human and Peoples' Rights (ACommHPR) underscored that branding persons with mental illnesses as "lunatics" and "idiots" serves to 'dehumanise and deny them any form of dignity'.[82]

The move to recognise states' positive obligations to reverse the pattern of "unseeing" – in effect, to see, has been patchy and inconsistent. There is a sense that human rights law is mainly focused on sanitising and making less repulsive the process of "unseeing". However, there are some important inroads in discrete areas, largely fuelled by the impact of the Convention on the Rights of Persons with Disabilities (CRPD).[83]

(i) Detention of persons who are homeless

In most countries, persons living in poverty are disproportionately represented in the criminal justice system, and this disproportionality is exacerbated when combined with other marginalising factors.[84] The detention of persons who are homeless and "vagrants" is a throwback to medieval vagrancy laws,[85] but has taken on new life with the neoliberal attacks on the poor. People are criminalised who display characteristics associated with homelessness, such as not having a fixed home or means of subsistence, loitering, trespassing, begging, hawking, vending, urinating, or washing clothes in public, and other nuisance-related or disorderly conduct. Laws are framed in vague and overbroad terms, making it unclear what actions are covered and leading to discretionary implementation and misuse (frequently in a discriminatory manner) by law enforcement.[86]

Homelessness laws are used to regulate public spaces and reflect different views and assumptions about what public space is for and who should have

---

[81] Ibid para 80. See, also, ACommHPR, 'Principles on the Decriminalisation of Petty Offences in Africa' (2017) <http://apcof.org/wp-content/uploads/apcof-principles-on-the-decriminalisation-of-petty-offences-in-africa-eng-fr-pr-ar.pdf> accessed 23 July 2023, para 7.

[82] *Purohit and Moore v Gambia* (n 79) para 59.

[83] CRPD.

[84] Karen Dolan, *The Poor Get Prison: the Alarming Spread of the Criminalization of Poverty* (Institute for Policy Studies 2015).

[85] Lee Beier and Paul Ocobock (eds), *Cast Out: Vagrancy and Homelessness in Global and Historical Perspective* (Ohio University Press 2008); Christopher Roberts, 'Vagrancy and Vagrancy-Type Laws in Colonial History and Today', Transnational Legal History Group (City University Hong Kong 2022).

[86] Leslie Sebba, 'The Creation and Evolution of Criminal Law in Colonial and Post-Colonial Societies' (1999) 3 *Crime, Hist & Soc'y* 71.

access to it. As Sepúlveda Carmona explains, behaviours are prohibited because they are classified as 'dangerous, conflicting with the demands of public safety or order, disturbing the normal activities for which public spaces are intended, or contrary to the images and preconceptions that authorities want to associate with such places'.[87] The presence of people who are homeless is 'a danger, or a disturbance of the normal activities for which public spaces are intended, or they are seen as contradicting the images and symbols of those spaces'.[88]

The laws are used to justify "sweep-up" operations to forcibly remove undesirable persons and to demolish informal settlements to improve tourist traffic and economic prospects of urban areas and to aid gentrification, in violation of the right to housing.[89] Arbitrary detention of homeless persons is thus part of the hostile strategies used to get persons to move along, to encourage them to stop seeing certain locations as safe or welcoming. Often it is sex workers, homeless children, unemployed persons, persons who beg, street vendors, or migrant or displaced persons groups that are targeted. The practice is global, including in Africa,[90] Asia,[91] Europe[92] and the Americas.[93] While often associated with urban areas, the criminalisation of poverty and homelessness can also stem from changes in economies and rural land use, resulting in evictions, forcing migration to cities, without any social infrastructure in place to receive the arrivals.[94] It can also stem from, or be exacerbated by, armed conflict, environmental or other disasters causing internal or external displacements of populations.[95]

---

[87] UNGA, 'Report of the Special Rapporteur on Extreme Poverty and Human Rights', UN Doc A/66/265 (4 August 2011) para 29. See, also, Antonio Tosi, 'Homelessness and the Control of Public Space – Criminalising the Poor?' (2007) 1 *Eur J Homelessness* 225, 226.

[88] Tosi (n 87) 226.

[89] UNGA, 'Guidelines for the Implementation of the Right to Adequate Housing' UN Doc A/HRC/43/43 (26 December 2019) para 35.

[90] ACtHPR, 'The Compatibility of Vagrancy Laws with the African Charter' (n 80); Lukas Muntingh and Kristen Petersen, 'Punished for Being Poor: Evidence and Arguments for the Decriminalisation and Declassification of Petty Offences' (Dullah Omar Institute and Pan-African Lawyers Union 2015).

[91] Simon Springer, 'The Violence of Homelessness: Exile and Arbitrary Detention in Cambodia's War on the Poor' (2020) 61 *Asia Pacific Viewpoint* 3; International Commission of Jurists, 'Sri Lanka's Vagrants Ordinance No 4 of 1841: a Colonial Relic Long Overdue for Repeal' (December 2021).

[92] Roberts (n 85).

[93] Roberts (n 85).

[94] Springer (n 91) 4.

[95] UN Commission on Human Rights, 'Report of the Special Rapporteur on Adequate Housing as a Component of the Right to an Adequate Standard of Living', UN Doc E/CN.4/2005/48 (3 March 2005) paras 21–63.

Constitutional or supreme courts,[96] regional courts,[97] human rights commissions, treaty bodies and special procedures[98] are recognising the insidiousness of vagrancy and related laws and determining that they are incompatible with fundamental human rights standards, including the prohibition on arbitrary detention. For instance, the African Court on Human and Peoples' Rights has indicated:

> [T]he enforcement of [vagrancy] laws often results in pretextual arrests, arrests without warrants and illegal pre-trial detention. This exposes vagrancy laws to constant potential abuse.
>
> The Court concedes that arrests under vagrancy laws may, ostensibly, satisfy the requirement that the deprivation of freedom must be based on reasons and conditions prescribed by law. Nevertheless, the manner in which vagrancy offences are framed, in most African countries,

---

[96] See, for example, *Gopalanachari v State of Kerala* 1981 AIR 674, 1981 SCR (1)1271: 'personal liberty is a prized value […] the Court itself having to be gravely concerned about using preventive provisions against helpless persons, not on formal testimony readily produced to order as we have noticed in a recent case, but on convincing testimony of clear and present danger to society'. See, also, *Gwanda v S (Constitutional Cause 5 of 2015)* [2017] MWHC 23 (10 January 2017) (striking down as unconstitutional the section of the Malawi criminal code which made it an offence to be a "rogue" or a "vagabond"); *The Sex Worker Education and Advocacy Taskforce v Minister of Safety and Security* (3378/07) [2009] ZAWCHC 64; 2009 (6) SA 513 (WCC) (20 April 2009) (the police practice of arresting women who engage in sex work, for purposes of harassing and punishing them, without any legitimate reason or intention to have them prosecuted is unlawful). See, also, *King v Attorney General* [1981] IR 233; *Papachristou v City of Jacksonville* 92 SCt 839 (1972).

[97] For instance, in *Njemanze v Nigeria* the ECOWAS (Economic Community of West African States) Court of Justice determined that the arbitrary detention of women labelled prostitutes because they were on the street late at night violated the women's human rights under the Charter, the Women's Rights Protocol, and various international human rights instruments: *Njemanze v Nigeria*, No ECW/CCJ/JUD/08/17 (12 October 2017). See, also, ACtHPR, 'The Compatibility of Vagrancy Laws with the African Charter' (n 80); *Villagran Morales v Guatemala* (Merits) Series C No 63 (IACtHR, 19 November 1999) (regarding the arbitrary detention, abduction and/or murder of children living on the streets); *Lăcătuş v Switzerland* App No 14065/15 (ECtHR, 19 January 2021) (finding a violation of the right to privacy in respect to the criminalisation of begging, the Court holding that a custodial sentence, which was liable to further increase an individual's distress and vulnerability, had been almost automatic and inevitable was not capable of justification in the public interest).

[98] See, for example, UNGA, 'Report of the Special Rapporteur on Extreme Poverty and Human Rights on his Mission to the United States of America', UN Doc A/HRC/38/33/Add.1 (4 May 2018) para 45; Human Rights Committee, 'Concluding Observations on the Third Periodic Report of Cambodia', UN Doc CCPR/C/KHM/CO/3 (18 May 2022) paras 28, 29; WGAD, Preliminary Findings from Its Visit to Sri Lanka, UN Doc A/HRC/39/45/Add.2 (23 July 2018) paras 61, 64, 66.

presents a danger due to their overly broad and ambiguous nature. One of the major challenges is that vagrancy laws do not, ex ante, sufficiently and clearly lay down the reasons and conditions on which one can be arrested and detained to enable the public to know what is within the scope of prohibition. In practice, therefore, many arrests for vagrancy offences are arbitrary.[99]

Many of these decisions call on states to amend or repeal vagrancy laws and to undertake all necessary measures to support vulnerable populations,[100] yet implementation remains weak, and the jurisprudence is inconsistent.

The main challenges with the laws and their implementation are as follows:

Vague laws: Vague vagrancy legislation gives law enforcement wide discretion, which can be influenced by discriminatory assumptions about criminality fuelled by biased views on poverty, gender, race, ethnicity, place of origin and social status. Initiatives like the African Court on Human and Peoples' Rights Advisory Opinion on the compatibility of vagrancy laws with the African Charter[101] are pathbreaking.

Regulation of space: Public space has become the location for the politicisation and penalisation of the homeless and the poor. There is increasing pressure on courts to privilege the interests of businesses and other highly valued groups over the rights of everyone (including homeless persons) to avail themselves of public spaces.

Revulsion of the poor: People are being targeted for their status as poor people and for their life-sustaining activities on account of their economic and social situations, and not for their criminal conduct. Communities should stop 'treating homeless persons as affronts to their sensibilities and neighbourhoods, should see in their presence a tragic indictment of community and government policies'.[102]

(ii) Detention on mental health grounds

Views about detention on mental health (including psychosocial and intellectual disabilities) grounds have evolved significantly in recent decades. This is due to the growing recognition of the human dignity of persons with mental health disabilities, and the understanding of the critical importance of autonomy, agency and non-discrimination to notions of human dignity.

---

[99] ACtHPR, 'The Compatibility of Vagrancy Laws with the African Charter' (n 80) paras 85, 86.
[100] Ibid.
[101] Ibid.
[102] UNGA, 'Report of the Special Rapporteur on Extreme Poverty and Human Rights on his Mission to the USA', UN Doc A/HRC/38/33/Add.1 (4 May 2018) para 45.

Much of this shift has been fostered by the advocacy for and the adoption of the CRPD.[103]

Prior to the adoption of the CRPD, detention was seen as an acceptable part of the toolbox, within boundaries. Automatic (involuntary) detentions of persons on mental health grounds without resort to individualised assessments were understood to violate the right to liberty and the prohibition of arbitrary arrest and detention.[104] Detention was only justifiable if specific conditions were met that were personal to the individual being detained, considering all relevant circumstances, and these needed to be reasoned.

First, the individual needed to suffer from a "true" mental illness or disorder with the condition diagnosed being of a kind or degree warranting compulsory confinement.[105] It would not be lawful to permit someone to be involuntarily confined simply because their views or behaviour deviated from the norms prevailing in a particular society.[106] Any disorder must have been established through objective medical expertise, assessed by an appropriate medical professional procedurally and substantively competent to certify the detention.[107]

Second, the disability should not in itself have been able to justify detention, but rather any deprivation of liberty must have been necessary and proportionate, for the purpose of protecting the individual in question from serious harm or preventing injury to others,[108] and any protective measure needed to reflect as far as possible the wishes of persons capable of expressing their will.[109] Most courts and adjudicative bodies refrained from outlawing mandatory committals outright, and assessed the lawfulness of committals on a case-by-case basis, considering the totality of the circumstances. This avoidance of sweeping statements of principle is consistent with some of the in-built incrementalism of human rights adjudication. But it is also problematic, as whether a person could be detained on mental health grounds became a question of degree, with human dignity and autonomy being measured against other "goods". Some recognition of the ability to detain on mental health grounds also appeared in international standards.[110]

---

[103] CRPD (n 44).

[104] *Purohit and Moore* (n 79) para 62.

[105] *Winterwerp v Netherlands* App No 6301/73 (ECtHR, 24 October 1979) para 39. See, also, *A v New Zealand*, UN Doc CCPR/C/66/D/754/1997 (3 August 1999).

[106] *Winterwerp* (n 105) para 37.

[107] *Purohit and Moore* (n 79) para 66.

[108] Human Rights Committee, General Comment No 35 (n 70) para 19.

[109] *Stanev v Bulgaria* (Grand Chamber) App No 36760/06 (ECtHR, 17 January 2012) para 153.

[110] The *Principles for the Protection of Persons with Mental Illness and the Improvement of Mental Health Care* provide: 'Domestic law may authorize a court or other competent authority, acting on the basis of competent and independent medical advice, to order that such persons be admitted to a mental health facility' (Principle 20(3) UNGA res

Third, authorities were obligated to ensure that any committal to a mental health facility complied with a modicum of procedural safeguards. It was not appropriate for an individual to be admitted "informally" to an institution where they did not have the mental capacity to consent to admission.[111] Individuals needed to be able to be heard and to be represented by counsel (and to be provided with legal aid if required) in determinations affecting their lives, livelihood, liberty, property or status[112] and to be able to seek a review of any decision on committal, and their ability to do so needed to be practical and achievable.[113]

Fourth, authorities were obliged to take appropriate initiatives to ensure that detainees received treatment adapted to their state of health and that was likely to help them regain their freedom. Detention for seven years in a psychiatric wing of a prison, which was supposed to be temporary, and which did not provide appropriate treatment, constituted a violation of the right to liberty and security.[114]

Moving to the present, the CRPD has shifted matters in several important ways.

First, while the CRPD itself is ambiguous on this point, the United Nations Committee on the Rights of Persons with Disabilities (CRPD Committee), the body of experts tasked with interpreting the CRPD, has determined that involuntary committals on mental health grounds constitute arbitrary detention; the practice is inherently arbitrary. The CRPD Committee

---

46/119 (17 December 1991)). See, similarly, Council of Europe, 'Recommendation No REC(2004)10 of the Committee of Ministers to Member States Concerning the Protection of the Human Rights and Dignity of Persons with Mental Disorder and Its Explanatory Memorandum' (22 September 2004) paras 18–26. The Human Rights Committee's General Comment No 35 ((n 70) para 19) provides a helpful outline of measures designed to avoid arbitrary detention in mental health settings, though it avoids recommending an outright ban on involuntary detention. The Inter-American Commission on Human Rights (IACommHR) has taken a similar approach to the Human Rights Committee: 'health systems [...] shall apply [...] with a view to gradually de-institutionalizing these people, and organizing alternative service models that facilitate the achievement of objectives that are compatible with an integrated, continuing, preventative, participatory, and community-based psychiatric care and health system, and in this way avoid unnecessary deprivation of liberty in hospitals or other institutions' (IACommHR, Principles and Best Practices on the Protection of Persons Deprived of Liberty in the Americas, Resolution 1/08 (13 March 2008) Principle III(3)).

[111] *HL v United Kingdom* App No 45508/99 (ECtHR, 5 October 2004).
[112] *Purohit and Moore* (n 79) para 72.
[113] *A v New Zealand* (n 105) paras 7.2, 7.3.
[114] *LB v Belgium* App No 22831/08 (ECtHR, 2 October 2012). See, similarly, *Claes v Belgium* App No 43418/09 (ECtHR, 10 January 2013).

'imbued with a sense of *urgency*, impatient with reformist "chipping away" at the legal and physical edifices of institutionalization',[115] indicated that:

> Involuntary commitment of persons with disabilities on health care grounds contradicts the absolute ban on deprivation of liberty on the basis of impairments (article 14(1)(b)) and the principle of free and informed consent for health care (article 25). The Committee has repeatedly stated that States parties should repeal provisions which allow for involuntary commitment of persons with disabilities in mental health institutions based on actual or perceived impairments. Involuntary commitment in mental health facilities carries with it the denial of the person's legal capacity to decide about care, treatment, and admission to a hospital or institution, and therefore violates article 12 in conjunction with article 14.[116]

This position aligns with the trajectory of the WGAD in respect to persons with disabilities.[117]

The CRPD Committee has applied this reasoning in its adjudication of several individual complaints. *Leo v Australia*[118] concerned an Aboriginal man from Australia who, during an apparent psychotic episode, assaulted a woman on the street. He was deemed unfit to stand trial and found not guilty due to his mental impairment. The court placed a custodial supervision order on him, under which he was to remain in prison for 12 months, a sentence he might have received had he been convicted. Ultimately, he remained in maximum-security prison for a total of five years and ten months, about

---

[115] Lucy Series, *Deprivation of Liberty in the Shadows of the Institution* (Bristol University Press 2022) 98–99.

[116] CRPD Committee, *Guidelines on Article 14 of the CRPD*, UN Doc A/72/55 (2016) Annex para 10.

[117] WGAD, 'UN Basic Principles and Guidelines on Remedies and Procedures on the Right of Anyone Deprived of Their Liberty to Bring Proceedings Before a Court', UN Doc A/HRC/30/37 (6 July 2015) Principle 20 para 38, which reminds of states' 'obligation to prohibit involuntary committal or internment on the grounds of the existence of an impairment or perceived impairment, particularly on the basis of psychosocial or intellectual disability or perceived psychosocial or intellectual disability, as well as [with] their obligation to design and implement de-institutionalization strategies based on the human rights model of disability.' The WGAD has determined similarly in its individual opinions. See, for example, WGAD, *Opinion No 70/2018 Concerning Ms. H (whose name is known by the Working Group) (Japan)*, UN Doc A/HRC/WGAD/2018/70 (16 January 2019) para 50; *Opinion No 8/2018 Concerning Mr. N (whose name is known by the Working Group) (Japan)*, UN Doc A/HRC/WGAD/2018/8 (23 May 2018) para 46.

[118] *Leo v Australia*, UN Doc CRPD/C/22/D/17/2013 (18 October 2019). See, also, the earlier case of *Noble v Australia*, UN Doc CRPD/C/16/D/7/2012 (10 October 2016).

six times longer than if he had not been declared mentally impaired, had stood trial and been convicted.[119] He was given very limited or no mental health support and, consequently, his mental health further deteriorated. The Committee determined that the differential treatment provided by Australian law, which allowed for the potentially indefinite detention of persons found unfit to stand trial, was discriminatory because it did not eliminate barriers to gaining equal access to the law to assert rights.[120] By detaining Mr Leo without a criminal conviction, but on the basis of the potential consequences of his disability, Australia 'convert[ed] his disability into the core cause of his detention',[121] resulting in discriminatory treatment.

This reform of mental health practices required by the CRPD has not yet been fully implemented by many states. According to Minkowitz, frameworks that recognise the right to detain and compulsory treatment but have progressively introduced procedural safeguards 'represent a first attempt to come to grips with the human rights implications of this regime, while demonstrating an unwillingness to challenge the supposed necessity for segregation, confinement and compulsion of those labelled as "mentally ill"'.[122] She argues that no laws that allow for involuntary confinement of persons with psychosocial disabilities for the purpose of treatment or preventive detention will be capable of complying with Article 14 CRPD, because such laws always justify detention on the basis of disability.[123] A new World Health Organization/Office of the High Commissioner for Human Rights Guidance document, which was still in draft at the time of writing, recognises that 'ending coercive practices in mental health – such as involuntary commitment, forced medication, seclusion and restraints – is essential in order to respect the rights of people using mental health services'.[124] Dainius Pūras, former UN Special Rapporteur on the right to health, has gone so far as to recommend states to 'stop directing investment to institutional care and redirect it to community-based services'.[125] Following this reasoning to its logical conclusion, proper implementation of Article 14

---

[119] *Leo v Australia* (n 118) para 2.4.

[120] Ibid paras 8.4–8.7.

[121] Ibid para 8.8.

[122] Tina Minkowitz, 'Why Mental Health Laws Contravene the CRPD – An Application of Article 14 with Implications for the Obligations of States Parties' (2011) *SSRN Electronic Journal* <https://papers.ssrn.com/sol3/papers.cfm?abstract_id=1928600> accessed 23 July 2023.

[123] Ibid.

[124] WHO/OHCHR, 'Guidance on Mental Health, Human Rights and Legislation' (Draft June 2022) 52.

[125] HRC, 'Report of the Special Rapporteur on the Right of Everyone to the Enjoyment of the Highest Attainable Standard of Physical and Mental Health', UN Doc A/HRC/35/21 (28 March 2017) para 95(b).

CRPD would require states to put in place alternatives that would allow a person to be appropriately supervised in a non-custodial setting, which would constitute a significant, but important, commitment to the implementation of the Convention.

Second, the CRPD privileges individuals' autonomy and agency in all matters affecting their health and well-being. The CRPD provides the most up-to-date statement on the legal capacity of persons with mental health challenges to consent to mandatory committal.[126] Article 12 of the CRPD requires states parties to *inter alia*, take appropriate measures to provide access by persons with disabilities to the support they may require in exercising their legal capacity, and that measures provide for appropriate and effective safeguards to prevent abuse:

> [These] shall ensure that measures relating to the exercise of legal capacity respect the rights, will and preferences of the person, are free of conflict of interest and undue influence, are proportional and tailored to the person's circumstances, apply for the shortest time possible and are subject to regular review by a competent, independent, and impartial authority or judicial body. The safeguards shall be proportional to the degree to which such measures affect the person's rights and interests.[127]

In *Leo v Australia*, the CRPD Committee made clear that disability must never be a ground for denying legal capacity. Australia should have provided, or at least considered providing, Mr Leo with the support or accommodation he needed to stand trial, exercise legal capacity and access justice.[128] This second aspect too has major implications for guardianship regimes in place in many states, and for the removal of mandatory treatment regimes that continue to operate in many closed facilities. Juan Méndez, former Special Rapporteur on Torture, has underscored that 'involuntary treatment and other psychiatric interventions in health-care facilities are forms of torture and ill-treatment'.[129]

---

[126] Art 12 CRPD.

[127] Art 12(4) CRPD.

[128] *Leo v Australia* (n 118) para 8.6. On the fallout associated with the Committee's stance on legal capacity and supported decision-making, see, George Szmukler, ' "Capacity", "Best Interests", "Will and Preferences" and the UN Convention on the Rights of Persons with Disabilities' (2019) 18 *World Psychiatry* 34.

[129] HRC, 'Report of the Special Rapporteur on Torture and Other Cruel, Inhuman or Degrading Treatment or Punishment, Juan E. Méndez', UN Doc A/HRC/22/53 (1 February 2013) para 64.

(iii) Detention of people who use drugs

People who use drugs, regularly portrayed as evil, as social deviants, sinners and criminals, are often detained in compulsory drug detention centres,[130] sometimes referred to as drug treatment centres or re-education through labour centres or camps, which are 'commonly run by military or paramilitary, police or security forces, or private companies'.[131] Such detention – which results from acts of "unseeing" and the denial of social protections – is frequently without medical assessment, judicial review or appeal, or clear standards for release, and will amount to arbitrary detention.[132] In addition to the detention of persons suspected of using drugs, the centres often house other individuals deemed threatening to national security or public order, as well as homeless persons, sex workers and individuals with mental health conditions.[133] Exposure of the significant problems and abuses associated with compulsory centres has provided impetus for reforms, and UN agencies have repeatedly called for the centres' permanent closure.[134] However, according to Wolfe and Saucier, there is a challenge of mixed messages and lack of implementation,[135] and compulsory drug detention centres remain part of what is essentially a punitive landscape.

In addition to the resort to compulsory drug detention centres, drug control gives rise to a host of human rights violations that foster arbitrary detention.[136] The main challenges include:

Excessive resort to pre-trial detention. In some countries, pre-trial detention for drug-related offences is lengthy and/or mandatory.[137] The International Guidelines on Human Rights and Drugs Policy provide that states should 'ensure that pre-trial detention is never mandatory for drug-related charges

---

[130] UNODC and UNAIDS, *Compulsory Drug Treatment and Rehabilitation in East and Southeast Asia* (2022).

[131] UNGA, 'Report of the Special Rapporteur on Torture Juan E. Méndez' (n 129) para 40.

[132] *Arbitrary Detention Relating to Drug Policies* (n 48) paras 3, 82–97.

[133] UNODC and UNAIDS (n 130) 6.

[134] Thirteen UN agencies, 'Joint Statement: Compulsory Drug Detention and Rehabilitation Centres in Asia and the Pacific in the Context of COVID-19' (1 June 2020) <https://unaidsapnew.files.wordpress.com/2020/05/unjointstatement1june2020.pdf> accessed 23 July 2023; 'Joint Statement: Compulsory Drug Detention and Rehabilitation Centres' (March, 2012) <www.unodc.org/documents/southeastasiaandpacific/2012/03/drug-detention-centre/JC2310_Joint_Statement6March12FINAL_En.pdf> accessed 23 July 2023.

[135] Daniel Wolfe and Roxanne Saucier, 'Not Enough Stick? Drug Detention and the Limits of UN Norm Setting' (2022) 24(1) *Health Hum Rights* 175.

[136] Rick Lines, Julie Hannah and Giada Girelli, '"Treatment in Liberty" Human Rights and Compulsory Detention for Drug Use' (2022) 22 *Hum Rts L Rev* 1.

[137] *Arbitrary Detention Relating to Drug Policies* (n 48) paras 17–20. On the automatic imposition of pre-trial detention, see WGAD, *Opinion No 75/2018 Concerning Gerardo Pérez Camacho (Mexico)*, UN Doc A/HRC/WGAD/2018/75 (11 February 2019) para 78.

and is imposed only in exceptional circumstances where such detention is deemed reasonable, necessary, and proportional'.[138]

Disproportionate criminalisation and punishment: Minor drug offences may be over-criminalised and prison sentences for drug offences can be disproportionately long, even for crimes involving children,[139] sometimes matching or exceeding sentences for violent crimes.[140] In *Acosta Martínez v Argentina,* the Inter-American Court of Human Rights (IACtHR) determined that 'the State's punitive power can only be exercised to the extent strictly necessary to protect fundamental legal rights from attacks that damage or endanger them'.[141] It expressed its concerns over:

> the adoption of state measures that seek to punish drug-related conduct – specifically minor drug-related offenses, such as consumption and possession for personal use – and finds worrisome what appears to have been a notable increase in the number of persons deprived of liberty for drug-related criminal acts. In this context, the offenses related to drug use are characterized as "grave offenses" ("delitos graves"), and therefore, pretrial detention is applied automatically, and without the persons accused being able to benefit from alternatives to incarceration.[142] [...] all drug-related conduct is treated as "serious crimes" with no distinction whatsoever, thereby ignoring the principles on which the use of pretrial detention is based, especially proportionality.[143]

---

[138] *International Guidelines on Human Rights and Drug Policy* (2019) <www.humanrights-drugpolicy.org> accessed 23 July 2023, Principle 7(ii).

[139] WGAD, *Opinion No 60/2019 Concerning four minors (Minors A, B, C and D, whose names are known to the Working Group) (Belarus),* UN Doc A/HRC/WGAD/2019/60 (23 July 2020) para 129; *Opinion No 90/2018 Concerning Mohd Redzuan Bin Saibon (Malaysia),* UN Doc A/HRC/WGAD/2018/90 (31 January 2019) para 51.

[140] *Arbitrary Detention Relating to Drug Policies* (n 48) paras 36–40. See, also, UNGA, 'Report of the Special Rapporteur on the Right to Health' (n 23) paras 62–69, where the Special Rapporteur encourages states to consider decriminalisation. Decriminalisation of drug possession for personal use, and to promote the principle of proportionality is also aligned with the UN system common position supporting the implementation of the international drug control policy through effective inter-agency collaboration, UN Doc CEB/2018/2, Annex I (2018) and with the ACommHPR, *Principles on the Decriminalisation of Petty Offences in Africa* (n 81).

[141] *Acosta Martínez et al v Argentina* (Merits, Reparations and Costs) Series C No 410 (31 August 2020) para 87.

[142] IACommHR, 'Report on Measures Aimed at Reducing the Use of Pretrial Detention in the Americas', OEA/Ser.L/V/II.163 Doc 105 (3 July 2017) para 9.

[143] Ibid para 28. See, also, para 90.

Discriminatory drug control measures directed at and/or differentially impacting vulnerable and marginalised groups, which may result in arbitrary detention.[144] Human Rights Watch research, conducted in respect of the Somsanga drug detention centre in Lao People's Democratic Republic, concluded: 'Somsanga not only detains those dependent on drugs. For Lao authorities, Somsanga functions as a convenient dumping ground for those considered socially "undesirable." People who might have a genuine need for drug dependency treatment are locked in alongside beggars, the homeless, street children, and people with mental disabilities.'[145] Similar findings have been made in respect of other countries.[146]

4.4.2 The "reviled and resented": racism, xenophobia, and other discriminatory treatment

The second typology has to do with the rise in xenophobia and hate. It concerns the discriminatory targeting of certain marginalised groups because they are perceived as different or less worthy of membership in the "imagined" society and indeed, to some, as an existential threat to that society. These groups are discriminated against based on race, ethnicity, national origin, gender, gender identity or sexual orientation. They are also indigenous peoples, religious minorities and non-citizens. These labels, which are imposed on them, serve as a vector for their containment and result in their increased susceptibility to arrest and detention. The groups are targeted because of the labels others place upon them, but also as a method to repress their autonomy and subjecthood. When these groups seek to insist upon their subjecthood – when they cease to be invisible simply by existing and engaging within the society – the "imagined" dominant majorities who control the public sphere respond with suppression, a theme that is also explored in Chapter 5: Deterring Dissent. Thus, in this sense, it is the groups that are feared for their unknowability, however they are also repressed when they appear to force upon the "imagined society" their visibility.[147] Scarry captures this conundrum when she explains: 'There exists a circular

---

[144] *Arbitrary Detention Relating to Drug Policies* (n 48) paras 51–71.

[145] HRW, 'Somsanga's Secrets Arbitrary Detention, Physical Abuse, and Suicide inside a Lao Drug Detention Centre' (2011) 11.

[146] See for similar concerns expressed by HRW in respect to Cambodia and Vietnam, HRW, *'They Treat Us Like Animals' Mistreatment of Drug Users and 'Undesirables' in Cambodia's Drug Detention Centers* (2013) 21; HRW, *The Rehab Archipelago: Forced Labor and Other Abuses in Drug Detention Centers in Southern Vietnam* (2011).

[147] Elaine Scarry, 'The Difficulty of Imagining Other Persons', in Martha Nussbaum (ed), *For Love of Country?: a New Democracy Forum on the Limits of Patriotism* (Beacon Press 2002) 98.

relation between the infliction of pain and the problem of otherness. The difficulty of imagining others is both the cause of, and the problem displayed by, the action of injuring.'[148] These groups are being locked up to foster the dignity of the "imagined" streets and picket fences, and as a figurative form of punishment when they push against that imagined decorum. It is yet another form of sanitisation.

This section considers the connection between racism, xenophobia and other discriminatory treatment, and the practice of arbitrary detention. Race, ethnicity, national origin status, religion and gender are socially constructed identities that have been employed and essentialised in the construction and exploitation of difference to impose and maintain privileges and hierarchies. These identities create privileges in some and disadvantages in others.[149] Membership of each of these identities may be self-defined and subjectively meaningful to individuals, but also imposed (and contested) by others in a society and by the society.

While discrimination can take many forms, this section focuses on three areas of identity-based discrimination and how discrimination in these areas fuels arbitrary detention: (i) groups discriminated against based on race, ethnicity or religion; (ii) indigenous peoples; and (iii) persons discriminated against on the basis of gender or gendered roles.

(i) Groups discriminated against based on race, ethnicity or religious identity

The 2001 Declaration adopted in Durban by the World Conference against Racism, Racial Discrimination, Xenophobia and Related Intolerance expressed:

> profound repudiation of the racism, racial discrimination, xenophobia and related intolerance that persist in some States in the functioning of the penal system and in the application of the law, as well as in the actions and attitudes of institutions and individuals responsible for law enforcement, especially where this has contributed to certain groups being overrepresented among persons under detention or imprisoned.[150]

---

[148] Scarry (n 147) 102.
[149] Stephanie Wildman and Adrienne Davis, 'Language and Silence: Making Systems of Privilege Visible', in Richard Delgado and Jean Stefancic (eds), *Critical Race Theory: the Cutting Edge* (3rd edn, Temple University Press 2013) 794, 795.
[150] World Conference against Racism, Racial Discrimination, Xenophobia and Related Intolerance, Declaration (31 August – 8 September 2001) para 25.

The Committee on the Elimination of Racial Discrimination (CERD Committee), in its General Recommendation 31 highlighted the importance of combatting all forms of discrimination in the administration and functioning of the criminal justice system against persons belonging to racial or ethnic groups.[151] The Recommendation encourages states parties to pay particular attention to the number and percentage of such persons, 'who are held in prison or preventive detention, including internment centres, penal establishments, psychiatric establishments or holding areas in airports',[152] and reminds that:

> the mere fact of belonging to a racial or ethnic group or one of the aforementioned groups is not a sufficient reason, de jure or de facto, to place a person in pretrial detention. Such pretrial detention can be justified only on objective grounds stipulated in the law, such as the risk of flight, the risk that the person might destroy evidence or influence witnesses, or the risk of a serious disturbance of public order.[153]

Despite these missives, arbitrary detention stemming from racial and ethnic discrimination, as well as religious identity, continues unabated. The WGAD has adopted numerous opinions that stem from discrimination on these bases. It has found a *prima facie* case of discrimination on the basis of a consistent pattern of behaviour involving the targeting of the groups concerned,[154] the making of discriminatory insults or the perpetration of

---

[151] CERD Committee, 'General Recommendation 31 on the Prevention of Racial Discrimination in the Administration and Functioning of the Criminal Justice System', UN Doc A/60/18 (2005) preamble.

[152] Ibid 3.

[153] Ibid 9.

[154] See, for example, WGAD, *Opinion No 8/2021 Concerning Layan Kayed, Elyaa Abu Hijla and Ruba Asi (Israel)*, UN Doc A/HRC/WGAD/2021/8 (7 June 2021) (involving the targeting of female Palestinian students); *Opinion No 7/2018 Concerning Vital Ndikumwenayo et al (Burundi)*, UN Doc A/HRC/WGAD/2018/7 (27 August 2018) (involving harassment of soldiers belonging to the Tutsi ethnic group); *Opinion No 29/2017 Concerning Aramais Avakyan (Uzbekistan)*, UN Doc A/HRC/WGAD/2017/29 (8 June 2017) (concerning the consistent practice of punishing Armenian Christians in Uzbekistan for their faith); *Opinion No 36/2016 Concerning Biram Dah Abeid, Brahim Bilal Ramdane and Djibril Sow (Mauritania)*, UN Doc A/HRC/WGAD/2016/36 (28 December 2016) (discrimination against the Haratine minority in Mauritania); *Opinion No 24/2014 Concerning La Ring (Myanmar)*, UN Doc A/HRC/WGAD/2014/24 (21 November 2014) (consistent with the numerous arrests of Kachins and serious allegations of human rights abuses against villagers from Kachin); *Opinion No 9/2017 Concerning Hana Aghighian et al (Iran)*, UN Doc A/HRC/WGAD/2017/9 (29 May 2017) (pattern of religious discrimination against Bahai's, coupled with a failure to recognise the group as a protected religious minority in the Constitution, unlike other minorities).

conduct directed against the ethnicity or religion of the detainees,[155] and the application of discriminatory laws targeting particular groups.[156] The WGAD also determined, in relation to the US, that racial disparities are among the areas causing systemic problems within the criminal justice system that result in arbitrary detention[157]: '[C]ompared to the Caucasian population, African Americans are more likely to be stopped and searched by law enforcement officers; more likely to be arrested for marijuana possession, despite equal levels of use; and more likely to be sentenced to longer terms of imprisonment.'[158] In the prisons it visited, African American and Hispanic detainees were over-represented.[159]

A European Parliament report found extensive profiling by police of persons of African descent/Black Europeans (24% of people of African descent/Black Europeans in the 12 member states for which data was collected had been stopped by the police in the previous five years),[160] with discriminatory detention practices impacting people of African descent/Black Europeans, Roma, and migrants and refugees.[161] In France, a national survey determined that young men of Arab and African descent are 20 times more likely to be stopped and searched than any other male group, whereas in the UK Black people were nine and a half times more likely to be stopped as compared to white people.[162] The Parliamentary Assembly of the Council of Europe has indicated that '[t]he over-representation of foreign nationals among pretrial detainees gives rise to concerns that the legal grounds for detention are applied in a discriminatory way', and has recommended states to take 'appropriate action to redress any discriminatory application of the rules governing pretrial detention with regard to foreign

---

[155] WGAD, *Opinion No 40/2020 Concerning Jean Claude Hamenyimana (Burundi)*, UN Doc A/HRC/WGAD/2020/40 (2 October 2020) (insults against the Tutsi ethnicity); *Opinion No 50/2013 Concerning Laphai Gam (Myanmar)*, UN Doc A/HRC/WGAD/2013/50 (2 April 2014) (forced to stand in a crucifixion position, during which time he was subjected to mocking statements about his Christian faith); *Opinion No 37/2012 Concerning Adnam El Hadj (Spain)*, UN Doc A/HRC/WGAD/2012/37 (26 November 2012) (racist insults).

[156] WGAD, *Opinion No 71/2020 Concerning Mohammad Qais Niazy (Australia)*, UN Doc A/HRC/WGAD/2020/71 (12 February 2021).

[157] UNGA, 'Report of the WGAD on its Visit to the USA', UN Doc A/HRC/36/37/Add.2 (17 July 2017) para 50.

[158] Ibid para 58.

[159] Ibid para 59.

[160] Quentin Liger and Mirja Guhteil, 'Protection against Racism, Xenophobia and Racial Discrimination, and the EU Anti-Racism Action Plan', European Parliament Policy Department for Citizens' Rights and Constitutional Affairs, PE 730.304 (May 2022) 33.

[161] Ibid, 50, 167, 189.

[162] Council of Europe Commissioner for Human Rights, 'Ethnic Profiling: a Persisting Practice in Europe' (9 May 2019).

nationals, in particular by clarifying that being a foreigner does not per se constitute an increased risk of absconding'.[163]

International human rights case law and, accordingly, formal judicial pronouncements on the matter, is still developing. The ACommHPR, in an unfortunately timed decision, determined that arrests and detentions carried out by the (ousted genocidal) Rwandan Government 'on grounds of ethnic origin alone, [...] constitute arbitrary deprivation of the liberty of an individual'; such acts are thus 'clear evidence of a violation' of Article 6 of the African Charter on Human and Peoples' Rights.[164] The UN Human Rights Committee indicated in a case concerning racial profiling that:

> [T]he physical or ethnic characteristics of the people subjected thereto should not by themselves be deemed indicative of their possible illegal presence in the country. Nor should they be carried out in such a way as to target only people with specific physical or ethnic characteristics. To act otherwise would not only negatively affect the dignity of the people concerned, but would also contribute to the spread of xenophobic attitudes in the public at large and would run counter to an effective policy aimed at combating racial discrimination.[165]

The IACtHR has recognised, in *Acosta Martínez v Argentina*, that the context of racial discrimination and police persecution experienced by persons of African descent in Argentina is a relevant consideration to take into account when considering whether a deprivation of liberty was arbitrary.[166] It determined that the use of vague legislation to justify the arrest obscured the use of racial profiling as the primary reason for the detention. The arrest was therefore arbitrary.[167]

The ECtHR determined that the use of ethnic profiling that resulted in differential treatment between persons of Chechen and non-Chechen ethnic origin in the enjoyment of their right to freedom of movement had no objective and reasonable justification, and therefore constituted

---

[163] Parliamentary Assembly of the Council of Europe (PACE), 'Abuse of Pretrial Detention in States Parties to the European Convention on Human Rights', Doc 13863 (7 September 2015) paras 8 and 12.1.4.

[164] *Organisation Contre la Torture v Rwanda*, Comm Nos 27/89, 46/91, 49/91, and 99/93 (ACommHPR, October 1996) para 28.

[165] *Rosalind Williams Lecraft v Spain*, UN Doc CCPR/C/96/D/1493/2006 (17 August 2009) para 7.2.

[166] *Acosta Martínez et al v Argentina* (Merits, Reparations and Costs) Series C No 410 (31 August 2020) para 94.

[167] Ibid para 100.

discrimination.[168] The Court was not called upon to consider the impact of discrimination on arbitrary detention, though it indicated generally that 'no difference in treatment which is based exclusively or to a decisive extent on a person's ethnic origin is capable of being objectively justified in a contemporary democratic society built on the principles of pluralism and respect for different cultures'.[169] Similarly, there are several cases in which a separate regime for the indefinite detention of non-nationals,[170] or the decision not to afford bail to non-nationals on the basis that they present greater flight risks,[171] were held to be an insufficient basis for distinction and thus not justifiable under Article 5 of the Convention.

In an unrelated case, the ECtHR indicated that 'where there is evidence of patterns of violence and intolerance against an ethnic minority, the positive obligations incumbent on member states require a higher standard of response to alleged bias-motivated incidents'.[172] However, the nature of the positive obligation remains vaguely framed. Do states have an obligation to stop racial profiling that is discriminatory in itself and ultimately leads to additional serious violations of human rights, including arbitrary detention? In *Basu v Germany*[173] and *Muhammad v Spain*,[174] two ECtHR decisions on racial profiling during identity checks decided on the same day, the Court was confronted with parts of this question. However, the majority in each case takes a narrow view of states' positive obligations. Both chambers determined that, once an arguable case of discrimination has been made, there is an obligation on the authorities to investigate. But the judgments do not provide a clear assessment of what petitioners must demonstrate to shift the burden to the state, and what the states must do once that burden shifts is framed in a narrow, procedural way. In *Basu*, the investigation that followed was deemed inadequate, whereas the *Muhammad* investigation was determined to be sufficient, though with strong dissents.[175] As has been argued by commentators, the judgments failed to consider whether the states had adequate structures in place to prevent racial profiling.[176] Furthermore,

---

[168] *Timishev v Russia* App Nos 55762/00, 55974/00 (ECtHR, 13 December 2005) paras 56–59. See, also, *Gillan and Quinton v United Kingdom* App No 4158/05 (ECtHR, 12 January 2010) para 85.
[169] *Timishev* (n 168) para 58.
[170] *A v United Kingdom* (Grand Chamber) App No 3455/05 (ECtHR, 19 February 2009).
[171] *Tomasi v France* App No 12850/87 (ECtHR, 27 August 1992) para 87.
[172] *Lingurar v Romania* App No 48474/14 (ECTHR, 16 April 2019) para 80.
[173] *Basu v Germany* App No 215/19 (ECtHR, 18 October 2022).
[174] *Muhammad v Spain* App No 34085/17 (ECTHR, 18 October 2022).
[175] *Muhammad v Spain* (n 174).
[176] Julie Ringelheim, 'Basu v. Germany and Muhammad v. Spain: Why the First European Court of Human Rights' Judgments on Racial Profiling in Identity Checks Are Disappointing', *EJIL:Talk!* (7 February 2023).

following the inadequate investigation in *Basu*, the Court determined that it was unable to make a positive determination on discrimination,[177] which, as Ringelheim has argued, 'amounts to requiring the applicant to pay the cost of state authorities' failure to comply with their obligation to investigate'.[178] As Judge Pavli notes in his partial dissent in Basu:

> The facts of the present case, as well as the applicant's specific submissions, invited the Court to begin to delineate the substantive standards to be applied in this field, beyond the preliminary (albeit essential) requirements of an effective domestic investigation. The majority have declined that invitation by stopping at a finding of a procedural violation. While minimalism may have its fans, both as a legal doctrine and as a school of architecture and design, it is not necessarily the best way to ensure equality for all in our diverse societies; which are here to stay.[179]

What do *Basu* and *Muhammad* say about positive obligations to eradicate discrimination? Very little. The focus is maintained on states' procedural obligations to investigate particular incidents raised by aggrieved individuals, and much too little on how to address what are invariably systemic challenges. One can only hope that the Committee of Ministers will press states to address the wider issues in their general measures, as part of the execution of the judgments.

(ii) Indigenous peoples

The over-representation of indigenous peoples in all forms of detention is a global problem linked to the continued impact of land dispossession, colonialism and ongoing discrimination. While such discrimination can increase their susceptibility to arbitrary detention in much the same way as it does for other ethnic, racialised and marginalised groups, the experience of colonialism, dispossession and subjugation is a crucial lens through which to analyse susceptibility to detention and, in particular, 'the long-term social and economic marginalisation, the denial of citizenship rights for Indigenous peoples, and the limited recognition of Indigenous law and governance'.[180]

---

[177] *Basu v Germany* (n 173) para 38.
[178] Ibid, partly dissenting opinion of Judge Pavli.
[179] Ibid, partly dissenting opinion of Judge Pavli, para 21.
[180] Chris Cunneen and Juan Tauri, *Indigenous Criminology* (Bristol University Press 2016) 46.

This is also underscored by the UN Expert Mechanism on the Rights of Indigenous Peoples.[181]

The UN Special Rapporteur on the Rights of Indigenous Persons has explained that indigenous peoples are 'overrepresented in every stage of criminal justice processes'.[182] They are additionally subjected to arbitrary detentions as part of the crackdowns against their engagement in the defence of their fundamental rights, their land, culture and ways of life.[183]

The applicability of principles of equality and non-discrimination in indigenous peoples' access to human rights protections has been recognised in several treaties and declaratory texts.[184] The CERD Committee's General Recommendation 31 recommends states parties to give preference to alternatives to imprisonment and to other forms of punishment that are better adapted to indigenous persons' legal systems.[185] The susceptibility of indigenous persons to arbitrary detention has also been considered in WGAD opinions, both in respect of their experience of discrimination within the criminal justice system[186] and their vulnerability as activists.[187] It also features in the jurisprudence of regional and international courts and treaty bodies.

The IACtHR has addressed the arbitrary detention of indigenous persons in several of its judgments[188] and, in so doing, has recognised that because

---

[181] HRC, UN Expert Mechanism on the Rights of Indigenous Peoples, 'Advice No 5 (2013): Access to Justice in the Promotion and Protection of the Rights of Indigenous Peoples', in 'Access to Justice in the Promotion and Protection of the Rights of Indigenous Peoples' UN Doc A/HRC/24/50 (30 July 2013) Annex.

[182] HRC, 'Report of the Special Rapporteur on the Rights of Indigenous Peoples', UN Doc A/HRC/42/37 (2 August 2019) para 42.

[183] This is canvassed in Chapter 5: Deterring Dissent.

[184] ILO Indigenous and Tribal Peoples Convention (No. 169) (adopted 27 June 1989, entered into force 5 September 1991); UN Declaration on the Rights of Indigenous Peoples, UN Doc A/RES/61/295 (13 September 2007); American Declaration on the Rights of Indigenous Peoples, AG/RES. 2888 (XLVI-O/16) (15 June 2016).

[185] CERD Committee, General Recommendation 31 (n 151) para 36. This recommendation to implement measures to reduce the number of indigenous persons in prison, including non-custodial options, such as traditional restorative and rehabilitative approaches, has also been part of the country recommendations of the UN Expert Mechanism on the Rights of Indigenous Peoples (EMRIP). See, for example, EMRIP, Country Engagement Mission (8–13 April 2019) – New Zealand (14 July 2019) para 23.

[186] WGAD, *Opinion No 35/2021 Concerning Juana Alonzo Santizo (Mexico)*, UN Doc A/HRC/WGAD/2021/35 (4 November 2021).

[187] See, for example, WGAD, *Opinion No 64/2018 Concerning Francisca Linconao Huircapán (Chile)*, UN Doc A/HRC/WGAD/2018/64 (28 February 2019); WGAD, *Opinion No 18/2015 Concerning Pedro Celestino Canché Herrera (Mexico)*, UN Doc A/HRC/WGAD/2015/18 (13 July 2015).

[188] See, for example, *López Álvarez v Honduras* (Merits, Reparations, and Costs) Series C No 141 (1 February 2006) paras 67, 75; *Norín Catrimán et al v Chile* (Merits, Reparations, and Costs) Series C No 279 (29 May 2014).

indigenous persons deprived of their liberty belong to culturally distinct peoples, states should adopt specific measures to account for this particularity. This stems from a general principle when assessing the scope and content of rights that states must take into account the specific characteristics that differentiate members of indigenous peoples from the general population and that constitute their cultural identity.[189]

The IACtHR introduced indigenous-specific factors into its consideration of the impact of detention in *Norín Catrimán v Chile*.[190] For their alleged roles in fomenting protests about land dispossession, Mapuche traditional leaders, members of the Mapuche people as well as an activist were convicted of crimes linked to terrorism and given lengthy terms of imprisonment. The IACtHR determined that the adoption and maintenance of pre-trial detention, on vague grounds linked to the danger they posed to the security of society, constituted arbitrary detention, as it was not exceptional in nature, did not respect the presumption of innocence, and also the principles of legality, necessity and proportionality that are essential in a democratic society.[191] Further, the state had not taken into account the impact the detention of Mapuche traditional leaders and members of the Mapuche people would have on the Mapuche communities.[192]

Considering critical perspectives on what differentiates indigenous peoples from the general population, including the colonial history of dispossession, repression and marginalisation, helps to "centre" these experiences in the delivery of justice. But does it go far enough? Some countries have begun to differentiate indigenous peoples' experiences in criminal sentencing processes. For instance, the Penal Code of Peru 'includes several provisions intended to ensure consideration of indigenous peoples' cultural rights, including a reduction or exemption of sentences in cases where an indigenous defendant has committed a crime under different cultural parameters'.[193] In Australia, while race and indigeneity, in themselves, cannot be used as mitigating or aggravating factors in sentencing,[194] the 'Fernando Principles'[195] provide courts with some scope to take into account the circumstances behind a particular offence or offender, in the context of sentencing,[196] though the

---

[189] *Yakye Axa Indigenous Community v Paraguay* (Merits, Reparations and Costs) Series C No 125 (17 June 2005) para 51.
[190] *Norín Catrimán et al v Chile* (n 188).
[191] Ibid paras 310–312.
[192] Ibid para 357.
[193] HRC, UN EMRIP, 'Access to Justice in the Promotion and Protection of the Rights of Indigenous Peoples' (n 181) para 48.
[194] *Bugmy v The Queen* [2013] HCA 37.
[195] *R v Fernando* (1992) 76 A Crim R 58.
[196] Janet Manuell SC, 'The Fernando Principles: the Sentencing of Indigenous Offenders in NSW', Discussion Paper prepared for the NSW Sentencing Council (December

principles have not been uniformly or fully applied.[197] Cunneen and Tauri also note certain foundational problems:

> The communicative and performative aspects of Fernando are seen in the act of first determining the actual harms of colonialism and then deciding which Indigenous individuals may have suffered social, economic and psychological damage as a result. This individualising discourse has left open the subsequent reading down of these principles to the extent that they apply to fewer and fewer Aboriginal people before the courts.[198]

In Canada, efforts to address high indigenous incarceration levels include the *Gladue* sentencing principles. *R v Gladue* involved a guilty plea by 19-year-old Jamie Tanis Gladue for manslaughter for the killing of her fiancé while she was intoxicated.[199] The Supreme Court recognised that Aboriginal people face unique circumstances, and judges must give those circumstances special consideration when setting bail or assigning a sentence:

> [T]he judge must consider: (a) the unique systemic or background factors which may have played a part in bringing the particular [A]boriginal offender before the courts; and (b) the types of sentencing procedures and sanctions which may be appropriate in the circumstances for the offender because of his or her particular [A]boriginal heritage or connection [...]. Judges may take judicial notice of the broad systemic and background factors affecting [A]boriginal people, and of the priority given in aboriginal cultures to a restorative approach to sentencing.[200]

Judges are also obligated to consider all options other than imprisonment, including community sentences focused on rehabilitation and healing, when determining the appropriate sentence.[201] *Gladue* focused on the need

---

2009) <www.publicdefenders.nsw.gov.au/Documents/sentencing_indigenous_offenders_nsw.pdf> accessed 24 July 2023.

[197] Anthony Hopkins, 'The Relevance of Aboriginality in Sentencing: "Sentencing A Person for Who They Are"' (2012) 16(1) *Austr Indigenous L Rev* 37.

[198] Cunneen and Tauri (n 180) 115.

[199] *R v Gladue* [1999] 1 SCR 688. See, also, *R v Ipeelee* [2012] 1 SCR 433.

[200] *Gladue* (n 199) para 93.

[201] See, however, *R v Sharma* [2022] SCC 39, which upholds the constitutionality of section 742.1(c) of the Criminal Code, which made conditional sentences unavailable for any offence with a maximum term of imprisonment of 14 years or life (and thereby making a conditional sentence unavailable to Ms Sharma despite her indigenous background and, thus, according to her, undermining the applicability of the *Gladue* criteria and further perpetuating the overincarceration of Indigenous people in Canada). See particularly, the

to take account of indigenous differentiation in relation to criminal justice matters, though it has inspired conversations in Canada about extending this decolonisation of the law, or 'contextualized decision-making', to child welfare and family law, and beyond indigenous offenders to other visible minority groups.[202] *Gladue* contextualisation or differentiation could have as much relevance in other areas of detention considered in this chapter, particularly detention on mental health grounds, drug-related detention, and the detention of persons who are homeless.

While greater consideration of indigeneity is important, the approaches referred to have not reduced overrepresentation, which was their intended purpose.[203] Cunneen and Tauri argue that both these Canadian and Australian approaches 'remain predicated on the centrality of the non-Indigenous legal system'.[204] In this respect, they see more promise in the developing practice of indigenous sentencing courts.[205] Similarly, Arbel argues in relation to the Canadian system that 'it does little to challenge the operation of Indigenous mass imprisonment or disrupt its ordering'.[206]

(iii) Discrimination based on gender or gendered roles

The impact of gender-based discrimination (including discrimination pertaining to gender identity, gender expression, sex characteristics and sexual orientation) on detention and detention practices bears both similarities and some differences to other forms of discrimination set out earlier in this section.

The similarities stem from situations in which persons are being arbitrarily detained for deigning to exist in the public sphere. Arbitrary detention is used here as a tool to regulate behaviour and to punish. This phenomenon occurs most often in conjunction with a culture of misogyny, homophobia

---

R v Sharma dissent of Karakatsanis J (Martin, Kasirer and Jamal JJ concurring). Following the *Sharma* judgment, the Canadian Senate passed Bill C-5, which repeals the provisions on the inapplicability of conditional sentences at issue in the case. See, further, Azka Anees, '"Unsolicited, Unnecessary, and Contrary to Stare Decisis": Dissent Criticizes SCC's Majority Opinion in *R v Sharma*' (12 December 2022) <www.thecourt.ca/unsolicited-unnecessary-and-contrary-to-stare-decisis-dissent-criticizes-sccs-majority-opinion-in-r-v-sharma/> accessed 24 July 2023.

[202] Jane Dickson and Michele Stewart, 'Risk, Rights and Deservedness: Navigating the Tensions of Gladue, Fetal Alcohol Spectrum Disorder and Settler Colonialism in Canadian Courts' (2022) 40(1) *Behavioral Sciences & the Law* 14, 15.

[203] Cunneen and Tauri (n 180); Efrat Arbel, 'Rethinking the "Crisis" of Indigenous Mass Imprisonment' (2019) 34(3) *Cdn J L & Soc* 437, 438.

[204] Cunneen and Tauri (n 180) 119.

[205] Cunneen and Tauri (n 180) 120–127.

[206] Arbel (n 203) 439.

and transphobia in policing, where homosexuality is criminalised, and where discrimination by public officials occurs with impunity. In *Toonen v Australia*, the UN Human Rights Committee determined that the criminalisation of homosexual practices was incompatible with Article 17 ICCPR (right to privacy),[207] and the WGAD in a series of opinions made clear that detaining individuals pursuant to laws that criminalise homosexuality constituted arbitrary detention.[208] Principle 7 of the Yogyakarta Principles finds similarly.[209] Other examples of the practice include where police officers mock and harass members of the LGBTI+ community, use vague and discretionary dress and behavioural codes to extort money from them or threaten them with detention, sometimes carrying out the detention.[210] For example, Azul Rojas Marín (at the time of the incident a gay man, who subsequently transitioned to a woman) was arrested by Peruvian police and was raped with a baton by three police officers while detained. The IACtHR held that the detention was unlawful as there was no lawful basis for it. It was arbitrary because it was carried out for discriminatory purposes based on her sexual orientation, which was supported by the derogatory remarks made during the incident; she was shouted at 'cabro concha de tu madre' (queer, motherfucker).[211]

In a related sense, persons are frequently being detained for not conforming with stereotypical gendered roles or, as Madrigal-Borloz explains, 'preconceived notions of what the victim's sexual orientation or gender

---

[207] *Toonen v Australia*, UN Doc CCPR/C/50/D/488/1992 (31 March 1994). Principle 6 of the Yogyakarta Principles focuses similarly on the multiple privacy concerns associated with the denial of freedoms related to sexual orientation or gender identity. Principle 6(e) calls on states to: 'Release all those held on remand or on the basis of a criminal conviction, if their detention is related to consensual sexual activity among persons who are over the age of consent, or is related to gender identity': International Panel of Experts in International Human Rights Law and on Sexual Orientation and Gender Identity, Principles on the Application of International Human Rights Law in relation to Sexual Orientation and Gender Identity (Yogyakarta Principles) (2006).

[208] WGAD, *Opinion No 7/2002 Concerning Yasser Mohamed Salah et al. (Egypt)*, UN Doc E/CN.4/2003/8/Add.1 21 June (2002); *Opinion No 22/2006 Concerning François Ayissi et al (Cameroon)*, UN Doc A/HRC/4/40/Add.1 (31 August 2006); *Opinion No 14/2017 Concerning Cornelius Fonya (Cameroon)*, UN Doc A/HRC/WGAD/2017/14 (3 July 2017); *Opinion No 20/2021 Concerning Douglas Tumuhimbise et al (Uganda)*, UN Doc A/HRC/WGAD/2021/20 (9 July 2021). See, also, WGAD, 'Visit to Qatar', UN Doc A/HRC/45/16/Add.2 (30 July 2020) paras 44, 45; 'Visit to Bhutan', UN Doc A/HRC/42/39/Add.1 (31 July 2019) paras 51, 52.

[209] Yogyakarta Principles (n 207) Principle 7.

[210] Jonathon Egerton-Peters et al, *Injustice Exposed: the Criminalisation of Transgender People and its Impacts* (Human Dignity Trust 2019) 14–313.

[211] *Azul Rojas Marín et al v Peru* (Preliminary objections merits, reparations, and costs) Series C No 402 (IACtHR, 12 March 2020).

identity should be, with a binary understanding of what constitutes a male and a female or the masculine and the feminine, or with stereotypes of gender sexuality'.[212] Detention as punishment for failing to conform to stereotypical gendered roles may also involve punishing women for displaying 'unfeminine' behaviour, failing 'to demonstrate adequate compliance and submission'.[213] It can include sexual or public behaviour that does not comply with a society's moral sensibilities linked to gendered roles, such as the detention of women and children in mother and baby homes in Ireland.[214] Another notorious example is the detention of Jina Mahsa Amini, and the thousands of protesters who followed her, for failing to wear the veil in the way stipulated, and for demanding their rights.[215] It also relates to the punishment of women for exercising reproductive autonomy. For example, the WGAD examined the situation of three young women living in rural areas in El Salvador with limited access to health services who had suffered obstetric emergencies, but were charged with alleged aggravated homicide offences. It found that the women's incarceration was arbitrary, as it amounted to discrimination against the women on the basis of their sex or gender and socio-economic status.[216] Similarly, women human rights defenders or other women who 'seek to participate in political, economic, social or cultural leadership in their communities or nations may be acting in defiance of stereotypes obliging women to stay quiet and invisible and defer to male governance' and 'may thus be stigmatized, or even criminalized or confined, to prevent them from speaking out or taking action'.[217] Equally, men may be penalised and face arbitrary detention for failing to exhibit stereotypical notions of masculinity.

Persons are also subjected to "detentions" in the private or non-state spheres for reasons linked to gender, such as persons subjected to forced marriages, women confined to the home unless they have a male chaperone, LGBTI+ persons forcibly confined by family or community members to undergo "rehabilitation" or other coercive rituals, and persons confined for the purpose of sexual slavery. The International Commission of Jurists

---

[212] HRC, 'Report of the Independent Expert on Protection against Violence and Discrimination Based on Sexual Orientation and Gender Identity', UN Doc A/HRC/38/43 (11 May 2018) para 48.

[213] HRC, 'Women Deprived of Liberty', Report of the Working Group on the Issue of Discrimination against Women in Law and in Practice, UN Doc A/HRC/41/33 (15 May 2019) para 23.

[214] Quinlan (n 47); Finnegan (n 47).

[215] HRC, 'Deteriorating Situation of Human Rights in the Islamic Republic of Iran', UN Doc A/HRC/S-35/L.1 (16 November 2022).

[216] *Opinion No 68/2019 Concerning Sara del Rosario Rogel Garcia, Berta Margarita Arana Hernandez and Evelyn Beatriz Hernandez Cruz (El Salvador)*, UN Doc A/HRC/WGAD/2019/68 (4 March 2020).

[217] Ibid para 25.

recounted a case of a lesbian woman who was forcibly confined by her family, taken to meet priests at religious shrines and forced to repeatedly denounce homosexuality as a sin. When one of her friends complained to the police about the woman's forced confinement, they were threatened.[218] These forms of private or non-state confinements do not fit seamlessly into the usual profile of arbitrary detention; however, they often contain all relevant elements of arbitrary detention or, alternatively, may lead to arbitrary detention.[219] States may only have an indirect role in these "detentions"; however, in some contexts, they will tolerate or even acquiesce to the practices and, in all cases, their due diligence obligations to protect these persons from such carceral contexts are engaged. For the most part these contexts have not been considered under the lens of arbitrary detention.[220] While there are good reasons not to blur the distinctions between the denial of freedom of movement and arbitrary detention, there is sense and great importance in continually evaluating whether current descriptions, focuses and lenses are sufficiently encompassing of all persons.

4.4.3 The "undeserving": refugees and other migrants

The third typology, which connects to the first two, relates to governments' resort to administrative (mainly non-penal, though these lines increasingly blur) detention to deter migrants and refugees from deigning to join the society, on whatever the terms. Aided by a process of reinforcement of borders, the narrative focuses on the criminalisation of migrants' quest to enter – *how dare they, they have no right, they must be punished for trying* – the criminalisation of the traffickers and smugglers who have coalesced around migrants to marketise their need to enter (because all lawful channels have been foreclosed), or selective humanitarianism – *we must deter people from making unsafe journeys* – while ignoring the reasons prompting many to

---

[218] Mathuri Thamilmaran, 'Sri Lanka: Stop Unnecessary "Psychiatric Evaluations" Based on Sexual Orientation', International Commission of Jurists (1 December 2022) <www.icj.org/sri-lanka-stop-unnecessary-psychiatric-evaluations-based-on-sexual-orientation/> accessed 26 July 2023.

[219] 'Women deprived of liberty' (n 213) para 22. See, also, *Rantsev v Cyprus and Russia* App No 25965/04 (ECtHR, 7 January 2010) paras 314–325.

[220] Sara Malkani, 'When Women Can't Escape: a Gender-Sensitive Approach to Arbitrary Detention' (2015) 30 *Wis J L Gender & Soc'y* 1. She argues, for example, that the WGAD 'has not addressed the effects of cultural and religious practices that lead to women's confinement within the home and restrict their movement in public spaces. Nor has the Working Group addressed the detention of women and girls coerced into forced marriages, or of women compelled to stay at home due to discriminatory laws that curtail their movement' (20).

leave their countries of origin in the first place. Detention thus becomes a tool of deterrence and a form of humanitarian charity: it is meted out as a salve to stop a problem, but is experienced punitively by extremely vulnerable persons.

The vast numbers of persons forcibly displaced because of fear of persecution and conflict and the many others seeking new lives elsewhere on account of poverty and lack of opportunities in their home countries have fuelled a rise in anti-immigrant sentiment, racism and xenophobia. Refugees and other migrants have become the epitome of Agamben's *homo sacer*.[221] This "othering" is premised on fear:

> [T]here is the public fear of the shadowy "Other" who brings crime and criminality into the country […] There is the securitization of migration and calls for stringent policing as the solution. There is the panic in the government that it will be portrayed as a "soft touch" and the consequent scramble to appear tough (i.e. exclusionary) on immigration issues. And there is the language that is used: "sneaking in", the "scourge of illegal immigration", "flows" and "attacks".[222]

The detention of refugees and migrants in many destination countries, particularly in the West, is a product of this constructed fear. It is about the ulterior purpose[223] of demonstrating resolve to local constituents, about optics and local politics, more so than it is about enabling applications to be processed or ensuring applicants do not abscond. The policies in some countries appear willfully blind to the fact that it is not a crime to seek asylum, and this blindness is aided at least in Europe by the ECtHR's exceptional approach to Article 5(1)(f) claims, discussed later. To seek asylum is a human right, and the Refugee Convention recognises that penalties should not be imposed on account of refugees' 'illegal entry or presence', who 'enter or are present in their territory without authorization, provided they present themselves without delay to the authorities and show good cause for their

---

[221] Agamben, *Homo Sacer* (n 2) 28–29, 126.

[222] Pia Oberoi, 'The Enemy at the Gates and the Enemy Within: Migrants, Social Control and Human Rights' (International Council on Human Rights Policy, 2009).

[223] This arguably engages Arts 17 and 18 ECHR in addition to Art 5, as has been argued by Garahan. See, Sabina Garahan, 'Opening the Door to Arbitrary Detention – Uncontrolled Detention Powers under the Illegal Migration Bill' *Public Law Journal* (forthcoming); Sabina Garahan and Matthew Gillett in their submission to the UK Parliament: UK Parliament Joint Committee on Human Rights, 'Legislative Scrutiny: Illegal Migration Bill', HC 1241, HL Paper 208 (11 June 2023), Written Evidence by Dr Sabina Garahan and Dr Matthew Gillett (IMB0015).

illegal entry or presence'.[224] Even for those who do not claim to be refugees, migrants in an irregular situation are not hardened criminals; at most, they should fall foul of administrative rules, though states are increasingly seeking to criminalise them.[225]

International law and standard-setting texts[226] make clear that immigration detention should be exceptional, used only as a last resort, and that all states should be actively pursuing alternatives to detention. This is further confirmed by UNHCR's Detention Guidelines.[227] Mandatory detention policies that do not consider the individual circumstances of applicants for entry violate this requirement of exceptionality.[228] Similarly, prolonged administrative custody without the possibility of administrative or judicial review or remedy is arbitrary.[229] Most standard-setting texts recognise that certain people should not be detained, including migrants with international protection needs and migrants in vulnerable situations, including pregnant women, breastfeeding women and victims of trafficking, and children.[230]

---

[224] Article 31(1) Convention Relating to the Status of Refugees (adopted 28 July 1951, entered into force 22 April 1954). Further, under Art 5 of the UN Protocol against the Smuggling of Migrants by Land, Sea and Air Supplementing the UN Convention against Transnational Organised Crime (adopted 15 November 2000, entered into force 28 January 2004), migrants who have been the object of smuggling shall not be subject to criminal prosecution.

[225] *Vélez Loor v Panama* (Preliminary Objections, Merits, Reparations and Costs) Series C No 218 (23 November 2010) para 170. See, also, HRC, 'Report of the Special Rapporteur on the Human Rights of Migrants, François Crépeau', UN Doc A/HRC/20/24 (2 April 2012) para 13: 'irregular entry or stay […] are not per se crimes against persons, property, or national security. It is important to emphasize that irregular migrants are not criminals per se and should not be treated as such.'

[226] Art 9 ICCPR and para 18, General Comment No 35 (n 70). See, also, the *Global Compact for Safe, Orderly and Regular Migration* (adopted 13 July 2018) Objective 13; IACommHR, 'Inter-American Principles on the Human Rights of all Migrants, Refugees, Stateless Persons and Victims of Human Trafficking', Resolution 04/19 (7 December 2019) principles 68, 69 and 71; WGAD, 'Report of the WGAD', UN Doc A/HRC/13/30 (18 January 2010) para 59.

[227] The detention of asylum seekers 'should be avoided' and only used as a measure of last resort when it proves 'necessary in the individual case, reasonable in all circumstances and proportionate to a legitimate purpose.' See UNHCR, 'Guidelines on the Applicable Criteria and Standards relating to the Detention of Asylum-Seekers and Alternatives to Detention' (2012) Introduction, para 2, and Guideline 4 para 18.

[228] General Comment No 35 (n 70) para 18; *Vélez Loor v Panama* (n 225) para 171; *Baban v Australia*, UN Doc CCPR/C/78/D/1014/2001 (18 September 2003).

[229] WGAD Methods of Work (n 75) para 8(d). See, also, WGAD, *Opinion No 69/2021 Concerning Navanitharasa Sivaguru (Australia)*, UN Doc A/HRC/WGAD/2021/69 A/HRC/WGAD/2021/69 (22 February 2022); *Opinion No 17/2021 Concerning Mirand Pjetri (Australia)*, UN Doc A/HRC/WGAD/2021/17 (4 June 2021).

[230] WGAD, 'Revised Deliberation No 5 on Deprivation of Liberty of Migrants' (7 February 2018) para 11; Committee on the Protection of the Rights of All Migrant Workers

There are only limited rationales to detain refugees and other migrants, and these are framed differently depending upon the legal framework. As has been explained, the general right to liberty and security of the person requires that any deprivation of liberty is not arbitrary, and may be permitted only on such grounds and in accordance with such procedures as are established by law.[231] The ECHR is different in that it has set out an exhaustive list of exceptions to the right to liberty. Article 5(1)(f) ECHR provides:

> 1. Everyone has the right to liberty and security of person. No one shall be deprived of his liberty save in the following cases and in accordance with a procedure prescribed by law:
> [...]
> (f) the lawful arrest or detention of a person to prevent his effecting an unauthorised entry into the country or of a person against whom action is being taken with a view to deportation or extradition.

In general, there is an equivalent approach to lawfulness and the principle of legality among regional and international human rights courts and bodies that have had occasion to assess the validity of laws allowing for immigration detention. A decision to detain must comply with domestic law and be consistent with international law. The law must be sufficiently precise to ensure that those subject to it can know its meaning and to avoid excessive discretion or inconsistencies in the law's application. This is a standard approach to lawfulness and legality that is broadly consistent across all areas of detention canvassed in this chapter.

With respect to arbitrariness, the UN Human Rights Committee has understood this to include elements of inappropriateness, injustice, lack of predictability or due process of law, unreasonableness, or where it is otherwise

---

and Members of Their Families, 'General Comment No 5 (2021) on Migrants' Rights to Liberty and Freedom from Arbitrary Detention and Their Connection with Other Human Rights', UN Doc CMW/C/GC/5 (21 July 2022) paras 46–53; Committee on the Protection of the Rights of All Migrant Workers and Members of Their Families and Committee on the Rights of the Child, 'Joint General Comment No 4 (2017) of the Committee on the Protection of the Rights of All Migrant Workers and Members of Their Families and No 23 (2017) of the Committee on the Rights of the Child on State Obligations Regarding the Human Rights of Children in the Context of International Migration in Countries of Origin, Transit, Destination and Return', UN Doc CMW/C/GC/4-CRC/C/GC/23 (16 November 2017) para 5; UNHCR and the International Detention Coalition, 'Vulnerability Screening Tool – Identifying and Addressing Vulnerability: a Tool for Asylum and Migration Systems' (2016).

[231] Art 9(1) ICCPR; Art 7(2) American Convention on Human Rights; Art 6 Banjul Charter; Convention on the Protection of the Rights of All Migrant Workers and Members of Their Families (adopted 18 December 1990, entered into force 1 July 2003) Art 16(4).

unnecessary or disproportionate.[232] It has recognised that all decisions to detain, and to maintain a person in detention, must pursue a legitimate aim, and meet the conditions of necessity and proportionality.[233] Detention that fails to consider the viability of alternatives to detention would likewise be arbitrary.[234] Detention which is initially considered lawful may become "arbitrary" if it is unduly prolonged or not subject to periodic review.[235] These criteria must be assessed on a case-by-case basis in light of the facts and circumstances presented.

This approach has also been taken by the IACtHR and by the WGAD.[236] For example, in *Vélez Loor v Panama*, the IACtHR set out the test as follows:

(i) that the purpose of measures that deprive or restrict a person's liberty is compatible with the Convention;
(ii) that the measures adopted are appropriate for complying with the intended purpose;
(iii) that the measures are necessary, in the sense that they are absolutely indispensable for achieving the intended purpose and that no other measure less onerous exists, in relation to the right involved, to achieve the intended purpose. Hence, the Court has indicated that the right to personal liberty assumes that any limitation of this right must be exceptional; and
iv) that the measures are strictly proportionate, so that the sacrifice inherent in the restriction of the right to liberty is not exaggerated or unreasonable compared to the advantages obtained from this restriction and the achievement of the intended purpose.[237]

These bodies can consider all circumstances when justifying a detention (the detention must simply meet the requirements for necessity and proportionality). For example, the Human Rights Committee concluded

---

[232] *Mukong v Cameroon*, UN Doc CCPR/C/51/D/458/1991 (21 July 1994) para 9.8. See, also, section 2.5 in this book: The "arbitrariness" in arbitrary detention.
[233] *van Alphen v The Netherlands*, UN Doc CCPR/C/39/D/305/1988 (23 July 1990) para 5.8.
[234] *C v Australia*, UN Doc CCPR/C/76/D/900/1999 (13 November 2002). See, similarly, the IACommHR's *Principles and Best Practices on the Protection of Persons Deprived of Liberty in the Americas* (n 110) Principle 4, which provides that OAS Member States 'shall establish by law a series of alternative or substitute measures for deprivation of liberty'.
[235] Human Rights Committee, General Comment No 35 (n 70) para 12.
[236] WGAD, 'Revised Deliberation No 5 on Deprivation of Liberty of Migrants' (7 February 2018) paras 13, 14, 19, 20, 24.
[237] *Vélez Loor v Panama* (n 225) para 166. See, similarly, the IACommHR's Principles and Best Practices on the Protection of Persons Deprived of Liberty in the Americas (n 110) Principle 2.

that detention could be justified 'to prevent flight or interference with evidence'.[238] It has also found that 'the lack of cooperation' may justify detention for a period.[239]

The UNHCR Detention Guidelines have likewise underscored the need for any detention to pursue a legitimate aim, and meet the conditions of necessity and proportionality.[240] The guidelines explain that there are three purposes for which detention may be necessary in an individual asylum case: public order (to prevent absconding and/or in cases of likelihood of non-cooperation, in connection with accelerated procedures for manifestly unfounded or clearly abusive claims, for initial identity and/or security verification or to record, within the context of a preliminary interview, the elements on which the application for international protection is based, which could not be obtained in the absence of detention), public health or national security.[241] Costello has argued that the grounds for detention identified in the Detention Guidelines are inordinately broad, and seem 'liable to undermine the commitment to ensuring that detention is an exceptional practice'.[242] Indeed, "public order" as a ground or a category appears overly expansive, though in the UNHCR's explanatory text it is clarified that:

> Decisions to detain on public order grounds might include initial screening for identity, documentation or health reasons, or exceptionally, in the context of mass influx and in the latter situation, only until order has been restored. In terms of a right of states to detain persons in order to assess the elements of their asylum claim, this applies only to an initial screening, and not generally during a full refugee status determination unless necessary in the individual case.[243]

As indicated, unlike other frameworks, Article 5(1)(f) ECHR provides an exhaustive list of permissible exceptions. It permits detention in two different situations: first, 'to prevent an unauthorised entry into the country' and,

---

[238] UN Human Rights Committee, *A v Australia*, UN Doc CCPR/C/59/D/560/1993 (30 April 1997) para 9.2.
[239] Ibid para 9.4.
[240] Detention Guidelines (n 223) Guideline 4.2, para 34.
[241] Ibid para 21.
[242] Cathryn Costello, 'Human Rights and the Elusive Universal Subject: Immigration Detention Under International Human Rights and EU Law' (2012) 19(1) *Indiana J Glob Leg St* 257, 276.
[243] Alice Edwards, 'Back to Basics: the Right to Liberty and Security of Person and "Alternatives to Detention" of Refugees, Asylum-Seekers, Stateless Persons and Other Migrants', PPLA/2011/01.Rev.1 (UNHCR, April 2011) 12.

second, detention 'of a person against whom action is being taken with a view to his or her deportation or extradition'.[244] In principle, this should reduce the grounds upon which detention would be acceptable. In practice, however, it has become easier for states to demonstrate that the detention of refugees and other migrants falls within either limb. This is because the ECtHR case law has determined that, taking into account the 'undeniable sovereign right to control aliens entry into and residence in their territory',[245] there is no overarching need to satisfy the requirements of necessity or proportionality, so long as the specific criteria in Article 5(1)(f) are met.

With respect to the first limb, the ECtHR has taken an expansive approach to what constitutes 'preventing authorised entry into the country'. In *Saadi v United Kingdom*, the Court made clear that states are entitled to detain individuals prior to formally authorising their entry, under this first limb.[246] In other words, there was no need to show that a person was trying to evade entry restrictions (and thus that they presented a risk of absconding or similar); the ability to detain encompassed any person seeking entry.[247] The ECtHR found in this way by giving credence to the rhetorical tool of crisis, 'given the difficult administrative problems with which the United Kingdom was confronted during the period in question, with increasingly high numbers of asylum-seekers'.[248] Even more controversially, it suggests that the detention is for the applicants' benefit because the ability to impose short-term detention avoided a further overwhelming of the immigration system, which would have resulted in even longer periods of detention.[249] Saadi is "othered" and has his detention justified on the basis of his own "otherness".[250]

---

[244] ECHR.

[245] *Saadi v United Kingdom* (Grand Chamber) App No 13229/03 (29 January 2008) para 64.

[246] *Saadi* (n 245) paras 64–66. See, also, *Suso Musa v Malta* App No 42337/12 (23 July 2013) paras 90–107.

[247] *Suso Musa v Malta* (n 246) para 90.

[248] *Saadi* (n 245) para 80.

[249] Ibid, joint partly dissenting opinion of Judges Rozakis, Tulkens, Kovler, Hajiyev, Spielmann and Hirvelä: 'Indeed, the policy behind the creation of the Oakington regime was generally to benefit asylum-seekers; detention was therefore in their best interests. […] to maintain that detention is in the interests of the person concerned appears to us an exceedingly dangerous stance to adopt. Furthermore, to contend in the present case that detention is in the interests not merely of the asylum-seekers themselves "but of those increasingly in the queue" is equally unacceptable. In no circumstances can the end justify the means; no person, no human being may be used as a means towards an end.'

[250] A similar "othering" is present in the Grand Chamber's judgment of *Ilias and Ahmed v Hungary* (Grand Chamber) App No 47287/15 (ECtHR, 21 November 2019) when the judges essentially hold that the migrants exercised their free will to enter the transit zone and were therefore consenting to their detention (paras 220–223).

With respect to the second limb, the Court determined in *Chahal* that there is no separate need to show that the detention was necessary to prevent a risk of absconding[251] or similar while deportation or extradition proceedings are ongoing.[252] The ECtHR has clarified that detention is justifiable under this second limb only to the extent that, and for as long as, deportation or extradition proceedings are in progress and being pursued with diligence.[253] If it is clear that it is impossible to proceed with the removal on any grounds, including a real risk of torture or persecution, this would prevent further detention from being justifiable.[254]

The right to detain in either of these two exhaustive circumstances was not understood as completely unrestrained, however. Though the ECtHR has maintained its finding that there was no need to demonstrate that detention was necessary, it has underscored that the detention needed to be: (1) carried out in good faith without deception by the authorities; (2) closely connected to the purpose of preventing unauthorised entry of the person; (3) in an appropriate place and under appropriate conditions bearing in mind that detainee has not 'committed criminal offences' but rather may have fled fearing for his life; and (4) the length of the detention should not exceed that reasonably required for the purpose pursued.[255]

A further distinction in the ECtHR's approach to immigration detention, and 'another nuance to its well-established point of departure in cases dealing with migrants,'[256] is how the Court understands what constitutes a deprivation of liberty. *Ilias and Ahmed v Hungary* involved two migrants who had arrived in the Röszke transit zone in Hungary, situated at the border between Hungary and Serbia. They had submitted asylum requests upon their arrival at the transit zone, which had been rejected and their expulsions ordered. They were ultimately removed to Serbia after spending 23 days at the transit zone. The Grand Chamber (different from the initial Chamber decision and distinguishing several prior judgments[257]) held that

---

[251] On absconding, see *Al Chodor* C-528/15 (CJEU, 15 March 2017).

[252] *Chahal v United Kingdom* (Grand Chamber) App No 22414/93 (15 November 1996) para 112.

[253] *Suso Musa* (n 242) para 91. *Chahal* (n 252) para 113.

[254] *A v United Kingdom* (Grand Chamber) App No 3455/05 (19 February 2009) paras 170, 171.

[255] *Chahal* (n 247) paras 69, 72–74.

[256] Vladislava Stoyanova, 'The Grand Chamber Judgment in *Ilias and Ahmed v Hungary*: Immigration Detention And How The Ground Beneath Our Feet Continues To Erode', strasbourgobservers.com (23 December 2019).

[257] *Amuur v France* App No 19776/92 (25 June 1996) (detention in the international zone of an airport; *Khlaifia v Italy* (Grand Chamber) App No 16483/12 (15 December 2016) (detention in a reception centre at the port of Lampedusa, and subsequently, detention on ships moored in Palermo harbour).

the applicants' time at the transit zone did not constitute a detention for the purposes of Article 5, therefore making the article inapplicable, because the applicants were at the transit zone by choice and could at any point have returned to Serbia (though the applicants disputed Serbia's status as a safe country). In arriving at this conclusion, the Grand Chamber noted (similar to its comments in the *Saadi* case[258]) that in the context of asylum-seekers, its approach should be 'practical and realistic, having regard to the present-day conditions and challenges. It is important in particular to recognise the States' right, subject to their international obligations, to control their borders and to take measures against foreigners circumventing restrictions on immigration.'[259] Judge Bianku, in his partial dissent, took issue with the majority's conclusion:

> An asylum-seeker wants protection, and his asylum request concerns the protection of a right secured under the Convention, namely the right not to suffer treatment contrary to Article 3, or else Article 2. This process concerns a necessity, not a choice. We can see from European history that such "choices" have cost hundreds of people their lives. I therefore find it difficult to conceive of the fact of asylum-seekers crossing a border as a "choice".[260]

Certainly, the ECtHR's approach to immigration detention has received criticisms[261] and strong dissents.[262] Nevertheless, it remains in place and is an important vehicle for states' ongoing resort to policies of exclusion.

Unlike some of the other contexts of detention explored in this chapter, particularly in respect to detention on mental health grounds, the ECtHR case law on immigration detention makes clear that immigration detention is not understood to be *prima facie* arbitrary. This stems from the different roles played by proportionality assessments, which ultimately justifies a fundamentally different approach to a highly vulnerable, highly marginalised and stigmatised category of persons. It must be queried whether the assumptions that give rise to these differences in result are sufficiently substantial, or whether they simply stem from the frame of "crisis" and

---

[258] *Saadi* (n 245) para 80.
[259] *Ilias and Ahmed v Hungary* (n 250) para 213.
[260] Ibid, partly dissenting opinion of Judge Bianku, joined by Judge Vučinić.
[261] Costello (n 242); Stoyanova (n 256); Helen O'Nions, 'No Right to Liberty: the Detention of Asylum Seekers for Administrative Convenience' (2008) 10 *Eur J Mig & L* 149.
[262] *Saadi* (n 245) joint partly dissenting opinion of Judges Rozakis, Tulkens, Kovler, Hajiyev, Spielmann and Hirvelä; *Ilias and Ahmed* (n 250) partly dissenting opinion of Judge Bianku, joined by Judge Vučinić.

"othering" from which judgments on immigration detention tend to be decided. Other regions are watching carefully.

4.5 Conclusions

This chapter has considered the various ways in which arbitrary detention serves as a strategy to enforce hostility and social control in relation to some of the most marginalised individuals and groups: the "unseen" – persons who are homeless, persons with mental health problems, or who use drugs; the "reviled and resented" – persons discriminated against on the basis of race, ethnicity or religious identity, indigenous peoples and persons discriminated against on the basis of gender or gendered roles; and the "underserving" – refugees and other migrants. Arbitrary detention does so in several ways:

- It keeps people already on the fringes of society locked away and, in so doing, prevents them from being able to confront the society socially and politically.
- It pathologises and punishes "degenerate" behaviour, to censure it and progressively erase it from existence.
- It makes hierarchies more fixed by punishing those that try to subvert them.
- It blocks new people from joining the society.

The logic has been about locking the doors to the imagined community so others cannot taint the vision of what is imagined. The spatial imagery is about borders, barriers, distinctions. There is a desire to exclude aspects of subjectivity that one refuses to acknowledge. And the result is the reduced toleration of marginalised groups in the community – a dystopic denial of their 'grievability'.[263]

Human rights law prohibits arbitrary detention and its mechanisms have had ample opportunity to consider the practice in all its diversity and complexity. But we can see that the law is struggling under the neoliberal weight of what is being thrown at it and the courts have generally been incapable whether because of mandate, formalism or conservatism to address what is largely systemic, intersectional discriminatory treatment. Certainly, the courts have been capable of identifying arbitrary treatment in individual cases. However, they are not managing to address the foundational issues about the over-representation of marginalised groups in detention. Nor do they manage to oppose resolutely, or even clearly, all phenomena of arbitrary detention.

---

[263] Judith Butler, *Precarious Life: the Powers of Mourning and Violence* (Verso 2004).

Courts are simply finding new ways to process persons that offend the sensibilities of the status quo and legitimise the discriminatory carceral state in the process. Consequently, the law shows itself incapable of being more than a fleeting comfort. As Iris Marion Young has said in a different time and place, but with words that still resonate:

> Social change to break the cycle of exclusion and disadvantage that women, people of color, disabled people, gay men and lesbians, old people, and others suffer will not be aided by the law unless courts are willing to require forward-looking remedies of institutions whose unconscious and unintended actions contribute to that disadvantage.[264]

Aside from some important exceptions in discrete areas, where the affected groups themselves have pushed their ways through the stagnancy of the law, such as the progressive recognition of the agency and autonomy of persons with disabilities or the taking into account of indigenous experiences of marginalisation and colonialism in sentencing, there has been an inability to identify, stop and change behaviour. The law is simply stirring the pot.

---

[264] Young (n 72) 151.

5

Deterring Dissent

5.1 Introduction

This chapter focuses on the use of arbitrary detention to quash dissent. In societies where pluralism and ideological diversity are seen as negative influences, those perceived to challenge the status quo may be subjected to repression, including to arbitrary detention. Tolerance for difference within societies is usually variable. In some societies, tolerance for any kind of difference will be low, whereas in others there may be great tolerance for some forms of difference and little for others. Even the most pluralistic societies have a privileged inside and a non-tolerated "outside".

States are encouraged to foster diverse views, perspectives, and voices within society.[1] Yet, in many countries, dissenting views are hardly tolerated if not actively suppressed. Toleration of dissent tends to be lowest when the dissent operates to undermine a governmental policy or practice that is "defining" for that government. In such instances, the dissenters are not just a rabble of unwelcome voices but seen to interfere in governments' ability to deliver policies that they believe are fundamental to their *raison d'être*. The focus here is on undermining and disempowering mainly those voices among the 'independent human rights and class-orientated grassroots organizations with a counterhegemonic potential'[2] that pose the greatest risk to states' hegemonic agendas, whatever those agendas might be.

---

[1] United Nations General Assembly (UNGA), 'Declaration on the Right and Responsibility of Individuals, Groups and Organs of Society to Promote and Protect Universally Recognized Human Rights and Fundamental Freedoms', UN Doc A/RES/53/144 (8 March 1999).

[2] Raul Delgado Wise, 'Is There a Space for Counterhegemonic Participation? Civil Society in the Global Governance of Migration' (2018) 15(6) *Globalizations* 746, 753 (who makes this argument in respect to the limited tolerance of 'counterhegemonic' voices in political debates on migration).

Those who present the greatest challenges to regimes that do not tolerate dissent are political opponents, human rights and social justice advocates, journalists, and protest movements. In some countries it will be civil society groups who advocate for the protection of the environment or indigenous communities opposing the legitimacy of the state and/or its approach to development projects.[3] In other countries it will be nongovernmental organisations (NGOs) and civic movements helping refugees and other migrants,[4] or journalists who, because of the nature of what they write, are seen as maligners or saboteurs, or wrongly accused of being affiliated with terrorist groups.[5] Or, the chosen targets may be groups promoting LGBTI+ rights,[6] or, women's groups,[7] particularly those that work to combat gender stereotypes.[8] In this regard the WGAD has explained:

---

[3] Débora Leão et al, 'Defenders of Our Planet: Resilience in the Face of Restrictions' (CIVICUS, November 2021); UN Economic Commission for Europe, 'Information Note on the Situation Regarding Environmental Defenders in Parties to the Aarhus Convention from 2017 to date', UN Doc AC/WGP-24/Inf.16 (1–3 July 2020); Article 19, 'A Deadly Shade of Green: Threats to Environmental Human Rights Defenders in Latin America' (2016).

[4] Carla Ferstman, 'Using Criminal Law to Restrict the Work of NGOs Supporting Refugees and Other Migrants in Council of Europe Member States' CONF/EXP(2019)1 (Expert Council on NGO Law, December 2019); Ben Hayes and Poonam Joshi, 'Rethinking Civic Space in an Age of Intersectional Crises: a Briefing for Funders' (Global Dialogue, May 2020) 22.

[5] *Bulaç v Turkey* App No 25939/17 (ECtHR, 8 June 2021).

[6] OHCHR, 'Diversity in Adversity: Stories from SOGI Rights Defenders', Video Testimonies (2022) <https://youtu.be/XLGO6-_ok3Y> accessed 30 July 2023. The UN Special Rapporteur on Torture has explained that sexual minorities are 'often subjected to violence of a sexual nature, such as rape or sexual assault in order to "punish" them for transgressing gender barriers or for challenging predominant conceptions of gender roles': UNGA, 'Report of the Special Rapporteur on the Question of Torture and Other Cruel, Inhuman or Degrading Treatment or Punishment', UN Doc A/56/156 (3 July 2001) para 17.

[7] *Magdulein Abaida v Libya*, UN Doc CEDAW/C/78/D/130/2018 (12 April 2021). See, also, HRC, 'Girls' and Young Women's Activism', UN Doc A/HRC/50/25 (10 May 2022) para 41; HRC, 'Report of the Special Rapporteur on the Situation of Human Rights Defenders', UN Doc A/HRC/40/60 (10 January 2019) paras 54, 55; and UN Doc A/HRC/16/44 (20 December 2010) para 70.

[8] According to the UN Working Group on the Issue of Discrimination against Women in Law and in Practice, 'Certain laws, including "complicity" laws, and "public order" laws or even anti-terrorism laws, may be particularly instrumentalized to target women human rights defenders. In some countries, forms of public expression dominated by women, such as religious observances (for example, how they are dressed) related to "disfavoured" or minority faiths, are criminalized or are grounds for restricting access to essential services': HRC, 'Women Deprived of Liberty', UN Doc A/HRC/41/33 (15 May 2019) para 25.

> Women human rights defenders have been arrested and subjected to gendered risks, including threats to publicize fabricated sexual images, denial of female hygiene products while in custody, death threats to a mother and her children, verbal attacks for believing in feminism, and virginity testing, suggesting detention on the discriminatory basis of their gender. […] Other human rights defenders have been detained for advocacy to remove a ban on women driving, seeking to change restrictive rules on male guardianship, calling for an end to sexual harassment, speaking out against the stoning of women for adultery, promoting free hygiene products for schoolgirls, attending a meeting on International Women's Day, and protecting women and children's rights and their education. Similarly, human rights defenders who sought to protect the rights of children with disabilities, of persons living with communicable diseases, and of LGBTIQ+ persons, have been detained and punished for their work.[9]

Those who advocate for better treatment of the "unseen"; the "reviled and resented"; and the "undeserving" are often targeted. This targeting is not simply about the "invisibilising" of such groups, which was explored in Chapter 4; it is about the targeting of those who refuse to tolerate the invisibilisation and who stand up against such practices. Often, special wrath is reserved for those coming from within marginalised groups who are actively seeking to claim their rights.

The physical imagery of the stifling of dissent is the muzzle, the pacifier, the hood, the dark closet, the prison cell. The emotional imagery is that of claustrophobia, though this chapter does not serve as a comment on the merits or weaknesses of open and pluralistic societies or those that are more insular. It is about how any society treats persons who act outside of the marginal space they have been accorded. Thus, it is about dissent, but it is also about how marginalised persons actively negotiate difference and social hierarchies.

Detention is only one of many strategies of repression and part of a trajectory of measures used to stifle or to punish dissenters. Other strategies that are part of this dynamic of repression but not the specific focus of this book or this chapter include: introducing and targeting undesirable critics of government policy or conduct with, abusive and arbitrary regulations that are designed to limit civil society space,[10] limiting the ability of courts to adjudicate claims related to the lawfulness of governmental decisions by

---

[9] HRC, 'Report of the WGAD', UN Doc A/HRC/48/55 (6 August 2021) para 49.

[10] HRC, 'Report of the Special Rapporteur on the Situation of Human Rights Defenders', UN Doc A/HRC/25/55 (23 December 2013) paras 54 *et seq*.

reducing the opportunities for administrative review, and increasing claimants' procedural costs associated with seeking justice,[11] and using strategic lawsuits against public participation (SLAPPs), which serve to harass, intimidate and silence critics on matters of public interest by burdening them with the high costs of a legal defence until they abandon their criticism or opposition.[12] Governments also subject professionals who use their skills to criticise government policies and practices, or to support others who do such work, to disciplinary proceedings, such as lawyer disbarment[13] or medical doctor fitness to practise hearings.[14] Dissenters are also subjected to surveillance,[15] their movements are restricted within and outside their countries of operation,[16] and they face additional barriers in their ability

---

[11] See, for example, IAComm HR, 'Access to Justice as a Guarantee of Economic, Social, and Cultural Rights: a Review of the Standards Adopted by the Inter-American System of Human Rights', OEA/Ser.L/V/II.129 Doc 4 (7 September 2007).

[12] George Pring and Penelope Canan, *SLAPPs: Getting Sued for Speaking Out* (Temple University Press 1996); Justin Borg-Barthet, Benedetta Lobina and Magdalena Zabrocka, 'The Use of SLAPPs to Silence Journalists, NGOs and Civil Society', European Parliament, Policy Department for Citizens' Rights and Constitutional Affairs, PE 694.782 (June 2021).

[13] *Communication of the Special Rapporteur on the Independence of Judges and Lawyers and the Special Rapporteur on the Situation of Human Rights Defenders*, AL IRQ 4/2022 (31 October 2022) (allegedly calling an Iraqi lawyer to the Professional Conduct Committee of the Iraqi Bar Association for tweets related to women's rights as well as his work, potentially resulting in disciplinary penalties); *Communication of the Special Rapporteur on the Independence of Judges and Lawyers, the Special Rapporteur on the Situation of Human Rights in Belarus and the Special Rapporteur on the Promotion and Protection of the Right to Freedom of Opinion and Expression*, AL BLR 5/2021 (18 May 2021) (concerned the revocation of the licences to practise law of five Belarussian lawyers who have been providing legal services to opposition leaders and peaceful protesters). See, also, Amnesty International, 'Against the Law: Crackdown on China's Human Rights Lawyers Deepens', AI Index ASA 17/018/2011 (2011) 9–16; International Commission of Jurists, 'Defenceless Defenders: Systemic Problems in the Legal Profession of Azerbaijan' (2016); Jeremy McBride, 'Study on the Feasibility of a New, Binding or Non-Binding, European Legal Instrument on the Profession of Lawyer: Possible Added-Value and Effectiveness' (April 2021).

[14] Marine Buissonniere et al, 'The Criminalization of Healthcare' (Safeguarding Health in Conflict, Centre for Public Health and Human Rights and University of Essex, June 2018) <www1.essex.ac.uk/hrc/documents/54198-criminalization-of-healthcare-web.pdf> accessed 30 July 2023; Joseph Leone, 'Silenced and Endangered: Clinicians' Human Rights and Health Concerns about Their Facilities' Response to COVID-19' (Physicians for Human Rights, February 2021); Center for Reproductive Rights, 'Defending Human Rights: Abortion Providers Facing Threats, Restrictions and Harassment' (2009).

[15] *Big Brother Watch v United Kingdom* (Grand Chamber) App Nos 58170/13, 62322/14 and 24960/15 (ECtHR, 25 May 2021); HRC, 'The Right to Privacy in the Digital Age', UN Doc A/HRC/51/17 (4 August 2022).

[16] See, for example, *Democracy and Human Rights Resource Centre and Mustafayev v Azerbaijan*, App Nos 74288/14, 64568/16 (ECtHR, 14 October 2021); HRW, 'Egypt: Arbitrary Travel Bans Throttle Civil Society' (6 July 2022); OHCHR, 'UN Experts Urge Azerbaijan

to interact with international organisations, foundations and donors. Also, governments seize and destroy dissenters' property,[17] charge advocates with unsubstantiated crimes and threaten members of their families.[18] Ultimately, many advocates and civil society workers have been tortured, disappeared and/or murdered for their advocacy.[19]

The chapter considers the different contexts in which arbitrary detention is used to suppress dissent, identifying and analysing trends and patterns. It then considers the main gaps in the law that fuel the practice. At times, the law simply accommodates and upholds governments' efforts to criminalise, securitise or pathologise dissent,[20] whereas occasionally, even if rarely, the law shows that it is capable to help "de-securitise" issues back to a more normal status.[21]

5.2 How arbitrary detention is used to deter dissent

Detention removes dissenters from public circulation. This can limit their ability to carry out their work, particularly if the detention is prolonged. It can also have a chilling effect on their future work as well as the work of the persons or groups they associate with. The stigma of detention can negatively impact the reputation of the persons detained and make it more difficult for them to operate effectively.[22] This, however, will depend upon the context; detention that is perceived by the public to be arbitrary or unfair can rally more supporters to the cause.[23]

---

to End Travel Ban on Award-Winning Investigative Journalist Khadija Ismayilova' (5 December 2017).

[17] IACommHR, 'IACHR Calls for Persecution of People Identified as Dissidents to End and for Democratic Guarantees to be Reestablished in Nicaragua' (10 October 2020).

[18] IACommHR, *Criminalization of Human Rights Defenders* OEA/Ser.L/V/II. Doc 49/15 (31 December 2015); HRC, 'Refusing to Turn Away: Human Rights Defenders Working on the Rights of Refugees, Migrants and Asylum-Seekers', UN Doc A/77/178 (18 July 2022).

[19] HRC, 'Final Warning: Death Threats and Killings of Human Rights Defenders', UN Doc A/HRC/46/35 (24 December 2020).

[20] This point is raised by Eichler and Barnier-Khawam in relation to Chile's application of anti-terrorism laws, upheld by domestic courts, as part of its response to Mapuche protest movements: Jessika Eichler and Pablo Barnier-Khawam, 'Criminalization, Securitization and Other Forms of Illegalizing Indigenous Contestations in Chile: Responses from Constitutional Law and Inter-American Jurisprudence on Mapuche People's Rights' (2021) *J Hum Rts Practice* 357, 373.

[21] Claudia Aradau, 'Security and the Democratic Scene: Desecuritization and Emancipation' (2004) 7 *J Intl Relations & Dev* 388.

[22] HRC, 'Report of the Special Rapporteur on the Situation of Human Rights Defenders', UN Doc A/HRC/13/22 (30 December 2009) para 32.

[23] Julia Norman, 'Negotiating Detention: the Radical Pragmatism of Prison-Based Resistance in Protracted Conflicts' (2022) 53(2) *Security Dialogue* 95.

5.2.1 Criminalisation

The principal route to detain political opponents, activists, journalists and other dissenters is to criminalise their behaviour. As canvassed in Chapter 3, criminalisation is mainly about what acts and omissions are prohibited and subject to the criminal law, as well as decisions about whom to prosecute and how to sentence offenders.[24] Some decisions to criminalise (including the decision to criminalise dissent) may involve biases and subjective considerations that result in over-criminalisation and/or selective and arbitrary criminalisation, which invariably lead to arbitrary detentions.

The criminalisation of dissent is about making certain types of advocacy, or related activity, a criminal offence, most frequently on the purported basis that the conduct breaches national security, terrorism or treason-related provisions. Here, criticism of the state, the government or its officials may be considered an act of terrorism or treason. This has the effect of stifling 'dissent and advocacy by peaceful critics, human rights activists and members of minority groups' and the 'arrests, detentions and convictions are meant to send a message to citizens that they will be prosecuted if they engage in these broadly defined activities'.[25] Additional rationales to criminalise are that dissenters' written or verbal statements are criminally libellous or slanderous. Further, some countries arrest and detain dissenters for unrelated criminal offences (such as tax evasion, finance, corruption or bribery offences, or regulatory breaches upgraded to criminal law offences).[26]

(i) Securitising dissent

Securitisation is a process by which the state's resort to extraordinary means is justified as necessary to protect against an existential threat.[27] States' choices about what constitutes an existential threat, and what actions to take or not to take, are securitised choices, based on national or political interests. When dissenters obstruct states from achieving their objectives, these obstructions too are seen from a securitised lens.

---

[24] Andrew Simester and Andreas von Hirsch, *Crimes, Harms, and Wrongs: On the Principles of Criminalisation* (Hart 2011) 3.

[25] HRC, 'Report of the Special Rapporteur on the Promotion and Protection of Human Rights and Fundamental Freedoms While Countering Terrorism on the Role of Measures to Address Terrorism and Violent Extremism on Closing Civic Space and Violating the Rights of Civil Society Actors and Human Rights Defenders', UN Doc A/HRC/40/52 (18 February 2019) para 39.

[26] UNGA, 'Report of the Special Rapporteur on the Situation of Human Rights Defenders', UN Doc A/64/226 (4 August 2009) paras 60–66.

[27] Michael Williams, 'Words, Images, Enemies: Securitization and International Politics' (2003) 47 *International Studies Quarterly* 511.

The securitisation of dissent involves the construction and use of security discourses to undermine dissent. As Bigo explains, the 'professionals in charge of the management of risk and fear especially transfer the legitimacy they gain from struggles against terrorists, criminals, spies, and counterfeiters toward other targets',[28] and these other (more benign) targets include the dissenters. The securitisation is done by producing narratives that show facets of dissent as matters of security,[29] often with the help of overly vague or broad definitions of national security, terrorism and counter-terrorism. For example, China's counter-terrorism law, adopted in 2015, includes in its definition of terrorism 'propositions and actions that create social panic, endanger public safety, violate person and property, or coerce national organs or international organizations, through methods such as violence, destruction, intimidation, so as to achieve political, ideological, or other objectives'.[30] The legislation has led to a 'growing number of arbitrary detentions and criminal charges linked to national security being imposed on human rights defenders and lawyers across China'.[31] Egypt's counter-terrorism legislation, which gives prosecutors extensive powers to detain suspects without judicial review, defines as a "terrorist act" any:

> use of force or violence or threat or terrorizing [that aims, among other things, to] [d]isrupt general order or endanger the safety, interests or security of society; harm individual liberties or rights; harm national unity, peace, security, the environment or buildings or property; prevent or hinder public authorities, judicial bodies, government facilities, and others from carrying out all or part of their work and activity.[32]

---

[28] Didier Bigo, 'Security and Immigration: Toward a Critique of the Governmentality of Unease' (2002) 27(1) *Alternatives* 63–92, 63.

[29] Barry Buzan, Ole Wæver and Jaap de Wilde, *Security: a New Framework for Analysis* (Lynne Rienner 1998) 26.

[30] Art 3 (adopted 18th session of the Standing Committee of the 12th National People's Congress, 27 December 2015, amended 27 April 2018). See International Campaign for Tibet and FIDH, *China's New Counter-Terrorism Law: Implications and Dangers for Tibetans and Uyghurs* (November 2016) 18. See, also, Lana Baydas and Shannon Green (eds), *Counterterrorism Measures and Civil Society: Changing the Will, Finding the Way* (CSIS 2018) 3–4. See, also, OHCHR, 'OHCHR Assessment of Human Rights Concerns in the Xinjiang Uyghur Autonomous Region, People's Republic of China' (31 August 2022) paras 17–24.

[31] OHCHR (n 30) 17, 33.

[32] Law 95 of 2015 for Confronting Terrorism. See HRW, 'Egypt: Counterterrorism Law Erodes Basic Rights: Broad "Terrorist Acts" List May Criminalize Civil Disobedience' (19 August 2015). See, also, Saskia Brechenmacher, 'Civil Society Under Assault: Repression and Responses in Russia, Egypt and Ethiopia' (Carnegie Endowment for International Peace, 2017) 37, 44–47.

It has led to the arrest of numerous activists, including blogger Alaa Abd El Fattah, lawyer and human rights defender Mohammed El-Baqer, and journalist Mohammed Ibrahim Radwan, all of whom were charged with the vague offence of spreading false news likely to pose a threat to national security.[33] Israel's vague and overly broad counter-terrorism legislation enabled the government to declare in 2021 six Palestinian human rights groups – Addameer Prisoner Support and Human Rights Association, Al-Haq, Bisan Center for Research and Development, Defense for Children International – Palestine, the Union of Agricultural Work Committees and the Union of Palestinian Women Committees – terrorist organisations.[34] These designations follow a pattern of securitising Palestinian advocacy work, which has resulted in the arbitrary detention of activists via administrative detention.[35] This has occurred, for example, with Salah Hammouri, a Palestinian lawyer for the NGO Addameer, who was arrested on the basis of a secret file, never charged or tried,[36] and eventually deported to France,[37] and Khalida Jarrar, former director of Addameer and a member of the Palestinian Legislative Council, who was arrested without a warrant and subjected to administrative detention, with charges subsequently lodged linked to her affiliation with an "illegal organisation", her role as a member of the Palestinian Legislative Council and a political leader, and her work campaigning for prisoners.[38] In Pakistan, some 70 human rights defenders and 150 lawyers were reportedly arrested in the context of a declaration of a state of emergency.[39] In respect of Russia, the UN Committee against Torture denounced the 'arbitrary detention […] of human rights defenders, lawyers, journalists and political opponents' and the 'consistent reports that provisions of the Criminal Code on combating terrorism are often used against civil activists'.[40] The WGAD considered that the detention of

---

[33] OHCHR, 'UN Experts Urge Release of Rights Defenders in Egypt, Condemn Misuse of Counter-Terrorism Measures', Press Release (1 December 2021).

[34] OHCHR, 'UN Experts Condemn Israel's Designation of Palestinian Human Rights Defenders as Terrorist Organisations', Press Release (25 October 2021).

[35] Military Order No 1651 (2009).

[36] WGAD, *Opinion No 34/2018 Concerning Salah Hammouri (Israel)*, UN Doc A/HRC/WGAD/2018/34 (29 May 2018).

[37] 'Israel Deports Palestinian Activist Salah Hammouri to France', *France24* (18 December 2022).

[38] WGAD, *Opinion No 15/2016 Concerning Khalida Jarrar (Israel)*, UN Doc A/HRC/WGAD/2016/15 (22 June 2016).

[39] HRC, 'Report Submitted by the Special Representative of the Secretary-General on the Situation of Human Rights Defenders, Hina Jilani, Addendum', UN Doc A/HRC/7/28/Add.1 (5 March 2008) paras 1553–1558.

[40] UN Committee against Torture, 'Concluding Observations on the Sixth Periodic Report of the Russian Federation', UN Doc CAT/C/RUS/CO/6 (28 August 2018) paras 28, 34.

Russian military reporter Grigory Pasko, who was detained on espionage and disclosing state secrets charges, for having reported on the failure of Russian authorities to process radioactive waste material generated from disused nuclear submarines, constituted arbitrary detention.[41]

In Turkey, Articles 1 and 7 of the Anti-Terrorism Law and Articles 314(1) and 220(6)–(7) of the Penal Code criminalise the establishment and/or commanding of an armed terrorist organisation, membership in an armed organisation, aiding and abetting such organisations as well as disseminating terrorist propaganda.[42] As there is no definition of what constitutes armed organisations nor what is meant by membership, the provisions are prone to arbitrary application. Many critics, including lawyers, political opponents, human rights advocates, public intellectuals and journalists, have been subjected to these laws for expressing opinions and, in consequence, have become victims of arbitrary detention.[43] Emblematic examples include the arbitrary detentions of: the chairperson of Amnesty International (Turkey branch) Taner Kılıç[44]; human rights activist, medical doctor and President of the Turkish Medical Association Şebnem Korur Fincancı[45]; philanthropist Osman Kavala[46]; and many lawyers, journalists and

---

[41] WGAD, *Opinion No 9/1999 Concerning Grigory Pasko (Russia)*, UN Doc E/CN.4/2000/4/Add.1 (20 May 1999).

[42] Zafer Yılmaz, 'Turkey's Regime Transformation and its Emerging Police state: the Judicialization of Politics, Everyday Emergency, and Marginalizing Citizenship', in Jürgen Mackert, Hannah Wolf and Bryan Turner (eds), *The Condition of Democracy*, vol. 2 (Routledge 2021); Bahar Baser, Samim Akgönül and Aandmet Erdi Öztürk, '"Academics for Peace" in Turkey: a Case of Criminalising Dissent and Critical Thought Via Counterterrorism Policy' (2017) 10(2) *Critical Studies on Terrorism* 274.

[43] Amnesty International, 'Weathering the Storm: Defending Human Rights in Turkey's Climate of Fear', AI Index EUR 44/8200/2018 (April 2018).

[44] *Taner Kılıç v Turkey (No. 2)* App No 208/18 (ECtHR, 31 May 2022); Amnesty International, 'Turkey: the Taner Kılıç Prosecution', AI Index EUR 44/7331/2017 (20 October 2017). Kılıç had been charged with membership of a terrorist organisation, principally on the basis that he had downloaded a secure mobile messaging application that had been said to have been used by terrorist organisations.

[45] Dr Korur Fincancı was detained in 2022 and 2023 due to her apparent remarks calling for an investigation into claims concerning the alleged use of chemical weapons by the Turkish military against Kurdish militants in northern Iraq. This led to charges of disseminating terrorganizationon propaganda. The arrest followed on from previous bouts of arbitrary detention. See, for example, Michele Heisler et al, 'Free Şebnem Korur Fincancı and End Systematic Silencing of Health Professionals' (2022) 400 (10366) *The Lancet* 1843–1844.

[46] *Kavala v Turkey* App No 28749/18 (ECtHR, 10 December 2019); *Proceedings under Article 46 § 4, in the Case of Kavala v Türkiye* (Grand Chamber) App No 28749/18 (11 July 2022). Mr Kavala has been detained since 2017 on charges connected to his alleged role in connection with the 2013 Gezi Park protests and the July 2016 failed coup attempt. The charges had been dismissed by Turkish courts twice, only to be immediately reinstated on the same facts. In April 2022, he was sentenced to life imprisonment for his said role

academics.[47] As Amnesty International has written, 'anybody critical of the government, fear, with justification, that at any moment they may be taken into police custody and subsequently remanded in pre-trial detention on baseless charges. Many defenders have either been detained themselves or will know someone who has.'[48] Despite the Council of Europe's Venice Commission pronouncement on the failure of many of the Penal Code provisions to satisfy the requirements of proportionality,[49] and several rulings of the ECtHR finding the same,[50] as well as further pronouncements by the UN Human Rights Committee[51] and WGAD,[52] at the time of writing the provisions remained in force with only minimal amendments and continued to be applied against numerous dissenters.

Dissenters need not be civil society representatives or hold other special roles to be accused of security-related offences linked to their critiques of government. In Iran, the Aban (People's) Tribunal recorded numerous incidents in which persons believed by the Iran government to be associated with the protests were arbitrarily detained on security-related offences. Others who sought answers about the deaths of loved ones were also subjected to arrests or threats of arrest.[53] For instance, Ministry of Intelligence

---

in relation to the Gezi Park protests (despite the ECtHR having held previously that the evidence proffered against him had not been sufficient even to detain him) which in December 2022 was confirmed on appeal: 'Turkish Court Upholds Life Sentence for Activist Kavala', *Deutsche Welle* (28 December 2022).

[47] Baser et al (n 42).

[48] Amnesty International, 'Weathering the Storm' (n 43) 7.

[49] Venice Commission Opinion on Articles 216, 299, 301 and 314 of the Penal Code of Turkey (CDL-AD(2016)002).

[50] *Selahattin Demirtaş v Turkey (No. 2)* (Grand Chamber) App No 14305/17 (ECtHR, 22 December 2020); *Acar v Turkey* App Nos 64251 and 49 others (28 June 2022); *Yılmaz and Kılıç v Turkey* App No 68514/01 (17 July 2008); *Taner Kılıç v Turkey (No. 2)* App No 208/18 (31 May 2022); *İmret v Turkey (No. 2)* App No 57316/10 (3 December 2018); *Işıkırık v Turkey* App No 41226/09 (14 November 2017); *Parmak & Bakır v Turkey* App Nos 22429/07 and 25195/07 (3 December 2019); *Akgün v Turkey* App No 19699/18 (20 July 2019).

[51] *Mukadder Alakus v Turkey* UN Doc CCPR/C/135/D/3736/2020 (15 November 2022) para 10.6; *Mümüne Acikkollu v Turkey* UN Doc CCPR/C/136/D/3730/2020 (30 November 2022) para 8.8.

[52] For example, WGAD, *Opinion No 38/2021 Concerning Cihan Erdal (Turkey)*, UN Doc A/HRC/WGAD/2021/38 (15 October 2021); *Opinion No 66/2020 Concerning Levent Kart (Turkey)*, UN Doc A/HRC/WGAD/2020/66 (2 February 2021); *Opinion No 41/2017 Concerning 10 individuals associated with the newspaper Cumhuriyet (Turkey)*, UN Doc A/HRC/WGAD/2017/41 (26 July 2017) paras 91–97.

[53] See, for example, the statement of witness 300 at para 276 of the judgment: International People's Tribunal on Iran's Atrocities (Aban Tribunal) Judgment (1 November 2022) <https://abantribunal.com/wp-content/uploads/2022/11/Aban-Judgment-Final.pdf> accessed 30 July 2023.

agents reportedly arbitrarily detained Elham Afkari (whose brother, the Iranian wrestler Navid Afkari, was executed by the regime) and placed her in solitary confinement for nine days, where she was accused of 'spreading propaganda against the system' and was told she would be charged with 'gathering and colluding to commit crimes against national security'.[54]

Securitisation narratives harness legitimate fears about insecurity and link these to wider concerns about pluralism. They produce anxiety about the destabilising potential of public debate. Also, the narratives link the dissenters and activists with the "toxicity" of their causes and portray the state as the beneficent saviour of security, order and all that is good. As Sombatpoonsiri argues in relation to the construction of security discourses to support military actions in Thailand:

> If we want to understand how authoritarian regimes can legitimize their political repression of nonviolent pro-democracy protestors, it is imperative that we examine the manner in which such regimes can define nonviolent activists as a threat to national security and succeed in getting such a securitized definition (or frame) publicly accepted.[55]

Securitising narratives have been used to link a range of dissenters to national security and terrorism-related offences, including LGBTI+ rights defenders, climate change activists, human rights defenders, journalists, minority groups, labour activists, indigenous peoples, and members of the political opposition.[56] As has been stated in relation to the crackdowns on Gezi park protesters in Turkey, 'government officials have increasingly resorted to rhetoric equating protest with "terrorism", opposition with "the enemy within"'.[57]

The second stage of the securitisation of dissent is about justifying or legitimising the use of "exceptional" measures to quash the dissent. This is achievable as an exceptional measure because of the panic engendered by the deployment of the existential threat narratives, and the "othering" of the persons and groups who will be subjected to the exceptional measures. For example, calling protesters "terrorists" justifies the use of violence against them. Detaining "terrorists" makes the general population feel safe.

---

[54] Amnesty International, Second Urgent Action: 66/21 Index: MDE 13/6280/2022 Iran (6 December 2022).

[55] Janjira Sombatpoonsiri, 'Securitization of Civil Resistance: Thailand's Military Junta and Beyond' (2021) 1(2) *Journal of Resistance Studies* 85, 87.

[56] Report of the Special Rapporteur on the Promotion and Protection of Human Rights and Fundamental Freedoms While Countering Terrorism (n 25) paras 8, 34.

[57] Anonymous, 'The Securitisation of Dissent and the Spectre of Gezi', *OpenDemocracy* (1 June 2014).

This legitimisation is what leaves the dissenters vulnerable, threatened, criminalised and, very often, subject to arbitrary detention.

(ii) Criminally defamatory speech acts

Dissenters, particularly journalists and human rights advocates, are frequently charged with defamation or other variations on criminal libel of slander following their critiques of government policies and practices.[58] This is even though the peaceful exercise of the right to freedom of opinion and expression (which does not amount to hate speech) should never result in criminal sanction. As the WGAD explained in several opinions,[59] holding and expressing views, or disseminating or receiving information, including opinions that do not accord with official government policy, are protected under the right to hold opinions without interference and the right to freedom of expression.[60] This includes charges of "lese-majesty" or the insulting of the king or supreme ruler,[61] and extends to other government officials exercising their functions.

Public officials should tolerate more criticism than private individuals, not less.[62] Politicians put themselves voluntarily into the spotlight and thus need

---

[58] HRC, 'Report of the Special Rapporteur on the Situation of Human Rights Defenders' (n 22) para 33.

[59] See, for example, WGAD, *Opinion No 88/2017 Concerning Thirumurugan Gandhi (India)*, UN Doc A/HRC/WGAD/2017/88 (23 January 2018) para 32; *Opinion No 8/2009 Concerning Mr. Hassan Ahmed Hassan Al-Diqqi (United Arab Emirates)*, UN Doc A/HRC/13/30/Add.1 (1 September 2009); *Opinion No 51/2017 Concerning Sasiphimon Patomwongfangam (Thailand)*, UN Doc A/HRC/WGAD/2017/51 (13 October 2017); *Opinion No 28/2015 Concerning Abdullah Fairouz Abdullah Abd al-Kareem (Kuwait)*, UN Doc A/HRC/WGAD/2015 (5 October 2015) para 41; *Opinion No 5/1999 Concerning Khemais Ksila (Tunisia)*, UN Doc E/CN.4/2000/4/Ad 1, 37 (17 December 1999) paras 11, 12; *Opinion No 25/2012 Concerning Agnès Uwimana Nkusi and Saïdati Mukakibibi (Rwanda)*, UN Doc A/HRC/WGAD/2012/25 (22 November 2012); *Opinion No 7/2008 Concerning Ko Than Htun and Mr. Ko Tin Htay (Myanmar)*, UN Doc A/HRC/10/21/Add.1 (4 February 2009) paras 8–10.

[60] Art 19 ICCPR.

[61] WGAD, *Opinion No 51/2017* (n 59) para 38. See, also, Human Rights Committee, General Comment No 34 on the Freedoms of Opinion and Expression, UN Doc CCPR/C/GC/34 (12 September 2011) para 38: 'the Committee expresses concern regarding laws on such matters as, lese majesty, *desacato*, disrespect for authority, disrespect for flags and symbols, defamation of the head of state and the protection of the honour of public officials, and laws should not provide for more severe penalties solely on the basis of the identity of the person that may have been impugned. States parties should not prohibit criticism of institutions, such as the army or the administration.' See, also, WGAD, *Opinion No 35/2012 Concerning Somyot Prueksakasemsuk (Thailand)*, UN Doc A/HRC/WGAD/2012/35 (23 November 2012).

[62] WGAD, *Opinion No 35/2008 Concerning Abdul Kareem Nabil Suliman Amer (Egypt)*, UN Doc A/HRC/13/30/Add.1 (20 November 2008) para 32. See, also, *Kenneth Good v Botswana*, App No 13/05 (African Commission on Human and Peoples' Rights (ACommHPR, 26 May 2010) para 198.

to have a "thicker skin".[63] In *Usón Ramírez v Venezuela*, Usón Ramírez, a retired member of the military, was convicted of the crime of 'insult against the Armed Forces', for criticising the performance of the military. The IACtHR determined that the application of the criminal law in this case was not suitable, necessary or proportionate, also taking into account that his expressions were worthy of special protection because they were made in the public interest.[64] Similarly, in *Lohé Issa Konaté v Burkina Faso*, which concerned the offence of criminal defamation levied against a journalist for articles published about the corruption of a public prosecutor, the African Court on Human and Peoples' Rights determined that, as a public figure, a prosecutor 'is more exposed than an ordinary individual and is subject to many and more severe criticisms', and 'a higher degree of tolerance is expected of him/her'.[65] Consequently, a deprivation of liberty that is applied on the sole ground of a person having made such criticisms or similar is arbitrary.[66]

Pursuant to Article 19(3) ICCPR, to be permissible, restrictions on the right to freedom of expression must be 'provided by law'. Any limitation must be in accordance with law, formulated with sufficient precision to enable individuals to regulate their conduct accordingly. No law should be so broad or vague to confer on the authorities an unfettered discretion to restrict freedom of expression.[67]

As a qualified right, restrictions on freedom of expression must also serve one of a narrow, specified list of "legitimate aims" (namely, respect for the rights or reputations of others or protection of national security, public order, public health or morals).[68] A legitimate purpose might be, for example, 'for the purposes of securing due recognition and respect for the rights and freedoms of others and of meeting the just requirements of morality, public order and the general welfare in a democratic society'.[69]

---

[63] *Castells v Spain* App No 11798/85 (ECtHR, 23 April 1992) para 46; *Lingens v Austria* App No 9815/82 (ECtHR, 8 July 1986) para 42.

[64] *Usón Ramírez v Venezuela* (Preliminary Objection, Merits, Reparations and Costs) Series C No 207 (IACtHR, 20 November 2009) para 83. See, similarly, *Palamara-Iribarne v Chile* (Merits, Reparations and Costs) Series C No 135 (IACtHR, 22 November 2005) para 83; *Herrera-Ulloa v Costa Rica* (Preliminary Objections, Merits, Reparations and Costs) Series C No 107 (IACtHR, 2 July 2004) para 82.

[65] *Lohé Issa Konaté v Burkina Faso*, App No 004/2013 (ACtHPR, 5 December 2014) para 156.

[66] WGAD, *Opinion No 28/2015* (n 59) para 38.

[67] WGAD, *Opinion No 75/2021 Concerning Ros Sokhet (Cambodia)*, UN Doc A/HRC/WGAD/2021/75 (27 January 2022) para 55.

[68] Art 19(3) ICCPR.

[69] WGAD, *Opinion No 88/2017* (n 59) para 35.

The restriction must also be proportionate and "necessary", in the sense that the interference with freedom of expression must be proportionate to the legitimate aim pursued and there must be no other, less intrusive, measures available to achieve that aim. According to the WGAD, criminal defamation (as opposed to a civil libel claim where required) is an overly intrusive response 'to achieve respect for the rights or reputations of others',[70] and will generally not satisfy the requirements of proportionality.[71] This principle has only very limited exceptions, for example, 'serious and very exceptional circumstances for example, incitement to international crimes, public incitement to hatred, discrimination or violence or threats against a person or a group of people, because of specific criteria such as race, colour, religion or nationality'.[72] This is consistent with the approach taken by the Inter-American Commission.[73]

The Mexican journalist Lydia Cacho Ribeiro founded in 2000 the Integral Centre for Women in Cancún, which provides services to women and children victims of domestic and sexual violence. In 2005, she published a book about child pornography, in which she exposed a corruption and child exploitation ring involving Mexican public authorities and business leaders. One business leader who was cited in the book brought against her a criminal complaint for defamation, which ultimately led to her arrest and detention. The conditions of her arrest and transfer to detention as well as the initial period of detention involved conduct amounting to both physical and psychological ill-treatment, including torture.[74] The UN Human Rights Committee underscored, in relation to her case, that even if it could be said that the detention was effectuated pursuant to a valid law, and the law

---

[70] WGAD, *Opinion No 51/2017* (n 59) para 38.
[71] See, for example, *Alexander Adonis v The Philippines*, UN Doc ICCPR/C/103/D/1815/2008/Rev.1 (26 October 2011) para 6. See, also, *Kimel v Argentina* (Merits, Reparations and Costs) Series C No 177 (2 May 2008) para 94; *FAJ v The Gambia*, ECW/CCJ/JUD/04/18 (13 February 2018).
[72] *Lohé Issa Konaté v Burkina Faso* (n 65) para 165. See similar at the ECtHR, *Mahmudov and Agazade v Azerbaijan* App No 35877/04 (18 December 2008) para 50.
[73] Principle 10 of the Declaration of Principles of Freedom of Expression, adopted by the IACommHR in 2000, underscores that the 'protection of a person's reputation should only be guaranteed through civil sanctions in those cases in which the person offended is a public official, a public person or a private person who has voluntarily become involved in matters of public interest. In addition, in these cases, it must be proven that in disseminating the news, the social communicator had the specific intent to inflict harm, was fully aware that false news was disseminated, or acted with gross negligence in efforts to determine the truth or falsity of such news': IACommHR, Declaration of Principles of Freedom of Expression (108th Regular Session, October 2000).
[74] *Lydia Cacho Ribeiro v Mexico*, UN Doc CCPR/C/123/D/2767/2016 (29 August 2018) paras 2.4, 2.5.

pursued a legitimate aim, such as protecting personal honour, detention was not a necessary or proportionate measure to achieve that aim, and violated Ribeiro's right to freedom of expression.[75]

5.2.2 Pathologising dissent

Certain governments have resorted to locking up dissenters in mental institutions alongside, or in lieu of, the criminalisation of their activities. This coincides with the history of certain states misusing 'psychiatric diagnosis, treatment and detention for the purposes of obstructing the fundamental human rights of certain individuals and groups in a given society'[76]; as a tool of political suppression.[77] The practice is objectionable on multiple grounds. As Bonnie and Polubinskaya note:

> [R]epression of dissent is problematic whether the dissenter is sent to jail or to a psychiatric hospital. However, it would be a mistake to regard the hospitalization of dissidents as only a derivative problem. To hospitalize a dissenter who is *not* mentally ill on grounds of non-imputability combines repression with moral fraud and magnifies the violation of human rights; it demeans the dissenter's dignity, devalues his or her message and establishes the legal authority for an indeterminate period of what can only be called psychiatric punishment.[78]

Erica-Irene Daes, in her then capacity as Special Rapporteur of the UN Sub-Commission on the Prevention of Discrimination and Protection of Minorities, produced Principles, Guidelines and Guarantees for the Protection of Persons Detained on Grounds of Mental Ill-Health or Suffering From Mental Disorder.[79] In her report, she noted that 'abuses of involuntary admission and detention in psychiatric hospitals are taking place in several parts of the world, especially against persons who defend fundamental freedoms and exercise their human rights',[80] and underscored that 'psychiatry shall never be used for the purpose of violating human rights and for the

---

[75] Ibid para 10.9.
[76] Robert van Voren, 'Ending Political Abuse of Psychiatry: Where We Are at and What Needs to be Done' (2016) 40 *BJPsych Bulletin* 30, 30.
[77] See, for example, Michael Perlin, 'International Human Rights and Comparative Mental Disability Law: the Role of Institutional Psychiatry in the Suppression of Political Dissent' (2006) 39(3) *Israel L Rev* 69.
[78] Richard Bonnie and Svetlana Polubinskaya, 'Unraveling Soviet Psychiatry' (1999) 10 *J Contemp Leg Issues* 279, 282.
[79] UN Doc E/CN.4/Sub.2/1983/17/Rev.1 (1986) Annex II.
[80] Ibid, iii.

subversion of the political and legal guarantees of the patient's freedom; in particular, it shall never serve as an instrument for enforcing political conformity'.[81] Yet Daes' recommendations have not been fully heeded.

The practice has mainly been associated in the past with the former Soviet Union,[82] former Soviet bloc countries and China,[83] though not exclusively so. Russia reportedly continues to carry out forced psychiatric evaluations on dissidents, including Mikhail Kozenko, Pyotr Pavlensky and certain members of the feminist punk band Pussy Riot.[84] Ilmi Umerov, an ethnic Crimean Tatar activist and deputy leader of the Mejlis, a representative body elected by Crimean Tatars, spent three weeks in forced psychiatric detention in 2016.[85] In Vietnam, Bui Kim Thành, who advocates on behalf of destitute women farmers, was reportedly committed twice to a mental hospital, without having any mental illness, and was forcibly injected with drugs during her stay.[86] In 2018, the Kazakh activist and blogger Ardak Ashym was reportedly forcibly placed in a psychiatric facility for over a month and subjected to psychiatric treatment, including with psychotropic drugs.[87] Elena Urlaeva, the Uzbek campaigner against forced labour, was reportedly detained in a psychiatric prison immediately preceding meetings she was due to hold with the World Bank, the International Labour Organization and the International Trade Union Confederation to discuss forced labour in Uzbekistan.[88]

---

[81] Ibid, v.

[82] Sidney Bloch and Peter Reddaway, *Soviet Psychiatric Abuse: the Shadow Over World Psychiatry* (1st edn, Routledge 1984); see, also, 'Report of the US Delegation to Assess Recent Changes in Soviet Psychiatry', reprinted in (1989) 15(4) (Supp) *Schizophrenia Bulletin* 1.

[83] Sidney Bloch and Peter Reddaway, *Psychiatric Terror: How Soviet Psychiatry Is Used to Suppress Dissent* (Basic Books 1977); Richard Bonnie, 'Political Abuse of Psychiatry in the Soviet Union and in China: Complexities and Controversies' (2002) 30 *J Amer Acad Psychiatry & L* 136; Robin Munro, 'Judicial Psychiatry in China and Its Political Abuse' (2000) 14 *Colum J Asian L* 1.

[84] Max Seddon, 'Russian Dissident Artist Transferred to Psychiatric Ward', *Financial Times* (28 January 2016); Maryana Torocheshnikova, 'Russian Psychologists "Appalled" by Expert Analysis in Pussy Riot Case' *Radio Free Europe Radio Liberty* (14 August 2012).

[85] Amnesty International, Urgent Action: 'Activist Released from Psychiatric Detention', AI Index: EUR 50/4786/2016 (9 September 2016). See, also, Viktor Davidoff, Madeline Roache and Robert van Voren, 'Psychiatry as a Tool of Coercion in Post-Soviet States (2012–2017)', Human Rights in Mental Health and Federation Global Initiative on Psychiatry (April 2017) <www.gip-global.org/files/pol-abuse-eng-april-2017-full.pdf> accessed 30 July 2023.

[86] Pen America, 'Internet Writer Bui Kim Thành Released' (19 August 2008).

[87] HRC, 'Report of the Special Rapporteur on the Situation of Human Rights Defenders', UN Doc A/HRC/40/60 (10 January 2019) para 55.

[88] Anti-Slavery International, 'Uzbek Activist Detained for Forced Labour Monitoring' (17 March 2017).

The rationale for using psychiatry to justify arbitrary confinement is said to stem from the "unique role" of state psychiatry 'in discrediting opinion and dehumanizing those with whom one disagrees'.[89] As Alexander notes:

> If people can transform their opponents from heroes or even martyrs to lunatics in the public's view, they have accomplished a great deal. In that sense, psychiatric incarceration may occasion a greater intrusion of the rights of the politically unpopular than mere jailing. […] The conjunction of the effect of stigmatization, disagreement as to what, if anything, constitutes mental illness and the laxness of procedural protections make the use of psychiatry effective as a tool of political oppression.[90]

China has a long-standing practice of using learning and re-education camps that operate outside of the legal system to modify the behaviours of dissidents, minority ethnic and religious groups and others perceived to hold anti-government views. Persons are reportedly left to languish in the camps until officials deem them "transformed". These are not, strictly speaking, psychiatric institutions, though they reportedly operate on similar bases: individuals are involuntarily detained on the basis that their behaviours are not acceptable in open society; they are "treated" including with "psychological punishments", sterilisations and the forcible administration of electroshocks in order for the behaviour to change, and will only be released if and when officials deem them satisfactorily re-educated.[91] According to a Communist Party audio recording, the persons selected for re-education 'have been infected by an ideological illness' and therefore 'they must seek treatment from a hospital as an inpatient'. If there is a failure to eradicate the "illness", terrorist incidents will 'grow and spread all over like an incurable malignant tumor'.[92] Similarly, some Iranians protesting in the aftermath of the death in detention of Mahsa Amini for allegedly wearing her head scarf

---

[89] George Alexander, 'International Human Rights Protection against Political Abuses' (1997) 37 *Santa Clara L Rev* 387, 392, referred to in Perlin (n 77) 70.

[90] Alexander, ibid, 392, 393.

[91] HRW, '"Break Their Lineage, Break Their Roots" China's Crimes against Humanity Targeting Uyghurs and Other Turkic Muslims' (April 2021) 20; Adrian Zenz, '"Wash Brains, Cleanse Hearts": Evidence from Chinese Government Documents about the Nature and Extent of Xinjiang's Extrajudicial Internment Campaign' (2019) 7(11) *J Political Risk*; Adrian Zenz, 'Sterilizations, IUDs, and Coercive Birth Prevention: the CCP's Campaign to Suppress Uyghur Birth Rates in Xinjiang' (2020) 20(12) *China Brief*. See, also, OHCHR, 'OHCHR Assessment of Human Rights Concerns in the Xinjiang Uyghur Autonomous Region, People's Republic of China' (31 August 2022).

[92] Reported in Sigal Samuel, 'China Is Treating Islam Like a Mental Illness', *The Atlantic* (28 August 2018).

incorrectly have reportedly been sent to re-education camps, referred to as 'psychological centres', to 'educate and amend' their behaviour so that they do not turn into 'anti-social people'.[93] Iran's resort to forced psychiatric and psychological treatment of protesters has been derided because the practice contributes to 'wrongly pathologising opinions and values that differ from that of a ruling regime'.[94]

Repressive politics that understand dissent as an anathema or an illogical impossibility allow for the conclusion to be drawn that the expression of dissent is symptomatic of severe mental illness.[95]

5.2.3 Isolating dissenters and using other non-traditional forms of detention

Governments have resorted to tactics of privation to isolate dissenters from their networks and supporters. Dissenters have sometimes been arrested preventively and typically arbitrarily to stop them from taking part in demonstrations, meetings or conferences. As often they are not formally charged or brought before a judge, detentions can simply be a tactic to undermine dissenters' activities.[96] Likewise, some dissenters' work has been stifled by their being prevented from travelling outside the country to attend meetings[97] and, within the country, prevented from accessing certain parts of the country, or from taking part in certain public events, including meetings, marches and demonstrations that convey messages that are critical of the authorities.[98] And some authorities have contained large groups of protesters participating in gatherings and demonstrations on public order grounds in ways that have significantly impeded their freedoms.[99]

Restrictive forms of control orders including requiring individuals to wear tracking devices and to remain at a specified place between

---

[93] Radio Free Europe, 'Iranian Officials Say Student Protesters Arrested, Sent to Reeducation Camps' (12 October 2022).

[94] Maryam Jay et al, 'Political Abuse of Iranian Psychiatry and Psychiatric Services' (2022) 400 (10367) *Lancet* 1923.

[95] Perlin (n 77) 79.

[96] UN Special Rapporteur on the Situation of Human Rights Defenders, 'Commentary to the Declaration on the Right and Responsibility of Individuals, Groups and Organs of Society to Promote and Protect Universally Recognized Human Rights and Fundamental Freedoms' (July 2011) 28–29.

[97] UNGA, 'Human Rights Defenders', UN Doc A/61/312 (5 September 2006) paras 57–60.

[98] OSCE Office for Democratic Institutions and Human Rights (ODIHR), *Guidelines on the Protection of Human Rights Defenders* (2014) paras 231, 232.

[99] *Austin v United Kingdom* (Grand Chamber) App Nos 39692/09, 40713/09 and 41008/09 (ECtHR, 15 March 2012).

certain times are notorious for their use against terror suspects,[100] and come exceedingly close to house arrest, which has been recognised as capable of constituting a deprivation of liberty.[101] Such measures have also been applied in cases involving political opponents,[102] human rights defenders,[103] journalists and others perceived as undermining governmental regimes.[104]

Invariably, significant parts of these measures have been understood as restrictions on movement as opposed to new or *de facto* forms of detention, though the distinction, as set out in Chapter 2,[105] is not always obvious. The particular circumstances of a confinement of any kind are relevant to determining whether there is a deprivation of liberty, or whether the facts reveal a lesser or different restriction on liberty or movement.[106] There is also a need to consider holistically the practical impact on the persons directly affected of rights restrictions, however they are labelled.

5.3 The dissenters

All kinds of dissenters have been subjected to arbitrary detention to quash or stifle their dissent. The sub-sections that follow provide some non-exhaustive, illustrative examples.

5.3.1 Opposition politicians

The IACtHR, in a case concerning the 1994 extrajudicial execution of then Colombian Senator Manuel Cepeda Vargas, recognised that 'opposition voices are essential in a democratic society; without them it is not possible to reach agreements that satisfy the different visions that prevail in society', and consequently states must take positive measures to ensure that opposition

---

[100] See, *Secretary of State for the Home Department v JJ (FC)* [2007] UKHL 45. See, also, Lucia Zedner, 'Preventive Justice or Pre-Punishment? The Case of Control Orders' (2007) 60(1) *Current Legal Problems* 174; Andrew Lynch, 'Control Order in Australia: a Further Case Study in the Migration of British Counter-Terrorism Law' (2008) 8(2) *Oxford University Commonwealth LJ* 159. This is discussed further in Chapter 6: The Securitisation of Detention.

[101] WGAD, Deliberation 01: 'House Arrest', UN Doc E/CN.4/1993/24 (12 January 1993) 9.

[102] See, for example, *Navalnyy v Russia (No. 2)* App No 43734/14 (ECtHR, 9 April 2019).

[103] HRW, *'Locked Inside Our Home': Movement Restrictions on Rights Activists in Vietnam* (2022).

[104] Ibid.

[105] See section 2.6 of Chapter 2: The "detention" in arbitrary detention and its impact on arbitrariness.

[106] WGAD, 'Report of the WGAD, Deliberation No 9', UN Doc A/HRC/22/44 (24 December 2012) para 59.

individuals, groups and political parties can participate effectively in debates on matters of public interest.[107]

Opposition politicians are regularly subjected to arbitrary detention. Typically, such detention occurs in the lead up to elections.[108] It may focus on preventing persons from participating in political assemblies, rallies or meetings,[109] or may occur in the immediate period of transition following a change in government.[110] Those targeted may be officials who voice their opposing views publicly,[111] or those who are simply known to represent opposing political views. This form of repression is embodied in the physical space of Robben Island, the notorious South African prison that was home to Nelson Mandela and many of the apartheid government's highest-profile political prisoners.[112] As Mandela famously said in his inaugural speech in 1994: 'The names of those who were incarcerated on Robben Island is a roll call of resistance fighters and democrats spanning over three centuries. If indeed this is a Cape of Good Hope, that hope owes much to the spirit of that legion of fighters and others of their calibre.'[113]

In its provisional measures decision ordering the Nicaraguan government to immediately free opposition leaders, the IACtHR has explained:

> The deprivation of liberty of these persons carries with it an implicit message of intimidation, aimed at dissuading and silencing other members of the political opposition, who may see themselves at risk of being deprived of their freedom. The issue assumes special importance given the imminence of the general elections to be held this year. If this situation persists, it would be eroding the rules of democracy and the Rule of Law.[114]

---

[107] *Manuel Cepeda Vargas v Colombia* (Preliminary Objections, Merits, Reparations and Costs) Series C No 213 (IACtHR, 26 May 2010) para 173.

[108] HRW, 'Critics Under Attack Harassment and Detention of Opponents, Rights Defenders, and Journalists Ahead of Elections in Nicaragua' (2021); IRIN, 'Zimbabwe: Spate of Arrests Ahead of Elections' (5 June 2008).

[109] See, for example, *Navalnyy v Russia* (Grand Chamber) App Nos 29580/12 and four others (15 November 2018) paras 71, 72; *Kasparov v Russia* App No 53659/07 (11 October 2016) paras 56, 69.

[110] *Lutsenko v Ukraine* App No 6492/11 (ECtHR, 3 July 2012).

[111] Amnesty International, 'Silenced by Force: Politically-Motivated Arbitrary Detentions In Venezuela', AI Index: AMR 53/6014/2017 (2017); WGAD, *Opinion No 61/2018 Concerning Leila Norma Eulalia Josefa De Lima (Philippines)*, UN Doc A/HRC/WGAD/2018/61 (30 November 2018).

[112] Fran Buntman, *Robben Island and Prisoner Resistance to Apartheid* (CUP 2004).

[113] Cape Town, 9 May 1994.

[114] *J v Peru* (Request for Provisional Measures and Monitoring Compliance with Judgment) Order of the IACtHR (24 June 2022) para 41.

Sometimes, what may have started out as a lawful detention transforms into an arbitrary detention when there is a failure to release the detainee when the circumstances justifying the initial detention become inapplicable.[115] Increasingly, countries are using cynical tactics like "rotation" to maintain individuals in detention after the expiry of the maximum periods for pre-trial detention or following the dismissal of charges.[116]

The targeting through arbitrary detention of opposition members of parliament and opposition leaders and political party activists has been documented in many African countries, including Burundi,[117] Cameroon,[118] Egypt,[119] Ethiopia,[120] Rwanda,[121] Sudan,[122] Tunisia[123] and Zimbabwe.[124] The detention of opposition political figures has also featured in many countries in Asia and the Middle East, including Bahrain,[125] Cambodia,[126] China,[127] Malaysia,[128] Maldives[129] and

---

[115] *Merabishvili v Georgia (Grand Chamber)* App No 72508/13 (28 November 2017) paras 234, 235.

[116] See, for example, Committee for Justice et al, 'Joint NGO Submission for the Review of Egypt by the Human Rights Committee', 137th session (27 February to 24 March 2023) (30 January 2023); *Kavala v Türkiye* (Grand Chamber) Proceedings under Art 46(4), App No 28749/18 (11 July 2022).

[117] HRC, 'Report of the Commission of Inquiry on Human Rights in Burundi', UN Doc A/HRC/48/68 (16 September 2021) para 38; 'Report of the Commission of Inquiry on Burundi', UN Doc A/HRC/45/32 (17 September 2020) paras 32, 37, 53.

[118] OHCHR, 'Cameroon: UN Human Rights Experts Call for End to Detention and Intimidation of Peaceful Protesters' (12 October 2020).

[119] International Commission of Jurists, 'Politicized and Unfair Trials Before the Emergency State Security Court the Case of Zyad el-Elaimy' (November 2022).

[120] HRW, 'Ethiopia: Opposition Figures Held Without Charge: Police Deny Lawyers, Relatives Access; Ignore Bail Orders' (15 August 2020).

[121] HRW, 'Politician Convicted for Harming Rwanda's Image' (18 January 2023).

[122] Sudan Tribune' '88 Political Detainees Are Still in Jail: Sudanese Lawyers' (8 May 2022).

[123] AFP, 'UN Rights Chief Decries "Deepening" Tunisia Crackdown' (14 February 2023).

[124] VOA, 'Zimbabwe's Tsvangirai Detained for Second Time in Three Days' (27 October 2009); WGAD, *Opinion No 15/2009 Concerning Messrs. Lloyd Tarumbwa, Fanny Tembo and Ms. Terry Musona (Zimbabwe)*, UN Doc A/HRC/13/30/Add.1 (4 March 2010).

[125] WGAD, *Opinion No 23/2015 Concerning Sheikh Ahmed Ali al-Salman (Bahrain)*, UN Doc A/HRC/WGAD/2015/23 (17 November 2015) 194.

[126] WGAD, *Opinion No 9/2018 Concerning Kem Sokha (Cambodia)*, UN Doc A/HRC/WGAD/2018/9 (5 June 2018).

[127] WGAD, *Opinion No 23/2011 Concerning Liu Xianbin (China)*, UN Doc A/HRC/WGAD/2011/23 (28 February 2012); *Opinion No 43/2005 Concerning Mr. Peng Ming (China)*, UN Doc A/HRC/4/40/Add.1 (2 February 2007).

[128] WGAD, *Opinion No 22/2015 Concerning Anwar Ibrahim (Malaysia)*, UN Doc A/HRC/WGAD/2015/22 (2 November 2015).

[129] WGAD, *Opinion No 33/2015 Concerning Mohamed Nasheed (Maldives)*, UN Doc A/HRC/WGAD/2015/33 (10 November 2015).

Myanmar.[130] Similar practices occur in some countries in the Americas.

For example, in Venezuela opposition members of the National Assembly[131] and others[132] at different levels in the power structure[133] have been subject to a campaign of repression, including arbitrary detention. As the Chairperson on the UN Human Rights Council Fact-Finding Mission on Venezuela stated in 2021: 'Repression […] continues against individuals perceived to be "internal enemies" or opponents of the government. Criminal proceedings are ongoing in over two-thirds of the 110 cases of arbitrary detentions against political and military dissidents that we investigated for our September 2020 report.'[134] Since 2014, the Supreme Court has requested that the immunity of many National Assembly parliamentarians be lifted, on the basis that their opposition activity put them *in flagrante delicto* for allegedly committing crimes of a permanent nature. This lift of immunity, which impedes the exercise of free speech and the separation of powers, has paved the way for arrests and criminal prosecutions,[135] a practice that has been widely condemned.[136] Juan Requesens, a member of the opposition political party Primero Justicia and a member of Venezuela's National Assembly, and an outspoken critic of President Maduro, was detained, in circumstances widely held to be arbitrary,[137] on 7 August 2018, on conspiracy and treason charges related to a drone attack on a military parade attended by President Maduro. Psychotropic drugs were reportedly used to induce a confession.[138] He was

---

[130] WGAD, *Opinion No 4/2010 Concerning Dr Tin Min Htut and Mr. U Nyi Pu (Myanmar)* UN Doc A/HRC/16/47/Add.1 (2 March 2011).

[131] Inter-Parliamentary Union, Venezuela: 'Decision Adopted Unanimously by the IPU Governing Council at its 210th Session' (Kigali, 15 October 2022).

[132] WGAD, *Opinion No 75/2019 Concerning Roberto Eugenio Marrero Borjas (Bolivarian Republic of Venezuela)*, UN Doc A/HRC/WGAD/2019/75 (26 February 2020); *Opinion No 28/2021 Concerning Luis Javier Sánchez Rangel (Bolivarian Republic of Venezuela)*, UN Doc A/HRC/WGAD/2021/28 (18 November 2021).

[133] IACommHR, 'Democratic Institutions, the Rule of Law and Human Rights in Venezuela', OEA/Ser.L/V/II. Doc 209 (31 December 2017) para 163.

[134] HRC, 'Statement by Marta Valiñas, Chairperson of the Independent International Fact-Finding Mission on the Bolivarian Republic of Venezuela' (10 March 2021).

[135] HRC, 'Detailed Findings of the Independent International Factfinding Mission on the Bolivarian Republic of Venezuela', UN Doc A/HRC/45/CRP.11 (15 September 2010) A/HRC/45/CRP.11 paras 253, 608.

[136] OAS Permanent Council, 'Respect for Parliamentary Immunity in Venezuela', OEA/Ser.G CP/RES. 1136 (2245/19) (11 September 2018).

[137] See, for example, WGAD, *Opinion No 40/2019 Concerning Juan Carlos Requesens Martínez (Bolivarian Republic of Venezuela)*, UN Doc A/HRC/WGAD/2019/40 (9 October 2019); HRC, Fact-Finding Report on Venezuela (n 135) para 633; IACommHR, *Venezuela: CIDH manifiesta preocupación por la situación de diputado de la Asamblea Nacional en Venezuela* (29 August 2018); European Parliament, Resolution on the Situation in Venezuela, 2018/2891(RSP) (25 October 2018).

[138] HRC, Fact-Finding Report on Venezuela (n 135) para 283.

placed under house arrest on 28 August 2020. On 4 August 2022, he was convicted and sentenced to eight years' imprisonment.

Georgian national Tengiz Assanidze, the former mayor of Batumi and a former member of the Ajarian Supreme Council, was arrested by Ajarian authorities in October 1993 on suspicion of illegal financial dealings and the possession of firearms. Ultimately he was acquitted, and his immediate release was ordered by the Georgian Supreme Court. According to the Grand Chamber of the ECtHR, the failure of the authorities to release him following the Supreme Court's acquittal constituted a violation of Assanidze's right to liberty.[139] In another Grand Chamber case, Selahattin Demirtaş, the former co-chair of the pro-Kurdish People's Democratic Party, who had run in Turkey's presidential elections, was detained in 2016 on terrorism-related charges. In 2020, the Grand Chamber held that Turkey's detention of Demirtaş was politically motivated and aimed to prevent him from carrying out his political activities.[140] The Grand Chamber determined that the protected political expression of a political actor could not be the basis upon which to derive a reasonable suspicion related to the commission of a crime.[141] The lifting of parliamentary immunity by the Turkish constitutional amendment of 20 May 2016 by which certain members of parliament lost their immunity from prosecution, when considered alongside Demirtaş' detention and the criminal proceedings brought against him, also interfered with his freedom of expression.[142] At the time of writing, Turkey had failed to implement the ECtHR's order for Demirtaş' release, and he continues to languish in detention.[143]

5.3.2 Environmental activists

The criminalisation of activists working on land rights, climate change and associated issues connected to the protection of the environment is another area that has led to arbitrary detention and other serious violations of human rights. For instance, Ken Saro-Wiwa Jr and others who were protesting oil production in Ogoniland were arrested and kept in detention pursuant to legislation then in place in Nigeria – the State Security (Detention of Persons) Act 1984 and the State Security (Detention of Persons) Amended

---

[139] *Assanidze v Georgia* (Grand Chamber) App No 71503/01 (8 April 2004) paras 172–176.
[140] *Selahattin Demirtaş v Turkey (No.2)* (Grand Chamber) App No 14305/17 (22 December 2020).
[141] Ibid paras 422–438.
[142] Ibid para 247.
[143] *Selahattin Demirtaş v Turkey (No.2) group v Turkey* (App No 14305/17) Supervision of the Execution of the European Court's Judgments, CM/Del/Dec(2022)1451/H46–39 (8 December 2022).

Decree No. 14 (1994). The law stipulated that the government could detain persons critical to the government without charge for as long as three months without providing an opportunity to the detainees to challenge their arrest and detention before a court of law.[144] Saro-Wiwa Jr and eight others were ultimately tried by a special military 'Civil Disturbances' tribunal in relation to charges that they had incited youth to murder four Ogoni politicians.[145] They were convicted, sentenced to death and, ultimately, hanged on 10 November 1995.

Nine environmentalists, members of the Persian World Heritage Foundation, were arrested in Iran in 2018 on charges of espionage,[146] prompting UN independent experts to call for the charges to be dropped and for the defenders to be immediately released: they argued: 'It is hard to fathom how working to preserve the Iranian flora and fauna can possibly be linked to conducting espionage against Iranian interests.'[147] Among those arrested was Kavous Seyed-Emami, who founded the NGO. He was found dead in detention, with the authorities reporting that he had committed suicide. His family's request for an autopsy and formal investigation into his death was denied, with the consequence that his wife was effectively detained and ultimately prevented from leaving the country for almost two years.[148]

At the heart of the repression of environmental dissenters is the state privileging of large corporate interests, and its wish to continue to do so away from the gaze of onlookers. Notably, however, the field has become more fluid and pluralistic, reflecting a variety of interests and alliances, not all of them competing.[149]

States' responses to environmental activism are similarly varied, depending upon the state's political culture, how open it is to dissent on environmental policies, and the strategies of dissent that have been employed by environmental activists. Actions by environmental activists have ranged

---

[144] *International Pen, Constitutional Rights Project, Interights on behalf of Ken Saro-Wiwa Jr. and Civil Liberties Organisation v Nigeria*, Comm Nos 137/94, 139/94, 154/96 and 161/97, ACommHPR (31 October 1998) para 88.

[145] Amnesty International, 'Nigeria: the Ogoni Trials and Detentions', AI Index: AFR 44/020/1995 (14 September 1995); HRW, *The Ogoni Crisis: a Case-Study of Military Repression in Southeastern Nigeria* (1 July 1995); International Commission of Jurists, *Nigeria, and the Rule of Law: a Study* (1996).

[146] Radio Free Europe, 'Iran Sentences Eight Environmental Activists on Charges of Spying for U.S.' (18 February 2020).

[147] OHCHR, 'Iran: Spying Charges against Wildlife Activists "Hard to Fathom", Say UN Experts', Press Release (23 February 2018).

[148] Rhianna Schmunk, 'After 582 Days, Woman Detained in Iran After Husband's Death Reunites with Sons in Vancouver', CBC News (11 October 2019).

[149] Robert Falkner, 'Business and Global Climate Governance: a Neo-Pluralist Perspective', in Morten Ougaard and Anna Leander (eds), *Business and Global Governance* (Routledge 2010).

from simple speech acts, public campaigning, dissemination of scientific or other information to counter official versions of the truth, public protests, disruption of traffic and/or trade (tree spiking, chaining oneself to trees, damaging corporate equipment). Given that many of the defenders who work on land rights, natural resources and environmental protection come from indigenous communities, it is also relevant and important to consider the intersectional impacts of those identities on rights abuses, including arbitrary detention.[150]

Some states have termed the public statements or reports disseminated by environmental activists as slanderous and evidence of criminal activity.[151] Some have termed as 'ecoterrorism' acts of public nuisance committed by activists on behalf of, or in defence of, the environment.[152] In Chile, the Counter-Terrorism Act had been applied to individuals belonging to the Mapuche people,[153] including to the son of a Mapuche leader who had protested against illegal logging.[154] The WGAD determined that Chile's decision under the Counter-Terrorism Act to detain Francisca Linconao Huircapán, an indigenous woman, environmental defender and spiritual leader who had successfully taken legal action against economic projects to exploit natural resources constituted arbitrary detention on discriminatory grounds.[155] Likewise, villagers demonstrating against massive development projects that threaten their environment and livelihood have been charged with conducting anti-state activities.[156]

The UN Special Rapporteur on the Situation of Human Rights Defenders noted, following his visit to Colombia in 2018, that he heard testimonies that human rights defenders were criminalised in the context of social protests. In such cases, he explained:

---

[150] UNGA, 'Report of the Special Representative of the Secretary-General on Human Rights Defenders', UN Doc A/62/225 (13 August 2007) para 87.

[151] WGAD, *Opinion No 43/2022 Concerning Nguyen Ngoc Anh (Viet Nam)*, UN Doc A/HRC/WGAD/2022/43 (10 November 2022).

[152] Rob White, 'Environmental Victims and Resistance to State Crime Through Transnational Activism (2009–2010) 36(3) *Social Justice* 46, 56.

[153] OHCHR, 'UN Experts Urge Chile Not to Use Anti-Terrorism Law against Mapuche Indigenous Peoples: Chile Law Appeal', Press Release (6 October 2017); Amnesty International, 'Chile: Authorities Must Stop Criminalizing Indigenous Mapuche People under the Anti-Terrorism Law' (5 May 2018). See, also, *Norín Catrimán et al v Chile* (Merits, Reparations, and Costs) Series C No 279 (29 May 2014) para 215.

[154] HRC, 'Report Submitted by the Special Representative of the Secretary-General on Human Rights Defenders, Hina Jilani', UN Doc A/HRC/4/37 (24 January 2007) para 88.

[155] WGAD, *Opinion No 64/2018 Concerning Francisca Linconao Huircapán (Chile)*, UN Doc A/HRC/WGAD/2018/64 (28 February 2019) para 55.

[156] UNGA, 'Report of the Special Representative of the Secretary General on Human Rights Defenders', UN Doc A/58/380 (18 September 2003) para 25.

defenders might be prosecuted for the crime of rebellion (*crimen de rebellion*), conspiracy to commit a crime (*concierto para delinquir*), terrorism, public road obstruction, attempted homicide, etc. Environmental defenders have been particularly affected and criminalized for their participation in peaceful assemblies against extractive and business projects for the defence of the environment.[157]

In Ecuador, indigenous communities protesting mining and other large-scale extraction projects in their communities have been subjected to regular acts of intimidation, including arrests.[158] Protesters have been charged with crimes such as 'harm to the good of another' and 'attack or resistance'.[159] Similarly, in Guatemala, indigenous communities protesting large-scale cement projects have reportedly been detained arbitrarily,[160] as have communities protesting hydroelectric dam and other land use projects, resulting in 'disproportionate criminal charges, such as those of resistance, attack, terrorism and illegal association'.[161]

Adopted largely in response to widescale climate protests, in the UK the Public Order Act 2023 introduces new offences for protesters who cause serious disruption, such as protesters who chain themselves to others, objects, or buildings, protesters who obstruct or interfere with the construction or maintenance of major transport projects or prevent or significantly delay the operation of key infrastructure. All these offences may give rise to sentences of imprisonment.[162] The Act also authorises the courts to impose special control orders, Serious Disruption Prevention Orders, which prohibit an individual from being in a particular place, being with particular people, having particular articles in their possession, and using the internet to facilitate or encourage people to commit a protest-related

---

[157] OHCHR, 'End of Mission Statement by the United Nations Special Rapporteur on the Situation of Human Rights Defenders, Michel Forst on His Visit to Colombia' (3 December 2018).

[158] Alianza de Organizaciones por los Derechos Humanos, *Rights Defenders Under Threat in Ecuador* (June 2021) <https://amazonwatch.org/assets/files/2021–06-rights-defenders-under-threat-in-ecuador.pdf> accessed 31 July 2023.

[159] Ibid, 34.

[160] Article 19, 'A Deadly Shade of Green: Threats to Environmental Human Rights Defenders in Latin America' (2016) 40.

[161] HRC, 'Report of the UN High Commissioner for Human Rights on the Activities of Her Office in Guatemala', UN Doc A/HRC/22/17/Add.1 (7 January 2013) para 49. See, also, Compliance Advisor Ombudsman, 'Compliance Investigation Report IFC Investment in *Corporación Interamericana para el Financiamiento de Infraestructura, S.A.* (Project #26031)' (19 December 2018).

[162] Public Order Act 2023 ch 15.

offence.¹⁶³ A breach of the control order may also give rise to a sentence of imprisonment.

In Vietnam, environmental activists who spoke out about the 2016 disaster in which the Formosa steel plant discharged toxic industrial waste into the ocean, causing extensive deaths to marine life, were subjected to arbitrary detentions. For example, Nguyễn Năng Tĩnh was charged under Article 117 of the Criminal Code with 'making, storing or spreading information, materials and items for the purpose of opposing the State of the Socialist Republic of Viet Nam', and was ultimately convicted and sentenced to a lengthy term of imprisonment.¹⁶⁴ In Uganda students have protested the construction by Total Energies of the East Africa Crude Oil Pipeline, which has caused many people to be displaced from their lands. This, too, has led to arbitrary arrests.¹⁶⁵

Subjects relating to the protection of nature and the environment, health and respect for animals are issues of general concern that, in principle, enjoy a high level of protection under the right to freedom of expression. Consequently, it is recognised that protests pertaining to environmental matters constitute the manifestation of an expression of a protected opinion. However, states are entitled to intervene when activists' actions are blocking or impeding lawful activities.¹⁶⁶ The issue then becomes whether detention is ever a proportionate state response to activists who block or impede lawful activities. When the acts of such activists are framed as crimes (as they are now in the UK, with punishments of periods of imprisonment up to six and 12 months, depending on the crime), this pushes the analysis from whether detention is ever justifiable to whether detention is a proportionate response in the circumstances. This is a major shift in policy and, ultimately, will also significantly impact upon practice.

5.3.3 Mass protest movements

Many people have been arrested and detained while exercising their right to protest. Most protests are 'rooted in political, socio-economic, ethnic,

---

[163] Ibid, Arts 20–29.
[164] WGAD, *Opinion No 36/2021 Concerning Nguyễn Năng Tĩnh (Viet Nam)*, UN Doc A/HRC/WGAD/2021/36 (4 November 2021). See, also, *Opinion No 81/2020 Concerning Ho Van Hai (Viet Nam)*, UN Doc A/HRC/WGAD/2020/81 (19 February 2021); *Opinion No 36/2020 Concerning Đào Quang Thực (Viet Nam)*, UN Doc A/HRC/WGAD/2020/36 (18 September 2020).
[165] Juliet Kigongo, 'Environment Activists Demand Release of Nine Students Remanded over EACOP Protest', *The Monitor* (8 October 2022).
[166] *Drieman v Norway* App No 33678/96 (4 May 2000); *Chernega v Ukraine* App No 74768/10 (18 June 2019).

racial, religious, or other tensions specific to particular national or regional situations'[167] or they may exemplify wider concerns with networks of civil society coordinating in multiple countries. Examples of this phenomenon include 'large-scale migration, protests of climate activists, human rights defenders, indigenous peoples, […] the Black Lives Matter movement', anti-globalisation protests, women's empowerment marches, anti-war movements, all of which can be affected by excessive use of force and police brutality.[168]

The international law pertaining to protests, and the ability for a state to resort lawfully to detention as part of its response to protests, is relatively straightforward. Protesters may express dissent and voice grievances, share those views and opinions even when these go against government policy or majority opinion or cause some disruption,[169] and even when the protests are spontaneous or not authorised.[170] The right to peaceful protest requires states to allow peaceful assemblies without unwarranted interference.[171] Though national legislation often imposes significant limits on protests,[172] human rights law obligates states to put in place a legal and institutional framework within which protests can take place effectively. Police should be ensuring that peaceful protests can take place unhindered and de-escalating situations that may lead to violence.[173] The militarisation of police forces, as well as the deployment of the military to police protests, should be curtailed, since they are trained to fight against enemies and not to protect civilians.[174]

Restrictions may sometimes be required, such as blocking off streets, redirecting traffic or providing security.[175] Such restrictions must conform with the law and may only be invoked if doing so is necessary[176] and proportionate, in the sense that the type and level of the force used and the harm that may reasonably be expected to result from it is proportionate to the threat posed. Consequently, states' ability to detain persons who are peacefully protesting is extremely limited. For instance, in the WGAD's opinion concerning Can Thi Theu, which concerned the detention of a Vietnamese

---

[167] OHCHR, 'UN Experts Call for an End to Police Brutality Worldwide', Press Release (11 August 2021).
[168] Ibid.
[169] General Comment No 37 (2020) on the Right of Peaceful Assembly (Article 21), UN Doc CCPR/C/GC/37 (17 September 2020) para 7.
[170] Ibid para 14.
[171] General Comment No 37 (n 169) para 23.
[172] For example, the UK government's introduction of wide and vague new offences related to public protests and related restrictions as part of the Public Order Act 2023.
[173] General Comment No 37 (n 169) para 78.
[174] *Montero Aranguren et al. (Detention Center of Catia) v Venezuela* (Preliminary Objection, Merits, Reparations and Costs) Series C No 150 (5 July 2006) para 78.
[175] General Comment No 37 (n 169) para 24.
[176] Ibid.

human rights defender who was brandishing banners calling for the release of a human rights lawyer, and was alleged to have obstructed officials attempting to contain protestors, which the authorities contended had a negative impact on public order, the WGAD determined that the authorities had not demonstrated how Theu's participation in a demonstration constituted a real threat to public order, nor why the imposition of a 20-month sentence was a necessary and proportionate response to the temporary obstruction of traffic.[177] A deprivation of liberty as a form of punishment for organising protests, for protesting or for monitoring protests,[178] to prevent individuals from participating in protests,[179] or from continuing with peaceful protests,[180] will be arbitrary.[181] Mass, collective or indiscriminate arrests in the context of protests will similarly be arbitrary.[182]

In contrast, the ECtHR determined in *Austin v United Kingdom* that "kettling" anti-capitalism and globalisation protesters and bystanders for up to seven hours without access to food, water or toilets did not even amount to a deprivation of liberty.[183] Clearly, the practice of "kettling" was not going to fall within any of the exhaustive exceptional lawful bases for detention under Article 5(1)(a)–(f) ECHR, and instead of ruling that the detention was unlawful on that basis, the Grand Chamber took a different route and determined that there was no detention to speak of. It arrived at this decision on the basis of 'the specific and exceptional facts of this case',[184] holding that it was necessary to prevent serious injury and damage to property. But the only thing special about the case appears to be that

---

[177] WGAD, *Opinion No 79/2017 Concerning Can Thi Theu (Viet Nam)*, UN Doc A/HRC/WGAD/2017/79 (12 December 2017) paras 11, 57.

[178] *Ilgar Mammadov v Azerbaijan* App No 15172/13 (22 May 2014) para 100; WGAD, *Opinion No 12/2013 Concerning Nabeel Abdulrasool Rajab (Bahrain)*, UN Doc A/HRC/WGAD/2013/12 (25 July 2013).

[179] *Shimovolos v Russia* App No 30194/09 (21 June 2011) paras 55–57; *Rashad Hasanov v Azerbaijan* App Nos 48653/13, 52464/13 and others (7 June 2018) paras 107–108. See, also, OHCHR, 'Egypt: UN Experts Alarmed by Restrictions on Civil Society Ahead of Climate Summit', Press Release (7 October 2022).

[180] *Shomorgunov v Ukraine* App Nos 15367/14 and 13 others (ECtHR, 21 January 2021) paras 464–478.

[181] Human Rights Committee, General Comment No 35, Article 9 (Liberty and Security of Person) UN Doc CCPR/C/GC/35 (16 December 2014) para 17; WGAD, *Report of the WGAD*, UN Doc A/HRC/22/44 (24 December 2012) para 38(b). See *Servellón-García et al v Honduras* (Merits, Reparations and Costs) Series C No 152 (IACtHR, 21 September 2006) para 93.

[182] *Bulacio v Argentina* (Merits, Reparations and Costs) Series C No 100 (18 September 2003) para 137.

[183] *Austin v United Kingdom* (n 99).

[184] Ibid para 68.

the Court was looking to find a way not to find an Article 5 violation.[185] It recalls Çali's concerns about the deference shown by the Court towards the 'good faith interpreters that it trusts'.[186]

States' responses to protests will consider an array of factors. To start with, the response will depend on the extent to which the state respects the right to protest peacefully, and how it understands the parameters of that right. Some countries have highly restrictive laws pertaining to protests, with all activity falling outside the narrow space for assemblies being criminalised, and potentially resulting in the arrest and detention of individuals and groups 'solely for having organised or taken part in peaceful protests or for having observed, monitored or recorded them'.[187] As the Aban Tribunal concluded in relation to national protests in Iran in November 2019, the only type of assemblies that were capable of being authorised were political party assemblies, with prior permission. Civilian protests were not capable of authorisation under the law and, consequently, such protests – even fully peaceful ones – were classed as illegal and those participating were invariably arrested and detained.[188]

In a similar pattern, the number of persons arrested in the context of the protests following the death of Mahsa Amini approaches, according to some sources, 20,000.[189] In the "Tishreen Demonstrations" that took place in Iraq in October 2019, Iraqis were protesting about corruption, economic conditions and abuse by security forces. The government crackdowns, which followed led to around 3000 protesters arrested, 20,000 injured and 600 killed.[190] When making arrests, Iraqi police invoked the crimes of defamation, destruction of public property and, to a lesser degree, terrorism.[191] In Hong Kong, protesters were reportedly arrested for waving flags or shouting slogans about independence, in breach of the national security law.[192] In Sudan, protests that followed the October 2021 coup have led to crackdowns in

---

[185] This appears to be the worry expressed by Naomi Oreb, 'Case Comment: the Legality of Kettling after Austin' (2013) 76 *Mod L Rev* 735.

[186] Başak Çali, 'Coping with Crisis: Whither the Variable Geometry in the Jurisprudence of the European Court of Human Rights' (2018) 35(2) *Wisc Intl LJ* 237, 261.

[187] HRC, 'Summary of the Panel Discussion on the Promotion and Protection of Human Rights in the Context of Peaceful Protests, with a Particular Focus on Achievements and Contemporary Challenges', UN Doc A/HRC/50/47 (8 April 2022) para 6.

[188] Aban Tribunal Judgment (n 53) paras 87, 88.

[189] VOA News on Iran, 'Monitor: 516 Killed Since Iran Protests Began' (3 January 2023).

[190] UNAMI/OHCHR, 'Rights Violations and Abuses in the Context of Demonstrations in Iraq October 2019 to April 2020' (27 August 2020); International Crisis Group, 'Iraq's Tishreen Uprising: From Barricades to Ballot Box', Report 223 (26 July 2021).

[191] International Crisis Group, ibid, 16.

[192] Helen Davidson and Lily Kuo, 'Hong Kong: Hundreds Arrested as Security Law Comes into Effect', *The Guardian* (1 July 2020).

which scores of protesters, civilian leaders, journalists and defenders have been arrested, relying on an emergency order that permits the arrest of any person who 'participates in a crime related to [the state of emergency]'.[193]

The response to protests may also depend on factors such as how the protesters are identified and what political capital the state sees them as possessing (this may also change over time, depending on the dynamics of the protest). While the right to participate in peaceful protests applies to all persons without distinction, in practice many states will respond more harshly to typically marginalised groups with less influence or power in the society such as ethnic, religious or sexual minorities, and indigenous peoples.[194] It may also depend upon the extent to which the changes called for by protesters are understood as tolerable to the regime, or whether the changes, if implemented, are so fundamental that they would impact key policy objectives or, indeed, the credibility – or even the existence – of the regime. Over time, some peaceful protest movements take on a life of their own and have served as catalysts to end foreign military engagements, to hasten the fall of communism in parts of Eastern Europe and to foster regime changes as part of the "Arab Spring".

5.4 Ulterior or pretextual motives

The prohibition on arbitrary detention is absolute, meaning that there is no circumstance in which arbitrary detention will be considered acceptable; it is always unacceptable. Thus, detention will only be acceptable if there is a clear rationale for the detention that aligns with the limitations set out in the relevant treaty regimes. Most "dissent" cases not only involve an absence of an acceptable rationale for detention; they often turn on the existence of ulterior or pretextual motives.

The UN Human Rights Committee specifies that arbitrariness includes 'elements of inappropriateness, injustice, lack of predictability and due process of law, as well as elements of reasonableness, necessity and proportionality'.[195] It has determined that detaining individuals based on irrelevant characteristics such as political views constitutes arbitrary detention. In *Zelaya Blanco v Nicaragua*, it determined that the decision to detain without a warrant

---

[193] REDRESS, PLACE, Darfur Bar Association, and the Emergency Lawyers' Group, *'Taken from Khartoum's Streets' Arbitrary Arrests, Incommunicado Detentions, and Enforced Disappearances under Sudan's Emergency Laws* (March 2022) 3.

[194] Amnesty International, ' "So That No One Can Demand Anything": Criminalizing the Right to Protest in Ecuador?', AI Index: AMR 28/002/2012 (2012); UN Committee on the Elimination of Racial Discrimination, 'Prevention of Racial Discrimination, including Early Warning and Urgent Action Procedures: France' Statement 3 (7 July 2023).

[195] Human Rights Committee, General Comment No 35 (n 181) para 12.

Roberto Zelaya Blanco the day after the Sandinista Government assumed power, on account of his outspoken criticism of the Sandinistas, was arbitrary.[196] Similarly, the claimant in *Mukong v Cameroon* was arrested after having given an interview to a BBC correspondent in which he had criticised both the President of Cameroon and the Government. When assessing "arbitrariness", the UN Human Rights Committee determined that 'remand in custody pursuant to lawful arrest must not only be lawful but reasonable'[197] and 'necessary in all the circumstances, for example to prevent flight, interference with evidence or the recurrence of crime'.[198]

The WGAD includes, as the second of its categories of arbitrary detention, where the arrest and subsequent detention results from the detainee's exercise of other recognised rights and freedoms. Most cases involving the arbitrary detention of dissenters fall within this second category. Given the abridged working procedures of the WGAD,[199] it tends to affirm the applicability of the category simply after reviewing the allegations made and any response by the state. For example, in its opinion concerning the detention of Akzam Turgunov, the failure of the Uzbekistan Government to refute the allegations of prior intimidation and harassment and denying him an exit visa on account of Turgunov's human rights work was sufficient to place the case within the WGAD's second category of arbitrary detention.[200] In the *Yorm Bopha Case*, the WGAD clarified:

> [W]here there is prima facie reliable information that a prominent human rights defender is being deprived of liberty for a regular crime, that the conviction was not supported by reliable evidence and that, in fact, the person was punished for exercising his or her fundamental rights, the burden is on the Government to provide the WGAD with a reference to at least some of the specific evidence on which the conviction is based.[201]

---

[196] *Blanco v Nicaragua*, UN Doc CCPR/C/51/D/328/1988 (18 August 1994) para 10.3.

[197] *Mukong v Cameroon*, Comm No 458/1991, UN Doc CCPR/C/51/D/458/1991 (21 July 1994) para 9.8. See, also, *Van Alphen v The Netherlands*, Comm No 305/1988, UN Doc A/45/40 (15 August 1990) para 5.8; *Fongum Gorji-Dinka v Cameroon*, Comm No 1134/2002, UN Doc CCPR/C/83/D/1134/2002 (17 March 2005) para 5.1; *Felix Kulov v Kyrgyzstan*, Comm No 1369/2005, UN Doc CCPR/C/99/D/1369/2005 (19 August 2010) para 8.3.

[198] *Mukong v Cameroon* (n 197).

[199] HRC, 'Methods of Work of the WGAD', UN Doc A/HRC/36/38 (13 July 2017).

[200] WGAD, *Opinion No 53/2011 Concerning Akzam Turgunov (Uzbekistan)*, UN Doc A/HRC/WGAD/2011/53 (20 June 2012).

[201] WGAD, *Opinion No 24/2013 Concerning Yorm Bopha (Cambodia)*, UN Doc A/HRC/WGAD/2013/24 (14 January 2014). See, similarly, *Opinion No 21/2014 Concerning Wang Hanfei (China)*, UN Doc A/HRC/WGAD/2014/21 (21 November 2014).

The ECtHR is clear that the only detentions that comply with the Convention are those that are set out in Article 5, paragraph 1(a)–(f). As an exhaustive list, if the factual circumstances of the detention do not align with any of the enumerated exceptions, the individual's right to liberty will have been violated and the proportionality or necessity of the detention never arises.[202] Note, however, that the ECtHR has found a number of routes to avoid this formalism, such as holding that certain scenarios do not fulfil the characteristics of detention,[203] or interpreting Article 5(1)(a)–(f) as allowing for additional bases to detain when those bases stem from other applicable legal regimes.[204] Only if it is determined that a particular exception is applicable will the Court analyse the context of the detention and determine whether it satisfied the criteria of lawfulness and absence of arbitrariness (the latter of which includes an analysis of proportionality and necessity).[205]

Cases before the ECtHR involving the detention of the kinds of dissenters explored in this chapter have had little difficulty to convince the Court that none of the exceptions in Article 5(1)(a)–(c) apply to justify the detention in the first place. For instance, in the *Kavala* and *Demirtaş* cases against Turkey, in which the respective detentions were justified by Turkey on the basis that there was a reasonable suspicion of the detainees having committed an offence, the Court determined that there was no reasonable basis upon which to ground the detention.[206]

Where there is no "reasonable suspicion" that the detainee committed an offence, but this is the rationale provided by the authorities to detain, the detention will be considered arbitrary. A "reasonable suspicion" that a criminal offence has been committed 'presupposes the existence of facts or information which would satisfy an objective observer that the person concerned may have committed an offence. The question then is whether the arrest and detention were based on sufficient objective elements to justify a "reasonable suspicion" that the facts at issue had actually occurred.'[207]

---

[202] *James, Wells and Lee v United Kingdom* App Nos 25119/09 and 2 others (18 September 2012) paras 191–195.

[203] For example, *Austin v United Kingdom* (n 99).

[204] For example, *Hassan v United Kingdom*, App No 29750/09 (16 September 2004), discussed further in Chapter 6.

[205] *S, V and A v Denmark* (Grand Chamber) App Nos 35553/12, 36678/12 and 36711/12 (22 October 2018) paras 73–77.

[206] *Demirtaş* (n 51) paras 323, 331, 337, 338; *Kavala v Turkey* App No 28749/18 (10 December 2019) paras 127, 128, 131, 136, 137, 156, 157.

[207] *Włoch v Poland* App No 27785/95 (ECtHR, 19 October 2000) para 108. See, also, *Fox, Campbell and Hartley v United Kingdom* App Nos 12244/86, 12245/86, 12383/86 (ECtHR, 30 August 1990) paras 32–24; *Başer and Özçelik v Türkiye* App Nos 30694/15, 30803/15 (ECtHR, 13 September 2022) para 202.

The Court's consideration of arbitrariness in these cases stems from its conclusion that there is an absence of a reasonable basis to detain, and the decision to detain without such a reasonable basis arguably introduces *ipso facto* an element of abuse of power, bad faith or deception on the part of the authorities.[208] This is part of the reason why the ECtHR has increasingly been resorting to Article 18 (the restriction of rights for an ulterior purpose) in conjunction with Article 5 for the detention of dissenters, particularly political opponents and human rights defenders. As Çalı argues, 'it may be difficult to distinguish an act or omission that is manifestly arbitrary from one that pursues a malicious agenda beyond arbitrariness'.[209] Tsampi argues that, beyond the usual absence of a legitimate basis to detain that characterises Article 5 rulings, '[t]he finding of a violation under Article 18 implies a systemic malfunction of the State machinery, to the extent that the criminal justice system is perverted into an instrument of suppression'.[210] Thus, according to Tsampi, it is this systematicity that is captured by the Article 18 breach, which goes beyond the Article 5 context: 'Such an alarming situation, both for the democracy and the rule of law, entails the crossing of the "significantly high threshold" required by the Court for the finding of a violation of the Article 18.'[211]

5.5 Interpol and the cross-border persecution of dissenters

Dissidents, including human rights defenders, civil society activists, journalists and opposition politicians may be pursued beyond the borders of the countries in which they express dissent. This too has led to arbitrary detention. Interpol fugitive offender tracking systems circulate alerts known as "notices", which are used by police services to seek cross-border cooperation and assistance to

---

[208] This brings the analysis of cases involving the detention of dissenters in the absence of a reasonable basis to detain very close to the analysis of whether the state in proceeding with the detention was operating under an ulterior "bad faith" motive (such as punishing and silencing the dissenter and/or impeding his/her activities) in accordance with Art 18 of the Convention, in so far as the improper motive constituted a fundamental aspect of the case. This is perhaps why so many wrongful detentions of dissenters cases have proceeded under both Arts 5 and 18.

[209] Başak Çalı, 'Proving Bad Faith in International Law: Lessons from the Article 18 Case Law of the European Court of Human Rights', in Gábor Kajtár, Basak Çali and Marko Milanovic (eds), *Secondary Rules of Primary Importance in International Law: Attribution, Causality, Evidence, and Standards of Review in the Practice of International Courts and Tribunals* (OUP 2022)186.

[210] Aikaterini Tsampi, 'The New Doctrine on Misuse of Power Under Article 18 ECHR: Is It About the System of Contre-Pouvoirs Within the State After All?' (2020) 38(2) *Neth Q Hum Rts* 134, 150.

[211] Ibid.

seek the location and arrest of persons wanted for prosecution or to serve a sentence. These notices have been misused by some states to have dissenters arrested abroad on politically motivated or fabricated charges with a view to their extradition. While some of these wrongful notices have ultimately failed (on political grounds) to result in extraditions, some have succeeded. Further, the notice process has impeded many dissenters' travels and has led to many, often lengthy, arrests and detentions.[212]

By way of example, in January 2022 Serbian authorities extradited Bahraini dissident Ahmed Jaafar Mohamed Ali back to Bahrain, in violation of an injunction of the ECtHR issued only days prior, on the basis of the real risk of torture or inhuman or degrading treatment he faced if returned.[213] Uyghur activist Yidiresi Aishan was arrested by Morocco on the basis of a Chinese terrorism warrant distributed by Interpol, which cited him as being a member of a terrorist organisation.[214] While the Interpol Red Notice was ultimately cancelled, the Morocco Court of Cassation approved his extradition.[215] The Al-Jazeera journalist Ahmed Mansour was detained in Germany as a result of an Egyptian arrest warrant. He had previously been convicted by Egyptian courts *in absentia* in 2014 of torturing a lawyer in Tahrir Square in 2011.[216] He was ultimately released.

While Interpol has reformed some of its procedures to address the abuse of its procedures,[217] there is still considerable room for misuse.[218]

5.6 Conclusions

This chapter has set out the ways in which governments' targeting of activists, opposition leaders, journalists and other dissenters leads to arbitrary

---

[212] According to the organisation Fair Trials, it took Azerbaijani dissident and refugee Azer Samadov eight years to have a wrongful Interpol notice removed from its records: Fair Trials, 'Azer Samadov: Victim of INTERPOL abuse' (20 March 2018).

[213] *Mohamed v Serbia* App No 4662/22 (14 June 2022).

[214] Amnesty International, 'Morocco and Western Sahara: Ethnic Uyghur at Risk of Extradition to China: Idris Hasan (Official Name Yidiresi Aishan)', AI Index: MDE 29/5262/2022 (2 March 2022).

[215] OHCHR, 'Morocco: UN Experts Say Extradition of Uyghur Asylum Seeker to China Violates Principle of Non-Refoulement' (16 December 2021).

[216] Jared Maslin and Ben Knight, 'Al-Jazeera Journalist Ahmed Mansour Held in Germany on Egyptian Warrant', *The Guardian* (21 June 2015).

[217] Wui Ling Cheah, 'Policing Interpol: the Commission for the Control of Interpol's Files and the Right to Remedy' (2010) 7 *Intl Org L Rev* 379.

[218] Rasmus Wandall, Dan Suter and Gabriela Ivan-Cucu, 'Misuse of Interpol's Red Notices and Impact on Human Rights – Recent Developments', European Parliament, PE603.472, EP/EXPO/B/COMMITTEE/FWC/2013–08/Lot8/22 (January 2019); Fair Trials, 'Strengthening INTERPOL: an Update' (February 2018).

detention. It explains how states criminalise speech and conduct by resorting to narratives on security and defamation, how states pathologise dissent and how they deploy additional isolating tactics to impede dissenters from being able to engage effectively in their communities and societies. While at the global level the importance of fostering civil society space has been recognised and affirmed, in practice many states use detention and other forms of repression to quash voices they deem undesirable.

Regional and international courts and treaty bodies continue to issue decisions that identify instances in which dissenters have been arbitrarily detained; however, it has been difficult for them to keep pace with the scale of arbitrary detentions meted out against dissenters. To detain persons on the basis of the legitimate exercise of their fundamental right to opinion and expression, assembly, association, religion and/or privacy is arbitrary.[219] This is regardless of the efforts of an increasing number of states to criminalise speech acts and other forms of dissent. And it is irrespective of whether those states are perceived as authoritarian states, as liberal democracies, or as anything in between.

---

[219] Human Rights Committee, General Comment No 35 (n 181) paras 17, 53.

6

The Securitisation of Detention: Exceptional Regimes, Security Frameworks and Counter-Terrorism Measures

6.1 Introduction

The detention of combatants and civilians is a common feature of military, security and counter-terrorism operations. In these scenarios, each with their own permutations, the usual laws on detention may be displaced at least to an extent. This displacement stems from the special legal regimes that may apply, the exigent circumstances and the "othered" persons against whom detention is contemplated. Exigent circumstances involving "othered" persons will significantly heighten the risks of arbitrary detention. And, in these challenging, securitised contexts, some government decisions that may appear extraneous to detention can also increase the likelihood that individuals are arbitrarily detained.

In this chapter I consider how governments and others operating in these contexts address decisions to detain or to maintain in detention, and I assess the impact such decisions have on the resort to arbitrary detention. As will be argued, law and policy-makers have not sufficiently addressed the heightened risks of arbitrary detention in these situations. The designation of certain events as exigent or exceptional, while sometimes justified on the facts, can legitimise a range of ills – policies or practices that would normally be caught out by ordinary applications of the rule of law. This may reify power structures. These events, circumstances or contexts are framed as exceptional not because of their exceptional characteristics but because of the desire to legitimise the resort, as Neal explains, to 'exceptional sovereign power'[1] or, more simply put, to justify responses to such events that do not abide by the ordinary rules.

The "crisis-speak" can go beyond military or national security prerogatives, as Otto notes. Emergencies or other crises:

> have been declared with respect to issues of the everyday, such as the environment, immigration, poverty, health, and scarcities of food and water [...] crisis has provided the means of garnering new public support for racialized policing and security agencies acting outside the law, for blatant disregard of long-standing norms of human rights and fundamental freedoms, and for military and economic interventions that shore up the inequitable global order.[2]

There is thus a process of co-option or manipulation that underpins the rationale for the location and framing of the exception that is tied closely to the response of the powerful. Indeed, '[t]he tradition of the oppressed teaches us that the "state of emergency" in which we live is not the exception but the rule'.[3] Thus we must be wary of the unexceptionable exception and acknowledge its character as 'an opportunistic positionless position which recognizes that the terror in such disruption is no less than that of the order it is bent on eliminating'.[4]

There are calls and efforts to garner greater certainty, consistency and transparency about the rules governing detention particularly for non-international armed conflicts (NIACs) and other "exigent" contexts and how these rules are applied.[5] Yet the murkiness of the status quo gives

---

[1] Andrew Neal, 'Foucault in Guantánamo: Towards an Archaeology of the Exception' (2006) 37(1) *Security Dialogue* 31, 32 referring to Carl Schmitt, *Political Theology: Four Chapters on the Concept of Sovereignty* (trans. George Schwab) (MIT Press 1985).

[2] Dianne Otto, 'Decoding Crisis in International Law: a Queer Feminist Perspective', in Barbara Stark (ed), *International Law and its Discontents: Confronting Crises* (CUP 2015) 116, 117.

[3] Walter Benjamin, 'On the Concept of History' XIII, in Hannah Arendt (ed), *Illuminations* (Fontana/Collins 1973) 255–266.

[4] Mick Taussig, 'Terror as Usual: Walter Benjamin's Theory of History as a State of Siege' (1989) 23 *Social Text* 3, 4.

[5] Bruce Oswald CSC, 'Detention of Civilians on Military Operations: Reasons for and Challenges to Developing a Special Law of Detention' (2008) *Melb J Intl L* 524; Tilman Rodenhäuser, 'Strengthening IHL Protecting Persons Deprived of their Liberty: Main Aspects of the Consultations and Discussions Since 2011' (2016) 98(3) *Intl Rev Red Cross* 941. See, also, 'The Copenhagen Process on the Handling of Detainees in International Military Operations: Principles and Guidelines' (October 2012) (Copenhagen Principles and Guidelines) and Annexed Commentary, <www.onlinelibrary.iihl.org/wp-content/uploads/2021/05/Copenhagen-Process-Principles-and-Guidelines-EN.pdf> accessed 4 August 2023, Principles and Guidelines 4, Commentary paras 4.4, 4.5.

greatest flexibility and space for strategic manoeuvring, though it lends to arbitrariness.

6.2 The power of the exception and the shunning of the everyday

Much of international law is focused on responding to events understood to be crises, 'whether real or imagined'.[6] The sense of crisis permeates our understanding of space, time and personhood. It also influences what role we see for the law and the law's interaction with politics and security apparatuses.

6.2.1 The exigent exception: emergencies, exceptions and derogations

Much of the legislation put in place in response to conflict, terrorism and other security threats in recent years has been adopted through usual law-making processes.[7] However, the rationale for the introduction of such reforms is the exigent exception. New rules that provide enhanced powers to security, intelligence and policing authorities reduce the rights of categories of persons and often limit the role of the courts in providing oversight, and are justified as necessary to deal with the extraordinary situation that presents itself. Such laws and procedures often result in security detention – detaining persons said to represent a threat to national security not in contemplation of prosecution on a criminal charge.[8]

Human rights treaties tend to use the general principles of lawfulness and non-arbitrariness to assess the legality of security detention.[9] However, security detention frameworks can be just the opposite; what constitutes a threat to public security may be vaguely framed,[10] the length of detention can

---

[6] Otto (n 2) 115.

[7] Lutz Oette and Silvia Borelli, 'Extraordinary Measures, Predictable Consequences: Security Legislation and the Prohibition of Torture', REDRESS (2012) 7.

[8] Steven Greer, 'Preventive Detention and Public Security – Towards a General Model', in Andrew Harding and John Hatchard (eds), *Preventive Detention and Security Law* (Brill/Nijhoff 1993) 23–39.

[9] WGAD, 'Deliberation No 9 Concerning the Definition and Scope of Arbitrary Deprivation of Liberty under Customary International Law', HRC, 'Report of the Working Group on Arbitrary Detention', UN Doc A/HRC/22/44 (24 December 2012) paras 61–63; IACommHR, 'Report on Terrorism and Human Rights', OEA/Ser.L/V/II.116 (22 October 2002) para 378.

[10] HRC, 'Report of the Special Rapporteur on the Promotion and Protection of Human Rights and Fundamental Freedoms While Countering Terrorism, Mission to Egypt', UN Doc A/HRC/13/37/Add.2 (14 October 2009) para 20; HRC, 'Report of the Special Rapporteur on the Promotion and Protection of Human Rights and Fundamental Freedoms While Countering Terrorism, Visit to Sri Lanka', UN Doc A/HRC/40/52/Add.3 (14 December 2018) para 13.

be open-ended,[11] opening up the prospect for indefinite detention, and the judiciary's powers of oversight may be significantly curtailed.[12] As was set out in Chapter 5, security discourses can also be co-opted to undermine dissent.

The Human Rights Committee makes clear that:

> [Security] detention would normally amount to arbitrary detention as other effective measures addressing the threat, including the criminal justice system, would be available. If, under the most exceptional circumstances, a present, direct and imperative threat is invoked to justify the detention of persons considered to present such a threat, the burden of proof lies on States parties to show that the individual poses such a threat and that it cannot be addressed by alternative measures, and that burden increases with the length of the detention. States parties also need to show that detention does not last longer than absolutely necessary, that the overall length of possible detention is limited and that they fully respect the guarantees provided for by article 9 in all cases.[13]

An exception is the ECHR, which provides for an exhaustive list of lawful forms of detention (which does not include security detention); detention that falls outside what is listed will be impermissible unless the state has made a specific derogation, with minimal exceptions for IHL-compliant detentions in international armed conflicts (IACs).[14]

The state of emergency is the rationale for the adoption of security legislation that derogates from those usual, permissible limitations.[15] When

---

[11] Mission to Egypt (n 10) para 21; Mission to Sri Lanka (n 10) para 15.

[12] Mission to Sri Lanka (n 10) para 13.

[13] Human Rights Committee, General Comment No 35, Article 9 (Liberty and Security of Person) (16 December 2014) UN Doc CCPR/C/GC/35 para 15.

[14] In *Hassan*, which involved a civilian detained by British forces in Iraq on security grounds when the armed conflict was considered international in character, the ECtHR recognised that there was no need for the UK to derogate from Art 5 (liberty and security of the person) when it is a party to an IAC, so long as it complies with the rules of detention stipulated in the third and fourth Geneva Conventions: *Hassan v United Kingdom* App No 29750/09 (ECtHR, 16 September 2004) para 97. Derogations under the ECHR are crucial, however, for detentions in NIACs where the ordinary human rights rules on liberty and security of the person will invariably apply but for a valid derogation: *Al-Jedda v United Kingdom* (Grand Chamber) App No 27021/08 (ECtHR, 7 July 2011) paras 98–99.

[15] ICCPR, ECHR and ACHR derogation clauses provide that certain measures, which would normally violate the treaty would not constitute violations if those measures were taken in exceptional situations and only to the extent absolutely necessary. Other human rights treaties rely only on the general limitation clauses which outlaw arbitrary interference with rights (for example, Art 27(2) ACHPR; Arts 15, 16 ACHR; Art 24(7) Arab Charter on Human Rights (adopted 15 September 1994, League of Arab States); Arts 12(3), 17, 21, 22 ICCPR.

faced with a genuine, public emergency that 'threatens the life of the nation', some international human rights treaties – and many national constitutions – permit states to suspend the protection of certain human rights, to the extent that the measures to be introduced are strictly required by the exigencies of the situation.[16] Derogations are frequently resorted to in the aftermath of military coups or coup attempts,[17] terrorist attacks[18] and military invasions.[19] They can also be resorted to following natural disasters, health or other emergencies.

The Human Rights Committee has held that derogations cannot exceed those strictly required by the exigencies of the situation, and 'must be consistent with states' other obligations under international law, including provisions of international humanitarian law relating to deprivation of liberty, and nondiscriminatory.'[20] It should be underscored that no situation of insecurity or lawfully declared state of emergency can validate arbitrary detention, which is never permissible.[21] Likewise, given its essential role in protecting non-derogable rights, the right to be brought before a judge at the earliest opportunity to challenge the legality of detention (*habeas corpus*, *amparo*) cannot be derogated from in an emergency.[22] This has been recognised by the Inter-American system for the protection of human rights,[23] the

---

[16] Art 4 ICCPR; Art 15 ECHR; Art 27 ACHR.

[17] For example, the 2016 failed coup attempt in Turkey. See, *Mehmet Hasan Altan v Turkey* App No 13237/17 (ECtHR, 20 March 2018) paras 91–93; *Şahin Alpay v Turkey* App No 16538/17 (ECtHR, 20 March 2018) paras 75–77.

[18] For example, UK derogation from the ECHR regarding Northern Ireland: *Ireland v United Kingdom* App No 5310/71 (ECtHR, 18 January 1978) paras 205, 212; *Brannigan and McBride v United Kingdom* App Nos 14553/89, 14554/89 (ECtHR, 26 May 1993) para 48. See, also, *A v United Kingdom* (Grand Chamber) App No 3455/05 (ECtHR, 19 February 2009) where the Grand Chamber gives the state a wide margin of appreciation in assessing whether the life of the national was threatened 'as the guardian of their own people's safety' (para 175) though ultimately it finds the derogation invalid.

[19] Ukraine notified the UN Secretary-General of its derogation from certain articles of the ICCPR, following Russia's military invasion in March 2022. See, *Ukraine: Notification under Article 4(3)*, UN Doc C.N.65.2022.TREATIES-IV.4, 4132/28-110-17626 (Depositary Notification) (1 March 2022).

[20] General Comment No 35 (n 13) para 65. See, also, Human Rights Committee, General Comment No 29: Derogations During a State of Emergency (31 August 2001) UN Doc CCPR/C/21/Rev.1/Add.1, para 11.

[21] *Lindo v Peru*, IACommHR, Case 11.182, Report No 49/00 (IACommHR, 13 April 2000) paras 84–86. See, also, Human Rights Committee, General Comment No 35 (n 13) para 66.

[22] Human Rights Committee, General Comment No 29 (n 20) para 16.

[23] *Habeas Corpus in Emergency Situations*, Advisory Opinion OC-8/87 (IACtHR, 30 January 1987) paras 35, 43 and *Judicial Guarantees in States of Emergency*, Advisory Opinion OC-9/87 (IACtHR, 16 October 1987) paras 38–40; *Neira-Alegría et al. v Peru* (Merits) Series C No 20 (IACtHR, 19 January 1995) para 84.

ACommHPR[24] and the ECtHR.[25]

The Human Rights Committee has been relatively robust in its consideration of states' notifications of derogations to the ICCPR.[26] In contrast, the ECtHR's approach to derogations has afforded states a wide margin of appreciation both in relation to the qualification of the emergency and the measures taken,[27] which has been criticised by some commentators as being too deferential, allowing for too much limitation of rights on the basis of executive assertions of power. The Court has been accused in its early cases of 'having applied a level of scrutiny sufficient to deter flagrant abuse of the derogation privilege' but applying 'standards which remain disturbingly vague and inconsistent'[28] and, more recently, of affording states an overly wide margin of appreciation in determining whether the test for derogation is met.[29]

At times the due deference afforded to states in emergency situations has led courts to refrain from inquiring behind the lawfulness of detentions occurring in such contexts or conducting only superficial inquiries that have the effect of legitimising arbitrary detentions. The same deference is often at play with domestic courts, guided as they are by principles of the separation of powers, political questions and non-justiciability doctrines that insulate certain types of governmental action from review by the courts by invoking 'general notions of governmental expertise or superior democratic credentials', and 'effectively plac[ing] administrative discretion beyond the purview of the rule of law'.[30] An egregious example of this is *Korematsu v*

---

[24] *Amnesty International v Sudan*, Comm Nos 48/90, 50/91, 52/91, 89/93, 26th sess. (1–15 November 1999) paras 59, 60; *Constitutional Rights Project and Civil Liberties Organisation v Nigeria*, Comm Nos 143/95, 159/96, 26th sess. (1–15 November 1999) para 31.

[25] *Lawless v Ireland (No. 3)* App No 332/57 (ECtHR, 1 July 1961) para 14; *Ireland v UK* (n 18) paras 199, 200.

[26] Human Rights Committee, General Comment No 29 (n 20) para 3; *Camargo (on behalf of Suarez de Guerrero) v Colombia*, UN Doc CCPR/C/15/D/45/1979 (31 March 1982).

[27] *A v UK* (n 18) para 180 (though ultimately finding that, while there had been a public emergency threatening the life of the nation, the measures taken in response, which consisted of the indefinite detention of non-nationals, were discriminatory and had thus not been strictly required by the exigencies of the situation). See, also, *Brannigan and McBride v UK* (n 18).

[28] Joan Hartman, 'Derogation from Human Rights Treaties in Public Emergencies – A Critique of Implementation by the European Commission and Court of Human Rights and the Human Rights Committee of the United Nations' (1981) 22 *Harv Intl LJ* 1, 3.

[29] Emre Turkut, 'The Turkish Post-Coup Emergency and European Responses: Shortcomings in the European System Revisited' (2022) *Eur Ybk Hum Rts* 445.

[30] TRS Allan, 'Human Rights and Judicial Review: a Critique of Due Deference' (2006) *Cambridge Law Journal* 671.

United States,[31] in which the US decided that it would not look behind the view taken by the military and Congress that it was impossible for military authorities to immediately segregate disloyal from loyal Japanese Americans,[32] and thus justifying a widescale policy of internment.

6.2.2 The exception of place: denial of extraterritoriality

The sense of place underpins how we understand where threats of insecurity come from and frames the responses to those threats.

Sites of exception are places that most exemplify the politics of exceptionalism, and increasingly these are associated with detention. They are the Soviet Gulag, the Nazi concentration camp, the detention centre at Guantánamo Bay, the Khmer Rouge's Tuol Sleng, Bosnia and Herzegovina's Omarska camp, South Africa's Robben Island, and the stadiums, military grounds, and naval vessels used by the Dirección de Inteligencia Nacional (DINA) in Pinochet's Chile. They are set up as places where the ordinary rules can be bypassed, because of who is detained there (the *homo sacer* of the day[33]; today the marginalised and racialised "other", the migrant, the non-citizen), or because of where the sites are located (outside the boundaries of where the ordinary rules apply).[34]

Spatial techniques are used to demarcate the boundaries where the law is said to apply. There are two countervailing tendencies that, when operating in tandem, produce the perfect conditions for impunity.

First, there is the tendency in highly securitised contexts for hegemonic states to frame the boundaries in which they exercise power as beyond the territorial confines of the state. The context they are seeking to address is framed as global or, at least, transnational and, consequently, they assert, the response to such events should not be confined by the classical territorial limits of the state. Sometimes this will entail military aggression, such as Russia's invasion of Ukraine or the invasion by US-led coalition forces of Iraq, both of which involved wide-scale resort to arbitrary detention.[35] Or,

---

[31] *Korematsu v United States*, 323 US 214 (1944).

[32] Ibid, 223.

[33] Giorgio Agamben, *Homo Sacer: Sovereign Power and Bare Life* (trans. Daniel Heller-Roazen, Stanford University Press 1998); Giorgio Agamben, *State of Exception* (trans Kevin Attell) (University of Chicago Press 2005).

[34] Derek Gregory, 'The Black Flag: Guantánamo Bay and the Space of Exception' (2006) 88(4) *Geografiska Annaler. Series B, Human Geography* 405; Claudia Aradau, 'Law Transformed: Guantanamo and the "Other" Exception' (2007) 28(3) *Third World Quarterly* 489.

[35] HRC, 'Report of the Independent International Commission of Inquiry on Ukraine', UN Doc A/77/533 (18 October 2022) paras 75–80; Brian Bill, 'Detention Operations in Iraq: a View from the Ground' (2010) 86 *Intl Law Stud* 411.

it may involve other forms of extraterritorial military action, such as drone strikes and targeted killings, hostage-taking and renditions, extraterritorial involvements in NIACs, or proxy warfare by training and equipping foreign militaries and security agencies, or non-state armed groups.[36] At times these extraterritorial forays gain legitimacy through the involvement and support of regional and international organisations, such as UN Security Council mandated actions pursued under the guise of addressing threats to international peace and security, and other military, peace-enforcement or security mandates pursued by NATO (North Atlantic Treaty Organization) and regional and sub-regional organisations such as the African Union, the Economic Community of West African States or the European Union.[37]

Another example is the global framing of the terrorism threat that has influenced recent counter-terrorism responses, particularly the US's global war on terror in the aftermath of the 11 September 2001 terrorist attacks. The associated detention policy took many forms. The US Central Intelligence Agency (CIA) established its own secret detention facilities to interrogate so-called "high value detainees". It also transferred people to other states with poor human rights records to secretly detain and interrogate persons on its behalf.[38] When the conflicts in Afghanistan and Iraq started, the US also secretly held persons in battlefield detention sites for prolonged periods of time.[39] Certainly, these framings have been helped by hegemonic

---

[36] Peter Rowe, 'Is There a Right to Detain Civilians by Foreign Armed Forces During a Non-International Armed Conflict?' (2012) 61(3) *Intl & Comp LQ* 697; HRC, 'Follow-up Report to the Joint Study on Global Practices in Relation to Secret Detention in the Context of Countering Terrorism, Report of the Special Rapporteur on the Promotion and Protection of Human Rights and Fundamental Freedoms While Countering Terrorism, Fionnuala Ní Aoláin', UN Doc A/HRC/49/45 (25 March 2022); Rights & Security International, 'Europe's Guantanamo: the Indefinite Detention of European Women and Children in Northeast Syria' (17 February 2021) <www.rightsandsecurity.org/assets/downloads/Europes-guantanamo-THE_REPORT.pdf> accessed 5 August 2023.

[37] Jacques Hartmann, 'Detention in the Context of Multinational Military Operations', in Heike Krieger and Robin Geiss (eds), *The Legal Pluriverse Surrounding Extraterritorial Military Operations* (OUP 2020).

[38] In the update to the Joint Study on Global Practices, the Special Rapporteur on Human Rights and Counter-Terrorism listed the following countries as engaged in secret detention practices: Algeria, China, the Democratic Republic of the Congo, Egypt, Equatorial Guinea, Eritrea, the Gambia, India, Iran (Islamic Republic of), Iraq, Israel, Jordan, Libya, Nepal, Pakistan, the Philippines, the Russian Federation, Saudi Arabia, Sri Lanka, the Sudan, the Syrian Arab Republic, Turkmenistan, Uganda, Uzbekistan, Yemen and Zimbabwe: HRC, 'Follow-Up Report to the Joint Study on Global Practices in Relation to Secret Detention' (n 36) para 9.

[39] HRC, 'Joint Study on Global Practices in Relation to Secret Detention in the Context of Countering Terrorism of the Special Rapporteur on the Promotion and Protection of Human Rights and Fundamental Freedoms While Countering Terrorism, Martin Scheinin and Others', UN Doc A/HRC/13/42 (20 May 2010) paras 102, 141.

positionalities, though this does not detract from their salience as strategies to apply to "othered" individuals and groups. At the time of writing, almost 25 years after the September 2001 attacks, individuals, many not even charged with an offence, remain arbitrarily detained at Guantánamo Bay.

Second, there is the opposite, but very much connected, tendency for states to frame their human rights obligations as narrowly as possible. These they frame territorially, taking advantage of a general presumption against extraterritorial application of laws, despite the wording of most human rights treaties about their application both within the territory and subject to the state's jurisdiction, which has been taken to include circumstances when the state is exercising effective control extraterritorially.[40] This has been a strategy used in relation to security and military operations taking place outside states' national borders, as has the resort by the US government to "extraordinary rendition" to move suspects from one jurisdiction to other countries with a long history of torturing prisoners. This is done to enable (or at least to operate in an ambivalent grey zone in which the law does not strictly prohibit or the reach of the law is more tenuous) extra-legal interrogations that would otherwise not comply with domestic constitutional law if conducted on domestic soil. Similarly, the US government has housed detainees at the detention centre at Guantánamo Bay, Cuba and elsewhere[41] to avoid the reach of the US Constitution and the implementation of the right to *habeas corpus* or to a speedy trial.[42] Eventually, judgments like *Rasul v Bush* recognised that Guantánamo detainees were entitled to challenge the lawfulness of their detention.[43] Yet, more than 20 years after many of the individuals were first detained, the problem is the failure to give practical meaning to *habeas corpus* and a host of other rights.

---

[40] See, generally, Marko Milanovic, *Extraterritorial Application of Human Rights Treaties: Law, Principles, and Policy* (OUP 2011).

[41] Other securitised locations of detention where similar extra-legal arguments have been made include the detention facility run by US CIA operatives at Bagram airbase, Afghanistan, and the facility on the island of Diego Garcia. See, for example, *Al Maqaleh v Gates*, 605 F.3d 84 (DC Cir 2010); Reprieve, 'Ghost Detention on Diego Garcia' (2008).

[42] Memorandum of Patrick F Philbin, Deputy Assistant Attorney General, and John Yoo, Deputy Assistant Attorney General, to William J Haynes II, 'Possible Habeas Jurisdiction over Aliens Held in Guantanamo Bay, Cuba' (28 December 2001) <https://nsarchive2.gwu.edu/torturingdemocracy/documents/20011228.pdf> accessed 5 August 2023.

[43] *Rasul v Bush*, 542 US 466 (2004) (the US Supreme Court determined that, because of the complete jurisdiction and control the US government exercised over the naval base, the detention centre was not extraterritorial for the purposes of applying the federal habeas statute). See, also, *Boumediene v Bush*, 553 US 723 (2008).

These spatial techniques, however inconsistent, may work well with local electorates or courts, but have less success with regional and international courts and treaty bodies, given their relatively clear recognition of extraterritorial obligations. The latter have found situations, such as military occupations in which the level of the control exercised by a state is sufficient to render at least some of its human rights obligations applicable extraterritorially, including those relating to the treatment of persons in detention.[44] Even where a state operating extraterritorially exercises something less than effective control over an area, it may still incur state responsibility for its role in aiding or assisting another state in the commission of a wrongful act where this aiding or assisting was done with the knowledge of the circumstances of the wrongful act and the act would be internationally wrongful if it committed the act directly.[45]

These principles of responsibility have given rise to new political narratives about the imperatives for derogation. Where derogation too is still too feeble a solution, some states have resorted to exceptionalist reframings and, ultimately, have called for the renouncement of membership in certain treaties or international institutions.

6.2.3 The person as exception: "terrorists", "non-combatants" and other rhetorical labels

Part of the narrative of exception focusses on the status of the person or group being subjected to the exceptional practice. They are "other", typically marginalised, discriminated against, and sometimes feared, the Schmittian 'outlaw of humanity'[46] and Agamben's *homo sacer* stripped of political and legal attributes.[47] Their identity is part of the rationale to deploy the exception. Certainly, some exemptions are justifiable restrictions, such as the right to vote in national elections (often limited to citizens) or the need for migrants to have special permission to enter the territory that citizens or long-term residents do not require. Other more dubious distinctions, such as invoking a power to detain indefinitely through house arrest and electronic tagging

---

[44] *Al-Skeini v United Kingdom* (Grand Chamber) App No 55721/07 (ECtHR, 7 July 2011) paras 136–140, 149–150.

[45] ILC, 'Articles on the Responsibility of States for Internationally Wrongful Acts', Report of the International Law Commission on the Work of Its 53rd Session (23 April–1 June and 2 July–10 August 2001) UN Doc A/CN.4/SER.A/2001/Add.1 [ARS] Art 16.

[46] Carl Schmitt, *The Concept of the Political* (trans. George Schwab) (expanded edn, University of Chicago Press 2007) 54, 79. Note however, Schmitt's Nazi affiliations, which underpin his ideas and the corpus of his work. See Joseph Weiler, 'Cancelling Carl Schmitt?' *EJIL:Talk!* (13 August 2021).

[47] Agamben, *Homo Sacer* (n 33).

only non-nationals,[48] or classifying the context after the 11 September 2001 terrorist attacks as a global war on terrorism, but without recognising for the principal non-citizen combatants the usual status under IHL related to IACs,[49] can be discriminatory and incompatible with constitutional principles.

Commenting on then US President Bush's military order of 13 November 2001 authorising the indefinite detention and trial by military commissions of non-citizen terror suspects with minimal procedural guarantees,[50] Agamben writes:

> [I]t radically erases any legal status of the individual, thus producing a legally unnamable and unclassifiable being. Not only do the Taliban captured in Afghanistan not enjoy the status of POWs as defined by the Geneva Convention, they do not even have the status of persons charged with a crime according to American laws. Neither prisoners nor persons accused, but simply "detainees", they are the object of a pure de facto rule, of a detention that is indefinite not only in the temporal sense but in its very nature as well, since it is entirely removed from the law and from judicial oversight. The only thing to which it could possibly be compared is the legal situation of the Jews in the Nazi Lager [camps], who, along with their citizenship, had lost every legal identity, but at least retained their identity as Jews. As Judith Butler has effectively shown, in the detainee at Guantánamo, bare life reaches its maximum indeterminacy.[51]

The titles "terrorist" or "non-combatant" given to these "othered" groups are too often simply rhetorical labels that operate as mediatic devices to sway public opinion and justify government policy. Whether to distinguish treatment based on categories of persons is accepted as lawful and appropriate by the courts is a secondary consideration. The establishment at Guantánamo Bay of a prison where legal safeguards do not apply is a consequence of the US's war on terror with its "us vs them" clash of civilisations ethos. The US administration's position appears to be that persons who took up arms in the "war on terror" without complying with the customary prerequisites for belligerent immunity, and were then captured, are "unlawful

---

[48] *A v Secretary of State for the Home Department* [2004] UKHL 56, paras 97, 132, 158.
[49] While parts of the then war against the then Taliban government in Afghanistan could be framed as an IAC, the US war against Al Qaeda would invariably be considered a NIAC (with extraterritorial components) if it is considered a conflict at all. See, for example, Adam Roberts, 'The Laws of War in the War on Terror' (2003) 79 *Intl Law Studies* 175.
[50] Military Order of 13 November 2001: Detention, Treatment, and Trial of Certain Non-Citizens in the War against Terrorism, 3 CFR 918 (2001).
[51] Agamben, *State of Exception* (n 33) 3–4.

combatants" without rights under the Geneva Conventions, including the basic protections under Common Article 3. However, there is no person or group that is wholly outside the law.[52] At least, such persons are still covered by minimum standards of humane treatment in Additional Protocol 1, which makes clear that persons arrested, detained or interned must be 'released with the minimum delay possible and in any event as soon as the circumstances justifying the arrest, detention or internment have ceased to exist'.[53] The use of a war narrative to characterise the struggle against international terrorism has been widely rejected.[54]

The persons doing the detaining have also widened under this securitised framing. It is not just law enforcement (in peacetime) or military officials (during NIACs or IACs) detaining persons in accordance with the limits of IHL. The context of terrorism and national insecurity has increased the prominence of security and intelligence agencies carrying out detentions and officials of one state detaining suspects at the request of the agents of another, both scenarios with much weaker frameworks for oversight.

6.2.4 *The exception of law: lawfare and other narrative devices*

The importance of the rule of law to the proper functioning of democracies has been affirmed by the UN[55] and the Council of Europe's Venice Commission,[56] among others. Respect for the rule of law means that even the rights and interests of those who are derided in society are safeguarded

---

[52] Silvia Borelli, 'Casting Light on the Legal Black Hole: International Law and Detentions Abroad in the "War on Terror"' (2005) 87 (857) *Intl Rev Red Cross* 37. This point is also made in the original Commentary to the Fourth Geneva Convention: 'Every person in enemy hands must have some status under international law: he is either a prisoner of war and, as such, covered by the Third Convention, a civilian covered by the Fourth Convention, or again, a member of the medical personnel of the armed forces who is covered by the First Convention. There is no intermediate status; nobody in enemy hands can be outside the law': Jean Pictet (ed), *Commentary on Geneva Convention Relative to the Protection of Civilian Persons in Time of War* (ICRC 1958) 51.

[53] Protocol Additional to the Geneva Conventions of 12 August 1949, and relating to the Protection of Victims of International Armed Conflicts (adopted 8 June 1977, entered into force 7 December 1978) 1125 UNTS 3 (AP1) Art 75(3).

[54] Commission on Human Rights, 'Situation of Detainees at Guantánamo Bay', UN Doc E/CN.4/2006/120 (26 February 2006) paras 22–26, 83. See, also, WGAD, *Opinion No 89/2017 Concerning Ammar al Baluchi (USA)*, UN Doc A/HRC/WGAD/2017/89 (24 January 2018) para 42.

[55] UN Secretary-General, 'The Rule of Law and Transitional Justice in Conflict and Post-Conflict Societies', UN Doc S/2004/616 (23 August 2004).

[56] Venice Commission, 'Report on the Rule of Law', CDL-AD(2011)003rev-e (Venice, 25–26 March 2011).

in the same way as anyone else. Yet, the principle of equal rights for all is most vulnerable in times of conflict and insecurity.

During periods of exception, legislation is often introduced that seeks to restrict access to justice, constrain the powers of the courts to decide or award remedies, and/or introduces new arbitrary powers. This is done by introducing emergency legislation and formal derogation processes, as already discussed,[57] though such measures still have to respect the overriding conditions of lawfulness and non-arbitrariness.

Exceptionalism has also been advanced by the rhetoric and actions of politicians wishing to put an end to what they perceive as an encroaching, unhelpful hyper-legalism.[58] They have sought to concentrate power in the hands of the executive and simultaneously block or severely limit the role of the judicial and legislative branches of government, which traditionally afford the safeguards for the rule of law. This rhetoric has been progressed with the help of arguments that legal principles have been used strategically as a substitute for traditional military means to achieve an operational objective[59] or, more broadly, the instrumentalisation of the law to constrain the legitimate and necessary actions of militaries and other security agencies. This anti-encroachment of the law or, to some, an anti-law agenda, has fit in easily with the populist politics against "wokeness" and a hyper-educated, cosmopolitan "elite" that is out of touch with "real people", which pervades some societies.[60]

It is also exhibited by over-cautious courts refraining from adjudicating or exhibiting extreme deference when adjudicating matters involving political questions[61] despite the major ramifications for individuals' safety, freedom

---

[57] See section 6.2.1 of this chapter.
[58] David Luban, 'Carl Schmitt and the Critique of Lawfare' (2010) 43 *Case W Res J Intl L* 457, 458–460.
[59] Charles Dunlap Jr, 'Law and Military Interventions: Preserving Humanitarian Values in 21st Century Conflicts', Address at the Humanitarian Challenges in Military Intervention Conference, Harvard Carr Center (29 November 2001). See, also, Charles Dunlap Jr, 'Lawfare: a Decisive Element of 21st Century Conflicts?' (2009) 54 *Joint Force Quarterly* 34; Orde Kittrie, *Lawfare: Law as a Weapon of War* (OUP 2017).
[60] Randy Barnett et al, 'Law, Social Justice, Wokeness and the Protests: Where Do We Go from Here?' (2021) 33(2) *Regent U L Rev* 315; Bart Cammaerts, 'The Abnormalisation of Social Justice: the "Anti-Woke Culture War" Discourse in the UK' (2022) 33(6) *Discourse & Society* 730.
[61] Samuel Issacharoff and Richard Pildes, 'Between Civil Libertarianism and Executive Unilateralism: an Institutional Process Approach to Rights During Wartime' (2004) 5 *Theoretical Inquiries L* 1; Stephen Cody, 'Dark Law: Legalistic Autocrats, Judicial Deference, and the Global Transformation of National Security' (2021) 6(4) *U Pa JL & Pub Aff* 643; Rodric Schoen, 'A Strange Silence: Vietnam and the Supreme Court' (1884) 33 *Washburn LJ* 275, 278–303.

and autonomy.[62] Hill-Cawthorne makes this point in respect of the ongoing litigation concerning Guantánamo Bay detainees. As the US government has continued to maintain that the "war on terror" constitutes an ongoing conflict, US courts have refrained from scrutinising substantive challenges pertaining to the length of detention (for many now exceeding 20 years). In *Al Hela*, the Circuit Court held:

> Courts lack the authority or the competence to decide when hostilities have come to an end. The 'termination' of hostilities is 'a political act'. [...] [s]o long as the record establishes the United States military is involved in combat against Al Qaeda, the Taliban, or associated forces, we have no warrant to second guess fundamental war and peace decisions by the political branches.[63]

6.3 Detention during armed conflicts

Arbitrary detention (referred to as unlawful confinement in certain IHL texts) is prohibited in situations of armed conflict, both in IACs and NIACs.[64]

With respect to IACs, all four 1949 Geneva Conventions safeguard against unlawful and arbitrary detention by stipulating the grounds on which persons may be detained by a party to the conflict,[65] as well as the procedural guarantees that detainees must be afforded. The rules are status-based and

---

[62] See, however, Andrew Kent, 'Disappearing Legal Black Holes and Converging Domains: Changing Individual Rights Protection in National Security and Foreign Affairs' (2015) 115 *Columbia L Rev* 1029, who argues differently that there is a progressive trajectory toward the closing of legal black holes.

[63] *Al-Hela v Trump* (2020) 972 F.3d 120, 135 (referred to in Lawrence Hill-Cawthorne, 'Detention in the Context of Counterterrorism and Armed Conflict: Continuities and New Challenges' (2021) 103(916–917) *Intl Rev Red Cross* 555, 561.

[64] ICRC, 'Customary International Law Database' (undated) Rule 99 <www.icrc.org/customary-ihl/eng/docs/home> accessed 5 August 2023.

[65] Convention (I) for the Amelioration of the Condition of the Wounded and Sick in Armed Forces in the Field (adopted 12 August 1949, entered into force 21 October 1950) 75 UNTS 31 (GC1) Arts 28, 30, 32 (regarding the detention of medical and religious personnel); Convention (II) for the Amelioration of the Condition of Wounded, Sick and Shipwrecked Members of Armed Forces at Sea (adopted 12 August 1949, entered into force 21 October 1950) 75 UNTS 85 (GC2) Arts 36, 27 (regarding the detention of medical and religious personnel of hospital ships); Convention (III) relative to the Treatment of Prisoners of War (adopted 12 August 1949, entered into force 21 October 1950) 75 UNTS 135 (GC3) Arts 21, 90. 95, 103, 109, 118 (regarding the internment of prisoners of war for the duration of active hostilities); Convention (IV) relative to the Protection of Civilian Persons in Time of War (adopted 12 August 1949, entered into force 21 October 1950) 75 UNTS 287 (GC4) Arts 27(4), 42, 78 (regarding the internment or placement in an assigned residence of civilians).

depend on whether the detainees are combatants or civilians. Combatants who have been placed *hors de combat* through capture or injury are treated as prisoners of war and are protected under the Third Geneva Convention.[66] Prisoners of war may be detained until the end of active hostilities, after which time they must be released and where appropriate, repatriated. An unjustifiable delay in their release and repatriation would constitute a grave breach under Additional Protocol 1,[67] and continued detention would constitute arbitrary detention.[68] In contrast, civilian detainees are protected under the Fourth Geneva Convention. Civilians may only be detained where strictly required, where 'absolutely necessary', or only where there are 'serious and legitimate reasons'.[69] The Fourth Geneva Convention specifies that a civilian may only be interned or placed in assigned residence if 'the security of the Detaining Power makes it absolutely necessary'[70] or, in occupied territory, on an exceptional basis,[71] for 'imperative reasons of security'.[72] The unlawful confinement of civilians is a grave breach of the Geneva Conventions.[73] Similarly, detention of civilians pursuant to the Fourth Geneva Convention must cease as soon as the reasons for it cease,[74] otherwise the continued detention would be arbitrary.

In NIACs, detention is generally accepted as a matter of state practice, though IHL standards related to detention are less specific. The lack of clear rules is problematic, given that most modern armed conflicts are non-international and their typology is expanding.[75] A prisoner of war category as set out in the Third Geneva Convention with respect to IACs does not exist for NIACs, and there is nothing in either Common Article 3 or Additional Protocol II (dealing with NIACs) explicitly authorising detention, though detention is referred to.[76] Some have argued that the

---

[66] GC3 Art 21.
[67] AP1 Art 85(4)(b).
[68] ICRC, Official Commentary to GC3 (2020) para 4464 <https://ihl-databases.icrc.org/ihl/full/GCIII-commentary> accessed 5 August 2023.
[69] *Prosecutor v Delalić, Mucić, Delić and Landžo (Čelebići case)* Trial Chamber Judgment, IT-96-21-T (ICTY, 16 November 1998) para 576: 'Clearly, internment is only permitted when absolutely necessary' where the detaining party 'has *serious and legitimate reasons* to think that they may seriously prejudice its security by means such as sabotage or espionage'.
[70] GC4 Art 42.
[71] *Delalić* (n 68) paras 578, 583.
[72] GC4 Art 78.
[73] GC4 Art 147.
[74] GC4 Art 132; AP1 Art 75(3).
[75] Jelena Pejic, 'Conflict Classification and the Law Applicable to Detention and the Use of Force', in Elizabeth Wilmshurst (ed), *International Law and the Classification of Conflicts* (OUP 2012) 80, 84.
[76] Common Article 3 refers to 'Persons taking no active part in the hostilities, including members of armed forces who have laid down their arms and those placed "hors de

authorisation to detain (and the concomitant obligation to refrain from unlawful or arbitrary detention) in NIACs can be derived from IHL and is implicit in Common Article 3 of the four Geneva Conventions and Additional Protocol II.[77] Others have claimed that to infer an authorisation to detain when this is not evident from the texts cannot be reconciled with the need for any deprivation of liberty to be free from arbitrariness; any law authorising detention must be sufficiently clear in defining the circumstances in which it applies.[78] It has been suggested that the authorisation to detain derives instead from domestic criminal law and international human rights law, and/or in limited circumstances, from the enforcement of mandatory resolutions of the UN Security Council.[79] The latter position makes little difference in terms of the rights of states to detain in NIACs, though it arguably makes human rights law more firmly applicable in the context of such detentions.[80] And it maintains a legal grey zone for detentions carried out by other parties to NIACs – particularly non-state actors.

Given these considerations, detentions occurring in NIACs are permissible when carried out by the state and cannot be arbitrary, according to human rights law and/or IHL. The ICRC explains it thus:

> In a "traditional" NIAC occurring in the territory of a State between government armed forces and one or more non-State armed groups, domestic law, informed by the State's human rights obligations, and IHL, constitutes the legal framework for the possible internment by States of persons whose activity is deemed to pose a serious security

---

combat" by sickness, wounds, detention, or any other cause' (GC1 Art 3; GC2 Art 3; GC3 Art 3; GC4 Art 3) whereas AP2 refers in Arts 4(1) and 5 to 'persons whose liberty has been restricted.': Protocol Additional to the Geneva Conventions of 12 August 1949, and relating to the Protection of Victims of Non-International Armed Conflicts (adopted 8 June 1977, entered into force 7 December 1978) 1125 UNTS 609 (AP2)).

[77] See, for example, ICRC, 'Internment in Armed Conflict: Basic Rules and Challenges' (Opinion Paper, November 2014) 7 <www.icrc.org/en/download/file/3223/security-detention-position-paper-icrc-11–2014.pdf> accessed 5 August 2023. See, also, Sean Aughey and Aurel Sari, 'Targeting and Detention in NonInternational Armed Conflict: Serdar Mohammed and the Limits of Human Rights Convergence' (2015) 91 *Intl L Stud* 60, 116; Jelena Plamenac, *Unravelling Unlawful Confinement in Contemporary Armed Conflicts* (Brill 2021) 35–37; Ryan Goodman, 'The Detention of Civilians in Armed Conflict' (2009) 103(1) *Am J Intl L* 48.

[78] This position is summarised in *Mohammed (Respondents) v Ministry of Defence (Appellant)* [2017] UKSC 1 and [2017] UKSC 2, paras 268–270.

[79] Lawrence Hill-Cawthorne, *Detention in Non-International Armed Conflict* (OUP 2016); Lawrence Hill-Cawthorne and Dapo Akande, 'Does IHL Provide a Legal Basis for Detention in Non-International Armed Conflicts?' *EJILTalk!* (7 May 2014).

[80] *Mohammed* (n 78).

threat. A careful examination of the interplay between national law and the applicable international legal regimes will be necessary.[81]

Whether detentions by other parties to such conflicts may lawfully be carried out is arguable under international humanitarian law but remains subject to debate.[82]

Thus, arbitrary detention will arise in IACs when prisoners of war are maintained in detention unjustifiably after the end of hostilities or when civilians or other protected persons are interned outside circumstances deemed to be strictly necessary for imperative reasons of security. It will arise in NIACs either when the detention does not comply with human rights standards pertaining to liberty and security of the person operable within the state, accommodating for the circumstances of the conflict, and/or by virtue of the application of IHL. In the case of the ECHR, which provides an exhaustive basis for lawful detention (and without mentioning military or security detention), the ECtHR has held that such detention may be recognised as an additional exception if there is another accepted international law basis to detain, such as a clear ability to detain pursuant to the Geneva Conventions in an IAC[83] or, and as further discussed in section 6.3.2, on some readings, pursuant to a binding UN Security Council resolution that requires detention.[84]

6.3.1 Detention by multinational forces

Many modern conflicts, often non-international, involve coalitions of states working together under the rubric of international organisation mandates or simply through multilateral or bilateral partnerships. Foreign (and often multinational) armed troops may be fighting alongside the armed forces of the host state against armed opposition groups operating within that state. Despite the involvement of foreign troops, this type of engagement would not in and of itself change a non-international classification into an IAC, as it does not involve two or more states in opposition to each other.

Detention in such contexts is common. Persons will be detained because they are suspected of a crime or because they are believed to pose a security threat[85] though, as already explained, the basis for security internment in

---

[81] ICRC, 'Internment in Armed Conflict' (n 77) 7.
[82] See, for example, Pavle Kilibarda and Gloria Gaggioli, 'Detention of Suspected Terrorists in Connection with Armed Conflict: a Focus on Release and Repatriation', in Michael Schmitt and Christopher Koschnitzky (eds), *Prisoners of War in Contemporary Conflict* (OUP 2023) 253, 290–295.
[83] *Hassan* (n 14).
[84] See section 6.3.2. See, also, *Mohammed* (n 78); *Al-Jedda* (n 14).
[85] Hartmann (n 37) 163.

NIACs is contested. Aid and assistance to the host state through methods other than on the ground troops including supply of funds, equipment, training and/or logistical support which contributes to regimes of detention will not usually engage the responsibility of those providing the support.[86] Nevertheless, the more involved the supporting state becomes, the greater the possibility of it exercising power over detainees.[87]

As was seen with multinational forces operating in Afghanistan, forces will not always use the same basis for detaining persons. Some have engaged as part of the International Security Assistance Force (ISAF) in support of the Afghanistan government to maintain security in parts of the country, as opposed to a more focused mission against al Qaida. As Waxman has noted:

> [T]he spectrum of views spans differing judgments on such basic questions as what type of conflict exists (international versus internal), what body of law applies (law of armed conflict versus human rights law versus domestic Afghan law, or some combination) and what specific minimum requirements those bodies of law impose (mandatory provisions versus a sliding scale depending on practicability).[88]

These divergences, coupled with significant power imbalances, a general disregard for detainees' humanity, and the near impossibility to access detainees owing to a mixture of insecurity and lack of transparency, constituted a perfect recipe for prolonged arbitrary detention, torture and extraordinary rendition. A part of the consequences of this is described in the WGAD's 2021 Opinion concerning Ravil Mingazov, an ethnic Tatar from Russia, who was sold for bounty by Pakistan leading to his arrest by US security forces in Afghanistan and rendition to Guantánamo Bay, and eventual release to the United Arab Emirates where he remains detained. Mingazov was never charged with a crime but has spent more than 21 years and counting in detention.[89]

Similarly, in Iraq, thousands of persons were detained or interned following the US-led invasion in March 2003, during what was then an IAC.

---

[86] ARS (n 45) commentary on Art 8, paras 4, 5.
[87] Tilman Rodenhäuser, 'Partnering in Detention and Detainee Transfer Operations', in Robert Kolb, Gloria Gaggioli and Pavle Kilibarda (eds), *Research Handbook on Human Rights and Humanitarian Law* (Edward Elgar 2022) 393. See, also, ICRC, 'International Humanitarian Law and the Challenges of Contemporary Armed Conflicts', 32IC/15/11, 32nd International Conference of the Red Cross and Red Crescent (2015) 22–23.
[88] Matthew Waxman, 'The Law of Armed Conflict and Detention Operations in Afghanistan' (2009) 85 *Intl Law Studies* 343, 350.
[89] UN WGAD, *Opinion No 32/2021 Concerning Ravil Mingazov (USA and UAE)*, UN Doc A/HRC/WGAD/2021/32 (8 October 2021).

Once power was handed over to Iraqi authorities in June 2004, the conflict became non-international in character, with the multinational force and the Iraqi security forces operating in cooperation against Iraqi insurgents. Since the handover, the legal basis to detain was derived through UN Security Council Resolution 1546 which, while not referring specifically to detention, provided that 'the multinational force shall have the authority to take all necessary measures to contribute to the maintenance of security and stability in Iraq'[90] including 'internment where this is necessary for imperative reasons of security'.[91] This was further operationalised by a Coalition Provisional Authority memorandum on criminal procedures.[92] The vagaries of these rules and general disregard for detainees and their welfare led to inordinately prolonged internment amounting to arbitrary detention[93] and, as became well-known, significant ill-treatment including torture.[94]

Detention also occurs in peace operations, which increasingly operate in close contact with local populations.[95] Peace operations may be obliged to temporarily detain individuals while carrying out their protection of civilians mandates.[96] They may also need to detain to protect peacekeepers or mission property. The Standard Operating Procedure pertaining to the handling of detention in UN peacekeeping operations and special political missions[97] makes clear that UN field missions cannot subject anyone to arbitrary or unlawful detention.[98] In addition, UN peace operations are obliged to act in a manner consistent with IHL.[99] The Standard Operating Procedure only applies to operations established by the UN Security Council or General Assembly as appropriate. Other procedures are in place for operations

---

[90] UNSC, Resolution 1546 (2004), UN Doc S/RES/1546 (8 June 2004) para 10.

[91] Ibid, Annex, 10. The resolution made no mention of legal safeguards against arbitrary detention.

[92] CPA Memorandum No 3 (revised): Criminal Procedures (27 June 2004).

[93] WGAD, *Opinion No 5/2014 Concerning Shawqi Ahmad Omar (Iraq)*, UN Doc A/HRC/WGAD/2014/5 (15 July 2014).

[94] HRW, 'The Road to Abu Ghraib' (June 2004); ICC Office of the Prosecutor, 'Situation in Iraq/UK Final Report' (9 December 2020).

[95] UNGA and UNSC, 'Report of the Panel on United Nations Peace Operations', UN Doc A/55/305–S/2000/809 (21 August 2000).

[96] UN Department of Peacekeeping Operations, 'DPO Policy on the Protection of Civilians in UN Peacekeeping' (1 November 2019) para 69.

[97] DPO, DPPA and DSS, 'Standard Operating Procedure on the Handling of Detention in UN Peacekeeping Operations and Special Political Missions', UN Doc Ref. 2020.13 (1 January 2021).

[98] Ibid para 9.

[99] UN Secretary-General, 'Observance by UN Forces of International Humanitarian Law' (6 August 1999) UN Doc ST/SGB/1999/13.

taking place under the auspices of NATO,[100] the African Union[101] and other intergovernmental organisations.

The authority to detain derives from the consent of the host state and the mandate of the operation emanating from the Security Council or General Assembly or other body that either authorises detention specifically or authorises the use of 'all necessary means' to undertake certain tasks.[102] Where detention occurring in a UN peace operation exceeds what is lawful and/or is arbitrary, there will be limited and sometimes no remedy, which has been recognised as highly problematic.[103] This impunity results from the combined problem of conduct by troops occurring within the context of a UN Security Council mandated operation exercising effective control (and consequently the conduct being attributed solely to the UN), and the UN ultimately being immune from suit before most courts.[104] In contrast, where it is the troop-contributing country that has retained effective control or ultimate authority and control over the acts and omissions of its troops, the conduct may be attributed to that state and a measure of accountability may follow, at least in principle.

In Kosovo, authority to detain by Executive Order of the Special Representative of the Secretary-General was said to be derived from Security Council Resolution 1244,[105] in conjunction with UNMIK (United Nations Interim Administration Mission in Kosovo) regulations put in place by the mission.[106] KFOR, the NATO-led peacekeeping

---

[100] Mark Dakers, 'NATO Responsibility for Detention', in Gregory Rose and Bruce Oswald (eds), *Detention of Non-State Actors Engaged in Hostilities: the Future Law* (Brill 2016).

[101] African Union, 'Guidelines on Detention and DDR', Defense and Security Division of the Peace and Security Department of the AU Commission (2014).

[102] UNSC, Resolution 1546 (n 90) para 10 and Annex, 10.

[103] David Marshall and Shelley Inglis, 'The Disempowerment of Human Rights-Based Justice in the United Nations Mission in Kosovo' (2003) 16 *Harvard Hum Rts J* 95, 112. See, generally, on the inadequate remedial framework for international organizations, Carla Ferstman, *International Organizations and the Fight for Accountability: the Remedies and Reparations Gap* (OUP 2017).

[104] See, *Behrami and Behrami v France*; *Saramati v France, Germany and Norway* (Grand Chamber) App Nos 71412/01, 78166/01 (ECtHR, 2 May 2007). See, also, *Stichting Mothers of Srebrenica v Netherlands and United Nations*, Supreme Court [HR] LJN: BW1999, ILDC 1760 (NL 2012) (13 April 2012); Ferstman (n 103).

[105] UNSC, UN Doc S/RES/1244 (10 June 1999) authorising 'all necessary means to fulfil its responsibilities' (para 7).

[106] UNMIK, 'Regulation 1999/26 on the Extension of Periods of Pre-trial Detention' (22 December 1999). The OSCE called Regulation 1999/26 'unlawful', arguing that it fails 'to strike a proper balance between the imperative duty to safeguard the right to liberty and the need to detain those charged with serious criminal offences, pending the establishment of a fair and adequately functioning criminal justice system': OSCE Mission in Kosovo, 'Report No 6 – Extension of Custody Time Limits and the Rights off Detainees: the Unlawfulness of Regulation 1999/26' (29 April 2000). See, also, Gisela

force in Kosovo, in contrast, argued that its mandate provided it with the authority to detain, where detention was necessary to address a 'threat to KFOR' or under its mandate to provide 'a safe and secure environment [for as long as] civilian authorities are unable or unwilling to take responsibility for the matter'.[107] These extra-legal administrative detentions were a quick fix to what was 'a dysfunctional justice system'[108] when UNMIK and KFOR were getting started and, according to Foley, 'it was clear that they were using administrative detentions because they did not trust the Kosovan judiciary'.[109] The approach arguably did little to strengthen the rule of law in Kosovo or UN accountability, and led to arbitrary detentions in a number of well-publicised cases.[110] These extra-legal detentions with minimal safeguards were also criticised by the Ombudsperson Institution of Kosovo,[111] as well as the UN Human Rights Committee.[112]

"Peace" operations with offensive military mandates, such as the Intervention Brigade of the UN Stabilization Mission in the Democratic Republic of the Congo (DRC) (MONUSCO), with its mandate to use all necessary means to neutralise armed groups,[113] will invariably engage in detention activities. Because of the heightened probability of detentions, there are mission-specific internment procedures that apply to persons captured during the offensive operations of the Brigade.[114] As Wohlfahrt has noted, for this there is a need for detention oversight mechanisms, and Brigade members require training and support:

Hirschmann, 'Guarding the Guards: Pluralist Accountability for Human Rights Violations by International Organisations' (2019) 45(1) *Rev Intl Studies* 20, 33–36.

[107] As cited by Marshall and Inglis (n 103) 110.

[108] Conor Foley, *The Protection Paradox: How the UN Can Get Better at Saving Civilian Lives* (Palgrave Macmillan 2023) 26.

[109] Ibid.

[110] For example, the case of Afrim Zeqiri (detained under executive order for nearly two years) referred to by Marshall and Inglis (n 103) 111.

[111] Ombudsperson Institution in Kosovo, 'Special Report No 3 on the Conformity of Deprivations of Liberty under "Executive Orders" with Recognised International Standards' (2001).

[112] Human Rights Committee, 'Concluding Observations of the Human Rights Committee: Kosovo (Serbia)', UN Doc CCPR/C/UNK/CO/1 (14 August 2006) para 17.

[113] UNSC, Resolution 2098, UN Doc S/RES/2098 (2013) (28 March 2013) paras 9, 12(b).

[114] Scott Sheeran and Stephanie Case, 'The Intervention Brigade: Legal Issues for the UN in the Democratic Republic of the Congo' (International Peace Institute November 2014). See, also, Stéphane Wohlfahrt, 'Implementing the Legal Framework Relating to the Deprivation of Liberty by Peacekeeping Forces: a Practical Example', 41st Round Table on Current Issues of International Humanitarian Law, International Institute of Humanitarian Law (San Remo, 6–8 September 2018) 14.

> [U]niformed personnel often fail to provide timely notification of detentions and that they have difficulties filling out the required forms under the ISOP. They also have a limited knowledge and understanding of the steps they must follow when detaining an individual. Confusion is sometimes apparent, with a detaining unit reporting the detention of individuals who merely sought protection from the Mission, or failing to report a detention on the basis that a person was "immediately" handed over to national authorities.[115]

Much of the Brigade's work will be joint operations with the DRC armed forces. Consequently, it is likely that the Brigade will refrain from detaining directly where this can be done safely and effectively by local government forces, or it will transfer detainees to those forces as soon as practicable. The Security Council resolution establishing the Brigade anticipates these challenges and refers to the need for its actions, whether undertaken unilaterally or jointly, to be done 'in a robust, highly mobile and versatile manner and in strict compliance with international law, including international humanitarian law and with the human rights due diligence policy on UN-support to non-UN forces (HRDDP [Human Rights Due Diligence Policy])'.[116]

The UN's human rights due diligence policy[117] requires UN entities contemplating or involved in providing support to non-UN security forces to assess the risk of the recipient committing grave violations of IHL, human rights law or refugee law. Where there are substantial grounds to believe that there is a real risk of such outcomes, mitigatory measures must be identified, failing which if the risk is of an unacceptable level, support must be suspended or withdrawn.[118]

Evidence that international organisations' aid or assistance or other support to governments may contribute to or result in significant human rights violations is available for Libya. In March 2023, the Independent Fact-Finding Mission on Libya found 'grounds to believe that the European Union and its member States, directly or indirectly, provided monetary, technical, and logistical support to the LCG [Libya Coast Guard] and DCIM [Directorate for Combatting Illegal Migration] that was used in the context

---

[115] Wohlfahrt (n 114) 14.
[116] UNSC, Resolution 2098 (n 113) para 9.
[117] UN, 'Human Rights Due Diligence Policy on UN Support to Non-UN Security Forces, Guidance Note and Text of the Policy' (2015).
[118] On the challenges associated with the implementation of the HRDDP by MONUSCO in DRC, see, CIVIC, 'Enabling Support by Mitigating Risk: MONUSCO's Implementation of the HRPPP in the DRC' (June 2020).

of interception and detention of migrants'.[119] Intercepted migrants were returned directly to Libyan detention centres where they were subjected to prolonged arbitrary detention, cruel, inhuman and degrading treatment including torture and related grievous abuses.

Similar challenges arose with French military engagement in the Sahel region. French operation Barkhane supported African forces and the peace operation in Mali (United Nations Multidimensional Integrated Stabilization Mission in Mali (MINUSMA)) in fighting terrorism in the region. According to Guiffard, these operations:

> allowed French forces (alongside troops from Mali, Niger and Burkina Faso) to neutralize (i.e. either kill, or arrest and hand over to local authorities) the emirs ("princes" or leaders) of AQIM's four katibats (battalion), several dozen of their operational leaders, the emirs of Al-Mourabitoun and MUJAO, a large number of Ansar al-Din leaders, three of JNIM's five emirs, and the emirs of the Islamic State in the Greater Sahara.[120]

France ultimately decided to stop joint operations with Mali following the military coups in that country in 2021,[121] and a number of governments have subsequently decided to pull their troops from MINUSMA.[122] Cooperation with Mali was also not helped by Mali's growing alliance with the Wagner Group, the Russian security company that had at least at that time been operating in some relationship with the Russian government. MINUSMA has confirmed that its support was conditioned by the UN's HRDDP, already referred to.[123] The policy would not extend to France's Operation Barkhane, and thus it is less clear how France undertook due diligence in the course of its joint operations, particularly when arresting and handing over suspects to local authorities.

Another permutation pertaining to the extraterritorial engagement of foreign states in armed conflicts is their support to non-state opposition groups fighting against government forces to change a conflict's balance

---

[119] HRC, 'Detailed Findings of the Independent Fact-Finding Mission on Libya', UN Doc A/HRC/52/CRP.8 (24 March 2023) para 129.

[120] Jonathan Guiffard, 'Operation Barkhane: Success? Failure? Mixed Bag?', *Institut Montaigne* (30 March 2023).

[121] Tangi Salaün and John Irish, 'France Ends West African Barkhane Military Operation' *Reuters* (10 June 2021).

[122] International Crisis Group, 'MINUSMA at a Crossroads' (1 December 2022).

[123] UNSC, 'Situation in Mali: Report of the Secretary-General', UN Doc S/2021/519 (1 June 2021) para 42.

of power or to engage in proxy warfare.[124] Whether the foreign state engagement would be sufficient for such states to exert "effective" or similar degree of control[125] over the armed group they are supporting (and whether this impacts on the characterisation of the conflict) will depend on the particular facts and the applicable standard of control. Some scenarios involving detention help to clarify the challenges.

First, the US-led Global Coalition against Da'esh support to Kurdish People's Protection Units (YPG) (part of the non-state armed group Syrian Defence Forces, SDF) were the main proxy force that led ground operations against Da'esh in Syria from 2016. After overtaking Da'esh, the SDF began to oversee the detention facilities in the northeast of the country where thousands of foreign fighter detainees associated with Da'esh, as well as displaced Syrians and Iraqi refugees and others remain arbitrarily detained, outside any legal process. There are tens of thousands of mostly women and children who remain housed in camps with extremely poor conditions.[126] The Turkish military, having branded the SDF a terrorist organisation, mounted a military offensive against them, which included arresting persons and extrajudicially removing them to Turkey to face terrorism-related charges.[127] There are many questions that can be posed, not least whether, in addition to the SDF, the Global Coalition bears any responsibility for providing a modicum of support to the detention facilities in which the most basic of standards are not adhered to or, conversely, whether the Global Coalition's responsibility is engaged by failing to do more to strengthen the legality of the detention regime that it had a hand in fostering. It is hard to see how it can be both doing too much and too little.

Second is the military and operational support provided by Rwanda (though this is denied by Rwanda) to the Mouvement du 23 mars/Armée révolutionnaire congolaise (M23/ARC), a sanctioned armed group operating in north Kivu, eastern DRC. According to the UN Group of Experts on the DRC, the group is responsible for grievous violations, including attacks against peacekeepers, torture and inhuman treatment, rapes, deliberate killings and indiscriminate shelling of civilians. Several

---

[124] James Wither, 'Outsourcing Warfare: Proxy Forces in Contemporary Armed Conflicts' (2020) 31(4) *Security & Defence Quarterly* 17.

[125] The challenges associated with determining the appropriate test for control are canvassed in Djemila Carron, 'When Is a Conflict International? Time for New Control Tests in IHL' (2016) 98 *Intl Rev Red Cross* 1019.

[126] HRC, 'Report of the Independent International Commission of Inquiry on the Syrian Arab Republic', UN Doc A/HRC/52/69 (7 February 2023) paras 114–119.

[127] Amy Austin Holmes, 'Threats Perceived and Real: New Data and the Need for a New Approach to the Turkish–SDF Border Conflict', Wilson Center, Occasional Paper Series No 39 (May 2021).

testimonies of civilians who had been imprisoned explained how members of the M23/ARC would detain displaced civilians commuting to their fields located in the areas it controlled, in various M23 camps and beat them, some until death.[128] Rwandan Defence Force members were alleged not only to have afforded support to the M23/ARC but also to have directly intervened on the territory of the DRC, either to reinforce M23/ARC or to conduct military operations against Rwandan rebel forces operating from the DRC.[129] Again, to what extent are states obliged to ensure that the non-state actors they support refrain from serious violations of human rights, including arbitrary detention, torture and extrajudicial killings? Is there a direct relationship between the failure to exercise due diligence and the attribution of responsibility for the ensuing conduct? These questions are only partially answered in the ILC's Articles on the Responsibility of States (ARS).[130] This is not conduct carried out 'under the direction or control' of a state, in the sense of Article 8 ARS,[131] but conduct that the state knows about and acquiesced to, or did nothing to prevent. So, while the state would be held responsible for its own support for the armed group, only in certain individual instances would the acts of the M23/ARC be themselves held attributable to it, based upon actual participation of and directions given by the state.[132]

6.3.2 *"Extraterritorial NIACs", UN Security Council resolutions and the power to detain*

A traditional NIAC involves parties to a conflict engaging in hostilities on the territory of a single state. At times, the conflict may expand outside the state, for instance where armed opposition groups take refuge in a neighbouring country and are pursued in that country by the original state, often with the tacit consent of the government(s) concerned, or where foreign militaries are operating with the agreement of the territorial state, to help secure order or to address a particular security issue in the territorial state. As there is no conflict between two or more states these would still constitute NIACs, albeit ones pursued extraterritorially.[133]

---

[128] UNSC, 'Midterm Report of the Group of Experts on the DRC', UN Doc S/2022/967 (16 December 2022) para 57 and Annex 37.
[129] Ibid, 2.
[130] ARS (n 45) commentary on Art 8, para 4.
[131] Ibid. See, also, *Military and Paramilitary Activities in and against Nicaragua (Nicaragua v USA)* [1986] ICJ Rep 14, 51 para 86.
[132] ARS (n 45) commentary on Art 8, para 4.
[133] Sylvain Vité, 'Typology of Armed Conflicts in International Humanitarian Law: Legal Concepts and Actual Situations' (2009) 91(873) *Intl Rev Red Cross* 69, 89.

According to the ICRC, the framework for detentions occurring in such contexts stems from customary and treaty IHL, both of which 'contain an inherent power to intern and may in this respect be said to provide a legal basis for internment in NIAC'.[134] This contrasts somewhat with what the UK Supreme Court held in *Mohammed v Ministry of Defence,* a case involving security detention by British troops in Afghanistan. The Court ultimately held that 'subject to compliance with minimum standards of humane treatment, international humanitarian law leaves it to states to determine, usually under domestic law, in what circumstances, and subject to what procedural requirements, persons may be detained in situations of non-international armed conflict'.[135] Taking into account the ECtHR's *Hassan* decision,[136] the majority in *Mohammed* also recognised that Article 5(1) ECHR permits detention during extraterritorial NIACs that falls outside the permissible categories of detention listed in sub-paragraphs (a)–(f) whenever it was authorised by a Security Council resolution and detention was required for imperative reasons of security.[137] Thus, it is not the Security Council resolution itself that requires detention, but it authorises such detention in case 'imperative reasons of security' present themselves on the ground.

Mohammed can be contrasted with the ECtHR's own position on whether Security Council resolutions afford a further basis for detention under the ECHR, as expressed by the Grand Chamber in *Al-Jedda*.[138] In *Al-Jedda,* which concerned the indefinite detention of a dual British/Iraqi citizen in a British-run Basra detention facility, the UK House of Lords had previously held that the detention was lawful because the UK had been obligated by UN Security Council Resolution 1546[139] to detain, on the basis of the wording that the multinational force had 'the authority to take all necessary measures to contribute to the maintenance of security and stability in Iraq' (para 10), read together with Article 103 of the UN Charter,[140] which recognises that any obligations under the Charter trump any conflicting obligations under any other international agreement. This point was seized upon by Lord Bingham for the majority; Article 103 prevails over any other international agreement, including the ECHR,[141] and the effectiveness of the UN system required this kind of privileging. However, when *Al-Jedda* was ultimately

---

[134] ICRC, 'Internment in Armed Conflict' (n 76) 7.
[135] *Mohammed* (n 78) para 276.
[136] *Hassan* (n 14).
[137] *Mohammed* (n 78) paras 30, 119, 164.
[138] *Al-Jedda* (n 14).
[139] UNSC, Resolution 1546 (n 90).
[140] Charter of the United Nations and Statute of the International Court of Justice (adopted 26 June 1945, entered into force 24 October 1945) 1 UNTS XVI, Art 25.
[141] *R (Al-Jedda) v Secretary of State for Defence* [2007] UKHL 58, para 35.

considered by the ECtHR Grand Chamber, it determined that the Security Council resolution did not displace the UK government's obligations under Article 5. The Grand Chamber held that, when interpreting the Security Council's resolutions, one must have regard to the purposes for which the UN was created (which included promoting and encouraging respect for human rights and fundamental freedoms). Noting that the UN was obligated to act in accordance with its purposes and principles, there must be a presumption that the Council did not intend to impose any obligation on member states to breach fundamental principles of human rights. In the event of any ambiguity in the terms of a Security Council resolution, the Court had therefore to choose the interpretation that was most in harmony with the requirements of the ECHR and avoided any conflict of obligations.[142]

There is a valid question as to whether the Supreme Court in *Mohammed* simply chose not to follow the ECtHR in *Al-Jedda* or found a route to distinguish it (*Mohammed* was never taken to the ECtHR). Though it was well apprised of the ECtHR ruling in *Al-Jedda*, as already indicated, the majority held that the relevant Security Council resolution provided implied authority to capture and detain persons suspected of insurgency for imperative reasons of security (applying *Hassan*). The Supreme Court places much attention on the ECtHR's distinction as to whether the resolution was mandatory or simply authorised. Lord Sumption indicates:

> This was because the relevant Security Council Resolution left the choice of methods to the multinational force in Iraq. In the absence of sufficiently specific language the Security Council's authorisation to use 'all necessary measures' did not therefore create an obligation to detain even if it created a power to do so. [...]
>
> By declining to treat military detention as an obligation, as opposed to a discretionary power, the court was able to treat article 5 as consistent with the United Kingdom's obligations under the UN Charter.[143]

The Supreme Court goes on to cite *Hassan*, holding that the essential aspect of that case was whether Article 5:

> should be interpreted so as to accommodate an international law power of detention which was not among the permissible occasions for detention listed at article 5(1). The question is the same in the present cases, although the source of the international law power to

---

[142] *Al-Jedda* (n 14) para 102.
[143] *Mohammed* (n 78) paras 47, 50.

detain is a resolution of the Security Council under Chapter VII of the Charter instead of the Geneva Conventions.[144]

Thus, it holds that *Hassan* – a judgment where, as Jackson argues, 'a kind of pragmatism won out'[145] – has overtaken *Al Jedda*, and that there is no great leap to extend a permissible ground of detention from an IAC to a NIAC.

There is some logic to this leaping, in that NIAC detention is already happening, happening frequently and sometimes for good reason. But using a UN Security Council resolution as the basis for the detention when it simply provides the authority for the relevant forces to 'take all necessary measures to contribute to the maintenance of security and stability'[146] is arguably too vague and broad to satisfy the requirement for all detentions to have a clear, legal basis. Incongruously, the Security Council's 'take all necessary measures' framing for the extraterritorial NIACs referred to is looser than the standard to detain civilians in an IAC, only where strictly required, where 'absolutely necessary', or only where there are 'serious and legitimate reasons'.[147] The Human Rights Committee has underscored that the standard for detention in such circumstances must be exceedingly high: 'strict necessity and proportionality constrain any derogating measures involving security detention, which must be limited in duration and accompanied by procedures to prevent arbitrary application'.[148] Nevertheless, bringing NIAC security detention or internment into the spectre of permissible detention means that the ECtHR does not automatically find the claims to be inadmissible, but may engage substantively on the necessity, proportionality and legitimacy of the detentions (though by the time it may get to do so, the damage will invariably be done).

6.3.3 Challenges with the transfer of detainees

The right not to be forcibly expelled, deported, returned, removed or extradited to a country where the person faces a real risk of torture is a *sine qua non* of states' obligation to prohibit torture.[149] Non-refoulement to torture

---

[144] *Mohammed* (n 78) para 60.

[145] Miles Jackson, 'Judicial Avoidance at the European Court of Human Rights: Institutional Authority, the Procedural Turn, and Docket Control' (2022) 20(1) *Intl J Const L* 112, 127.

[146] UNSC, Resolution 1546 (n 90).

[147] See the outset of section 6.3.

[148] Human Rights Committee, General Comment No 35 (n 13) para 66.

[149] Convention against Torture and Other Cruel, Inhuman or Degrading Treatment or Punishment Art 3; UNCAT, 'General Comment No 4 (2017) on the Implementation of Article 3 of the Convention in the Context of Article 22, UN Doc CAT/C/GC/4 (4 September 2018). According to General Comment No 4, the refoulement prohibition may also apply to the risk of cruel, inhuman or degrading treatment or punishment: Ibid paras 26, 28.

is reflected in human rights treaties and derives from the non-refoulement principle under refugee law, which prevents states from expelling or returning a refugee in any manner whatsoever to the frontiers of territories where his life or freedom would be threatened on account of his race, religion, nationality, membership of a particular social group or political opinion.[150] The transfer of detainees or protected persons in circumstances that may realistically lead to torture or other fundamental violations of human rights is prohibited in times of IAC[151] and is also considered to extend to NIACs.[152]

Because non-refoulement to torture is absolute, states have sought to mitigate or lessen the risks associated with torture to an "acceptable" level so as to be able to lawfully proceed with transfers. In peacetime contexts, this has been done mainly by seeking assurances from the receiving states that they will refrain from subjecting the returnees to torture or other ill-treatment. Some commentators have questioned the effectiveness of unenforceable undertakings to reduce the likelihood of torture, particularly when many of the states concerned have already ratified binding treaties that prohibit them from carrying out torture or other cruel, inhuman, or degrading treatment or punishment.[153] The Special Rapporteur on the promotion and protection of human rights and fundamental freedoms while countering terrorism, Fionnuala Ní Aoláin, has called the practice of diplomatic assurances in counter-terrorism and national security-related transfers 'largely ineffective and quite cynical in seeking to circumvent fundamental treaty and customary law obligations'.[154] The case law has avoided making an overall finding related to the practice and has considered whether assurances reduce the risk of ill-treatment to an acceptable level on a case-by-case basis.[155]

The prohibition of refoulement also applies to states and others who engage in military, security or policing operations, including where these take place abroad. It applies 'in any territory under its jurisdiction or any area

---

[150] Refugee Convention Art 33(1).
[151] GC3 Art 12; GC4 Art 45(3)–(4). See, also, *Prosecutor v Mile Mrkšić (Vukovar Hospital Case)*, IT-95-13/1-A (ICTY, 5 May 2009) para 71.
[152] ICRC, *Commentary on the First Geneva Convention: Convention (I) for the Amelioration of the Condition of the Wounded and Sick in Armed Forces in the Field* (2nd edn, Geneva 2016) para 708.
[153] UNGA, 'Report of the Special Rapporteur on Torture and Other Cruel, Inhuman or Degrading Treatment or Punishment', UN Doc A/59/324 (1 September 2004) para 31; HRW, 'Still at Risk: Diplomatic Assurances No Safeguard against Torture' (April 2005) 6.
[154] HRC, 'Follow-up Report to the Joint Study on Global Practices in Relation to Secret Detention' (n 36) para 28.
[155] *HY v Switzerland*, UN Doc CAT/C/61/D/747/2016 (7 September 2017) para 10.6; *Saadi v Italy* (Grand Chamber) App No 37201/06 (ECtHR, 28 February 2008).

under its control or authority…',[156] including when foreign armed forces or peacekeeping troops operating abroad take custody over individuals in the course of their operations and thereafter wish to transfer them to local law enforcement or military troops. In the *Maya Evans* case,[157] which stemmed from a claim by a British peace activist that Afghan terror detainees transferred by the British armed forces to the Afghan National Directorate of Security (NDS) were at risk of being beaten and physically mistreated, thus making the transfers unlawful, UK courts banned transfers to NDS detention in Kabul. Transfers to other facilities were not banned, although the courts imposed a series of "safeguards" and monitoring arrangements on future transfers of detainees. These same issues arose in *Al Saadoon*,[158] which concerned the transfer to Iraqi custody of Iraqi detainees held by British forces without an assurance on the non-applicability of the death penalty. The ECtHR determined that the transfer violated Article 3 ECHR.[159] The prohibition on refoulement would also prohibit transfers to other states cooperating in an extraterritorial operation, where there is a real risk that those states may torture or transfer the detainees onward to locations or states where they face a real risk of torture (secondary refoulement).[160] Extraordinary rendition would also constitute refoulement among the range of violations it engenders.[161]

The Copenhagen Process recognised the particular challenges with transfers in NIAC and peacekeeping contexts, but its Principles and Guidelines[162] simply remind that states and international organisations must comply with their international law obligations when transferring a detainee to another state or authority. Similar to bilateral assurances sought between states regarding peacetime transfers, the Principles and Guidelines encourage the receiving state or authority to allow the sending state to undertake any necessary detainee monitoring, post transfer.[163] The challenges are significant, particularly in extraterritorial NIACs when states, present in the territory for only a limited time, may need to detain

---

[156] UN Committee against Torture, General Comment No 4 (n 149) para 10; see, also, UN Committee against Torture, General Comment No 2 'Implementation of Article 2 by States parties' UN Doc CAT/C/GC/2 (24 January 2008) para 16.

[157] *R (Maya Evans) v Secretary of State for Defence* [2010] EWHC 1445 (Admin) (UK).

[158] *Al-Saadoon v United Kingdom* App No 61498/08 (ECtHR, 2 March 2010) para 137.

[159] Ibid para 144.

[160] Human Rights Committee, 'General Comment No 31: Nature of the General Legal Obligation Imposed on States Parties to the ICCPR' (26 May 2004) UN Doc CCPR/C/21/Rev.1/Add.13, para 12.

[161] *El Masri v Former Yugoslav Republic of Macedonia* App No 39630/09 (ECtHR, 13 December 2012) para 220.

[162] Copenhagen Principles and Guidelines (n 5) Art 15.

[163] Ibid.

on security or other grounds. The inability to transfer detainees to the competent national authorities presents operational challenges in that it may delay missions intended to be short and ultimately may impede states from engaging in missions that may give rise to detentions. There are no easy solutions.

Often, cooperating states or international organisations have agreed transfer arrangements with host states,[164] have transferred to other foreign troops[165] or have undertaken more joint operations with local troops so that local troops can assume the detention function from the start, or they have immediately transferred detainees upon capture so as to avoid formal rules applicable to detention, though they are unlikely to avoid non-refoulement obligations.[166] This may be appropriate so long as adequate due diligence is undertaken and risks are sufficiently mitigated. Outside where the UN's human rights due diligence policy applies,[167] there is limited evidence to show that like models have been put in place or adequately implemented.[168]

6.4 National security, counter-terrorism and indefinite detention

Arbitrary detention is prevalent in responses to terrorism and insecurity because governments tend to approach strategies from a conflict lens (and thus import the challenges associated with such detentions set out in section 6.3), or they take an anti-law stance that results in certain persons or groups being prevented from accessing justice or certain issues from being adjudicated. A few particularly problematic areas are now highlighted.

---

[164] Cordula Droege, 'Transfers of Detainees: Legal Framework, Non-Refoulement and Contemporary Challenges' (2008) 90(871) *Intl Rev Red Cross* 669, 693.

[165] Marc Gionet, 'Canada the Failed Protector: Transfer of Canadian Captured Detainees to Third Parties in Afghanistan' (2009) *J Conflict Stud* 1; Public Interest Advocacy Centre, 'Military Detention: Uncovering the Truth, Story 1 – Australia's Detention, Custody and Transfer Policy in Afghanistan and Iraq' (1 July 2011).

[166] Droege (n 164) 683: 'The principle of non-refoulement applies to short- and long-term deprivation of liberty. So, if a transfer occurs immediately after a person is arrested, captured or even voluntarily surrenders to the authorities, the mere fact of being able to compel him or her to move from the control of one state to another against his or her will demonstrates that the authorities have control over that person.'

[167] UN Human Rights Due Diligence Policy (n 117).

[168] See, on the analogous situation of human rights due diligence in migrant return programmes in Libya, Carla Ferstman, 'Human Rights Due Diligence Policies Applied to Extraterritorial Cooperation to Prevent "Irregular" Migration: European Union and United Kingdom Support to Libya' (2020) 21(3) *German LJ* 459.

6.4.1 Counter-terrorism and forever prisoners

Using an IAC narrative to address terrorism is particularly problematic for the purposes of detention given the IAC focus on the release of prisoners of war 'after the cessation of active hostilities'.[169] While not only a problem for terrorism threats (some conflicts are also extremely protracted), active hostilities involving terrorism may have no obvious or objectively verifiable end. This may lead, as it has done in places like Guantánamo Bay, to the phenomenon of the "forever prisoner", a concept popularised in a documentary film about the experience of Saudi Arabian national Abu Zubaydah, who was taken into CIA custody in 2002 and transferred to Guantánamo Bay in 2006.[170]

At the time of writing in 2023 Abu Zubaydah remained detained there, never having been charged with an offence.[171] The Senate Intelligence Committee report on CIA torture explained the variety of torture practices meted out on him.[172] To agree the proposed interrogation tactics, a cable from the interrogation team stipulated that if Abu Zubaydah were to die during the interrogation, he would be cremated, and further indicated that 'regardless which [disposition] option we follow however, and especially in light of the planned psychological pressure techniques to be implemented, we need to get reasonable assurances that [Abu Zubaydah] will remain in isolation and incommunicado for the remainder of his life'.[173] As Hill-Cawthorne has explained, 'the presumption of indefinite administrative detention for the duration of hostilities remains the core part of the US's detention policy, even as the idea of ongoing hostilities against a defined enemy has long dissipated'.[174]

Indefinite, including severely protracted, detention stems from the failure to restrict security detention to those exceptional instances when it is strictly necessary to respond to a clear security risk, and for the shortest possible duration. The need for security detention is too often inappropriately presumed. As the WGAD explained in relation to Abu Zubaydah's continued detention:

---

[169] GC3 Art 118(1).
[170] See, Alex Gibney, *The Forever Prisoner* (HBO 2021).
[171] WGAD, *Opinion No 66/2022 Concerning Zayn al-Abidin Muhammad Husayn (Abu Zubaydah) (USA, Pakistan, Thailand, Poland, Morocco, Lithuania, Afghanistan and the United Kingdom)*, UN Doc A/HRC/WGAD/2022/66 (6 April 2023).
[172] Report of the Senate Select Committee on Intelligence Committee, 'Study of the Central Intelligence Agency's Detention and Interrogation Program', S. Report 113–288 (9 December 2014) 17–62.
[173] Senate Select Committee Report, ibid, 35.
[174] Hill-Cawthorne, 'Detention in the Context of Counterterrorism and Armed Conflict' (n 63) 564.

Administrative detention to address a security threat will normally amount to arbitrary detention when other effective measures, such as the criminal justice system, are not utilized. If, under the most exceptional circumstances, a present, direct and imperative threat is claimed to justify the detention of persons considered to present a threat, the burden of proof lies on States to demonstrate that it cannot be addressed by alternative measures, that the detention does not last longer than absolutely necessary, that the overall length of possible detention is limited and that they respect the guarantees of article 9 of the Covenant. The Government of the United States has not shown that Mr. Zubaydah constitutes a security threat for which there is no option other than keeping him in detention for more than two decades without charges.[175]

Indefinite detention is *ipso facto* arbitrary.[176] To ensure detention is not arbitrary, it must not only be subject to non-derogable protections, such as *habeas corpus* review at regular intervals by a competent judicial authority,[177] but there must also be a clear plan to ensure the detention does not become indefinite. For courts to simply affirm the continuation of detention at periodic intervals does not avoid that detention from being or becoming arbitrary.

The difficulty to transfer Guantánamo Bay detainees to other countries where they cannot be returned to their home countries[178] has been posited as an excuse for some to have been maintained in detention for so long. However, detainees' security assessments have progressed slowly and sporadically, delaying decisions to clear them for release, and the efforts to give effect to clearances have been marred with challenges. In some of the early cases, the US government required that receiving states agree to maintain the individuals in security detention or otherwise subject them to intensive security controls, irrespective of whether there was any proof of an

---

[175] WGAD, *Opinion No 66/2022 Concerning Abu Zubaydah* (n 171) para 80.
[176] WGAD, *Opinion No 18/2023 Concerning Mr. Mustafa Faraj Muhammad Masud al-Jadid al-Uzaybi (United States of America, Pakistan and Romania)*, UN Doc A/HRC/WGAD/2023/18 (2 June 2023) para 90.
[177] IACommHR, 'Toward the Closure of Guantanamo', OEA/Ser.L/V/II. Doc.20/15 (2015) 83–96.
[178] Usually this is because there is a real risk that returning them will expose them to torture. Other reasons may be because the country of nationality disputes or removes nationality, or the person is stateless. See, generally, Gaia Rietveld, Joris van Wijk and Maarten Bolhuis, 'Who Wants "the Worst of the Worst"? Rationales for and Consequences of Third Country Resettlement of Guantanamo Bay Detainees' (2021) 76 *Crime, Law & Social Change* 35.

ongoing and significant security threat.[179] Non-disclosure has also served as an additional barrier in some cases. In Djamel Ameziane's case (an Algerian national never charged with an offence), his lawyers were prevented from disclosing publicly that he had been cleared for transfer, complicating efforts to resettle him in a third country.[180] Also, the US government has chosen not to allow the detainees into US territorial jurisdiction.[181] It is, thus, far from blameless in the continued arbitrary detention of Guantánamo Bay inmates. As the *New York Times'* Editorial Board wrote at the end of April 2023:

> Clearing out the remaining prisoners requires cutting through a tangle of laws, policies, procedures and bureaucratic secrecy. These are not simple tasks, but they are well within the power of the White House to accomplish if the process is given a far higher priority. Mr. Biden can use his authority to order the Departments of Defense, Justice and State, the intelligence agencies and other agencies involved to coordinate their efforts and direct their resources to make it happen, as quickly as possible.[182]

A policy adopted by countries such as China to counter terrorism – mandatory, institutionalised re-education – has equally resulted in indefinite detention. The use of mandatory re-education centres was a practice discussed in Chapter 4 as a form of pathologisation of drug users and homeless persons.[183] Under this rubric, holding extremist ideologies is perceived as an illness, justifying mandatory, institutionalised re-education. While the practice has much in common with security detention, persons are not necessarily being detained because they pose a specific security threat, but more so because who they are and what values are ascribed to them is deemed to need changing. Commenting on mass detention and *incommunicado* detention of Uyghurs and other Turkic Muslims in Xinjiang, the Special Rapporteur on the promotion and protection of human rights

---

[179] Laurel Fletcher and Eric Stover, 'Guantánamo and Its Aftermath: US Detention and Interrogation Practices and Their Impact on Former Detainees', Human Rights Center University of California, Berkeley in partnership with Center for Constitutional Rights (November 2008) 61. See, also, IACommHR, 'Toward the Closure of Guantanamo' (n 175) paras 281–289.

[180] *Ameziane v USA*, Report No 20/29, Case 12.865, Merits (IACommHR, 22 April 2020) para 83.

[181] US S.1605, *National Defense Authorization Act for Fiscal Year 2022*, ss 1032, 1033.

[182] Editorial Board, 'Biden Can Close the Extrajudicial Prison at Guantánamo', *New York Times* (29 April 2023).

[183] See sections 4.3.2: Detention as pathologisation and 4.4.1: The "unseen": economic and social "degenerates".

and fundamental freedoms while countering terrorism has stipulated that the justification:

> of "re-education" to prevent extremism is incompatible with the Government's international law obligations. [...] the term "extremism" has no purchase in binding international legal standards, and when operative as a criminal legal category, it is irreconcilable with the principle of legal certainty, and is therefore, per se, incompatible with the exercise of certain fundamental human rights.[184]

As release depends on vague, extraneous factors, the prospect that detention is extended indefinitely is real.[185]

6.4.2 Da'esh and quasi-carceral zones of exclusion

Ní Aoláin has highlighted the plight of Da'esh alleged fighters and others caught in detention camps in northeast Syria, noting:

> [S]ince 2019, approximately 10,000 men and 750 boys, some as young as 9, have been detained for alleged association to Da'esh in approximately 14 detention centres – mostly converted schools and hospitals – throughout the north-east part of the Syrian Arab Republic. Of these, at least 2,000 men and 150 boys are third country nationals. [...] No judicial process has determined the legality or appropriateness of their detention.[186]

In the exceedingly complex operating environment, detention centres are run by the non-state SDF, which act as a quasi-governing force in this part of the country.[187] There is a continued threat from Da'esh insurgents still present in the area, who in 2022 launched an attack on a prison where Da'esh members are held in an attempt to break them out.[188] While there may be valid security and criminal law rationales for detention in some of the cases, the absence of any judicial process to determine their legality

---

[184] HRC, 'Follow-up Report to the Joint Study on Global Practices in Relation to Secret Detention' (n 36) para 33.
[185] HRW, '*Break Their Lineage, Break Their Roots*: Chinese Government Crimes against Humanity Targeting Uyghurs and Other Turkic Muslims' (2021) 12–19.
[186] HRC, 'Follow-up Report to the Joint Study on Global Practices in Relation to Secret Detention' (n 36) para 32.
[187] This is discussed in more detail in section 6.3.1.
[188] Al Jazeera, 'UN: Syria Prison Attack Shows Need to Deal with ISIL Detainees' (28 January 2022).

makes the detentions unlawful and arbitrary. That children make up a significant part of the detainee population makes the situation even more fraught and problematic.

There are obvious SDF capacity challenges, but the interest of many of the states that supported the fight against Da'esh in continuing that support to help institute a lawful detention regime and a justice process is much more limited. At the same time, support for a system of detention that is devoid of legal standards could make those states that would choose to extend support complicit in ongoing abuses. This is a point raised by Special Rapporteur Ní Aoláin: 'States that directly support or enable the building and maintenance of prisons within which no legal norms apply are, in the Special Rapporteur's view, complicit or responsible through the application of extraterritorial human rights obligations for the human rights violations that occur within them.'[189]

In addition to the thousands of Da'esh detainees, according to the Independent International Commission of Inquiry, there are also about 56,000 people – the majority of whom are women and children under the age of 12 – who remain confined in camps with extremely precarious conditions and limited healthcare and access to education.[190] With many repatriations of foreign nationals to their countries of nationality or long-term residency blocked or stalled, 'tens of thousands remain trapped, including children who have only known life in the camps, cut off from the rest of the world'.[191] Support for repatriations is variable in accordance with perceived national interests, often viewed from a short-term perspective.

Foreign fighters in a NIAC do not have a clear right to repatriation as prisoners of war or interned civilians would have at the end of an IAC,[192] nor would it be clear who would have the burden of repatriating foreign fighters in a NIAC where the states from where the fighters came were not involved in the conflict and, as here, the locations of the detention centres and camps are in a quasi-autonomous zone of Syria under non-state actor control. Nevertheless, outside a clear IHL basis for repatriations, returns that would not be barred because of refoulement problems could (and should) proceed based on nationality and citizenship laws or other human rights protections related to the right to family life. However, the practice of certain states to deprive nationals of their citizenship and barring them from re-entry to the country when they have been linked to terrorism (albeit without

---

[189] HRC, 'Follow-up Report to the Joint Study on Global Practices in Relation to Secret Detention' (n 36) para 32.
[190] 'Report of the Independent International Commission of Inquiry on the Syrian Arab Republic' (n 126) paras 114–119.
[191] Ibid para 118.
[192] GC3 Art 118; GC4 Arts 132, 134.

any formal charges or trial) has not been held by the ECtHR to necessarily violate their right to respect for private and family life.[193]

If a deprivation of citizenship case that also resulted in the applicant becoming stateless arose before the ECtHR, it is possible that the ECtHR would find a violation. In *Ramadan v Malta*, which involved the revocation of citizenship acquired through marriage following an annulment, which potentially would result in the applicant becoming stateless, the ECtHR held:

> [A]lthough the right to citizenship is not as such guaranteed by the Convention or its Protocols, it cannot be ruled out that an arbitrary denial of citizenship might in certain circumstances raise an issue under Article 8 of the Convention because of the impact of such a denial on the private life of the individual.[194]

Ultimately, though, it did not find a violation.[195] In *Usmanov v Russia*, in finding a violation, the ECtHR underscored that it was necessary to consider the consequences of the citizenship annulment (whether it resulted in a deprivation of legal status, an entry ban, and so on) and whether the annulment of citizenship was "arbitrary" (for example, was it done in accordance with law, accompanied by appropriate procedural safeguards, including the opportunity to challenge the decision before the courts, and whether the authorities acted diligently and swiftly). Ultimately the ECtHR determined that the annulment had serious consequences for the applicant and failed to give the individual adequate protection against arbitrary interference and, consequently, violated Article 8 ECHR.[196]

This is a question the ECtHR will be faced with should Shamima Begum's case come before it, following the exhaustion of domestic remedies in the UK.[197] Begum was allegedly lured (and it was determined by UK courts that there was 'credible suspicion that she had been recruited, transferred and then harboured for the purpose of sexual exploitation'[198]) to join Da'esh when she was a child. She married an Islamic State fighter and lived under Islamic State rule for more than three years. She bore three children who have since died. She was located in 2019 and remains in the al Roj camp in the al-Hasakah region, a camp described by the UN as having deplorable living conditions and limited access to healthcare, leading to suffering and preventable deaths

---

[193] *K2 v United Kingdom* App No 42387/13 (ECTHR, 7 February 2017) (decision on admissibility).
[194] *Ramadan v Malta* App No 76136/12 (ECTHR, 21 June 2016) para 84.
[195] See, however, the dissenting opinion of Judge Pinto De Albuquerque.
[196] *Usmanov v Russia* App No 43936/18 (ECTHR, 22 December 2020) paras 58–71.
[197] *Shamima Begum v Secretary of State for the Home Department* [2023] 2 WLUK 353.
[198] Ibid paras 219, 252.

among children and women.[199] The UK government stripped her of her citizenship based on national security concerns, which arguably made her stateless given her inability to give effect to her Bangladeshi nationality now that she has become an adult. The decision to revoke her British citizenship and deny her entry to the UK not only makes her stateless but assigns her to a situation of indefinite detention, as there is nowhere for her to go but where she is currently encamped. The encampment in this sense is not self-imposed; she cannot simply leave without major ramifications.[200] Thus, there is a valid question as to whether the UK's policy of citizenship revocation and denial of entry is the cause of her arbitrary detention for which it is responsible.

6.5 Conclusions

There are three main conclusions that can be drawn from this chapter.

First, there is a risk that, as insecurity becomes normalised, so does security detention. Security detention is supposed to be exceptional, in response to an exceptional risk. But when the risks it is supposed to address become commonplace, the inevitable outcome is that the measure used to address those risks also becomes commonplace. It is an expedient response and the rationales succeed largely because they are focused on addressing the security risk (still deemed exceptional but actually commonplace) rather than the rights of the largely "othered" persons subject to the security detention. In the process one conveniently forgets or ignores the harms associated with arbitrary detention, particularly when it is indefinite or prolonged.

Connected to this conundrum is the tendency for security detention to undergo lesser forms of judicial oversight or related scrutiny than ordinary detention, and much of this in closed proceedings, despite the heightened risks of arbitrary detention for those affected. Further, the status of these detainees as "othered", undesirable or otherwise marginalised places them even further away from recourse to their rights. Thus, there is a combination of factors that conspire not only to lead to situations of arbitrary detention but to ensure those situations are maintained. In some cases, it is courts through formulaic review processes that are "rubber-stamping" and, in effect, legitimising regimes of indefinite, arbitrary detention.

Second, there is a need to recognise the fiction of territoriality, particularly in the context of conflict and insecurity. States, intergovernmental

---

[199] 'Report of the Independent International Commission of Inquiry on the Syrian Arab Republic' (n 126) para 109.
[200] WGAD, *Opinion No 54/2015 Concerning Julian Assange (Sweden and the United Kingdom)*, UN Doc A/HRC/WGAD/2015 (22 January 2016) para 10.

organisations and other non-state actors increasingly operate in different forms of collaboration or opposition. It is rarely the case that a conflict or emergency situation is purely territorial. One must recognise the factual basis for this and ensure that one does not hold on inappropriately to the legal fictions of territoriality in terms of conduct, accountability and redress. Individuals should never be in situations that are outside the law, particularly when it is states that place them there through the use of legal fictions.

Third, there is a problem of stasis. Authorities are aware of the problems and injustices, but have shown themselves unwilling to resolve them. There is a certain contentment with the status quo, mainly for domestic political reasons, which makes those with the power to effect change reluctant to do so. A part of this relates to the fact that there are multiple actors, each with their own responsibilities and capacities to act. This gives rise to the tendency to shift blame onto others, and to sink below the parapet. Countless international and regional experts, treaty bodies and judicial authorities have called upon authorities to adopt concrete measures to end the stasis, but it continues. The answer lies in outlining and giving effect to states' positive obligations, including their obligations to exercise due diligence to ensure that both their acts and omissions, including their policies, do not contribute to, or foster in any way, regimes of arbitrary detention. Also, there is the need to recognise that more than one actor can be responsible for acts in which they play a part.

7

Detention of Dual and Foreign Nationals for Leverage

7.1 Introduction

Globalisation increases interconnectivity between countries, peoples, cultures and ideas. But the removal of some barriers causes others to be reified, as a response to 'globalising tendencies'.[1] A consequence of this is heightened protectionism in some countries as well as distrust between countries. Persons who are present in protectionist societies, but exemplify the openness that those societies reject, may be monitored and targeted. This has led, among other outcomes, to an increase in arbitrary detentions of foreigners and persons with foreign connections in countries that value insularity. These detentions serve two primary functions: First, insular societies use them to suppress external influences within their own societies, in much the same way as detention is deployed by many societies as a tool of social control. Second, these detentions are used as a form of state-to-state leverage to improve the detaining state's bargaining power vis-à-vis the state of nationality in relation to any number of possible bilateral or multilateral issues.

This chapter considers the phenomenon of states arbitrarily detaining dual or foreign nationals with a view to exerting pressure on their (other) states of nationality. The practice has become notorious in recent decades, and is often associated with countries such as China, Iran and Russia perpetrating the abuse against nationals predominantly coming from, or with second nationalities in, or close ties to, countries in the West. However, the phenomenon has a much longer history,[2] and involves a wider array

---

[1] Anthony Giddens, *Runaway World* (Profile Books 2011) 19.
[2] Chi-Kwan Mark, 'Hostage Diplomacy: Britain, China, and the Politics of Negotiation, 1967–1969' (2009) 20(3) *Diplomacy & Statecraft* 473; Anthony Grey, *Hostage in Peking* (Doubleday 1971). See, also, *United States Diplomatic and Consular Staff in Tehran United States Diplomatic and Consular Staff in Tehran* [1980] ICJ Rep 3, 35, para 74.

of countries,[3] both those responsible for the detentions and those whose nationals have been detained.

The chapter provides an overview of these detentions, focusing on some of the countries that have been most involved. The phenomenon clearly constitutes arbitrary detention in that the persons are detained without there being a reasonable suspicion that they committed an offence,[4] and without there being any other lawful purpose for the detention. As will be explained, the phenomenon also constitutes a crime. It aligns with understandings of hostage-taking, though the perpetrators are states and state officials as opposed to members of terrorist groups, militias or armed opposition movements.[5] It also resembles the crime of kidnapping, where the gaolers (usually armed gangs, or common criminals) are extorting funds or some other kind of benefit from their captives to secure release, as well as corruption or bribery, where officials falsely accuse or threaten to arrest persons with wealth or influence with a view to securing a bribe to avoid the arrest. As the detaining state is seeking to obtain some kind of leverage from the state of nationality, the act also constitutes unlawful coercion, which breaches the fundamental international law principle of non-intervention.

The phenomenon described in this chapter involves states using the full arsenal of their justice systems to exert pressure on the state of nationality. Indeed, the co-option of the detaining state's justice system to perpetrate the abuse is an essential feature. It serves to disorient diplomats who are caught between the need to show respect for and allow the foreign justice system to run its course under the classic international law duty not to interfere in the internal affairs of another state,[6] and the need to provide effective assistance to

---

[3] Associated Press, 'Venezuela Frees Seven Americans as Part of the Largest Prisoner Swap under Biden' (2 October 2022); Dominic Oo and Thompson Chau, 'Myanmar Court Sentences Ex-UK Envoy, Husband to Year in Prison', *Al Jazeera* (2 September 2022). The states involved in detentions for state-to-state leverage tend to operate outside of the rule of law, though that itself is a controversial characterisation, and it would be incorrect to suggest that arbitrary detentions are not also a feature within a rules-based order, though perhaps in different ways and not necessarily for reasons of state-to-state leverage. Colonial-era rulers and apartheid regimes regularly detained people they saw as agitators in which release was not necessarily predicated on legal rulings, but more so on concessions, states of contrition or similar.

[4] *Wloch v Poland* App No 27785/95 (ECtHR, 19 October 2000) para 108. See, also, *Fox, Campbell and Hartley v United Kingdom* App Nos 12244/86, 12245/86, 12383/86 (ECtHR, 30 August 1990) paras 23–24.

[5] Cynthia Loertscher, 'Bringing Americans Home 2020: a Non-Governmental Assessment of U.S. Hostage Policy and Family Engagement', New America and the James W Foley Legacy Foundation (April 2020) 10.

[6] Art 55(1) Vienna Convention on Consular Relations (adopted 24 April 1963, entered into force 19 March 1967); Art 41(1) Vienna Convention on Diplomatic Relations (adopted 18 April 1961, entered into force 24 April 1964); UNGA, 'Declaration on

their citizens. It is for this and related reasons that some have referred to the practice as an 'attempt to undermine the Rules-Based International Order'.[7]

As the target is not simply the victimised detainees or their families, but also their states of nationality, the victims are typically unable to solve the issue alone (for example, by hiring lawyers to prove their innocence and/ or negotiate with the detaining state, or to pay bribes) without their state of nationality's active involvement. Indeed, 'courts and routine diplomacy are of limited utility in these cases'; there is a need for concerted, tailored measures to address the particular challenges presented.[8] This three-way relationship between the detaining state, the victims and family members, and the state of nationality can become messy, however. For, while victims and family members will be focused only on securing release, both the detaining state and the state of nationality will have multiple, often competing interests to navigate, such as national security, trade and diplomatic relations. Harper, a negotiator, has made this point:

> [Y]ou would assume that that [release] was our No. 1 goal, but it actually might be our fourth or fifth goal. For example, I have been deployed before where the reputation of His Majesty's Government is No. 1, diplomatic relations can be No. 2, compliance with policy can be No. 3, prevention of harm can be No. 4 and release is No. 5. There needs to be an understanding of what our strategy is before we go in.[9]

As Snell argues in relation to the arbitrary detention by Iran of dual British Iranian national Nazanin Zaghari-Ratcliffe:

> Unlike the United States, Britain has never bowed from its stated desire to trade more with Iran and to accept Iran's government as it stands. These commercial and political relationships trump any concerns Britain either feels or expresses about Iran's numerous expeditionary wars abroad; its gunning down of protestors in neighbouring countries; its acts of international economic terrorism against Saudi Arabia and even Britain; its posturing threat to close now-open sea lanes; and,

---

Principles of International Law, Friendly Relations and Co-Operation Among States in Accordance with the Charter of the United Nations', UN Doc A/RES/2625(XXV) (24 October 1970).

[7] UK Parliament Foreign Affairs Committee, *Stolen Years: Combatting State Hostage Diplomacy* (4 April 2023) HC 166 para 101.

[8] Loertscher (n 5).

[9] UK Parliament Foreign Affairs Committee, Oral Evidence: the FCDO's Approach to State Level Hostage Situations, HC 166 (7 February 2023) Witness Phil Harper, Q190.

indeed, Iran's continual taking of hostages from Britain and other allied countries.

None of these things cause Britain to doubt its engagement with Iran, or eagerness to conclude whatever deal proves eventually acceptable to the Americans.

For Richard Ratcliffe's part, one can see the absurdity in all of this. Britain is willing to excuse Iran so much – and yet the nominal reasons for his wife's imprisonment have proven intractable.[10]

This tripartite relationship and array of competing interests may complicate the resolution process and breed resentment and distrust with victims' families. This is especially so in circumstances where the state of nationality appears to be dragging its heels, and/or where there is no political consensus as to what steps should be taken to progress the negotiations and ultimately to resolve the detentions.

In this chapter I provide an overview of the recent state practice of detention of dual and foreign nationals as a form of leverage on the state of nationality. I explain the different ways in which the phenomenon has been labelled and explore the tensions and the limits of such labels, considering the legal definitions and concomitant gaps in the law. The act of labelling is not neutral. It impacts how rights and responsibilities are framed and sets in motion the likely trajectory of how disputes will be raised and ultimately resolved. I follow this trajectory and analyse the challenges associated with negotiating access to the detainees and securing their release, which underscore the complex intersections between international law and international relations. I then consider multilateral approaches to the problems identified and how such approaches might be strengthened.

7.2 Arbitrary detentions and state-to-state leverage: the practice

The practice involves the arbitrary detention of foreign and dual nationals for reasons linked to their nationality(ies) so that the detaining state can secure an advantage or benefit from the (other) state of nationality in exchange for the release of the detainees. The persons are detained not for anything they may have done or any serious risk they may pose, but for who they are. The victims are present in the detaining state for all sorts of reasons. In this sense they are detained simply because they are foreign or have foreign connections and they are accessible to the detaining state. The detentions are mainly opportunistic.

---

[10] James Snell, 'Iran's Hostage Diplomacy', Artillery Row, *The Critic* (6 May 2021).

Sometimes individuals, particularly dual nationals, are in the country to visit family, as with Nazanin Zaghari-Ratcliffe, who was visiting family in Iran with her young daughter when she was arbitrarily detained. On other occasions individuals are taken when they visit the country as tourists, like American student Otto Warmbier, who was part of a guided tour group in North Korea when he was arrested at the airport when trying to leave the country. Or individuals are detained while undertaking authorised research or attending conferences, such as Briton Matthew Hedges, who was conducting doctoral research in the United Arab Emirates in 2018 when he was arrested on spurious charges of spying for the British government, or Canadian Iranian anthropology professor Homa Hoodfar and Swedish Iranian professor of disaster medicine Ahmad Reza Djalali, both of whom were arbitrarily detained in Iran, the latter who was, at the time of writing, under a death sentence. Xiyue Wang, a doctoral student from Princeton University, was arbitrarily detained in Iran in 2016 while there on a student visa issued by the Iranian Ministry of Foreign Affairs, whereas Kylie Moore-Gilbert was taken while conducting field research on Bahraini exiles in Iran.

Foreign correspondents have also been targeted, such as the *Wall Street Journal*'s Evan Gershkovich, who was arbitrarily arrested in Yekaterinburg, Russia on 29 March 2023; *Washington Post* journalist Jason Rezaian, arrested in Tehran, Iran on 22 July 2014, and Al Jazeera journalists Peter Greste and Mohamed Fahmy and others in Cairo, Egypt in December 2013. Others working for humanitarian or religious organisations have likewise been taken, such as Olivier Vandecasteele, who was arbitrarily detained in Iran on 24 February 2022; American pastor Andrew Brunson, who was arbitrarily detained in Turkey in October 2016; representatives of international policy groups, such as Michael Kovrig, who worked as a senior adviser for the International Crisis Group, and was arbitrarily detained in Beijing, China on 10 December 2018; and Michael Spavor, the Director of Paektu Cultural Exchange, an organisation that facilitated cultural and other exchanges involving North Korea, was arrested in China at around the same time. Kenneth Bae, a Korean American evangelical Christian, was likewise arbitrarily arrested and ultimately wrongfully convicted by North Korea of trying to overthrow the government.

The detained individuals are accused of vague national security–related offences such as espionage or coup plotting, collaborating with foreign governments, terrorism or of being a member of an illegal organisation.[11]

---

[11] Leigh Toomey, 'The Declaration against Arbitrary Detention in State-to-State Relations: a New Means of Addressing Discrimination against Foreign and Dual Nationals?' (2022) 35 *Harv Hum Rts J* 233, 243; Aykan Erdemir and Eric Edelman, 'Erdogan's Hostage Diplomacy: Western Nationals in Turkish Prisons' (Foundation for Defense of Democracies Press, June 2018); WGAD, *Opinion No 29/2021 Concerning Aras Amiri*

Invariably the charges are not accompanied by credible evidence in the sense of 'facts or information which would satisfy an objective observer that the person concerned may have committed an offence'.[12] Sometimes, there is no evidence at all; on other occasions, authorities have fabricated evidence or have made bald assumptions of criminality based on detainees' jobs or patterns of travel, unsupported by evidence.

Access to consular assistance for foreign[13] (including dual[14]) nationals is either denied by the detaining state outright or is severely curtailed.[15]

The ability to communicate with family, respect for fair trial guarantees – such as access to a lawyer of one's choice and being able to review the evidence and to mount an effective defence[16] – are generally restricted and, in some cases, used as part of the bargaining. For example, the WGAD noted in its opinion concerning Andrew Brunson that, while his arrest by Turkish authorities was authorised by a warrant, he was not notified of any charges against him until two months after the warrant had been issued, during which time his lawyer had no access to his file, which impeded efforts to seek to review the legality of the detention.[17]

Despite the absence of credible evidence of wrongdoing, the detainees tend to be either held without formal charges or trial for extended periods, or they are convicted of the charges proffered after summary trials that fall short of the most basic of fair trial guarantees,[18] with excessively long sentences of imprisonment then imposed. For such reasons, detentions falling within

---

(Islamic Republic of Iran), UN Doc A/HRC/WGAD/2021/29 (1 October 2021) paras 52, 53.

[12] *Wloch v Poland* (n 4) para 108. See, also, *Fox, Campbell and Hartley v United Kingdom* (n 4) paras 23–24; *Başer and Özçelik v Türkiye* App Nos 30694/15, 30803/15 (ECtHR, 13 September 2022) para 202.

[13] WGAD, *Opinion No 51/2019 Concerning Nizar Zakka (Islamic Republic of Iran)*, UN Doc A/HRC/WGAD/2019/51 (8 October 2019) paras 68–73; *Opinion No 51/2021 Concerning Mehmet Ali Öztürk (United Arab Emirates)*, UN Doc A/HRC/WGAD/2021/51 (8 February 2022) para 90; WGAD, *Opinion No 84/2018 Concerning Andrew Craig Brunson (Turkey)*, UN Doc A/HRC/WGAD/2018/84 (15 February 2019) paras 68–69.

[14] WGAD, *Opinion 27/2021 Concerning Kamran Ghaderi (Islamic Republic of Iran)*, UN Doc A/HRC/WGAD/2021/27 (8 October 2021).

[15] For example, OHCHR, 'Iran: UN Experts Say Arbitrary Detention of Belgian Aid Worker a Flagrant Violation of International Law' (17 January 2023) (regarding Olivier Vandecasteele).

[16] WGAD, *Opinion Concerning Aras Amiri* (n 11) para 66; *Opinion Concerning Nizar Zakka* (n 13) paras 64, 65; *Opinion Concerning Andrew Craig Brunson* (n 13) paras 63–64.

[17] WGAD, *Opinion Concerning Andrew Craig Brunson* (n 16) paras 58–62.

[18] WGAD, *Opinion Concerning Aras Amiri* (n 11); WGAD, *Opinion No 28/2016 Concerning Nazanin Zaghari-Ratcliffe (Islamic Republic of Iran)*, UN Doc A/HRC/WGAD/2016/28 (21 September 2016) para 52. See, also, *Yeğer v Turkey* App No 4099/12 (ECtHR, 7 June 2022) para 46.

this general pattern have been recognised by the WGAD as arbitrary, and to constitute discrimination based on national or social origin.[19]

The decision to detain or to maintain in detention is taken pursuant to a state decision to detain that operates as part of, but nevertheless outside, the usual functioning of a state's justice system. The justice system is simply the method used to orchestrate the decision. Co-option of the justice system is able to happen because the system lacks independence or is otherwise being manipulated in the taking of its decisions about the administration of justice. International standards on the independence of the judiciary make clear that justice sector actors and judges in particular must 'decide matters before them impartially, on the basis of facts and in accordance with the law, without any restrictions, improper influences, inducements, pressures, threats or interferences, direct or indirect, from any quarter or for any reason'.[20] Where justice actors are incapable of acting autonomously and there are insufficient guarantees in place to ensure that they are free from control, pressure, or undue influence from other organs of the state, the prospect of the law being abused by the state for an ulterior purpose becomes high.

In other circumstances, a foreign or dual national may be detained because of the initial decision of competent justice actors acting autonomously. However, after news of the initial detention spreads within the state of detention, the executive might intervene unlawfully to instruct the competent justice actors to maintain inappropriately the individual in detention pending the result of the executive's efforts to exert leverage on the state of nationality. In doing so, the state acknowledges and adopts the detentions as its own, in the sense of approving of and deciding to perpetuate or indeed exacerbate the unlawful situation.[21]

The lack of autonomy in the decision to detain may be demonstrated by showing that it fits within a wider pattern of detentions carried out for reasons unrelated to the lawful exercise of authority to detain.[22] In its assessment of whether detentions occurred for discriminatory purposes, the WGAD has

---

[19] See, for example, WGAD, *Opinion No 85/2021 Concerning Anoosheh Ashoori (Islamic Republic of Iran)*, UN Doc A/HRC/WGAD/2021/85 (14 February 2022) para 96. See, also, Toomey (n 11) 241.

[20] 'Basic Principles on the Independence of the Judiciary' (Milan, 6 September 1985) Seventh UN Congress on the Prevention of Crime and the Treatment of Offenders, para 2.

[21] ILC, 'Articles on the Responsibility of States for Internationally Wrongful Acts', Report of the International Law Commission on the Work of its 53rd Session (23 April–1 June and 2 July–10 August 2001) UN Doc A/CN.4/SER.A/2001/Add.1 (ARS) Art 11. See, also, *Iran Hostages case* (n 2) para 74.

[22] *Merabishvili v Georgia* (Grand Chamber) App No 72508/13 (ECtHR, 28 November 2017); *Kavala v Turkey* App No 28749/18 (ECtHR, 10 December 2019); *Mammadli v Azerbaijan* App No 47145/14 (ECtHR, 19 April 2018); *Navalnyy v Russia* (Grand Chamber) App Nos 29580/12 and four others (ECtHR, 15 November 2018).

considered *inter alia* whether there was a pattern of persecution of persons with similar distinguishing characteristics that would indicate discrimination against a particular group.[23] The WGAD has also considered as relevant reports and statements made by a government that draw attention to the characteristics of the detainee as a justification for the arrest or detention,[24] as well as the absence of any relevant indicia or reasonable suspicion that the detainee did what the detaining state alleged that they had done.[25] This approach to discriminatory decision-making is similar to how "systematic"[26] has been interpreted in several international judgments pertaining to crimes against humanity, having regard to its patterns, and its non-accidental and non-isolated nature.[27] Acts that are systematic 'follow a regular pattern on the basis of a common policy involving substantial public or private resources'.[28]

The detaining state will often not articulate the purpose of the detention in a direct way. This is because a specific intention to exercise leverage in order to compel the state of nationality to act or refrain from acting contradicts the usual official narrative that accompanies these cases – that the persons detained are criminal suspects appropriately detained prior to trial or convicted criminals serving out sentences, and not, on the face of it, detained for any ulterior purpose.[29] However, the intention of the detaining state may be inferred from the wider context, including the actions or statements of relevant officials, or a culmination of actions that coincide so closely in time that it is difficult to conclude otherwise.[30] In *Demirtaş v*

---

[23] HRC, 'Report of the Working Group on Arbitrary Detention', UN Doc A/HRC/36/37 (19 July 2017) para 48(b).

[24] WGAD, *Opinion Concerning Nazanin Zaghari-Ratcliffe* (n 18) para 47; *Opinion Concerning Aras Amiri* (n 11) paras 67–69.

[25] WGAD, *Opinion Concerning Nazanin Zaghari-Ratcliffe* (n 18) para 49; *Opinion Concerning Aras Amiri* (n 18) para 70; *Opinion Concerning Mehmet Ali Öztürk* (n 13) paras 94–98. See, also, *Fox, Campbell and Hartley v United Kingdom* (n 4) para 32.

[26] Art 7(1), Rome Statute of the International Criminal Court.

[27] *Prosecutor v Kunarac,* Trial Judgment, IT-96-23-T and IT-96-23/1-T (ICTY, 33 February 2001) para 429; *Prosecutor v Gbagbo*, Decision on the confirmation of charges against Laurent Gbagbo, ICC-02/11–01/11–656-Red (ICC, 12 June 2014) para 223.

[28] *Prosecutor v Akayesu*, Trial Judgment, ICTR-96-4-T (ICTR, 2 September 1998) para 580.

[29] Carla Ferstman and Marina Sharpe, 'Iran's Arbitrary Detention of Foreign and Dual Nationals as Hostage-taking and Crimes against Humanity' (2022) 20(2) *J Intl Crim J* 403, 412–413.

[30] For instance, Danielle Gilbert considered that 'when China arrested Canadian citizens Michael Kovrig and Michael Spavor in 2018, the Chinese government never announced that the Canadians were taken to pressure the release of Huawei CFO Meng Wanzhou from Canada. However, any time there was an update in Meng's case – from arrest to formal charges, to her release in late 2021 – there was a coincident update in the two Michaels' status. Such observed tit-for-tat behavior strongly suggests a case of hostage diplomacy. Nevertheless, state hostage takers maintain the guise of a legal process': *Stolen Years: Combatting State Hostage Diplomacy* (n 7), Written Evidence submitted to the UK

Turkey, after having found an absence of reasonable suspicion, the Grand Chamber of the ECtHR identified an ulterior purpose by taking into account a variety of mainly circumstantial evidence and using inferences. It determined that 'the concordant inferences drawn from this background support the argument' that the applicant was detained for an ulterior political purpose,[31] in that case 'of stifling pluralism and limiting freedom of political debate, which is at the very core of the concept of a democratic society'.[32] The ability to infer the intention of the detaining state from the wider context and circumstances is consistent with international criminal law jurisprudence on the assessment of intent,[33] as it is for transnational crimes such as hostage-taking.

Often the bargaining currency for release is prisoner exchanges, though ordinarily this is simply inferred from the timings of releases. For instance, Jason Rezaian and three other American detainees held in Iran were released in exchange for the release of seven Iranian prisoners and the dropping of charges against 14 others[34]; Michael Kovrig and Michael Spavor were reportedly exchanged for Meng Wanzhou,[35] as was Russian arms dealer Viktor Bout for American basketball player Brittney Griner.[36]

Transfers are not straightforward, however, and they can arguably incentivise further detentions, with the victims of arbitrary detention caught in the middle. Indeed, a constitutional challenge was brought in Belgium by the National Council of Resistance of Iran (the exiled Iranian opposition group that was the target of the foiled Paris bomb plot, which led to the conviction and imprisonment of Iranian diplomat Assadolah Assadi for attempted terrorism) to prevent Belgium from agreeing a bilateral treaty on prisoner exchanges with Iran,[37] which they argued would potentially open

---

Parliament Foreign Affairs Committee Inquiry by Danielle Gilbert (SLH0020). They were both released within hours after the US extradition request against Meng Wanzhou was dropped.

[31] *Selahattin Demirtaş v Turkey (No. 2)* (Grand Chamber) App No 14305/17 (ECtHR, 22 December 2020) paras 423, 436, 437.

[32] Ibid para 437.

[33] See, for example, *Prosecutor v Issa Hassan Sesay, Morris Kallon and Augustine Gbao,* Appeals Judgment, SCSL-04-15-A (SCSL, 26 October 2009) para 580; *Prosecutor v Akayesu*, Trial Judgment (n 28) para 523.

[34] Thomas Erdbrink and Rick Gladstone, 'Iran Frees Americans, Including Jason Rezaian, in Prisoner Swap', *New York Times* (16 January 2018).

[35] Gilbert (n 30).

[36] Niko Vorobyov, 'Griner-Bout Prisoner Swap: a Sign of Easing US–Russia Tensions?' *Al Jazeera* (9 December 2022).

[37] *Le Traité entre le Royaume de Belgique et la République islamique d'Iran sur le transfèrement de personnes condamnées* (Brussels, 11 March 2022).

the door for a significant increase in state hostage-takings.[38] The Belgian Constitutional Court's ruling in March 2023 affirmed the legality of the treaty, though it stipulated a number of conditions that would need to be complied with in the event of a transfer. At the end of May 2023, with the diplomatic assistance of Oman, Iranian authorities released Belgian aid worker Olivier Vandecasteele[39] and Belgian authorities released Iranian convicted diplomat Assadolah Assadi.[40]

Other currency, while not usually confirmed by either the detaining state or the state of nationality and not always agreed to, has included the release of funds frozen under sanctions regimes, negotiation of multilateral deals,[41] the repayment of debts,[42] agreement to extradition requests that had otherwise been blocked,[43] agreements to repatriate bodies and end criminal investigations,[44] and the desire to show goodwill in advance of major diplomatic talks.[45]

---

[38] Belgian Constitutional Court, *Arrêt n° 36/2023 du 3 mars 2023, Numéro du rôle: 7871*. See, Belgian Constitutional Court, Press Release: Judgment: 36/2023, 'The Court rejects the appeal against the law assenting to the Belgian-Iranian treaty, but the victims of a convicted person must be informed of his transfer so as to be able to submit this for the review of the legality by a judge' (3 March 2023).

[39] Olivier Vandecasteele, sentenced to a 40-year cumulative sentence on espionage charges. OHCHR, 'Iran: UN Experts Say Arbitrary Detention of Belgian Aid Worker a Flagrant Violation of International Law' (17 January 2023).

[40] Patrick Wintour, 'Belgium Aid Worker Freed in Prisoner Swap with Iranian Diplomat Jailed for Bomb Plot', *The Guardian* (26 May 2023); DW, 'Iran-Belgium Prisoner Swap Denounced as "Shameful"' (26 May 2023). See, also, Sunniva Rose, 'Inside Belgium's "Operation Blackstone" to Free Vandecasteele from Iran', NWorld (thenationalnews.com) (26 May 2023) (reporting that Belgian authorities sought and received Belgium King Philippe's approval for the transfer, to expedite the process).

[41] Foundation or Defense of Democracies, 'Release of Hostages in Iran May be Linked to US Sanctions Relief' (4 October 2022). American Iranian journalist Jason Rezaian recounted that his release was a 'point of negotiation' 'in the […] talks being held about Iran's nuclear program': Jason Rezaian, *Prisoner: My 544 Days in an Iranian Prison – Solitary Confinement, a Sham Trial, High-Stakes Diplomacy, and the Extraordinary Efforts it Took to Get Me Out* (Anthony Bourdain/Ecco 2019) 95.

[42] As was arguably the case with the arbitrary detention by Iran of UK nationals, in which it became progressively clear that the repayment of the International Military Services debt related to the aborted supply of 1,500 Chieftain tanks and 250 repair vehicles to Iran despite receipt of payment up front, became a precondition for their release. See *Stolen Years: Combatting State Hostage Diplomacy* (n 7) paras 81–88.

[43] Turkey has indicated that pastor Andrew Brunson would be released if the US agreed to extradite Fethullah Gulen. See 'Turkey's Erdogan Links Fate of Detained U.S. Pastor to Wanted Cleric Gulen' *Reuters* (28 September 2017).

[44] *The Economist*, 'North Korea Takes 11 Malaysians Hostage' (9 March 2017).

[45] Benjamin Haas, 'Trump Welcomes Home Three Americans Released by North Korea' *The Guardian* (10 May 2018).

7.3 The salience of labels: arbitrary detention, hostage-taking and unlawful coercion

While there are divergences in approaches taken depending on the detaining country and sometimes within countries, the overall pattern of detention of foreign or dual nationals for international leverage appears relatively clear in the sense that we "know it when we see it". The practice has been described colloquially in diverse ways – as hostage diplomacy; hostage-taking; state detentions for leverage; unlawful and arbitrary detention; or detaining innocent foreign civilians with a view to making political gains.[46] However, there is no single, accepted nomenclature. The absence of a universally accepted term or label to refer to the phenomenon means that its outer edges – what incidents form part of the pattern and what incidents fall outside – is subject to debate. When dual or foreign nationals are detained, this too is a broader phenomenon than what is described in this chapter. Such persons may be appropriately charged with an offence for which there is sufficient evidence, or they may be falsely accused of a crime and subject to the whims of a corrupt official who may maintain them in detention to elicit a bribe. Or the individuals may become the victims of an unfair trial that results in an unsound conviction and sentenced to a term of imprisonment. This does not necessarily mean that they were arbitrarily detained for state-to-state leverage. Thus, it will only be a narrow subset of detention cases that will be arbitrary, and state-sponsored, and effectuated for the ulterior purpose of securing a benefit or advantage from the (other) state of nationality.

The lack of clarity as to which incidents form part of the phenomenon and which fall outside delays and may also hamper the effectiveness of the state of nationality's response, which has led both families and advocates to call for greater clarity, so that the political situation can be analysed and appropriate actions can be taken much sooner in the process.[47] As Rezaian has explained in respect of the recent clarifying of US practice, stemming from the adoption of the Robert Levinson Hostage Recovery and Hostage-Taking Accountability Act[48] and the establishment of a Special Envoy for Hostage Affairs (SPEHA),[49] 'traditionally, [...] it becomes a Consular matter

---

[46] Antony Blinken, 'Conviction and Sentencing of U.S. Citizen Brittney Griner in Russia' Press Statement (4 August 2022); Global Affairs Canada, 'Statement on Passing of 1,000 Days Since Michael Kovrig and Michael Spavor Were Arbitrarily Detained in China' (5 September 2021); Council of the European Union, 'Iran: EU Adopts Council Conclusions and Additional Restrictive Measures' (12 December 2022).

[47] Loertscher (n 5).

[48] *Robert Levinson Hostage Recovery and Hostage-Taking Accountability Act* 22 USC 1741 (27 December 2020).

[49] See, website of the Office of the SPEHA <www.state.gov/bureaus-offices/secretary-of-state/special-presidential-envoy-for-hostage-affairs/> accessed 7 August 2023.

that might take months or years to get dealt with, the Hostage Envoy Office is, as you know, more proactive about these things, because there is a presumption that the person is being held unjustly'.[50] However, it is not unusual for events or practices to be difficult to classify; each incident will have its own permutations. And one must be mindful that the challenges of classification can be used as a justification for political paralysis. Also, states will under or over classify depending on their political interests and what impact they think it will have on the detaining state. Some variability therefore is to be expected. Nevertheless, the absence of a clear definition feeds into this variability and exploits it at the expense of transparency. This is difficult to fathom for families that have a legitimate interest and arguably also a right to know what support they might expect from their state of nationality and to be able to see the practical and effective implementation of that support.

Classification is indeed important, but states should be taking steps to ensure that the rights of their nationals are respected in all scenarios, not only in those cases that fall within a narrow subset of conditions. States of nationality should be calling for their nationals' release from detention whenever it is clear that the detention is arbitrary,[51] not only in instances of arbitrary detention that involve state-to-state leveraging or hostage-taking.[52] However, when state-to-state leveraging or hostage-taking is involved, this would constitute a further breach by the detaining state of its commitment to resolving international disputes by lawful means (without resorting to internationally wrongful acts to fuel unlawful coercion)[53] and there will be additional steps states of nationality should be taking to ensure that their full diplomatic arsenal is ready to be deployed to negotiate and secure the release.

A single classification is made difficult, however, because several regimes of responsibility are simultaneously engaged.

---

[50] Chatham House, 'State Sponsored Hostage-Taking' (22 October 2021) <https://chathamhouse.soutron.net/Portal/Public/en-GB/DownloadImageFile.ashx?objectId=4974&ownerType=0&ownerId=189821> accessed 7 August 2023.

[51] WGAD, 'UN Basic Principles and Guidelines on Remedies and Procedures on the Right of Anyone Deprived of their Liberty to Bring Proceedings Before a Court', UN Doc A/HRC/30/37 (6 July 2015) Principle 15 para 26.

[52] This is indeed a point made by the UK's Foreign Affairs Committee in *Stolen Years: Combatting State Hostage Diplomacy* (n 7) para 13 where it provides that 'All arbitrary detentions are illegal and unacceptable. The UK Government should be working toward their immediate resolution.' The WGAD regularly calls on states to immediately release persons who are detained arbitrarily. See, also, *Stolen Years: Combatting State Hostage Diplomacy* (ibid) 'Written Evidence Submitted by Professor Carla Ferstman and Dr Marina Sharpe (SLH0018)' para 9.

[53] Declaration on Friendly Relations 123.

7.3.1 The human rights violation of arbitrary detention

The phenomenon described in this chapter fits easily within the rubric of the human rights violation of arbitrary detention as there is necessarily no lawful basis to detain. Individuals subject to the practice will ordinarily be charged with security-related crimes and detained prior to trial. However, invariably, these laws will not satisfy the principle of legality because of vague and overly broad terms incapable of being consistently or predictably applied,[54] and when they inappropriately target persons based on their national or social origin they are discriminatory. This is made worse when states fail to follow the procedures required by law, such as to present the individual with an arrest warrant and to explain the reasons for the arrest,[55] to ensure access to independent counsel,[56] and to promptly ensure a genuine review of the lawfulness of detention.[57]

If a trial that has led to a conviction and sentence of imprisonment fell short of the most basic of fair trial guarantees,[58] where the "conviction" was the result of a flagrant denial of justice,[59] or the individual was sentenced to imprisonment without having had a trial, the persons may be considered *inter alia* to be victims of arbitrary detention.[60] Examples would include the

---

[54] WGAD, 'Deliberation No 9 Concerning the Definition and Scope of Arbitrary Deprivation of Liberty Under Customary International Law' UN Doc A/HRC/22/44 (24 December 2012) para 63; WGAD, *Opinion Concerning Mehmet Ali Öztürk* (n 13) paras 95–97.

[55] WGAD, *Opinion Concerning Nizar Zakka* (n 13) paras 55–57; WGAD, *Opinion Concerning Mehmet Ali Öztürk* (n 13) paras 64–67.

[56] In Kamran Ghaderi's case, the WGAD considered that 'the failure to provide Mr. Ghaderi with access to his lawyer from the outset, and the subsequent limitation of his meetings with counsel to mere minutes, violated his right to adequate time and facilities for the preparation of his defence and to communicate with counsel of his own choosing under article 14(3)(b) of the Covenant': (n 14) para 44. See, also, WGAD, *Opinion Concerning Aras Amiri* (n 11) paras 55–58; WGAD, *Opinion Concerning Nizar Zakka* (n 13) para 63; *Opinion Concerning Mehmet Ali Öztürk* (n 13) paras 75–80; Body of Principles for the Protection of All Persons under any Form of Detention or Imprisonment, UNGA Resolution 43/173 (9 December 1988); UN Standard Minimum Rules for the Treatment of Prisoners (Mandela Rules), UNGA resolution 70/175, annex (17 December 2015).

[57] WGAD, *Opinion Concerning Nizar Zakka* (n 13) para 59; *Savalanli v Azerbaijan* App Nos 54151/11 76631/14 et al (ECtHR, 15 December 2022) para 102.

[58] WGAD, *Opinion Concerning Nazanin Zaghari-Ratcliffe* (n 18) para 52. See, also, *Yeğer v Turkey* App No 4099/12 (ECtHR, 7 June 2022) para 46.

[59] *Ilaşcu v Moldova and Russia* (Grand Chamber) App No 48787/99 (ECtHR, 8 July 2004) para 461.

[60] See, for example, HRC, 'Report of the Detailed Findings of the Commission of Inquiry on Human Rights in the Democratic People's Republic of Korea', UN Doc A/HRC/25/CRP.1 (7 February 2014) paras 793, 820, 844.

absence of a fair hearing by an independent and impartial tribunal,[61] the resort to torture or other cruel, inhuman, or degrading treatment or punishment to coerce a confession,[62] the failure to provide to the detainee and/or their counsel the indictment and case particulars,[63] the failure to produce a duly reasoned written judgment of the findings of the trial,[64] and the denial of consular assistance for foreign[65] (including dual[66]) nationals. Similarly, if the individual's sentence was excessively lengthy, taking into account the offence for which the individual was convicted, or the person was maintained in detention after the expiry of the sentence,[67] then these circumstances too may give rise to arbitrary detention.

The human rights framing of arbitrary detention is important because it recognises not only the obligation on states to refrain from arbitrary detention but states' positive obligations to protect individuals and groups against arbitrary detention and to take positive action to facilitate the enjoyment of the right to liberty and security of the person.[68] Accordingly, legal and procedural safeguards must be put in place to prevent unlawful and arbitrary detention, and to prevent its continuance and recurrence. Fundamental among these are the obligations to put in place an adequate legal framework to ensure that there is a lawful basis to detain, which aligns with the right to liberty and security of the person and which clarifies the boundaries of who can be arrested, by whom and on what basis, and to ensure that adequate measures are in place to prevent persons from being detained outside those boundaries.[69] Additionally, procedures must be in place to inform detainees of the reasons for their arrest and of the charges proffered, to comply fully with consular rights and respect for the right to counsel, and to ensure that

---

[61] WGAD, *Opinion Concerning Aras Amiri*, ibid.

[62] WGAD, *Opinion Concerning Nizar Zakka* (n 13) para 67.

[63] WGAD, *Opinion Concerning Aras Amiri* (n 11) para 66; *Opinion Concerning Nizar Zakka* (n 13) paras 64, 65; *Opinion Concerning Andrew Craig Brunson* (n 13) paras 63–64.

[64] WGAD, *Opinion re Kamran Ghaderi* (n 14) paras 52, 53.

[65] WGAD, *Opinion Concerning Nizar Zakka* (n 13) paras 68–73; *Opinion Concerning Mehmet Ali Öztürk* (n 13) para 90; *Opinion Concerning Andrew Craig Brunson* (n 13) paras 68–69.

[66] WGAD, *Opinion Concerning Kamran Ghaderi* (n 14).

[67] See, for example, HRC, 'Detailed Findings of the Independent International Fact-Finding Mission on the Bolivarian Republic of Venezuela: Crimes against Humanity Committed Through the State's Intelligence Services: Structures and Individuals Involved in the Implementation of the Plan to Repress Opposition to the Government', UN Doc A/HRC/51/CRP.3 (20 September 2022) para 393.

[68] Human Rights Committee, 'General Comment No 31: Nature of the General Legal Obligation Imposed on States Parties to the International Covenant on Civil and Political Rights' (26 May 2004) UN Doc CCPR/C/21/Rev.1/Add.13, para 7.

[69] Human Rights Committee, General Comment No 35, Article 9 (Liberty and Security of Person) (16 December 2014) UN Doc CCPR/C/GC/35 paras 14–23.

detainees are promptly brought before the competent judicial authorities so that they can challenge the legality of their detention as appropriate.[70]

States have an obligation to investigate with a view to prosecuting those elements of arbitrary detention that amount to torture, enforced disappearances or hostage-taking, or when satisfying the conditions for a crime against humanity (when committed as part of a widespread or systematic attack directed against any civilian population, with knowledge of the attack) or a war crime. The obligation to investigate or prosecute may extend to additional forms of arbitrary detention if adjudged to be the most appropriate way to protect and fulfil the right to liberty and security of the person in the particular context.

It will necessarily be difficult for victims to access the legal systems of the states that engage in the practice to assert and demand enforcement of their rights to be free from arbitrary detention, because these same legal systems have been co-opted by those states to maintain unlawfully the victims in detention. Nevertheless, a determination (whether by an international quasi-adjudicative body like the WGAD or UN Human Rights Committee, or by a domestic panel set up by the state of nationality) that a national was subjected to arbitrary detention will greatly assist the state of nationality in pressing the detaining state to proceed with release, given that a confirmed case of arbitrary detention in state-to-state relations constitutes an internationally wrongful act.[71] It may also assist the detainees and their families to press their state of nationality to respond with due attention, speed and vigour to the plight of the detainees, though the normalisation of arbitrary detention discussed elsewhere in this book risks diluting the robustness of any response. Whereas some countries recognise a constitutional obligation to vigorously defend their nationals who require assistance abroad, in other countries the level of support governments provide is discretionary.[72]

7.3.2 The crime of hostage-taking

The phenomenon of states arbitrarily detaining dual or foreign nationals with a view to exerting pressure on their (other) states of nationality fits the principal criteria of the offence of hostage-taking within the meaning of the 1979 Convention on the Taking of Hostages (the Hostages Convention).[73]

---

[70] Human Rights Committee, General Comment No 35 (n 69) para 24 et seq.
[71] *Iran Hostages case* (n 2). See, further, section 7.3.3 of this chapter.
[72] ILC, 'Draft Articles on Diplomatic Protection and Commentaries', UN Doc A/61/10 (2006). See, also, John Dugard, 'Diplomatic Protection and Human Rights: the Draft Articles of the International Law Commission' (2005) 24 *Australian YB of Intl L* 75.
[73] International Convention against the Taking of Hostages.

To constitute the crime of hostage-taking within the meaning of the Hostages Convention, Article 1 of the Convention refers to:

> any person who seizes or detains and threatens to kill, to injure or to continue to detain a hostage in order to compel a State, an international intergovernmental organization, a natural or juridical person, or a group of persons, to do or abstain from doing any act as an explicit or implicit condition for the release of the hostage.

(i) 'Any person'

The reference to 'any person' underscores that the offence may be carried out by any person, whether a non-state or state actor. Lambert explains that the words 'any person':

> make it clear that the Convention applies regardless of the identity of, or cause espoused by, the offender. They also make it clear that the Convention is directed towards individual liability, rather than State action. This is not to say, however, that the Convention does not apply to acts committed by a person acting at the behest of a State. No exception for State agents can be implied from this wording. Indeed, the draftsmen made it clear that this definition includes acts by such persons. […] it may be assumed that the words 'Any person', unconditional as they stand, cover acts committed by State agents as well as those committed by private persons.[74]

Aust finds similarly that 'the act can be committed by a private individual or by the agent of a State'.[75] In a similar sense, state engagement in hostage-taking is a recognised though prohibited feature of armed conflict.[76]

Domestic law statutes implementing the Hostages Convention adopt the wording "any person" or "a person" when referring to offences. This is the case with the UK Taking of Hostages Act 1982,[77] and the equivalent

---

[74] Joseph Lambert, *Terrorism and Hostages in International Law: a Commentary on the Hostages Convention 1979* (Grotius 1990) 79–80.

[75] Anthony Aust, 'Implementation Kits for the International Counter-Terrorism Conventions' (Legal and Constitutional Affairs Division, Commonwealth Secretariat, London 2002) 142.

[76] See, *United States v Wilhelm List, et al.*, 'The Hostages Case', United States, Military Tribunal at Nuremberg, 15 ILR 632 (19 February 1948). See, also, ICRC, 'Customary International Law Database' (undated) Rule 96 <www.icrc.org/customary-ihl/eng/docs/home> accessed 7 August 2023; UNSC Resolution 687 (8 April 1991) UN Doc S/RES/687 concerning the invasion by Iraq of Kuwait.

[77] Art 1(1) Taking of Hostages Act (1982) c 28.

legislation in Australia,[78] New Zealand,[79] the US,[80] and many other states' implementing legislation.[81]

However, several recent considerations of the practice at the policy level appear to distinguish state-sponsored acts (framed as arbitrary or wrongful detention for leverage) from those carried out by non-state actors (framed as hostage-taking). For example, the UK government expressed the view that it is 'wary of using the term [hostage-taking], arguing that the Hostage Convention refers to individual, rather than state, liability' and it has argued that 'there was a significant risk of making Mrs Zaghari-Ratcliffe's situation worse by referring to her as a hostage of Iran'.[82] Nevertheless, the UK Parliament's Foreign Affairs Committee has recommended that 'the government uses the strongest possible language to call out situations of state hostage-taking as soon as it becomes clear detentions are being used for leverage'.[83]

The US is the only state that has legislated domestically against the practice. The Robert Levinson Hostage Recovery and Hostage-Taking Accountability Act,[84] named for former FBI agent Robert Levinson, who disappeared in March 2007 on Kish Island, Iran,[85] codifies key elements of hostage and wrongful detention policy and provides a framework for the US Secretary of State to review cases and make wrongful detention determinations where appropriate. While it does not define hostage-taking or other wrongful detentions per se, it sets out an open-ended checklist of 11 criteria developed to determine if the circumstances of detention suggest that the detainee was arrested on discriminatory or arbitrary grounds[86] or, differently put, as being detained 'unlawfully or wrongfully'[87]:

(1) US officials receive or possess credible information indicating the innocence of the detained individual.

---

[78] Crimes (Hostages) Act 1989, s 7.
[79] Crimes (Internationally Protected Persons, United Nations and Associated Personnel, and Hostages) Act 1980, s 8(1).
[80] Hostage Taking Act 18 USC 1203 (12 October 1984).
[81] German Criminal Code, s 2139(b); Kenya Prevention of Terrorism Act, Art 28; Thomson Reuters Foundation, 'Held Hostage? A Legal Report on Hostage-Taking by States in Peacetime and the Victim Protection Gap' (September 2018).
[82] *Stolen Years: Combatting State Hostage Diplomacy* (n 7) para 11.
[83] Ibid para 55.
[84] 22 USC 1741 (27 December 2020).
[85] WGAD, *Opinion No 50/2016 Concerning Robert Levinson (Islamic Republic of Iran)*, UN Doc A/HRC/WGAD/2016/50 (17 January 2017).
[86] US Department of State, 'Resource Guide for Families of Wrongful Detainees' (26 July 2021) 10.
[87] Robert Levinson Hostage Recovery and Hostage-Taking Accountability Act (n 48), s 2(a).

(2) The individual is being detained solely or substantially because he or she is a US national.
(3) The individual is being detained solely or substantially to influence US government policy or to secure economic or political concessions from the US government.
(4) The detention appears to be because the individual sought to obtain, exercise, defend, or promote freedom of the press, freedom of religion, or the right to peacefully assemble.
(5) The individual is being detained in violation of the laws of the detaining country.
(6) Independent NGOs or journalists have raised legitimate questions about the innocence of the detained individual.
(7) The US mission in the country where the individual is being detained has received credible reports that the detention is a pretext for an illegitimate purpose.
(8) The individual is detained in a country where the Department of State has determined in its annual human rights reports that the judicial system is not independent or impartial, is susceptible to corruption, or is incapable of rendering just verdicts.
(9) The individual is being detained in inhumane conditions.
(10) Due process of law has been sufficiently impaired so as to render the detention arbitrary.
(11) US diplomatic engagement is likely to be necessary to secure the release of the detained individual.[88]

Under this American model, subsidiary texts define a hostage as a person held by a non-state actor against their will in order to compel a third person or governmental organisation to do or abstain from doing any act as a condition for the release of the person detained.[89] Consequently, state-to-state detentions for leverage are not understood pursuant to these texts as hostage-taking, whereas detentions by non-state actors for leverage would be considered hostage-taking.[90] While this approach understates the practice of state-sponsored arbitrary detentions, distinguishing between cases in which states ordinarily apply their criminal laws to detain foreign or dual nationals and cases in which such detentions are "wrongful" or "unlawful" at least provides a clear space for states of nationality to seek their nationals'

---

[88] Ibid.
[89] Resource Guide for Families of Wrongful Detainees (n 86) Glossary of Acronyms and Terms, 45. See, also, Presidential Policy Directive PPD-30 (24 June 2015) para 7.
[90] Resource Guide for Families of Wrongful Detainees (n 86) 9.

release and return, as opposed to simply monitoring their well-being.[91] And the different label has not significantly impeded the capacity of the SPEHA to coordinate diplomatic efforts to recover Americans wrongfully detained abroad.[92]

(ii) 'In order to compel'

The definition of hostage-taking requires that the act of seizing, detaining, threatening to kill, to injure or to continue to detain, is done 'in order to compel a State, an international intergovernmental organization, a natural or juridical person, or a group of persons, to do or abstain from doing any act as an explicit or implicit condition for the release of the hostage'.[93]

As set out in section 7.2, the detaining state may not always articulate the actual purpose of a detention, and a failure to do so would not impede a finding that the detaining state carried out the detention 'in order to compel'. As Lambert has explained in relation to the Hostages Convention:

> [W]hile the seizure and threat will usually be accompanied or followed by a demand that a third party act in a certain way, there is no actual requirement that a demand be uttered. Thus, if there is a detention and threat, yet no demands, there will still be a hostage-taking if the offender is seeking to compel a third party.[94]

Intention may be derived from the wider context and circumstances surrounding the detention.[95]

Courts and other treaty bodies or special procedures frequently determine on the basis of the facts of a particular case that there was no reasonable basis to detain an individual, and that the detention was undertaken for an ulterior purpose unconnected with any lawful purpose to detain.[96] This

---

[91] Gilbert, Written Evidence (n 30) para 8. See, also, UK Parliament Foreign Affairs Committee, Oral Evidence: the FCDO's approach to state level hostage situations, HC 166 (7 February 2023), Witness Mickey Bergman, Q201.
[92] Gilbert (n 30) para 9.
[93] Art 1 Hostages Convention.
[94] Lambert (n 74) 85.
[95] *Demirtaş v Turkey (No. 2)* (n 31) paras 436, 437; *Prosecutor v Sesay, Kallon and Gbao*, Appeals Judgment (n 33) para 580.
[96] For example, *Demirtaş v Turkey (No. 2)* (n 31); *Merabishvili v Georgia* (Grand Chamber) (n 22); WGAD, *Opinion No 52/2018 Concerning Xiyue Wang (Islamic Republic of Iran)*, UN Doc A/HRC/WGAD/2018/52 (21 September 2018) paras 74, 81, 82; WGAD, *Opinion No 49/2017 Concerning Siamak Namazi and Mohammed Baquer Namazi (Islamic Republic of Iran)*, UN Doc A/HRC/WGAD/2017/49 (22 September 2017) paras 45, 49.

has frequently led to findings of arbitrary detention.[97] This may then be connected to other circumstantial evidence or contextual information that can form the basis for inferences such as the timing of releases, statements in the media or similar that point to negotiated releases.[98]

(iii) Application to dual nationals detained in one of their states of nationality

The Hostages Convention does not apply when the offence is committed within a single state, the hostage and the alleged offender are nationals of that state, and the alleged offender is found in the territory of that state.[99] The phenomenon of states arbitrarily detaining individuals with a view to exerting pressure on their (other) states of nationality will invariably not be caught by this limitation as it will involve the detention of foreign nationals. The applicability of the Hostages Convention to the detention of dual nationals who possess the nationality of the detaining state is more contentious.

There are three interlinked arguments that can be made to demonstrate how the Hostages Convention can apply to dual nationals who possess the nationality of the detaining state.

First, if the detainee's nationality that coincides with the detaining state is ineffective, given significant ties elsewhere,[100] then, pursuant to Article 13 of the Hostages Convention, the detention would not be purely domestic. This would require a factual determination as to which nationality is effective, which, according to the *Nottebohm Case*, is the jurisdiction where the person concerned has 'stronger factual ties', inviting consideration of different factors such as 'the habitual residence of the individual concerned', 'the centre of his interests, his family ties, his participation in public life, attachment shown by him for a given country and inculcated in his children, etc'.[101] While determinations of which nationality is 'effective' have been made in the context of assessing a state's competence to bring a claim,[102] there is no reason why the same logic cannot apply to determinations under Article 13 of the Hostages Convention.

---

[97] Ibid.
[98] *Merabishvili v Georgia* (Grand Chamber) (n 22) paras 309–317; see further, Ferstman and Sharpe (n 29) 412–416.
[99] Art 13 Hostages Convention.
[100] ILC, 'Draft Articles on Diplomatic Protection with Commentaries' (n 72) Art 7.
[101] *Case Concerning Nottebohm* (*Liechtenstein v Guatemala*) [1955] ICJ Rep 4, 22.
[102] Ibid. See, also, *Esphahanian v Bank Tejarat*, Iran-USCRT, vol 2 (1983), 166; *Ataollah Golpira v Government of Islamic Republic of Iran*, IranUSCTR vol 2 (1983) 174 and ILR vol 72, 493.

Second, if the arbitrary detentions are carried out as part of a broader pattern involving the detention of persons with several different nationalities, and the dual nationals are part of this broader pattern then, logically, they should not be excluded from being considered as hostages as the international dimension of the hostage situation has been demonstrated. This is an argument that has been made by Lambert.[103] He argues that for 'the offence to remain outside of the scope of the Hostages Convention, *all* the hostages and *all* the offenders must be nationals of the State in which the offence was committed'; 'the mere fact that one of the hostages is of a different nationality than all the others will be enough for this [Hostages] Convention to apply, even to an otherwise solely internal offence'.[104]

Third, the international dimension is derived from the international purpose of the detention, which is to exert leverage on another state.[105] Lambert also considered this argument in his text, but expressed doubts that the argument reflected the state of the law at that time (in 1990 when his text was published).[106] However, the position has evolved since his text was published. Three transnational crime treaties that have subsequently come into force recognise an additional basis for the applicability of the instruments: when the criminal act was directed at the national of a (foreign) state.[107]

The Declaration against Arbitrary Detention in State-to-State Relations, launched by the Canadian government on 15 February 2021, does not refer within the text to "hostage-taking"; it refers to the practice of 'arbitrary arrest or detention of foreign nationals to compel action or to exercise leverage over a foreign government'.[108] Nevertheless, the hostage-taking label is important because it aligns with how many detainees and their families perceive their experiences, also giving due weight to those experiences.[109]

From a legal perspective, the hostage-taking vocabulary also brings to the fore the range of obligations on states parties to the Hostages Convention. These include the obligation to take all practical measures to prevent

---

[103] Lambert (n 74) 312, 300.
[104] Lambert (n 74) 312.
[105] Lambert (n 74) 302–303. See, also, Ferstman and Sharpe (n 29) 417–419.
[106] Lambert (n 74) 302–308.
[107] See, Arts 3 and 6(2) International Convention for the Suppression of Terrorist Bombings (adopted 15 December 1997, entered into force 23 May 2001) 2149 UNTS 256; Arts 3 and 7(2) International Convention for the Suppression of the Financing of Terrorism (adopted 10 January 2000, entered into force 10 April 2002) 2178 UNTS 197; Arts 3 and 9(2) International Convention for the Suppression of Acts of Nuclear Terrorism (adopted 14 September 2005, entered into force 7 July 2007) 2445 UNTS 89.
[108] Declaration against Arbitrary Detention in State-to-State Relations (15 February 2021) preamble.
[109] Ferstman and Sharpe (n 29) 419–420.

preparations for the taking of hostages within or outside their territories, and to cooperate with each other to prevent the commission of such offences.[110] The Convention also requires the detaining state to secure the release and facilitate the departure of hostages from the territory.[111] Like many transnational or international criminal law treaties, the Hostages Convention requires states parties to criminalise acts of hostage-taking,[112] and obliges them to prosecute or extradite suspects found on their territory.[113]

7.3.3 Violating the principle of non-intervention

The inter-state principle of non-intervention, outlawed in the Friendly Relations Declaration,[114] and also constituting a rule of customary international law reflected in Article 2(7) of the UN Charter,[115] is relevant when considering whether any particular form of coercive diplomacy reaches beyond lawful or permissible forms of persuasion.[116] It entails the right of every state to conduct its internal affairs without outside interference, which is a reflection of state sovereignty.[117] The Friendly Relations Declaration makes clear that no state or group of states can intervene 'directly or indirectly, for any reason whatever, in the internal or external affairs of any other State'.[118] Further it makes clear that no state can 'use or encourage the use of economic, political or any other type of measures to coerce another State in order to obtain from it the subordination of the exercise of its sovereign rights and to secure from it advantages of any kind'.[119] The importance of friendly

---

[110] Art 4 Hostages Convention.
[111] Art 3(1) Hostages Convention.
[112] Art 2 Hostages Convention.
[113] Art 5(2) Hostages Convention.
[114] Declaration on Friendly Relations.
[115] Charter of the United Nations and Statute of the International Court of Justice.
[116] Mohamed Helal, 'On Coercion in International Law' (2019) 52 *NYU J Intl L & P* 1, 7.
[117] See, *Military and Paramilitary Activities in and against Nicaragua (Nicaragua v USA)* (Merits) [1986] ICJ Rep 14, para 202. See, also, Art 2(1) of the UN Charter (n 115); *Armed Activities on the Territory of the Congo (Democratic Republic of the Congo v Uganda)* [2005] ICJ Rep 168, para 162.
[118] Friendly Relations Declaration Principle 3 (explanatory text). See, also, UNGA, 'The Essentials of Peace', UNGA Res 290 [V] (1 December 1949); UNGA, 'Declaration on the Inadmissibility of Intervention in the Domestic Affairs of States and the Protection of their Independence and Sovereignty' UNGA Res 2131 [XX] (21 December 1965); UNGA, 'Declaration on the Enhancement of the Effectiveness of the Principle of Refraining from the Threat or Use of Force in International Relations', UNGA Res 42/22 (18 November 1987).
[119] Friendly Relations Declaration.

relations are also underscored, *inter alia*, in the preambles of the Hostages Convention[120] and the Vienna Convention on Consular Relations.[121]

In the *Nicaragua Case*, the ICJ determined that the principle of non-intervention (beyond the specific context of the use of force) applies to one state's actions in relation to another, where:

(1) one state exercises coercion against the other state (what actions might be considered coercive will depend on the particular facts of a matter and the context; but the pressure must be such that it is difficult to resist; 'Only acts of a certain magnitude are likely to qualify as coercive'.[122] Principle 3 of the Friendly Relations Declaration provides: 'No State may [...] coerce another State in order to obtain from it the subordination of the exercise of its sovereign rights and to secure from it advantages of any kind');
(2) in relation to or in a manner to influence 'matters in which each State is permitted, by the principle of State sovereignty, to decide freely. One of these is the choice of a political, economic, social and cultural system, and the formulation of foreign policy.'[123]

Interventions targeting foreign policy involve using some kind of conduct or behaviour as a foreign policy tool against another countries, as a form of 'coercive diplomacy'.[124] Examples of prohibited interventions include compromising:

> the integrity of a State's external affairs to the extent such relations are the sole prerogative of the State. Accordingly, matters protected by this Rule include the choice of extending diplomatic and consular relations, recognition of States or governments, membership in international organisations, and the formation or abrogation of treaties.[125]

---

[120] Hostages Convention preamble.

[121] Vienna Convention on Consular Relations preamble.

[122] Maziar Jamnejad and Michael Wood, 'The Principle of Non-Intervention' (2009) 22(2) *Leiden J Intl L* 2009 345, 248.

[123] *Nicaragua v USA* (n 117) para 205. See Harriet Moynihan, 'The Application of International Law to State Cyberattacks: Sovereignty and Non-Intervention' (Chatham House, 2 December 2019) para 81.

[124] UK Parliament Foreign Affairs Committee, *The FCDO's Approach to State Level Hostage Situations*, Oral Evidence: Rachel Briggs, Chief Executive Officer, The Clarity Factory; Brian Jenkins, Senior Advisor, RAND Corporation (24 May 2022) HC 166.

[125] Michael Schmitt (ed), *Tallinn Manual 2.0 on the International Law Applicable to Cyber Operations* (2nd edn, CUP 2017) 'Rule 66 – Intervention by States: a State may not intervene, including by cyber means, in the internal or external affairs of another State', para 16.

Other examples might include one state demanding that another abandon ambitions to join an international security alliance, or one state imposing a crippling trade embargo to coerce another to change its form of government or associated political alliances. Or there may be examples in which the victim state is coerced into taking specific actions (such as repay debts or release frozen assets), where the timing and modalities of such actions would involve questions of policy involving autonomous decision-making that are part of the victim state's *domaine réservé*.

Carrying out, or threatening to carry out, internationally wrongful acts that breach the fundamental human rights of nationals of the victim state would constitute a further example. The ICJ has observed: 'Wrongfully to deprive human beings of their freedom and to subject them to physical constraint in conditions of hardship is in itself manifestly incompatible with the principles of the Charter of the United Nations.'[126]

When a state violates the principle of non-intervention, or otherwise commits an internationally wrongful act for which it bears responsibility, it will incur the secondary obligations to cease the wrongful conduct if it is continuing.[127] Cases of ongoing arbitrary detention such as 'unlawful detention of a foreign official or unlawful occupation of embassy premises' have been recognised in the commentaries to the ARS as examples of continuing wrongful acts.[128] In cases of arbitrary detention, the obligation of cessation has been taken to mean the immediate release of the detainee from detention,[129] and under the Hostages Convention the additional requirement to facilitate the detainee's departure, where relevant.[130] The WGAD has explained:

> In the case of arbitrary deprivation of liberty, restitution must be in its most direct form, which is the restoration of the liberty of the individual, including in the context of health detention policies. In

---

[126] *Iran Hostages case* (n 2) para 91.
[127] Art 30 ARS.
[128] ARS Commentary to Art 14, para 3.
[129] See, for example, *Assanidze v Georgia* (Grand Chamber) App No 71503/01 (ECtHR, 8 April 2004) para 203: 'by its very nature, the violation found in the instant case did not leave any real choice as to the measures required to remedy it. In these conditions, […], the Court considers that the respondent State must secure the applicant's release at the earliest possible date.' See, also, *Loayza Tamayo v Peru* (Merits) Ser C No 33 (IACtHR, 17 September 1997) para 84; *Fermín Ramírez v Guatemala* (Merits, Reparations, Costs) Ser C No 126 (IACtHR, 20 June 2005) para 130(c).
[130] Art 3(1) Hostages Convention.

addition to releasing the individual, competent authorities should review the reasons for the deprivation of liberty or retry the case.[131]

Beyond cessation, it will also be required to offer appropriate assurances and guarantees of non-repetition, if circumstances so require, and make full reparation for the injury caused by the internationally wrongful act, which would ordinarily take the form of restitution, compensation and/or satisfaction.[132] In the *Iran Hostages Case*, the ICJ determined that the appropriate remedies included immediately terminating the unlawful detention, ensuring that all the said persons have the necessary means of leaving Iranian territory, and making reparation for the injury caused.[133]

7.4 Negotiating release

The state of nationality will usually become aware of the detention when families of the detainee contact the government and inform it of the detention of their loved one. Typically contact will be made through a member of parliament or via consular staff in the detaining country. Under the Vienna Convention on Consular Relations, the detaining state is obliged to advise detained foreigners of their right to contact a representative from their embassy, and to notify the state of nationality of the detention.[134] However, this treaty requirement is not always complied with in detentions involving arbitrary detentions for leverage.[135] In some detaining countries, the practice is to keep the detainee *incommunicado* for weeks and sometimes months at the outset of the detention as part of efforts to interrogate the detainee.[136] Not only is that tendency a violation of detainees' procedural rights,[137] it can

---

[131] WGAD, 'Deliberation No 10 on Reparations for Arbitrary Deprivation of Liberty' (4 May 2020).

[132] Arts 30, 31 ARS.

[133] *Iran Hostages case* (n 2) para 95.

[134] Art 36(1) Vienna Convention on Consular Relations (n 6). See, also, *Avena and Other Mexican Nationals (Mexico v USA)* [2004] ICJ Rep 12.

[135] The former Chair of the WGAD, Dr Elina Steinerte, has advised that 'the jurisprudence of the WGAD strongly indicates that prompt provision of consular assistance, which should be professional and confidential, coupled with the effective legal assistance from the moment of detention, are key safeguards against arbitrary detention of foreign nationals. The practice suggests that this may often require the consular authorities to actively insist on their right to provide such assistance as the authorities of the detaining State may fail to provide prompt notification of the detention and/or allow prompt access to the detainee': see *Stolen Years: Combatting State Hostage Diplomacy* (n 7), Written Evidence submitted by Dr Elina Steinerte (SLH0041) para 11.

[136] See, for example, WGAD, *Opinion No 85/2021 Concerning Anoosheh Ashoori* (n 19); WGAD, *Opinion Concerning Aras Amiri* (n 11).

[137] Ibid.

also constitute an enforced disappearance, may fuel torture or other cruel, inhuman, or degrading treatment, and will be deeply traumatising both for the detainees who experience total isolation and the families who may have no information about the fate of their loved ones.[138]

When the state of nationality learns of an arrest, it will typically operate on the assumption that the detainee has been lawfully detained, and will simply seek to afford the usual, though in practice quite limited, consular support of communicating with the detained national, inquiring about the detainee's health and well-being, and supplying general information to the detainee and/or their family, such as contact details for local lawyers.[139] States' approach to consular assistance is mainly regulated at the domestic level by the state of nationality. It is understood predominantly as a right of the state of nationality (the state of nationality has the right to afford consular assistance). All countries will provide some level of consular support, but not all states will provide regular or robust assistance to their nationals. The scope and content of support provided will depend on the policy of the state of nationality towards consular assistance. It will also depend on the extent of diplomatic relations with the detaining state, the availability of consular representatives in the territory of the detaining state, or what other arrangements the state of nationality could put in place.[140] In some cases, the detaining state may limit access to the detainee where the detainee is a dual national and holds the nationality of the detaining state and the detaining state does not recognise dual nationality. The state of nationality will usually take a pragmatic approach to restrictions on access, particularly at the outset, unless there is a specific reason to fear that the individual is being ill-treated. Often, family members will need to plead with their state of nationality to demand timely and more regular access.

The state of nationality will not easily displace its assumption about the lawful motives for the detention. Given the need to show respect for and allow the foreign justice system to run its course under the duty

---

[138] 'Istanbul Statement on the Use and Effects of Solitary Confinement' International Psychological Trauma Symposium, Istanbul (9 December 2007) <https://drive.reindex.net/RCT/101/TORT2008.1.8.pdf> accessed 10 August 2023.

[139] Dewi Avilia, 'Consular Assistance for Nationals Detained by a Foreign Government: States' Policies and Practises' (2017) 7(1) *Indonesia L Rev* 113.

[140] When a state does not have diplomatic representatives in a country, it may occasionally agree with another state with whom it has close ties to assume consular duties on its behalf. For instance, Switzerland provides limited consular services to US citizens in Iran. EU citizens are entitled to seek help from the embassy or consulate of any other EU country if there is no embassy or consulate from the citizen's own country able to assist. See EU, 'Council Directive 2015/637 on the Coordination and Cooperation Measures to Facilitate Consular Protection for Unrepresented Citizens of the Union in Third Countries and Repealing Decision 95/553/EC' (20 April 2015) OJ L 106, 1–13.

of non-interference (considered in section 7.3.3) and the likely negative impact on diplomatic relations of any interference, the state of nationality is unlikely to make assertions about arbitrary or wrongful detentions unless the evidence of wrongfulness is clear. Even where such clear evidence exists, the state of nationality may nevertheless be reluctant to make, or may delay making, such an assertion, though this might depend also on the relationship between the respective states. At times, a delay may simply be because the state wishes to be careful and avoid overstepping and making a mistake that could negatively impact diplomatic relations. On the surface, what is happening is the detention of a person for the commission of a crime – a purely domestic matter. The state of nationality will be overstepping its authority if it intervenes in such a matter. Of course, the state of nationality should intervene vigorously if it is a case of arbitrary detention for leverage, but it will be very cautious in arriving at such a conclusion.[141] Or it may be that the state has already formed a view about the wrongfulness of the detention but does not wish to confirm that view to the family, to the detaining state, or to the wider public given the potential impact on diplomatic relations with the detaining state, or there are different views within government about what approach to take in the face of the wrongful detention (resulting in paralysis).

Even when the state of nationality has realised that the detention of its national is for an ulterior purpose, it may not always be clear from the outset what the actual purpose of the detention is. Thus, the state of nationality must ascertain the motivations so that negotiations on release can be serious and productive. But this is not a clear process, and there may be domestic political factors that have precipitated a detention that have little to do with the state of nationality, at least at the outset. Those carrying out the detaining may take their time in articulating why they detain, and may do so indirectly. And, for the governments seeking their nationals' release, they may not wish to openly engage in negotiations, as their domestic policies may prevent them from making concessions such as cash payments, prisoner swaps, trade deals or diplomatic support or recognition (for fear of encouraging further detentions), though this may depend on the nature of the perpetrator.[142]

---

[141] Beatrice Lau has explained the dilemma of the state of nationality in these words: 'without a proper framework to differentiate whether the criminalisation or detention of the individual is a pretense to achieve other ulterior motives, victim states may have limited legal avenues to sanction the practice without, ironically, being accused of intervening in the *domaine réservé* of the perpetrating state': Beatrice Lau, 'Who Gets to Say Who is Wrongfully Detained? The Muddy Contours of "Hostage Diplomacy"', *Opinio Juris* (4 October 2022).

[142] For example, Gilbert and Rivard Piché explain, in relation to US practice, that US law prohibits the payment of ransoms to those designated by the State Department as foreign terrorist organisations, but there are no comparable prohibitions to afford concessions

Some of this dance of smoke and mirrors becomes apparent in Mark's depiction of the negotiations in the late 1960s to secure the release of Anthony Grey in Beijing:

> Negotiating with the Chinese over the Reuters correspondent proved a delicate task for the British government. Although London had little doubt that his detention was related to the Hong Kong disturbance, Beijing was reluctant to 'formally name a definite price for the release of Mr. Grey.' In July 1967, the Chinese had linked Grey's house arrest with the imprisonment of the NCNA correspondent, Xue Ping, and seven other news workers in the colony. But by late 1968, they referred to the detention of thirteen – later eleven – 'patriotic journalists' probably because, as the British assessed it, the release of Ping and the seven news workers had deprived Beijing of justifying the continued detention of Grey. Over Grey, British officials had to bargain not only with China but also among themselves. Serious differences existed between the British diplomats in Beijing, who approached the problem from the wider perspective of Anglo–Chinese relations, and the colonial governor, who saw Hong Kong's security as the top priority.[143]

Many victims and families have expressed frustration about the length of time it has taken for their states of nationality to recognise that the detention is wrongful or arbitrary or being effectuated for ulterior purposes. The delays will be frustrating for many families given that, in cases involving state-to-state leverage, progress towards release will only occur once the state of nationality stops treating the matter as an ordinary consular case and applies its full diplomatic arsenal to the goal of finding a solution. Families have also regularly expressed concern about being kept in the dark or feeling as if their governments are patronising them with platitudes, as weeks, months and sometimes years go past without any appreciable progress.[144]

The detainees and their families have little power to compel their state of nationality to respond in any particular way, especially to espouse their claim as a state-to-state dispute, to engage vigorously for the release of their loved ones and, thereafter, to seek a remedy for the harms already suffered. This is because the decision whether and how a state decides to intervene internationally on behalf of their nationals is determined mainly at the

---

to state actors. See, Danielle Gilbert and Gaëlle Rivard Piché, 'Caught Between Giants: Hostage Diplomacy and Negotiation Strategy for Middle Powers' (2021/22) 5(1) *Texas Nat Sec Rev* 1, 16.

[143] Mark (n 2) 487.

[144] See, for example, Loertscher (n 5) 29–34; REDRESS, 'Beyond Discretion: the Protection of British Nationals Abroad from Torture and Ill-Treatment' (January 2018) 43–46.

domestic level.[145] In many states, domestic law affords the state of nationality near absolute discretion to determine how a matter will be pursued, if it is pursued at all. At most, victims and their families may seek to compel their states of nationality not to fetter the exercise of that discretion,[146] and to be informed of the decision-making process about the exercise of discretion. An English High Court has held in an arbitrary detention case that the UK government's very limited approach to consular assistance and failure to call publicly for the detainee's release was not challengeable by the detainee's family, because it fell within the government's discretion.[147] In some other countries, there is a constitutional expectation that states will act in support of their nationals whose rights are violated abroad.[148] John Dugard, in his then role as ILC Rapporteur on Diplomatic Protection, sought to include in the draft articles on diplomatic protection an 'emerging' right to diplomatic protection of states, in which the state of nationality had a legal duty to exercise diplomatic protection on behalf of the injured person upon request, if the injury resulted from a grave breach of a jus cogens norm attributable to another state, with some exceptions,[149] though this right was not included in the version of the draft articles on diplomatic protection ultimately adopted by the ILC.

What has helped prompt states of nationality to engage more effectively has depended upon the country. In some countries, resort to the media, pressure by parliamentarians and joint advocacy by multiple families similarly situated has assisted to raise the profile of ongoing detentions, which has, in turn, encouraged states of nationality to engage more vigorously. This approach has been adopted in part by families in the UK, with some success in pressing the government to become more visibly engaged.[150] In the US,

---

[145] ILC, 'Draft Articles on Diplomatic Protection with Commentaries' (n 72) Commentary to Art 2, para 2, referring to *Case Concerning the Barcelona Traction Light and Power Co Ltd (Belgium v Spain)* Second Phase, Judgment [1970] ICJ Rep 4, 44. See, also, Sevane Garibian. 'Vers l'émergence d'un droit individuel à la protection diplomatique?' (2008) 54 *Annuaire français de droit international* 119.

[146] *Hicks v Ruddock* (2007) 156 FCR 574; *Abbasi v Secretary of State* [2002] EWCA Civ 1598.

[147] *R v Secretary of State for Foreign and Commonwealth Affairs, ex parte Menabe Andargachew* [2016] EWHC 2881 (Admin). Note that the WGAD had called for his immediate release: WGAD, *Opinion No 2/2015 Concerning Andargachew Tsige (Ethiopia and Yemen)*, UN Doc A/HRC/WGAD/2015 (8 May 2015) para 27.

[148] ILC, 'First Report on Diplomatic Protection, by Mr. John R. Dugard, Special Rapporteur', UN Doc A/CN.4/506, I 36 (2000) paras 80–83.

[149] Ibid, Draft Article 4 and Commentaries. See, further, Dugard (n 72).

[150] *Stolen Years: Combatting State Hostage Diplomacy* (n 7) para 57: 'Anooshen Ashoori and his family regretted that they waited so long to go public with his case and that it was only this publicity which persuaded the Government to elevate the priority of his case in negotiations with Iran. Had they remained quiet he may not have been included in the March 2022 deal under which he was released. Richard Ratcliffe felt compelled to go

engagement by civil society groups, such as the James W. Foley Legacy Foundation and Hostages USA and others, led the US government to initiate a comprehensive review of US policy toward overseas hostage-takings and to adopt new policies and structures,[151] such as the Hostage Recovery Fusion Cell and the office of the SPEHA. The SPEHA office has been lauded by families and observers for serving as a crucial focal point for the high-level diplomatic efforts needed to secure releases, for coordinating the efforts within the government and for improving communications and information-sharing with families. The UK Parliament's Foreign Affairs Committee has recommended the UK government to adopt a like approach.[152]

7.5 Conclusions: the importance of multilateral approaches

Having worked on several of these cases, I have formed a view, however anecdotal, as to how many families and governments perceive these detentions and respond to them, and why multilateral approaches are vital, though they can be difficult to agree.

For the most part, states have tended to respond unilaterally to cases involving their nationals. Perhaps if they negotiate alone and identify some feature that distinguishes the national from others similarly detained, they believe they will have a better chance of securing an advantageous outcome. Or perhaps if they negotiate individually with the detaining state, they can secure a preferential deal that the detaining state would never agree to if it was negotiating with a block of states, and still find some way to preserve the diplomatic relationship with the detaining state.

This has also been the approach taken by certain families, at least at the outset of the detention, but for different reasons – *the other detainees may have done something to be arrested, but not our son/daughter/husband, they are different*. This type of reaction does not stem from narcissism or naïveté, but tends to be more of a psychological response to the idea that their loved one

---

on hunger strike to protest at the Government's lack of activity. Daniela Tejada, wife of Matthew Hedges, a UK academic detained in the United Arab Emirates, maintains that she was certain the only reason her husband's case received the attention it did from the FCDO was her choice to go public. There was a strong feeling amongst many we spoke to that Nazanin Zaghari-Ratcliffe's case received more attention from the Government because she had a more prominent public profile as a result of the attention the media gave to her family's campaign. Indeed, Lord Hammond, Foreign Secretary at the time of her arrest, suggested he did not become aware of her case until it was raised in a Parliamentary debate over a month after her arrest.'

[151] The White House, 'Report on U.S. Hostage Policy' (June 2015); PPD-30 (n 89) and Executive Order 13698 'Hostage Recovery Activities' (24 June 2015).

[152] *Stolen Years: Combatting State Hostage Diplomacy* (n 7) paras 41–43.

may be part of a horrific pattern, like the cases they read about in the news, that will take years to fix if they are to be fixed at all. Families want to hold onto the belief that the detaining state took their loved one by mistake; that once the truth of the mistake is revealed, the error will be rectified. They do not want to know about patterns, because the patterns are not helpful to the hope for early release that they must cling to, at least in the first weeks and months. Even much later, many families are still somehow hoping that if their loved one distinguishes themselves from the other detainees, then they can get to the front of the queue – if they complain less, if they remain quiet. But this second-guessing is part of the psychological torment that detainees and their families experience. It feeds into families' stress and fears, contributes to their sense of isolation, and prevents them from acting *en bloc*. Ultimately, of course, the timing of releases may have little to do with the detainees or their families.

It is a struggle to get out of this insular mindset, whether for the family members or the state of nationality. Over time, and as the patterns of the abuses have become much harder to ignore, some families have cautiously come together, to trade stories, for support and solidarity, and in an increasing number of cases to advance joint advocacy campaigns. Former hostages and family members have formed new advocacy and campaigning groups, such as Hostages Aid Worldwide,[153] to provide support and assistance and to advocate for releases and advance policy. Lawyers and legal support organisations have identified and drawn attention to patterns as part of strategies to engage both states of nationality and detaining states, and to seek the support of regional and international organisations, special procedures and rapporteurs.[154]

States too have realised that unilateral approaches can be ineffective. Many detentions will involve multiple states. The release by China of Canadians Michael Kovrig and Michael Spavor necessarily involved actions by both Canada and the US, because the resolution of the case required a US extradition request to be quashed.[155] The release by Iran of Belgian Olivier Vandecasteele required actions by both Belgium and France, because the

---

[153] https://hostageaid.org/.

[154] For instance, the recognition by the WGAD that there was a pattern of arbitrary detentions targeting foreign and dual nationals in Iran stemming from discrimination based on national or social origin served as a catalyst for families of detainees to consider joint advocacy strategies. See, for example, WGAD, *Opinion No 54/2022 Concerning Nahid Taghavi (Islamic Republic of Iran)*, UN Doc A/HRC/WGAD/2022/54 (29 November 2022) para 97 in which is lists its prior opinions in which it identified a practice in Iran of arbitrarily detaining persons who are foreign nationals, dual nationals and Iranian nationals with permanent residence in another country, a pattern also recognised by the Special Rapporteur on the situation of human rights in the Islamic Republic of Iran.

[155] Gilbert (n 30).

intended target of Assadollah Assadi's terror attack was a rally in France. Also, the release would not have been possible without the assistance of Oman, which helped broker the deal.[156] Given that some of these detentions have ostensibly been used to influence the trajectory of international treaty negotiations involving peace and security,[157] the implications are global and may, depending upon the context, entail threats to international peace and security that would engage Chapter VII of the UN Charter.[158]

It was in recognition of the global implications of the phenomenon of arbitrary detention in state-to-state relations that Canada initiated in February 2021 its Declaration against Arbitrary Detention in State-to-State Relations, with 72 endorsements at the time of writing.[159] The Declaration embodies a 'concerted commitment to core principles of human rights, consular relations, the rule of law and the independence of the judiciary',[160] and seeks to raise awareness and stop the practice of arbitrary detention by encouraging diplomatic collaboration among states. The Declaration itself restates basic and uncontroversial international law principles that outlaw arbitrary detention and underscore the importance of international consular law. What is most novel in the Declaration, however, is its commitment to solidarity, collaboration and joint action. The Partnership Action Plan accompanying the Declaration outlines six areas of cooperation and engagement that states can support to advance the goals of the Declaration, which consist of: advocacy and awareness raising; research and analysis; sharing of information; engaging civil society, academics and others with relevant expertise; supporting targeted and effective media campaigns; and meeting periodically to assess progress and advance practical proposals.

While these areas of cooperation are somewhat generic and non-specific, they serve as a useful starting point to build mutual trust and broaden the stakeholders committed to eradicating the practice. Some of the more practical areas for partnership engagement should ideally include: building frameworks for states to mutually support each other in the area of consular assistance and trial monitoring[161]; sharing intelligence and best practice

---

[156] Wintour, 'Belgium Aid Worker Freed in Prisoner Swap with Iranian Diplomat Jailed for Bomb Plot' (n 40).
[157] Rezaian (n 41).
[158] UN Charter (n 115).
[159] Global Affairs Canada, 'Initiative against Arbitrary Detention in State-to-State Relations', <www.international.gc.ca/world-monde/issues_development-enjeux_developpement/human_rights-droits_homme/arbitrary_detention-detention_arbitraire.aspx?lang=eng#a3> accessed 7 August 2023, list of endorsements.
[160] Ibid.
[161] Mike Blanchfield and Fen Osler Hampson, 'How the Free World Helped Free Two Canadians: Diplomacy and the Two Michaels', *Policy Magazine* (27 December 2022).

in identifying and addressing cases; engaging as appropriate the peace and security architecture of regional and international organisations for the purpose of sanctions or other counter-measures; and strengthening the international legal framework, as required, regarding state sponsored hostage-taking. As a general matter, however, when states work together to address these cases, they will ultimately reduce the power of perpetrator states to successfully isolate the state of nationality and to exert pressure or coercion on that state effectively. This is a powerful incentive to amplify multilateral approaches.

8

Detention and Pandemic Exceptionality

8.1 Introduction

This chapter considers the circumstances of persons deprived of their liberty in the context of epidemics, pandemics and other major health emergencies.[1] As described throughout this book, detention is intended to be exceptional, and this chapter explores the extent to which pandemics impact upon this exceptional character. Pandemics highlight and, in many respects, exacerbate inequalities, and consequently the chapter also considers how inequality impacts upon exceptionalisms and, particularly, the exceptionalism of detention.

The chapter analyses how governments, specialist agencies and courts have grappled with the legal, ethical and public health consequences associated with detention and infectious disease, looking particularly at the recent experience of COVID-19. I consider how lockdowns and quarantines were used to curb the spread of COVID-19. Here, I assess the potential over-reach of emergency regulations, discriminatory impacts, and the ways in which restrictions have been balanced with other rights, particularly for the most vulnerable in society.

The chapter then turns to consider how governments and others have sought to control the spread of COVID-19 in closed places of confinement, including prisons and criminal remand centres, immigration holding facilities, hospitals, psychiatric care establishments and social care institutions. In particular, I consider the imposition of no-visitation policies on highly vulnerable persons as well as COVID-inspired releases

---

[1] An early, abridged version of this chapter was published as: Carla Ferstman, 'Detention and Pandemic Exceptionality', in Carla Ferstman and Andrew Fagan (eds), *COVID-19, Law and Human Rights: Essex Dialogues* (Essex Law School and Human Rights Centre 2020).

from detention. I assess whether the goals of retribution and specific and general deterrence should be weighed against the rights to health and safety of prisoners and prison staff and, if so, in which ways. Arguably, the recognition of the heightened health risks for detainees associated with pandemics should serve as an important impetus to reduce reliance on detention – and thereby to make good on the intention for detention to be recognised as an exceptional measure. Yet, as will be shown, the selectivity of approaches, buoyed here too by inequalities, and the lack of transparency and oversight of decision-making has put some detainees – often those who are most vulnerable because they are "unseen", "reviled and resented", or "undeserving",[2] and with the least agency and voice – at even greater risk of harm. I also analyse to what extent the arbitrary resort to detention as well as the arbitrary decision to maintain someone in detention during a pandemic, which may heighten detainees' exposure to the disease and thereby increase prospects of illness and death, as well as produce extreme anxiety, give rise to violations of the right to life and cruel, inhuman, or degrading treatment or punishment, if not torture.

I conclude by assessing whether the experience of pandemics has helped to clarify understandings of "arbitrariness". By increasing the unacceptability of detention during pandemics and other health emergencies, have the rules regarding what may constitute "arbitrary detention" changed?

8.2 Human rights, infectious diseases and the positive obligation of non-discrimination

International human rights standards recognise the obligation on states to respect, protect and fulfil human rights. Each human right is comprised of different negative and positive obligations. These will depend on the nature of the right and what is judged necessary to make it practical and effective,[3] and how the right is characterised under treaty-based and/or customary international law.[4] Positive obligations, which are relevant when assessing states' responses to epidemics, pandemics and other major health emergencies, are the proactive steps states must take to ensure that human rights can be achieved. States generally have an obligation of means; they must exercise due diligence to prevent and respond to violations, which requires them to deploy their best efforts that adequately account for the risks, the underlying context, and their capacity to act.[5]

---

[2] These are categories of marginalisation developed in Chapter 4 of this book.
[3] *Öneryildiz v Turkey* App No 48939/99 (ECtHR, 30 November 2004) para 69.
[4] Dinah Shelton and Ariel Gould, 'Positive and Negative Obligations', in Dinah Shelton (ed), *The Oxford Handbook of International Human Rights Law* (OUP 2013) 563.
[5] *Velásquez-Rodríguez v Honduras* (Merits) Series C No 4 (IACtHR, 29 July 1989) para 172.

States' positive obligations in respect of the right to health[6] include the need to take appropriate measures to address infectious diseases. Notwithstanding the standard of "progressive realisation" that attaches to many economic, social and cultural rights, including the right to health,[7] Article 12(2)(c) of the ICESCR recognises that states must take measures to 'prevent, treat and control' epidemic and other diseases,[8] which has been taken to require prevention and education programmes, the creation of a system of urgent medical care, and the need to implement or enhance immunisation programmes and other strategies to control infectious diseases.[9]

When considering the right to life, the Human Rights Committee recognises that states cannot rely on economic hardship, lack of financial resources or other logistical problems to reduce their responsibility to take any necessary measures to protect the lives of individuals deprived of their liberty by the state.[10] States' positive obligations to safeguard life[11] apply in all detention settings, including health and social care settings.[12] Positive obligations to protect life also include the requirement to take appropriate measures to address the prevalence of life-threatening diseases.[13] Detaining authorities are obligated to take adequate steps to prevent the spread of contagious disease, and must introduce measures, such as screening detainees upon admission and prompt and effective treatment programmes.[14]

Severe overcrowding can amount to prohibited ill-treatment[15] on account of the distress or hardship it engenders, for example by being 'obliged to live, sleep and use the toilet in the same cell with so little personal space'.[16] It is not difficult to extend this logic to detainees who fear the spread of COVID-19 because of inadequate sanitation, poor ventilation, lack of protective gear for staff entering and exiting facilities and inadequate testing and medical care. The ECtHR has recognised that the failure to diagnose and provide adequate

---

[6] UN Committee on Economic, Social and Cultural Rights (CESCR), 'General Comment No 14: the Right to the Highest Attainable Standard of Health (Art 12)' UN Doc E/C.12/2000/4 (11 August 2000) para 33.

[7] Judith Bueno de Mesquita et al, 'Lodestar in the Time of Coronavirus? Interpreting International Obligations to Realise the Right to Health During the COVID-19 Pandemic' (2023) 23 *Hum Rts L Rev* 1, 15–20.

[8] ICESCR.

[9] CESCR General Comment No 14 (n 6) para 16.

[10] Human Rights Committee, 'General Comment No 36: Article 6: Right to Life' (3 September 2019) UN Doc CCPR/C/GC/36 para 25.

[11] Art 6(1) ICCPR.

[12] *Lopes de Sousa Fernandes v Portugal* App No 56080/13 (ECtHR, 19 December 2017).

[13] Human Rights Committee, General Comment No 36 (n 10) para 26.

[14] *Poghosyan v Georgia* App No 9870/07 (ECtHR, 24 February 2009) paras 69, 70.

[15] *Kalashnikov v Russia* App No 47095/99 (ECtHR, 15 July 2002) paras 96–97.

[16] *Khudoyorov v Russia* App No 6847/02 (ECtHR, 8 November 2005) para 107.

medical care to detainees can amount to degrading treatment on account of the considerable anxiety and strong feelings of insecurity this may give rise to[17]; lack of treatment resulting in death would also violate the right to life if the authorities knew or ought to have known at the time of the existence of a real and immediate risk to the life of the individual and failed to take measures within the scope of their powers that, judged reasonably, might have been expected to avoid that risk.[18] In *Gladkiy v Russia*, the ECtHR determined that, 'for lack of adequate medical treatment, the applicant was exposed to prolonged mental and physical suffering diminishing his human dignity'.[19] In accordance with the above-referenced standards, an arbitrary deprivation of life may occur when the state fails to act with due diligence to protect life. Similarly, a state may violate the prohibition on ill-treatment when, in the context of a pandemic, it places a detainee near other persons who could have posed a risk to health in the absence of any relevant health consideration for doing so.[20]

When persons are detained at the insistence of the state during a pandemic or other health emergency, the state has a special responsibility to ensure their well-being and lives, given detainees' complete reliance on the state. The Human Rights Committee has recognised that the obligation on states to care for detainees is a 'heightened duty of care' 'to protect the life of all detained individuals [and] includes providing them with the necessary medical care and appropriately regular monitoring of their health'.[21] Taking into account the heightened risks of disease transmission in places of detention, and the ultra-vulnerability of detainees, what is understood as necessary measures to protect life may be especially extensive, depending on the circumstances.

The enforcement of rights in a pandemic also invites consideration of whose rights (and not only which rights) are at stake. There are a multitude of "otherings" at play.[22] Pandemics and how one responds to them exacerbate the marginalisation of already oppressed groups, including their disproportionate effect on:

> individuals and groups who are marginalized and more vulnerable to racial discrimination, in particular persons belonging to national

---

[17] *Khudobin v Russia* App No 59696/00 (ECtHR, 26 October 2006) paras 94–96. See, also, *Asyukov v Russia* App No 2974/05 (ECtHR, 5 April 2011) para 76.

[18] *Salakhov and Islyamova v Ukraine* App No 28005/08 (ECtHR, 14 March 2013) paras 180–183.

[19] *Gladkiy v Russia* App No 3242/03 (ECtHR, 21 December 2010) para 96.

[20] *Feilazoo v Malta* App No 6865/19 (ECtHR, 11 March 2021) para 92.

[21] Human Rights Committee, General Comment No 36 (n 10) para 25.

[22] Kim Dionne and Fulya Turkmen, 'The Politics of Pandemic Othering: Putting COVID-19 in Global and Historical Context' (2020) 74(S1) *International Organization* E213.

or ethnic, religious and linguistic minorities as well as indigenous peoples, including those living in isolation, migrants, refugees and asylum-seekers, Roma, non-citizens, people of African descent and other groups who face discrimination based on descent.[23]

This discrimination is evident in discussions about the utility of herd immunity. As Butler has argued:

> [O]ne could say that herd immunity does not contain in itself a death verdict, and yet its implementation would certainly lead to the increased isolation, unemployment, and ostracism of those considered to be most vulnerable – it also makes explicit assumptions about mortality rates linked with rates of productivity. […] These populations are considered as on their way to death anyway, not worth safeguarding, and a metric is implicitly or explicitly adopted that determines whose life is valuable and whose is not. Any policy or institution that creates increased mortality rates for a group is engaged in a form of death dealing. When that group is black, it is a racist form of death dealing with clear links to other forms, including the carceral ones.[24]

This discrimination is also apparent in how the enforcement of rights impacts the relative weight and positioning of marginalised persons and groups, such as the higher proportions of persons from marginalised groups already subject to detention. The impact of inadequate precautionary measures, limited access to vaccinations and poor medical treatment and care in prisons affect disproportionally those groups that are over-represented in prison populations. This in and of itself can exacerbate the discrimination these groups experience. As the Office of the United Nations High Commissioner for Human Rights (OHCHR) has explained, the 'failure to address the heightened risks in places of detention, including through prisons release, also thus raises questions of racial discrimination and racial justice'.[25]

Differential impacts of lockdowns and isolation measures, including on job security, livelihoods, well-being, access to services, including education, and personal safety,[26] must also be considered from an anti-discrimination

---

[23] CERD Committee, 'Statement on the Coronavirus (COVID-19) Pandemic and its Implications Under the International Convention on the Elimination of All Forms of Racial Discrimination' (7 August 2020).

[24] Francis Wade, 'Judith Butler on the Violence of Neglect Amid a Health Crisis' *The Nation* (13 May 2020).

[25] OHCHR, 'Racial Discrimination in the Context of the Covid-19 Crisis' (22 June 2020) 3.

[26] UN Secretary-General, 'COVID-19 and Human Rights: We Are All in This Together' (April 2020) 10–12.

perspective. For example, COVID-19 lockdowns had a disproportionately severe impact on elderly persons, who already faced higher infection and mortality rates, were disadvantaged in some triage decisions, and faced neglect and social isolation under confinement.[27] Other persons significantly affected were those in menial or insecure jobs who could not simply shift their work online and persons without homes where they could isolate. Lockdowns have also significantly heightened the risk of domestic violence, which has been recognised as a major public health concern.[28]

These differential impacts all influence the nature of states' positive obligations to protect and fulfil human rights. Thus, the nature of the positive obligation to take appropriate steps to protect health and life in the context of a pandemic will be influenced directly by groups' differential risk profiles. A higher risk should lead to more concerted efforts on the part of authorities to address that risk. In line with the obligation to ensure that the measures states adopt account for multiple and intersecting forms of discrimination and inequalities, and do not disproportionally harm vulnerable people,[29] states must proactively identify and take those vulnerabilities into account when devising measures to comply with positive obligations to protect and fulfil human rights, and when determining the proportionality of operational measures that restrict certain human rights.[30] This may require added protections for groups most at risk or disproportionately impacted, in order to ensure substantive equality.[31] A blunt, uniform approach that exacerbates inequalities would not comply with states' obligations to respect the rights to life and health, the prohibition of ill-treatment, and the obligation not to discriminate.

---

[27] Richard Armitage and Laura Nellums, 'COVID-19 and the Consequences of Isolating the Elderly' (2020) 5 *The Lancet*, Correspondence e256.

[28] Jinan Usta et al, 'COVID-19 Lockdown and the Increased Violence Against Women: Understanding Domestic Violence During a Pandemic' (2021) 8(3) *Violence and Gender* 133.

[29] CESCR, General Comment No 14 (n 6) para 43(f).

[30] IACommHR, 'Human Rights of Persons with Covid-19', Resolution No 4/2020 (20 July 2020) para 24: 'measures must be adopted immediately that include gender equality and intersectional perspectives, as well as differential approaches, in order to highlight the added risks of violating the human rights of persons, groups, and collectivities in the region that are especially vulnerable or who have historically suffered exclusion, such as persons living in poverty or on the street, older adults, persons deprived of liberty, indigenous peoples, tribal communities, Afrodescendants, persons with disabilities, migrants, refugees, and displaced persons in other human mobility contexts, LGBTI persons, children and adolescents, and women, particularly pregnant women and victims of gender-based violence.'

[31] Sandra Fredman, 'Emerging from the Shadows: Substantive Equality and Article 14 of the European Convention on Human Rights' (2016) 16(2) *Hum Rts L Rev* 273, 282–284.

Accordingly, there is likely to be a violation of the right to life or right to health 'when the measures taken to control the pandemic have not – or have to an insufficient degree – taken into account these heightened risks',[32] or where:

> the government has neglected to adopt special protective measures in regard to the greater risk to life and health of certain groups, [...] e.g. a case in which persons with disabilities in residential care institutions are exposed to a disproportionate risk of infection because of lack of protective equipment, and failure to prioritise their needs.[33]

The law on equality and non-discrimination in ordinary times recognises the need to factor in disadvantage when adopting and implementing policies or programmes.[34] It is equally, if not more, important for it to do so in extraordinary times of pandemics and other serious health emergencies.

8.3 The proportionality of anti-COVID measures that deprive persons of their liberty

Proportionality tests are frequently used to determine the appropriateness of the limitation of rights. Thus, if a state action interferes with or limits individuals' human rights, and the human rights being interfered with are not absolute rights (like the prohibition on torture, which is incapable of being restricted or abrogated), then there is a need to consider whether the interference or limitation of the right in question is justifiable. This would involve assessing whether the interference or limitation meets the requirements of legality, necessity and proportionality, and is non-discriminatory.[35] In the context of a pandemic, as in all contexts, this results in evaluating different societal interests.

---

[32] Eva Brems, 'Unequal Human Rights impact of the COVID-19 Pandemic: the Added Value of Indirect Discrimination Framing', in *Indirect Discrimination and the COVID-19 Pandemic*: February 2021 Workshop Proceedings, Harvard Human Rights Program Research Working Paper Series 37, 38.

[33] Ibid, 42.

[34] For example, the obligation to take all appropriate steps to ensure that reasonable accommodation is provided. See, Art 5(3) CRPD.

[35] See, for example, Human Rights Committee, General Comment No 29: Derogations During a State of Emergency (31 August 2001) UN Doc CCPR/C/21/Rev.1/Add.1. See, also, UN Commission on Human Rights, 'The Siracusa Principles on the Limitation and Derogation Provisions in the International Covenant on Civil and Political Rights', UN Doc E/CN.4/1985/4 (28 September 1984).

The assessment whether a restriction or deprivation of liberty constitutes an appropriate response to the circumstances of a pandemic or other health emergency will depend firstly on whether it was undertaken in accordance with law. First, to avoid the arbitrary exercise of power, the rights-restricting measures would need to be adopted by way of a clear, transparent process that is prescribed by law. In this respect, COVID-19 has resulted in some states derogating from certain treaty obligations, arguing that the pandemic constituted a public health emergency threatening the life of the nation.[36] Even without a formal derogation, states have used the exigencies of the situation to introduce new laws and policies or reform existing ones, which restrict or limit certain fundamental rights and freedoms, in order to preserve others.[37] Thus "accordance to law" will already have several permutations depending on how it is activated and the extent to which the internal and external rules for the mode of application have been appropriately applied.[38] A second component concerns the measures themselves: whether they are sufficiently clear and precise to promote legal certainty. The measures should be publicly declared and accessible so that all are sufficiently aware of their existence and what steps they must take to comply.[39] Laws or regulations that are vague or unclear, or involve significant discretion in how they are applied, can result in arbitrary or disproportionate enforcement, with a potential to produce differential impacts for individuals coming from marginalised or vulnerable groups.

There is then a need to consider whether the restrictions or deprivations were undertaken for a legitimate purpose. Human rights texts tend to refer to the purposes of respecting the rights and reputations of others, protecting national security or public order, protecting public morals, public health[40]

---

[36] Audrey Lebret, 'Covid-19 Pandemic and Derogation to Human Rights' (2020) 7(1) *J Law & Biosciences* 1. See, also, Roman Girma Teshome, 'Derogations to Human Rights During a Global Pandemic: Unpacking Normative and Practical Challenges' (2022) 37(2) *Am U Intl L Rev* 307.

[37] Alain Zysset, 'To Derogate or to Restrict? The COVID-19 Pandemic, Proportionality, and the Justificatory Gap in European Human Rights Law' (2022) 4 *Jus Cogens* 285; Alessandra Spadaro, 'COVID-19: Testing the Limits of Human Rights' (2020) 11(2) *Eur J Risk Regulation* 317, 320–322.

[38] International Center for Not-for-Profit Law, 'COVID-19 Civic Freedom Tracker', <www.icnl.org/covid19tracker/> accessed 11 August 2023, which monitors government responses to the pandemic that affect civic freedoms and human rights, focusing on emergency laws. The tracker lists 112 countries with emergency declarations.

[39] Joelle Grogan, 'Impact of COVID-19 Measures on Democracy and Fundamental Rights: Best Practices and Lessons Learned in the Member States and Third Countries', European Parliament's special committee on the COVID-19 pandemic: lessons learned and recommendations for the future (COVI), PE 734.010 (November 2022) 48–52.

[40] For example, Art 29(2) Universal Declaration of Human Rights, UNGA Res 217(A)(III) (10 December 1948) (adopted by 48 votes to none, eight abstentions); Art 19(3) ICCPR.

of the general welfare of a democratic society.[41] Many lockdown measures, for instance, aim to reduce the spread of infection and to prevent health systems from being overwhelmed. These aims would both be consistent with protecting public health and, on that basis, are relatively uncontroversial.

Following such analyses, one must consider the appropriateness of the measures adopted. This involves considering the extent to which the limitations or restrictions are designed to meet, and are rationally connected to, the objective being sought. Thus, in the context of a pandemic or health emergency, there is a need for the measures adopted to be relevant and appropriate to reduce the spread of infection and/or promote health. Where a pandemic has served as the impetus to bring in legislative or regulatory reforms that consolidate power in the executive or to regulate matters that are unconcerned with the promotion of health, these would be inconsistent with this part of the proportionality analysis.[42]

The measures adopted must be strictly proportionate to the threat to the public caused by the emergency, they must reflect the least intrusive means to protect public health and be imposed only for the time required to combat the emergency.[43] Thus, it must be considered whether there are other ways to achieve the aims that are less intrusive or limiting in respect of the rights in question.[44] This invites consideration of whether, balancing the severity of the measures' effects on the rights of the persons to whom it applies against the importance of the objective, the former may, in certain circumstances, outweigh the latter. If the measures taken produce a discriminatory effect on certain protected groups or produce consequences for such groups that are so serious that they outweigh the potential general benefit to society they are designed to achieve, then this too would not satisfy a proportionality analysis.

The lawfulness of quarantines and/or other restrictions on movement or liberty are not treated in any depth by the ICESCR or by the Committee on Economic, Social and Cultural Rights (CESCR) in its General Comment on the right to the highest attainable standard of health, though the Committee makes clear that a state party that:

> restricts the movement of, or incarcerates, persons with transmissible diseases such as HIV/AIDS, refuses to allow doctors to treat persons

---

[41] Art 4 ICESCR.

[42] Venice Commission, 'Respect for Democracy, Human Rights and the Rule of Law During States of Emergency: Reflections', CDL-AD(2020)014 Study No 987/2020 (19 June 2020) para 10.

[43] WGAD, 'Deliberation No 11 on Prevention of Arbitrary Deprivation of Liberty in the Context of Public Health Emergencies', UN Doc A/HRC/45/16 (24 July 2020) Annex II, para 3.

[44] *Enhorn v Sweden* App No 56529/00 (25 January 2005) para 44.

believed to be opposed to a Government, or fails to provide immunization against the community's major infectious diseases, on grounds such as national security or the preservation of public order, has the burden of justifying such serious measures.[45]

Accordingly, states can adopt exceptional measures that restrict freedom of movement or the right to liberty in order to protect public health. However, such measures would need to satisfy the requirements of legality, the aims pursued must be legitimate, and the measures taken the least restrictive as possible to the enjoyment of the right. Only those restrictions that are strictly necessary would be permissible.

The differential impacts of the pandemic and pandemic responses on vulnerable and marginalised groups should also have a direct bearing on assessments of necessity and proportionality. When one assesses the appropriateness of quarantines, lockdowns, isolation measures and other pandemic-related restrictions on liberty or, indeed, the situation of persons in all forms of detention, it is necessary to look beyond the generalities.

8.4 Quarantines, lockdowns and other pandemic-related restrictions on liberty

Quarantines and lockdowns are restrictions that are placed on the society to reduce the spread of infectious diseases. They are put in place to protect not only the health and life of quarantined persons but also those of others in society. As Butler explains, they set out a vision of interconnectivity and solidarity – the idea of living as being bound up with others.[46]

Typically, quarantines separate and restrict the movement of people who were exposed to a contagious disease to see if they become sick. During pandemics, quarantines are often applied more broadly (in the form of lockdowns) to the society at large, to segments of society who are particularly vulnerable to infection, and to persons who are adjudged likely to have been exposed, for example because of their patterns of travel or for other reasons.

There is a history to the use of quarantines and related measures as a strategy to reduce transmission rates.[47] Quarantines have long been used in ports of entry, dating back to the times of the Bubonic Plague or Black Death, to

---

[45] CESCR General Comment No 14 (n 6) para 28.
[46] Judith Butler, *What World Is This? A Pandemic Phenomenology* (Columbia University Press 2022) 39.
[47] Eugenia Tognotti, 'Lessons from the History of Quarantine, from Plague to Influenza A' (2013) 19(2) *Emerg Infect Dis* 254; Lloyd Stanley, 'Influenza at San Quentin Prison, California' (1919) 34(19) *Public Health Reports* 996, 1005–1007.

monitor the health of persons before they were allowed to comingle with the society. This was done to prevent travellers (who were perceived as more likely to be infected) or other outsiders from bringing in disease to cities (or countries).[48] Isolation measures separate persons with a suspected or confirmed contagious disease from persons who are not sick. In the throe of the COVID-19 pandemic, members of the public with a suspected or confirmed COVID-19 diagnosis were routinely required to self-isolate and avoid contact with other people. Similarly, persons in detention situations were often required to isolate (depending on the institution and the country concerned) in their single-occupancy cell or room, or in isolation facilities identified within the place of detention for that purpose, mirroring a punitive form of solitary confinement.[49]

Whether a quarantine or isolation measure will be considered a deprivation of liberty (as opposed to a restriction on liberty or movement) will depend on the particular facts. According to the WGAD, 'if the person concerned is not at liberty to leave a premise, that person is to be regarded as deprived of his or her liberty'.[50] The WGAD has indicated that 'mandatory quarantine in a given premise, including in a person's own residence that the quarantined person may not leave for any reason, is a measure of de facto deprivation of liberty'.[51] Many countries instituted lockdowns that confined persons to their place of residence, subject to minimal (depending on the timing of the regulation and the location) exemptions to leave to buy food or medicine or to exercise. Despite the significant impacts, particularly for persons living in cramped quarters with no or limited outside space, in ordinary circumstances these types of lockdown measures would be likened to restrictions on liberty

---

[48] Gian Franco Gensini, Magdi Yacoub and Andrea Conti, 'The Concept of Quarantine in History: from Plague to SARS' (2004) 49 *Journal of Infection* 257.

[49] Erica Bryant, 'Solitary Confinement is Torture, Not COVID Medical Care', Vera Institute of Justice (25 March 2022). See, also, in respect to COVID social distancing measures in prisons in the UK, UK National Preventive Mechanism, 'Monitoring Places of Detention During COVID-19', 12th Annual Report 2020/2021 (February 2022) CP 607, 4: 'There was evidence of isolating prisoners being kept in conditions that meet the widely accepted definition of solitary confinement. Serious safeguarding concerns were raised about the lack of social care provision for some very vulnerable prisoners with disabilities. Some children spent extremely limited amounts of time out of cell, which was both disproportionate and avoidable. Almost all detainees in long-term detention settings in the UK faced issues in maintaining contact with their families as in-person social visits were suspended. We also report on patients detained in hospitals facing severe delays to their care pathways to less secure facilities or placements in the community due to COVID-19.' See, also, ibid, 31–35.

[50] WGAD, Deliberation No 11 (n 43) para 8; UNGA, 'Report of the WGAD', UN Doc A/HRC/36/37 (19 July 2017) para 56.

[51] WGAD, Deliberation No 11, Ibid para 8.

and movement as opposed to a deprivation of liberty,[52] though this is a line that is easily blurred.

There are several permutations to these practices, however, some of which would clearly bring the lockdowns into the sphere of deprivation of liberty. For example, lockdowns may have a disproportionate impact on homeless persons; their inability to self-isolate at home may give rise to a greater risk of detentions by the state for the violation of lockdown orders.[53] Similarly, during lockdowns, some open reception facilities for migrants (where persons were required to reside but there was still some freedom to come in and out) became closed facilities.[54] The Special Rapporteur on the situation of migrants has referred to this practice of tightening up of living conditions for persons in immigration dormitories, shelters and reception centres as 'de facto detention centres with conditions making physical distancing impossible to observe',[55] with some conditions 'so disproportionate and unnecessary or degrading that they could amount to ill-treatment'.[56] Reports of egregious conditions in COVID-19 detention centres housing mainly sub-Saharan African migrants in Saudi Arabia described 'emaciated men crippled by the Arabian heat lying shirtless in tightly packed rows in small rooms with barred windows', torturous and degrading conditions that have led to mental illness and suicides.[57] Similarly, COVID restrictions on persons residing in care and other live-in facilities have resulted in new circumstances that cross into the threshold of detention, where the individuals are subject to continuous supervision and control by those caring for them; they are not free to leave and they may lack the mental capacity to consent to these care arrangements. The removal of visitations in care and other live-in facilities housing extremely vulnerable people has led to prison-like conditions in some instances, particularly for persons unable to communicate effectively through telephones or the internet, with the deep anxiety, loneliness and accompanying loss of dignity violating, in certain instances, individuals'

---

[52] Ibid.
[53] Ana Santos, 'Poverty Punished as Philippines Gets Tough in Virus Pandemic', *Al Jazeera* (13 April 2020); Sunal Phasuk, 'Covid-19 Curfew Arrests of Thailand's Homeless', HRW (24 April 2020).
[54] Elspeth Guild and Kathryn Allinson, 'Detention of Refugees, Asylum Seekers and Migrants Under Corona Lockdown Risks Becoming Arbitrary', University of Bristol Law School Blog (1 May 2020).
[55] UNGA, 'One and a Half Years After: the Impact of COVID-19 on the Human Rights of Migrants', Report of the Special Rapporteur on the Human Rights of Migrants, UN Doc A/76/257 (30 July 2021) para 34. See, also, para 60.
[56] Ibid para 35.
[57] Will Brown, 'Investigation: African Migrants "Left to Die" in Saudi Arabia's Hellish Covid Detention Centres', *The Telegraph* (30 August 2020).

rights to be free from cruel, inhuman, or degrading treatment,[58] as well as their right to private and family life.[59]

During the COVID-19 pandemic, many countries, including Australia, Canada, China, Malaysia, Singapore and the UK, established quarantine hotels, where incoming persons were required to stay before being allowed to mingle with others in the destination country. I was forced to spend ten days in a Heathrow quarantine hotel in 2021 after having returned from a 'Red List country' in Africa.[60] Despite the context and a deep appreciation of the need for measures to quell the spread of the disease, I recall the experience not only as detention, but as punitive; a tiny, dirty room with a window that did not open, with guards on every floor, in a hotel run by the same international logistics companies, like G4S and Mitie,[61] that have been awarded contracts to run the UK's immigration detention facilities, among such facilities in other locations. At the time, I wrote that 'whilst quarantine itself is not arbitrary, the UK's maximalist approach to who must quarantine, and from what regions, does not in all cases align with infection rates – racist undertones need exploring'.[62]

The Red List policy subjected to mandatory quarantine persons travelling from countries in much of Africa and Asia, and a few countries in other parts of the world. The countries on the Red List did not align seamlessly with countries with the highest transmission rates; thus the spectre of arbitrariness certainly merits consideration.[63] Nevertheless, the issues are not

---

[58] Muhammad Rahman et al. 'Mental Distress and Human Rights Violations During COVID-19: a Rapid Review of the Evidence Informing Rights, Mental Health Needs, and Public Policy Around Vulnerable Populations' (2021) 11 *Frontiers in psychiatry* 603875.

[59] UK Joint Committee on Human Rights, 'The Government's Response to COVID-19: Human Rights Implications', HC 265, HL Paper 125 (21 September 2020) para 136.

[60] Schedule 11 to the Health Protection (Coronavirus, International Travel and Operator Liability) (England) Regulations 2021 (SI 2021 No 582). See, also, Rob Davies and Jamie Grierson, 'First Travellers Arrive at Covid Quarantine Hotels in England', *The Guardian* (15 February 2021); Diane Taylor, 'UK Travellers Complain of "Prison-Like" Conditions in Quarantine Hotels', *The Guardian* (11 May 2021).

[61] Sam Bright, '£1.55 Billion Contracts Awarded to Corporate Giants for COVID Quarantine Security', *Byline Times* (21 October 2021); Léonie Chao-Fong and Graeme Demianyk, 'Revealed: Tory-Linked Private Firm Awarded Government Hotel Quarantine Contract' *Huffpost* (19 February 2021); Niamh McIntyre, 'Private Contractors Paid Millions to Run UK Detention Centres', *The Guardian* (10 October 2018).

[62] Carla Ferstman, *Twitter* (12 June 2021) <https://twitter.com/CarlaFerstman/status/1403600230084485125?s=20> accessed 11 August 2023.

[63] This is a point raised in evidence to the UK Parliament: 'The lack of transparent criteria for countries to be on the "Red List" allows for no checks and balances on the Government's decisions, which is troubling given that those decisions have an immense, real-world impact on the economies of other countries, most of which are in the global south and share long-lasting historical, cultural, and economic ties with the UK that the Government should seek to protect': UK House of Commons Transport Committee, 'UK

straightforward: persons travelling during a pandemic will inevitably incur inconvenience – the question is the extent to which restrictions of their rights are appropriate, and whether the rules are applied fairly and transparently. And, unlike many of the persons subjected to arbitrary detention as explored in other chapters of this book, it was always clear how long my detention was going to last, and when I would be released. Whatever my personal annoyance, I was keenly aware that my situation of detention was not on a par with those described in other chapters of this book. Judges reviewing the scheme concluded similarly,[64] with similar rulings in the courts of other countries.[65] Even if such schemes constituted a veritable deprivation of liberty, the aim of reducing the public health risk posed by persons entering the country was understood as appropriate, and the means as necessary and proportionate, aside from inevitable exceptions.

8.5 Confinement: positive obligations in a state of hyper-engagement

Places of confinement are particularly dangerous for the spread of infectious diseases. This is regardless of whether they are prisons, police stations, hospitals, drug rehabilitation centres, ships, residential care homes, transit zones, refugee and migrant detention or removal centres or closed refugee or displaced persons camps. It is also irrespective of whether the goals of the places of confinement are to care for or protect the inhabitants, to respond to emergencies or to serve as some form of rehabilitation or punishment.

The dangers associated with places of confinement stem from the large number of persons forced to live in close proximity to one another and the inability to practise effective social distancing measures and hygiene best practice,[66] taken together with often poor ventilation, and delays in medical evaluation and treatment, and insufficient infection-control expertise.[67] Also, detainees may have a higher prevalence of underlying health conditions, which may make them more susceptible to contract infectious diseases.[68]

Aviation: Reform for Take-Off' (20 April 2022) HC 683, 'Written Evidence Submitted by PGMBM (AAS0006)'.

[64] *Hotta, R (on the application of) v Secretary of State for Health and Social Care* [2021] EWHC 3359 (Admin) para 26; *R (Khalid) v Secretary of State for Health and Social Care* [2021] EWHC 2156 (Admin).

[65] *Spencer v Canada (Attorney General)*, 2021 FC 621.

[66] OHCHR, 'Urgent Action Needed to Prevent COVID-19 "Rampaging Through Places of Detention" – Bachelet' (25 March 2020).

[67] Joseph Bick, 'Infection Control in Jails and Prisons' (2007) 45 *Healthcare Epidemiology* 1047.

[68] Gabrielle Beaudry et al, 'Managing Outbreaks of Highly Contagious diseases in Prisons: a Systematic Review' (2020) *BMJ Global Health* 1; Sara Wakefield and Christopher Uggen, 'Incarceration and Stratification' (2010) 36 *Ann Rev Sociology* 387; Meghan Novisky et al,

Consequently, detainees – as well as those working in detention settings – face a disproportionately high risk of infection as well as a higher mortality rate.[69] These heightened risks have been recognised by the World Health Organization, which has underscored that 'people in prisons and other places of detention are not only likely to be more vulnerable to infection with COVID-19, they are also especially vulnerable to human rights violations'.[70]

8.5.1 Reconciling the equivalence of care principle in a pandemic

The equivalence of care principle set out in the Mandela Rules recognises that detainees should have access to health and social care comparable to what is enjoyed by the population as a whole.[71] This principle is also reflected in the UN Principles of Medical Ethics, which recognise the responsibility of health personnel charged with the medical care of prisoners and detainees to provide them with 'protection of their physical and mental health and treatment of disease of the same quality and standard as is afforded to those who are not imprisoned or detained'.[72] The Inter-Agency Standing Committee (IASC)'s Interim Guidance further clarifies that the equivalence of care principle applies to all persons regardless of citizenship, nationality or migration status.[73] This principle of equivalence aligns with and is designed to underpin the fundamental precept that all persons possess human dignity in equal measure; 'respect for the dignity of detainees must be guaranteed under the same conditions as for that of free persons'.[74] The CESCR has further underscored that respecting the right to health requires states to refrain

---

'Incarceration as a Fundamental Social Cause of Health Inequalities: Jails, Prisons and Vulnerability to COVID-19' (2021) 61(6) *Brit J Crim* 1630.

[69] WGAD, Deliberation No 11 (n 43).

[70] WHO, 'Preparedness, Prevention and Control of COVID-19 in Prisons and Other Places of Detention' (15 March 2020) Principle 3.

[71] UNGA, 'UN Standard Minimum Rules for the Treatment of Prisoners' (Nelson Mandela Rules) UNGA Resolution 70/175, UN Doc A/RES./70/175 (8 January 2016) Rule 24(1); *Blokhin v Russia* (Grand Chamber) App No 47152/06 (ECtHR, 23 March 2016) para 137. See, also, CoE, 'Recommendation No R(98)71 of the Committee of Ministers to Member States Concerning the Ethical and Organisational Aspects of Health Care in Prison' (8 April 1998).

[72] UNGA, 'Principles of Medical Ethics relevant to the Role of Health Personnel, particularly Physicians, in the Protection of Prisoners and Detainees against Torture and Other Cruel, Inhuman or Degrading Treatment or Punishment', UNGA Resolution 37/194 (18 December 1982) Principle 1.

[73] IASC, 'Interim Guidance: Covid-19: Focus on Persons Deprived of Their Liberty' (March 2020) 4.

[74] Human Rights Committee, 'General Comment No 21: Article 10 (Humane Treatment of Persons Deprived of their Liberty)', UN Doc HRI/GEN/1/Rev.9 (Vol. I) 202 (10 April 1992) para 3.

'from denying or limiting equal access for all persons, including prisoners or detainees [...] to preventive, curative and palliative health services'.[75] Thus the principle of equivalence is mainly about ensuring that care for detainees is not sub-par simply because it is destined for detainees.

Yet, the provision of healthcare must also align with the specific needs of the prison population and conditions of detention. The Human Rights Committee has explained that states parties to the ICCPR have 'a positive obligation towards persons who are particularly vulnerable because of their status as persons deprived of liberty'.[76] The Inter-American Commission on Human Rights has recognised that prisoners should enjoy 'the highest possible level' of care.[77] The ECtHR has similarly recognised that the manner and method of the deprivation of liberty should not subject the detainee to distress or hardship of an intensity exceeding the unavoidable level of suffering inherent in detention and that, given the practical demands of imprisonment, the detainee's health and well-being are adequately secured by, among other things, providing the requisite medical assistance.[78]

As discussed throughout this chapter, it is known that COVID-19 has had a disproportionate impact on persons in all forms of detention, resulting in higher risks of infection and a greater proportion of deaths.[79] Given the lack of autonomy within detention settings, detainees are reliant on those responsible for their detention to address, both proactively and reactively, their health, safety and related needs.[80] This reliance exists at all times, but is accentuated in the time of a pandemic given the special health risks. The reliance heightens detainees' vulnerability, which in turn means that any acts or omissions of the authorities are likely to have a greater impact on detainees' psychological well-being on account of the feelings of powerlessness they engender.

Detaining authorities have a heightened or special duty of care to those they detain,[81] which, because of the greater risks of infection and higher

---

[75] CESCR, General Comment No 14 (n 6) para 34.
[76] Human Rights Committee, General Comment No 21 (n 74) para 3.
[77] IACommHR, 'Principles and Best Practices on the Protection of Persons Deprived of Liberty in the Americas', Resolution 1/08 (13 March 2008) Principle X.
[78] *Ramirez Sanchez v France* (Grand Chamber) App No 59450/00 (ECtHR, 4 July 2006) para 119; *Kudła v Poland* (Grand Chamber) App No 30210/96 (ECtHR, 26 October 2000) para 94.
[79] OHCHR, 'Covid-19 and the Rights of Persons with Disabilities: Guidance' (29 April 2020) 3.
[80] *Neira Alegría et al v Peru* (Merits) Series C No 20 (19 January 1995) para 60.
[81] Human Rights Committee, General Comment No 36 (n 10) paras 6, 25. See, also, *Rowson v Department of Justice and Community Safety* [2020] VSC 236 (1 May 2020) discussed in Human Rights Law Centre, 'Supreme Court Rules Victorian Government Prima Facie Breached Duty of Care to Person in Prison in their Response to COVID-19 Pandemic' (2 May 2020) <www.hrlc.org.au/> accessed 11 August 2023.

mortality rates, goes beyond the general duty recognised in the Mandela Rules to provide to detainees (irrespective of citizenship, nationality or migration status) the equivalent level of care inside detention as is available outside in the community.[82] This heightened duty of care is one of means rather than result. It is context-specific; it is focused on the reasonable steps detaining authorities must take in light of the specific and heightened risks posed by the pandemic in places of confinement, in terms of prevention of transmission, including: protective gear for staff; testing for detainees at the time of admission; ventilation and general air quality; hand sanitisers; and measures to improve physical distancing, access to vaccines and healthcare to those infected.

What follows from the recognition of a heightened or special duty of care, is that what is or should be equivalent is the equivalent right to health, not the equivalent level of care.[83] While many detention facilities are certainly far from achieving equivalent levels of care, an equivalent right to health would more aptly recognise that the level of care should depend on need and risk, not whether the person is detained or at liberty. This special duty of care will be breached if detention conditions and the policies relating to detention do not take adequate account of the specific contexts of detention and the special risks posed by COVID-19, and tailor services and measures to adequately protect against the infectious disease.

Courts and treaty bodies that have begun to assess the adequacy of anti-COVID measures in detention settings have mainly been faithful to the frame of equivalency of care set out in the Mandela Rules. For instance, the ECtHR has held that the authorities had the obligation to put measures in place aimed at avoiding infection, limiting the spread once it reached the prison, and providing adequate medical care in the case of contamination.[84] While it recognised that preventive measures had to be appropriate to address the risk at issue, the Court has effectively imposed an artificial ceiling on that proportionality when it underscored that the measures should not pose an excessive burden on the authorities in view of the practical demands of imprisonment, particularly when the authorities were confronted with a novel situation such as a global pandemic to which they had to react in

---

[82] Mandela Rules Rule 24(1). An argument on the inadequacy of the "equivalency of care" framework to determine the adequacy of psychiatric care in detention centres has been made by Tim Exworthy et al, 'Beyond Equivalence: Prisoners' Right to Health' (2011) 35(6) *Psychiatrist* 201.

[83] Exworthy et al (n 82). See, also, Dublin Declaration on HIV/AIDS in Prisons in Europe and Central Asia (23 February 2004): 'People in prison have the same right to health as people outside'.

[84] *Fenech v Malta* App No 19090/20 (1 March 2022) para 127.

a timely manner.[85] Equivalency, in the context of a pandemic, thus here becomes a form of "good enough" balancing when it focuses simply on ensuring that detainees do not receive sub-par care because they are detainees.

Because of the nature and seriousness of the risks and the vulnerability of detainees, states' positive obligations are not simply engaged – the pandemic puts them in a state of "hyper-engagement" given the significant, special risks posed.

The UN Committee on Economic, Social and Cultural Rights alludes to the need for such an approach in its statement on COVID-19. It reminds that, given the disproportionate impact of the pandemic on the most marginalised groups, 'allocation of resources should prioritize the special needs of these groups'.[86]

8.5.2 Anti-COVID measures in detention centres

Detention authorities have taken various measures to reduce the risk of COVID-19 spreading. Some measures have to do with releases, discussed in section 8.5.4. Other measures have to do with improving sanitation, increasing social distancing within detention facilities (through solitary cell confinement, reducing exercise and other mingling between detainees), and prohibiting or severely restricting access to outside visits. There is a question whether these measures are sufficient or appropriate in the circumstances, considering authorities' heightened positive obligations. There is also a question whether the measures taken may increase the risk of arbitrariness. This is because of the arbitrary way in which decisions tend to be taken. For example, the lack of transparency with respect to who may be subjected to new/additional restrictions on movement within places of confinement; as well as the failure of detaining authorities to consider adequately the impact on particularly vulnerable detainees of the removal of privileges (which tend to heighten vulnerability).

To increase social distancing, many institutions across the world severely restricted or even eliminated outside visits in the early phases of the COVID-19 pandemic.[87] Bans included visits from families and lawyers,

---

[85] Ibid para 129. See, also, para 128.
[86] CESCR, 'Statement on the Coronavirus Disease (COVID-19) Pandemic and Economic, Social and Cultural Rights', UN Doc E/C.12/2020/1 (17 April 2020) para 14.
[87] Lee-Fay Low et al, 'Safe Visiting at Care Homes During COVID-19: a Review of International Guidelines and Emerging Practices During the COVID-19 Pandemic', International Long Term Care Policy Network (19 January 2021); Lukas Muntingh, 'Africa, Prisons and COVID-19' (2020) 12 *J Hum Rts Practice* 284; EUROPRIS, 'Overview of European Prison Services' Responses to the COVID-19 Crisis' (20 April 2020); Sabrina Rapisarda and James Byrne, 'An Examination of COVID-19 Outbreaks in Prisons and Jails Throughout Asia' (2020) 15(7–8) *Victims & Offenders* 948.

and from some outside care providers, with some independent detention monitoring and oversight bodies also placed on hold. The bans also resulted in the rupture of educational and work programmes,[88] probation, mediation and religious services, and limited access to sports and exercise.[89] These measures contributed to detainee vulnerability, isolation, fears and anxieties, and led, at times, to riots,[90] suicidal thoughts and instances of self-harm.[91] They also impacted detainees' care regimes and access to food and other supplies, in those countries where the practice is for families to provide such necessities. Further, visitor bans have caused 'psychological distress, stigma and widespread disruption' for children unable to visit detained parents[92] and, significantly, for children in detention.[93]

The restrictions on access to counsel, associated denials of public trials,[94] as well as restrictions on outside monitoring of places of detention, raised fair trial concerns for criminal law detainees,[95] and have given rise to a variety of wider protection concerns for all detainees regardless of the circumstances.[96] The WGAD has recognised that the 'introduction of blanket measures restricting access to courts and legal counsel cannot be justified and could render the deprivation of liberty arbitrary'.[97] It determined: 'States must ensure the availability of other ways for legal counsel to communicate with their clients, including secured online communication or communication over the telephone, free of charge and in circumstances in which privileged and confidential discussions can take place.'[98] Access to counsel restrictions have

---

[88] Lina Marmolejo et al, 'Responding to COVID-19 in Latin American Prisons: the Cases of Argentina, Chile, Colombia, and Mexico' (2020) 15 *Victims & Offenders* 1062.

[89] EUROPRIS (n 87).

[90] Marcelo Bergman et al, 'The Effects of Coronavirus in Prisons in Latin America', Center for Latin American Studies on Insecurity and Violence (CELIV), Universidad Tres de Febrero, Argentina (June 2020).

[91] UK NPM, 'Monitoring Places of Detention During COVID-19' (n 49). See, also, User Voice and Queen's University Belfast, 'Coping with Covid in Prison: the Impact of the Prisoner Lockdown' (June 2022); Olga Suhomlinova et al, 'Locked up While Locked Down: Prisoners' Experiences of the COVID-19 Pandemic' (2021) XX *Brit J Crim* 1.

[92] EUROPRIS (n 87).

[93] UK HM Chief Inspector of Prisons, 'Report on Short Scrutiny Visits to Young Offender Institutions Holding Children' (21 April 2020).

[94] WGAD, *Opinion No 89/2020 Concerning Daler Sharipov (Tajikistan)*, UN Doc A/HRC/WGAD/2020/89 (10 March 2021) para 83.

[95] WGAD, *Opinion No 20/2021 Concerning Douglas Tumuhimbise et al (Uganda)*, UN Doc A/HRC/WGAD/2021/20 (9 July 2021) paras 24, 59, 60, 74–84.

[96] OMCT, 'Building Our Response on COVID-19 and Detention: OMCT Guidance Brief to the SOS-Torture Network and Partner Organizations' (April 2020) 12.

[97] WGAD, Deliberation No 11 (n 43) para 21.

[98] Ibid. See, also, IASC, 'Interim Guidance' (n 73); Fair Trials, 'The Public Health Need to Keep People out of Detention Practical Guidance' (March 2020).

been particularly egregious in offshore detention facilities like Guantánamo Bay, where in-person visits were virtually impossible at the height of the COVID-19 pandemic due to lengthy self-quarantine requirements pre and post visit, the suspension of the legal mail courier service and restrictions on remote access interviews, particularly for "high-value" detainees.[99]

The UN Subcommittee on the Prevention of Torture has stressed the importance of providing 'compensatory alternative methods' for detainees to maintain contact with families and others when normal visiting regimes were suspended during the COVID-19 regime, such as telephone, internet/email, video communication and other appropriate electronic means. They recommended that such measures should be both facilitated and encouraged, be frequent and free.[100] However important these measures are, the equipment may not be readily available,[101] or may not suffice for the size of the population, leading to significant delays.[102] The equipment can also be difficult to implement for persons with dementia or cognitive difficulties. This has been a particular challenge for some care home residents and persons in mental health facilities. Another difficulty is ensuring confidential communications with lawyers. The WGAD has received complaints from one detainee in India, who ultimately died in detention as a result of having contracted COVID-19, that telephone communications in detention with the lawyer were facilitated through an operator, which impeded their confidentiality.[103]

Any restrictions on visitations should be accompanied by other protective measures within detention facilities. This has often not happened. According to researchers on prisons in Latin America, governments have too often opted for 'quick and easy fixes' by locking down prisons and restricting contacts with the outside world. But they have failed 'to provide mass testing, guarantee unlimited and free access to personal protective equipment, implement clinical controls, and warrant access to health personnel for the at-risk groups'.[104]

---

[99] Scott Roehm, 'Guantanamo's COVID-19 Precautions Must Safeguard Detainees' Rights', *Just Security* (31 March 2020).
[100] Subcommittee on Prevention of Torture and Other Cruel, Inhuman or Degrading Treatment or Punishment (SPT), 'Advice of the Subcommittee on Prevention of Torture to States Parties and National Preventive Mechanisms relating to the Coronavirus Pandemic' (25 March 2020) para II(11). See, similarly, CPT, 'Statement of Principles Relating to the Treatment of Persons Deprived of their Liberty in the Context of the Coronavirus Disease (Covid-19) Pandemic', CPT/Inf(2020)13 (20 March 2020).
[101] EUROPRIS (n 87); UK HM Chief Inspector of Prisons, 'Report on Short Scrutiny Visits to Young Offender Institutions Holding Children' (n 93) para 4.4.
[102] Marmolejo et al (n 88).
[103] WGAD, *Opinion No 57/2021 Concerning Stan Swamy (India)*, UN Doc A/HRC/WGAD/2021/57 (14 February 2022) paras 44, 65.
[104] Marmolejo et al (n 88).

The detrimental impact of blanket visitor bans on vulnerable care home patients' well-being has led to some changed thinking about what precautionary measures best serve their interests. Low and others, whose research provides evidence-based recommendations to inform care home visitation policies, have found that it 'is possible that visitors may bring COVID-19 into facilities even with safe visiting practices, however the small additional risk should be considered against the benefits of visits. Therefore, safe on-site visiting should be required of care homes except under exceptional circumstances.'[105] Thus, while restricting contacts can be a legitimate means to prevent the transmission of infectious diseases such as COVID-19, the decision to introduce such measures must be part of a transparent and appropriate process, and the measures adopted must be proportionate, taking into account any mitigation strategies that can be deployed, and the impact of the measures not only on disease transmission within the country concerned, but on the detainee population and, in particularly, vulnerable groups within that detainee population. As has been stated by Penal Reform International, 'isolation or quarantine measures must be proportionate, authorised in law and not result in de facto solitary confinement'.[106] This would apply to all forms of confinement, whether the goal of those places is to care for or protect the inhabitants, to respond to emergencies or to serve as some form of rehabilitation or punishment.

8.5.3 *Access to vaccines and treatment for detainees*

The right to health includes the right to access (and states' positive obligation to provide) vaccines and treatment for infectious diseases such as COVID-19, including life-saving interventions as necessary.[107] While some states will have been constrained in their ability to access the COVID-19 vaccine and to vaccinate persons within their jurisdiction expeditiously, states' positive obligations to secure the right to health and the right to life required them to utilise their best efforts to the maximum available resources to embark on a vaccination programme of all persons who wish to be vaccinated. As part of the implementation of such a programme, they should have prioritised the roll-out of vaccines in a transparent, non-discriminatory manner that

---

[105] Low et al (n 87) 15.
[106] PRI, 'Coronavirus: Healthcare and Human Rights of People in Prison' Briefing Note (16 March 2020) 8.
[107] CESCR, 'Statement on Universal and Equitable Access to Vaccines for the Coronavirus Disease (COVID-19)' UN Doc E/C.12/2020/2 (15 December 2020) para 2. See, Ingrid Nifosi-Sutton, 'Realising the Right to Health During the COVID-19 Pandemic: an Antidote to the Pandemic and the Catalyst for Fulfilling a Long-Neglected Social Right?' (2022) 3(1) *Ybk Intl Disaster L* 126, 134 et seq.

aligned with medical needs and public health grounds.[108] This includes to persons in all forms of detention. The WHO SAGE values framework for the allocation and prioritization of COVID-19 vaccination issued in 2020 recognised detained persons as among the populations with a significantly elevated risk of being infected.[109] In the later 2022 iteration of the values framework, detained persons are no longer specifically listed, though they would arguably fall within the category of '[d]isadvantaged sociodemographic subpopulations at increased risk of severe disease and death because of higher burden of poor health, inadequate access to health services, underdiagnosis of comorbidities, and/or crowded living and working conditions'.[110]

The right of detainees to be vaccinated is clear under human rights law as part of the implementation of the right to life and the right to health, and the associated recognition of the dignity of all persons including detainees, as set out in section 8.2 of this chapter. It also forms part of international humanitarian law.[111] The obligation on states to factor in detainees' vulnerabilities and crowded living circumstances when developing and implementing rules on prioritisation of vaccine roll-outs and/or access to COVID-related treatments for all persons within a state or subject to its jurisdiction is equally clear. The OHCHR has encouraged that:

> [p]articular care should be taken to ensure that those who are often invisible in many ways, including people in institutional settings such as care homes, psychiatric institutions, homes for persons with disabilities, homeless shelters, immigration detention centres and prisons, are included without discrimination in vaccine distribution policies and plans.[112]

Nevertheless, to prioritise detainees (sometimes viewed as morally subordinate) over some other categories of persons can be fractious.[113] Ismail

---

[108] CESCR, 'Statement on Universal and Equitable Access to Vaccines' (n 107) para 5.
[109] WHO, 'WHO SAGE Values Framework for the Allocation and Prioritization of COVID-19 Vaccination' (14 September 2020).
[110] Ibid, version 21 January 2022.
[111] Oona Hathaway et al, 'COVID-19 and International Law Series: International Humanitarian Law – Treatment of Detainees', *Just Security* (16 November 2020). Regarding Guantánamo Bay detainees, it has been argued that detaining authorities are obliged to vaccinate (if the detainees elect to be vaccinated): Ryan Goodman et al, 'Why Guantánamo Detainees Should Have Access to COVID Vaccines Part I: Law of Armed Conflict and Good Policy', *Just Security* (1 February 2021).
[112] OHCHR, 'Human Rights and Access to Covid-19 Vaccines' (17 December 2020) Key Message 5.
[113] Ann Hinga Klein and Derek Norman, 'Covid Outbreaks Devastated Prisons, but State Inmates' Access to the Vaccine Varies Widely', *New York Times* (17 March 2021, updated 6 May 2021).

and others have referred to the de-prioritisation of certain categories of persons on supposed moral grounds as 'vaccine populism,'[114] particularly in respect to security detainees and other categories of detainees perceived as especially "unworthy". Liebrenz and others remind that '[u]nderprivileged populations especially those in prisons are stigmatized and ignored and more so in the current climate where they may be seen as deserving of infections. Public attitudes about safety and self-protection can further contribute to ignoring vulnerable groups.'[115] This is despite the Mandela Rules emphasis that detainees' access to health and social care should not be perceived as a privilege, or conversely, access to vaccines should not be withheld as a form of further punishment.[116] As with detainee access to care, detainees' access to vaccines should reflect their health status, not any view about their moral worthiness.[117] Despite these arguments, Ismail and others, who have reviewed data on COVID-19 vaccination strategies related to prisoners, found 'notable differences in considerations given to people who live and work in prisons.'[118] Some countries have explicitly prioritised people who live and work in prisons whereas others have not.

Beyond prisoners and criminal law detainees, other categories of detainees have faced vaccination prioritisation practices that are equally variable. Persons in care homes and hospitals have regularly been prioritised in vaccine rollouts, however migrants in detention centres or other irregular living situations such as transit zones or camps have had mixed access. It has been recognised that certain categories of migrants will be most exposed and vulnerable to COVID-19, such as migrants in irregular situations, low-income migrants, migrants living in camps or unsafe conditions, in immigration detention, or those in transit.[119] The UN Special Rapporteur on the Human Rights of Migrants has reported on certain countries that have established prioritisation criteria for access to testing, treatment and

---

[114] Nasrul Ismail et al, 'COVID-19 Vaccine for People Who Live and Work in Prisons Worldwide: a Scoping Review' (2022) 17(9) *PLoS ONE* e0267070, 1, 9, referring to the influence of politicians on debates about vaccine prioritisation in countries like Canada, Israel, South Africa and the US, claiming that people in prison are less morally deserving of vaccines.

[115] Michael Liebrenz and others, 'Prisoner's Dilemma: Ethical Questions and Mental Health Concerns About the COVID-19 Vaccination and People Living in Detention' (2021) 2 *Forensic Science International: Mind and Law* 100044, 2.

[116] Mandela Rule. See, also, Art 12 ICESCR.

[117] This argument has also been made by Justin Berk et al, 'Why We Vaccinate Incarcerated People First' (2021) 35 *The Lancet*, eClinicalMedicine 100864.

[118] Ismail (114) 7.

[119] 'Joint Guidance Note on Equitable Access to COVID-19 Vaccines for All Migrants' (8 March 2021) 1 <www.ohchr.org/Documents/Issues/Migration/JointGuidanceNoteCOVID-19-Vaccines-for-Migrants.pdf> accessed 11 August 2023.

vaccines taking into consideration the specific vulnerabilities and risks experienced by migrants, and which provide the same access to health care for migrants as for other members of the society.[120] He listed a range of countries in Asia, Europe, North Africa, the Middle East and the Americas which have provided free vaccine services for migrants during the COVID-19 pandemic.[121] Nevertheless, in some other countries like the US, some migrants were slow to be vaccinated,[122] and anti-Covid measures such as education, social distancing, hygiene and sanitation, COVID-19 testing and medical management were assessed as being inadequate in the early phases of the pandemic.[123]

8.5.4 COVID-19 and justifications for early release

Releasing persons from detention (whether temporarily or permanently) has been one of the principal strategies employed by many states to reduce infection rates and a clear recommendation by WHO and other expert bodies concerned with the spread of disease. Releases help underscore that detention should be exceptional, and particularly so in the context of a pandemic. Releases also encourage detaining authorities and policymakers to consider alternatives to detention. These could be applied to short-term pandemic needs but might in the longer term be incorporated as standard alternatives to detention.

The rules to determine whether a particular detention is arbitrary will not change because of a pandemic; it would still be necessary to consider whether a detention is subject to law, whether the law itself is just and appropriate, and whether the detention is necessary and proportionate to fulfil a legitimate purpose. However, the factors to consider whether a detention is necessary and proportionate certainly change in a pandemic such as COVID-19, given the higher risks of infection, serious illness and death faced by persons in all forms of detention (particularly at the height of the pandemic before vaccines became more widely available).

---

[120] UNGA, 'One and a Half Years After: the Impact of COVID-19 on the Human Rights of Migrants' (n 55) paras 67–69.
[121] Ibid para 70.
[122] Elizabeth Trovall, 'Few Texas ICE Detention Centers Are Vaccinating For COVID-19. Feds Say It's Up to Local Health Departments', *inDepth* (6 May 2021) <www.houstonpublicmedia.org> accessed 11 August 2023.
[123] Physicians for Human Rights, 'Praying for Hand Soap and Masks: Health and Human Rights Violations in U.S. Immigration Detention during the COVID-19 Pandemic' (12 January 2021); Caroline Lee et al, 'Individuals' Experiences in U.S. Immigration Detention During the Early Period of the COVID-19 Pandemic: Major Challenges and Public Health Implications' (2023) 11(8) *Health Justice* 1.

Thus, even though the proportionality test is unchanged, pandemics may change the outcome of considerations of necessity and proportionality. Certain detentions which would otherwise satisfy necessity and proportionality requirements may no longer do so, given the disproportionately high risk of infection in detention and higher mortality rate. Consequently, at the height of the pandemic it would have been necessary to assess whether, considering the change in circumstances occasioned by the pandemic, continued detention was still justified as necessary and proportionate in each detained case or class of cases.[124] The failure to do so would have increased the potential for arbitrariness of the detention by failing to allow individuals' changed circumstances to be considered as part of a review of the legality of their detention.[125]

Also, the consideration of the legitimate purpose of detention may have changed because of COVID-19. Proportionality requires some comparison between the detention and the purpose it is intended to achieve. Purposes will differ depending on the type of detention. The purpose of pre-trial detention is to ensure defendants appear at trial and the safety of accused and/or the public whereas the purpose of sentencing a person to a term of imprisonment is to ensure the various crime control punishment rationales (for example, specific, and general deterrence; retribution; rehabilitation). In other settings, purposes include to ensure physical or psychological care and protection in hospital and care settings; to ensure attendance at future legal proceedings or administrative processes for migrant and refugee processing or removal centres. These various purposes may change over time,[126] and sometimes, COVID-19 may render the purposes no longer applicable or justifiable. For instance, it may not be justifiable to detain a person on an extradition warrant, without any clarity about when extraditions could resume,[127] or a failed asylum seeker to await deportation, when deportation to the country of origin is not an option because that country is not expecting to accept entrants within a reasonable time, because of COVID-19.[128] Pre-trial detention may be harder to justify if trials in a particular country have been put on hold because of the pandemic. As explained by the Howard League for Penal Reform, in the UK, 'remand and sentenced prisoners alike are

---

[124] Landmark Chambers, 'Challenging Immigration Detention in the COVID-19 pandemic' (15 April 2020).

[125] Human Rights Committee, *A v Australia,* UN Doc CCPR/C/59/D/560/93 (3 April 1997) para 9.4.

[126] *Murray v The Netherlands* (Grand Chamber) App No 10511/10 (ECtHR, 26 April 2016) para 100.

[127] *Khokhlov v Cyprus* App No 53114/20 (ECtHR, 13 June 2023) para 101.

[128] *Murray v The Netherlands* (n 126). See, also, *R v Governor of Durham Prison ex parte Hardial Singh* [1984] 1 WLR 704.

being held in conditions amounting to solitary confinement, for extended periods as they await trials that have invariably been delayed. Nothing has been done to address this, for adults or children in the system.'[129]

Necessity is focussed on whether there are realistic alternatives to detention. Here, the negatives associated with detention during COVID-19 are augmented, but the alternatives to criminal law detention will also have been affected; due to lockdowns, there may be fewer available half-way houses or less temporary accommodation; community programmes to help integrate released detainees may not be operational and parole systems may be dysfunctional.[130] As OMCT highlights, 'release into confinement with families can also create difficulties and tensions with little time to prepare for release and appropriate post-release monitoring or support. There may also be detainees without clear places to go to, including foreigners, migrants, children, or women defenders whose family ties are broken, or street children.'[131]

Releases and commutations of sentences are an area where an absence of clear rules transparently implemented may result in other kinds of arbitrariness, particularly if there is no clear procedure for detainees to petition to have their cases considered. The WGAD has mainly taken a humanitarian approach to releases, recommending that persons it finds are arbitrarily detained are released, though usually without interrogating the COVID-19 release policies as part of its opinions.[132] The jurisprudence on the reducibility of life sentences is relevant, where the ECtHR has found a violation of Article 3 when legislation on clemency did not require the President 'to assess whether continued imprisonment is justified on legitimate penological grounds.' Nor did it 'set a time-frame in which the President must decide on the clemency application or to oblige him or the Minister of Justice […] to give reasons for the decision…'.[133] COVID-19 releases which are undertaken without transparency or without a clear framework

---

[129] Howard League for Penal Reform, 'Justice and Fairness under Covid-19 Restrictions' (May 2020).

[130] Ibid.

[131] OMCT (n 96).

[132] See, for example, WGAD, *Opinion No 83/2020 Concerning Youcef Nadarkhani (Islamic Republic of Iran)*, UN Doc A/HRC/WGAD/2020/83 (4 March 2021); *Opinion No 85/2020 Concerning José Daniel Márquez, Kelvin Alejandro Romero Martínez, José Abelino Cedillo, Porfirio Sorto Cedillo, Orbín Nahúm Hernández, Arnold Javier Alemán, Ewer Alexander Cedillo Cruz and Jeremías Martínez Díaz (Honduras)*, UN Doc A/HRC/WGAD/2020/85 (24 February 2021).

[133] *TP and AT v Hungary* App Nos 37871/14, 73986/14 (ECtHR, 4 October 2016) para 49. See, also, *Matiošaitis v Lithuania* App Nos 22662/13, 51059/13, 58823/13 (ECtHR, 23 May 2017) 157–181.

can also result in those who remain in detention feeling as if they are being doubly punished.

Monitoring and oversight bodies have recommended who should be prioritised for release.[134] The recommendations have tended to focus on factors connected to vulnerability, such as persons over a certain age, pregnant women and women who are breastfeeding, persons with underlying health conditions, and persons with disabilities, as well as children and women with children.[135] Who is considered vulnerable, and relative levels of vulnerability, particularly if connected to disease susceptibility, can be contested. Also, assessments of vulnerability can ignore or undervalue complex, intersecting vulnerabilities. Invariably, considerations of who should be released on account of their vulnerability will involve both ethics and science, and consideration of human rights. It is important that decisions to release are taken on clear and transparent grounds that are non-discriminatory. Monitoring bodies have also encouraged states to release detainees on the basis of the rationale for the detention (for example, persons unlawfully or arbitrarily detained should be released, as should the bulk of pre-trial detainees, persons held for non-penal reasons such as immigration detainees).[136] Regarding migrants, the WGAD noted that 'detention is only permissible as an exceptional measure of last resort, which is a particularly high threshold to be satisfied in the context of a pandemic or other public health emergency.'[137] Other factors taken into account include whether persons pose a danger to society (prisoners serving short prison sentences for non-violent crimes; prisoners who are almost at the end of their prison term).[138]

While in some states, there have been many arrests, often arbitrary, of persons accused of having breached pandemic lockdown or other restrictions,[139] many states have taken on board at least some of the recommendations

---

[134] WGAD, Deliberation No 11 (n 43) para 15, 16; UN Special Rapporteur on Extrajudicial, Summary or Arbitrary Killings, 'COVID-19 and Protection of Right to Life in Places of Detention', COVID-19 Human Rights Dispatch No 2 (5 May 2020); CPT, COVID-19 Statement of Principles (n 100), Principle 5; UN Office on Drugs and Crime, 'COVID-19 preparedness and responses in prison' (31 March 2020) 5; IASC (n 98) 3; SPT, 'Advice of the SPT to States Parties and National Preventive Mechanisms Relating to the Coronavirus Pandemic' (n 100) 3; Inter-American Commission on Human Rights, Resolution 1/20 'Pandemic and Human Rights in the Americas' (10 April 2020) paras 45–46.

[135] For example, WGAD, Deliberation No 11 (n 43) paras 15, 16; see, also, IASC (n 98).

[136] IASC (n 98); see, also, WGAD, Deliberation No 11 (n 43).

[137] WGAD, Deliberation No 11 (n 43) para 23.

[138] See, for example, CPT, COVID-19 Statement of Principles (n 100); IASC (n 98).

[139] Braema Mathiaparanam, 'Human Rights Derogations in Southeast Asian Countries During the Covid-19 Pandemic', Penang Institute (2 September 2020) 14–15 (discussing detentions and imprisonments for COVID-related violations in several Southeast Asian countries).

regarding social distancing in places of confinement, leading to an important number of temporary and permanent releases.[140] However, there are gaps. Some countries which have significant immigration detention programmes have been slow to implement releases or have simply refused to progress releases,[141] with dangerous consequences.[142] Many countries that routinely resort to arbitrary detention, particularly against protest movements, opposition groups, human rights defenders and journalists, have failed to proceed with releases of such detainees, even when they have released high numbers of detainees in the general prison population.[143] At times, this is because the individuals concerned have been charged or convicted of security-related offences, which have been deemed ineligible for full or conditional release.[144] At other times, it is because the state has introduced arbitrariness into the release process, picking and choosing who should benefit from this solution. For instance, it has been reported that in the context of the pandemic, Turkey introduced legislation to secure the release of up to 100,000 prisoners, but detained journalists and human rights activists were not included.[145] Similarly, Israel announced the release of thousands

---

[140] One major study of 53 jurisdictions worldwide estimates that more than one million criminal law detainees and prisoners have been either temporarily or permanently released because of COVID-19 measures. See, DLA Piper, 'A Global Analysis of Prisoner Releases in Response to COVID-19' (December 2020) 10. See, also, Justice Imman Ali, 'Releasing 20,000+ People from Prison in Bangladesh in 10 Days – the View from a Judge', Penal Reform International (11 June 2020); Marmolejo et al (n 88); Sabrina Rapisarda and James Byrne, 'An Examination of COVID-19 Outbreaks in Prisons and Jails Throughout Asia' (2020) 15(7–8) *Victims & Offenders* 948; Marcelo Aebi and Mélanie Tiago, 'Prisons and Prisoners in Europe in Pandemic Times: an Evaluation of the Short-Term Impact of the COVID-19 on Prison Populations' (Council of Europe, 2020), <https://www.europris.org/wp-content/uploads/2020/06/SPACE-I-Prisons-in-pandemic-time.pdf> accessed 11 August 2023.

[141] David Keegan and Arash Bordbar, 'Detention at All Costs: Covid-19 and Immigration Detention in Australia', in Vivienne Chew, Melissa Phillips and Min Jee Yamada Park (eds), *COVID-19 Impacts on Immigration Detention: Global Responses* (International Detention Coalition and HADRI/Western Sydney University 2020) 10–11; Australian Human Rights Commission, 'Management of COVID-19 Risks in Immigration Detention' (2021).

[142] Sam Levin, 'He Lived in the US for 40 Years. Then He Became the First to Die from Covid-19 in Immigration Jail' *The Guardian* (12 May 2020). See, also, Sophie Terp et al, 'Deaths in Immigration and Customs Enforcement (ICE) detention: FY2018–2020' (2021) 8(1) *AIMS Public Health* 81; John Openshaw and Mark Travassos, 'COVID-19 Outbreaks in US Immigrant Detention Centers: the Urgent Need to Adopt CDC Guidelines for Prevention and Evaluation' (2021) 72(1) *Clinical Infectious Diseases* 153.

[143] ICJ, 'Living Like People Who Die Slowly: the Need for Right to Health Compliant COVID-19 Responses' (September 2020) 86–87.

[144] OMCT (n 96).

[145] Emma Sinclair-Webb, 'Turkey Should Protect All Prisoners from Pandemic', HRW (23 March 2020). See, also, Ahmet Kuru, 'Turkey Releasing Murderers – But Not Political

of Israeli prisoners, including serious offenders. However, reportedly, it has failed to release Palestinian prisoners, even the minors, women, the elderly and infirm.[146] In Egypt, while thousands of prisoners have been pardoned, reportedly, none of those pardoned were "political" prisoners.[147] The UN Special Rapporteur on the human rights situation in Iran reported that prisoners convicted of national security offences remained ineligible for furlough under the criteria announced by the judiciary, with many of those who tested positive for COVID-19 in prison not granted temporary release or provided with sufficient health care. Several women political prisoners were subsequently granted leave.[148] For those forced to remain in detention it was a double punishment; arbitrarily detained and then condemned to anxiously await infection.

Several elderly and potentially frail convicted war criminals have been temporarily released from detention, on vulnerability considerations. Penological considerations such as retribution or rehabilitation have not been major considerations for such releases, particularly as they were intended to be temporary releases. These included Hissène Habré, who was sentenced to life imprisonment by the Extraordinary African Chambers seated in Senegal, for the torture and crimes against humanity he directly perpetrated and oversaw in Chad, who was given two months leave from prison (to house arrest) as a consequence of COVID-19 risks.[149] Victims of Habré's crimes expressed deep concern, given the failure to progress their reparations awards.[150] Habré was thereafter returned to prison and ultimately died of COVID-19 a year later. Many convicted war criminals have sought humanitarian releases around the world[151] and the human

---

Opponents – From Prison Amid Coronavirus Pandemic', *The Conversation* (23 April 2020). Beyond Turkey, HRW has reported that key human rights defenders remained in detention despite national release programmes making progress with other detainee groups in Bahrain, Egypt, Iran, Kyrgyzstan, Myanmar, Cambodia, Cameroon, Libya, South Sudan, Syria, Yemen and China. See, HRW, 'COVID-19: a Human Rights Checklist' (23 April 2020).

[146] Raji Sourani, 'COVID-19 and Human Rights: Interview with 2013 Laureate Raji Sourani', The Right Livelihood Foundation (8 May 2020).

[147] 'No Political Prisoners Freed as Egypt Pardons Thousands on Eid: President el-Sisi Grants Clemency to 3,157 People, Including Ex-Policeman Jailed for murder of Singer Suzanne Tamim', *Al Jazeera* (24 May 2020).

[148] HRC, 'Report of the Special Rapporteur on the Situation of Human Rights in the Islamic Republic of Iran, Javaid Rehman', UN Doc A/HRC/49/75 (13 January 2022) para 20.

[149] 'Chad: Ex-President Temporarily Released from Jail due to COVID-19', *Al Jazeera* (7 April 2020).

[150] Ephrem Rugiririza, 'COVID-19: Should We Release Vulnerable Convicts?', *Justiceinfo. Net* (16 April 2020).

[151] See, for example, Jo-Marie Burt, 'In Guatemala, COVID-19 Puts Justice on Hold, Emboldening Convicted War Criminals to Seek Their Freedom', *International Justice*

rights community has struggled with its response to such releases. The UN Special Rapporteur on the promotion of truth, justice, reparation and guarantees of non-recurrence has issued guidance on the issue, noting that 'the legitimate and necessary measures to protect against COVID-19 and overcrowding should not lead, *de jure or de facto,* to impunity for persons convicted in various parts of the world for serious violations of human rights, crimes against humanity, genocide, or war crimes.' He has underscored that temporary house arrest should only be afforded if it is impossible to relocate such prisoners to a prison facility with safe and healthy conditions.[152] OMCT has taken a more direct line, recommending to the organizations in its network that 'we should avoid advocating for the potential release of war criminals, those convicted of crimes against humanity, genocide or the crime of torture, whose prosecutions many of us have supported.'[153] But this presents an arbitrary exception to the application of vulnerability criteria, which cannot be appropriate. If individuals are no longer a danger to the public and they present health or other criteria which place them at a heightened risk for contracting COVID-19 and/or for dying from it, they should benefit as anyone from the possibility of a humanitarian release whether permanent or temporary. If not, the denial serves as a form of indirect punishment, connected to the moral opprobrium for the crime.

8.6 Conclusions: the transformative potential of positive obligations

As has been described, COVID-19 can accentuate the arbitrariness of detention in several important ways. First, detention may no longer satisfy the tests of proportionality and necessity. Second, inadequate prison conditions, including poor health and sanitation as well as distancing measures which isolate detainees for their own health and safety, but fail to provide reasonable accommodation, can make detentions arbitrary given the deleterious impacts such conditions have on the ability of detainees to exercise their fundamental rights which impacts on the proportionality of the measures adopted. Also, arbitrariness can infect decisions to release detainees as part of distancing measures. Lack of clarity, fairness, and transparency in decisions to release contributes to arbitrariness and increases the stress and anxiety of detainees

---

Monitor (17 April 2020). See, also, 'ADC-ICT Urges President of the UN International Residual Mechanism for Criminal Tribunals to Urgently Grant Early or Provisional Release to Detainees in Light of the COVID-19 Pandemic' (27 March 2020).

[152] UN Special Rapporteur on Truth, Justice and Reparation, 'COVID-19, Prison Overcrowding, and Serving Sentences for Serious Human Rights Violations' (29 April 2020).

[153] OMCT (n 96) 5.

and their families, which may constitute a double punishment which may rise to the level of cruel, inhuman, or degrading treatment.

The transformative potential of positive obligations in the context of pandemics is about the relationship between crisis and opportunity. COVID-19 exposed deep societal inequities with unusual clarity and has generated space for reflection and contestation in many areas of policy from the local to the global. The unequal impact of the pandemic has been widely recognised by governments, civil society, international organisations, and courts. It is hardly disputed that certain marginalised groups have been most affected financially, socially, and with respect to their health and mortality.

Many have argued that the stark inequalities so visibly experienced should serve as a catalyst for transformation,[154] as a rallying call to, as has euphemistically been referred to, 'build back better.'[155] The arbitrariness of detention is one key area for transformation. But, amidst all the political posturing about the need to build back better,[156] it is important to go beyond the slogans and consider what has been called for and what has been achieved.

Many governments have shown an ability to devise and efficiently implement strategies to reduce carceral populations in all parts of the world by releasing detainees and limiting new admissions. They have enacted new legislation, used executive powers, arranged approvals by competent government officials, decided executive pardons and clemency applications. They have done so when they had the will to do so. And they have refrained from doing so when that will was absent. "Building back better" would have required states to capitalise on and fuel forward the momentum generated by the COVID-19 push to reduce carceral populations and to transform the strategies into long-term, sustainable prerogatives. It would also have required interrogating and addressing why for the most part, the "unseen"; the "reviled and resented"; and the "undeserving"[157] benefited far less from COVID-19 releases and remain far more likely to be arbitrarily detained.

---

[154] Nifosi-Sutton (n 107) 151.

[155] OECD, 'Building Back Better: a Sustainable, Resilient Recovery after COVID-19' (5 June 2020); Global Facility for Disaster Reduction and Recovery, 'Building Back Better in Post-Disaster Recovery', Guidance Note (2017); UNA-UK, 'Sustainable Development Goals: Building Back Better' (2020); WHO Regional Committee for Southeast Asia, 'COVID-19 and Measures to "Build Back Better" Essential Health Services to Achieve UHC and the Health-Related SDGs', UN Doc SEA/RC74/3 (30 July 2021); Mark Pelling et al, 'Building Back Better from COVID-19: Knowledge, Emergence and Social Contracts' (2022) 46(1) *Progress in Human Geography* 121.

[156] The White House, 'Global COVID-19 Summit: Ending the Pandemic and Building Back Better', Statement (24 September 2021).

[157] Typologies developed in Chapter 4 of this book.

"Building back better" is thus not simply about strengthening economies, making health systems more robust or reducing the percentage of persons in detention. It is about identifying and seeking to address the structural bases for over-detention, and the social, economic, cultural, and political conditions that fuel over-detention and the hyper-susceptibility of certain marginalised and discriminated groups to be victims of that over-detention. It is about recognising and addressing the linkages between discrimination and arbitrariness and countering the rationales for mass detention.

These linkages will not be recognised or addressed by happenstance. They will be uncovered by harnessing the power of the positive obligations to fulfil the right to life, the right to liberty and security of the person, the right to health, and to ensure freedom from torture and other ill-treatment. And by applying the principle of non-discrimination to those rights.

9

Conclusions

In this book I sought to "conceptualise" arbitrary detention to better understand what the concept means, and to analyse how the concept is construed, applied, and at times, manipulated, and the consequences of such manipulations.

What is clear after many words and pages is that there are different perspectives about what arbitrary detention means. A minimalist perspective equates arbitrary detention with unlawful detention, though it recognises that detentions which comply with domestic law can nevertheless be arbitrary if they violate fundamental principles of international law. Minimalists understand that detention that is lawful can still be arbitrary if it is a disproportionate means to achieve the legitimate aim that the detention is seeking to address. However, minimalists afford an overabundance of deference to states' rationales for detention and give a wide berth to states to determine how best to achieve those rationales. Thus, there is little scope of a finding of arbitrariness for detentions which are lawful on their face. For the minimalist, arbitrary detention has already been normalised. And, once normalised, there is no need to see it as an exceptional measure. This is despite the sense of hopelessness and powerlessness it engenders, which as I set out in Chapter 3, may amount to torture or cruel, inhuman, or degrading treatment or punishment.

There is a spectrum of views about the role of proportionality in findings of arbitrary detention, also reflected in the divergent case law. The element of the proportionality test which has proven to be most relevant but also most contingent in arbitrary detention case law is the necessity requirement: the need to demonstrate that there were no less restrictive means aside from detention to achieve the legitimate aim sought by the state. This criterion has been of some help in ordinary pre-trial detention cases and to a limited extent on account of the Convention on the Rights of Persons with Disabilities, in cases involving the confinement of persons with disabilities. However, the criterion has been much less adept at addressing the more systemic regimes of arbitrary detention, such as immigration detention, and security detention, or those regimes of detention which are oriented at "unseeing" social issues, such as hiding away persons who are homeless or who use drugs. Without a robust necessity analysis, the principle of detention as a last resort has little practical meaning.

The more minimalist perspective is not overly concerned by the variances in proportionality standards depending on the category of detainee or reason for the detention, given the deference they hold for states' rationales to detain and how best to achieve those rationales. For the maximalist, these variances are evidence that arbitrary detention has become a tool of the powerful to exert their authority and social control, and more widely, as evidence of the erosion of the rule of law. But the more maximalist perspective is not focused on arbitrary detention at all. Its focus is liberty and security of the person, human dignity, and equality. Detention is an aberration and an abrogation of that fundamental starting point and therefore the maximalist understands the goal to be about safeguarding liberty rather than setting up a framework to legitimise or rationalise detention. The starting point is that all detention is arbitrary unless it is shown to be otherwise because liberty and security of the person is the right that one is seeking to protect.

From these different orientations one can consider how arbitrary detention is being construed, applied and at times, manipulated.

I have demonstrated that arbitrary detention is not ultimately or mainly about occasional departures from lawful detention affecting random persons in random places. It is an insidious policy tool used purposively by governments to exert social control on those who do not conform to the rules of the imagined society. It is a potent tool because it has an air of plausible deniability. Arbitrary detention removes the "unseen", the "reviled and resented", the "undeserving", as well as the dissenters and any other undesirables from the public sphere. But in so doing, it is they, the detainees, who are blamed for the loss of their freedom. Detention is a product of criminalisation, pathologisation and deterrence and as such, detention is not something that was done to detainees; it was done because of them. Confident in the effectiveness of the tool, it will be replicated, and expanded to a growing array of contexts. It is not difficult to hypothesise the response to the increasing number of "climate refugees" seeking to escape the erosion of their habitats, their ways of life and their security. The powerful become more powerful and confident in their privileged spaces and the marginalised simply remain detained.

I have shown how arbitrary detention has both procedural and substantive components. The procedural components are focused on ensuring that detention is subject to law, and that detainees have adequate and effective recourse to challenge the legality of their detention. Procedural safeguards are far more entrenched for ordinary criminal law detentions than they are for other forms of detention such as what is applied in situations of armed conflict or insecurity, or detentions in immigration holding facilities, hospitals, drug treatment facilities, psychiatric care establishments, and social care institutions. But procedural safeguards are only effective when detention is rightfully understood to be an exceptional measure. When detention is normalised and accepted as routine, procedural safeguards lose their usefulness; they become just *pro forma* endorsements of regimes of detention. Access to courts does not mean much if the systems of law that the courts enforce are ones which privilege detention. The judges and courts assessing detainees' confinement are simply affirming and legitimising the violence of the rules.

Substantive components of arbitrary detention involve considerations as to what is behind the decision to detain, and they grapple with how the presence or absence of race, gender or other morally arbitrary and discriminatory factors, impact upon who is detained, when, for how long and in what conditions. These components are about recognising and addressing the linkages between discrimination and arbitrariness and countering the rationales for mass detention. But courts are less effective at tackling systemic issues as they are entrenched in the everyday bureaucratic adjudication of the cases coming before them.

Furthermore, given the very limited consideration of what are states' positive obligations to secure and fulfil the right to liberty and security of the person, and particularly their positive obligations to ensure that any resort to detention is non-discriminatory, findings of arbitrary detention in individual cases have not led to the kinds of system-wide reflections and reform processes which are needed if states were to give full effect to the right.

What positive obligations do states have to ensure that detention is a last resort or that detention is not made indefinite? Outside of discrete areas, courts have been extremely limited in their articulation of principles, options or anything approaching what may be an answer to this question. Nor has any response been articulated to the related question about what obligations states or others with the means to act may have, to end circumstances of indefinite detention, regardless of whether they were the authors of the initial decision to detain. It should therefore be no surprise that the law has been unable to influence or address the scenario of 'forever prisoners,' whether they are the terrorist suspects trapped in the legal grey zones of Guantánamo Bay, the Da'esh suspects and persons loosely associated with them stuck in Northern Syria with their citizenships summarily revoked, or the Rwandans acquitted, or having served out their International Criminal Tribunal for Rwanda sentences, under permanent house arrest in Niger because there is literally nowhere for them to go.

The European Court of Human Rights, the human rights court with by far, the largest and most complex caseload and the greatest potential for influence, has taken a reductive approach to arbitrary detention. This has given the widest endorsement to states' efforts to normalise and expand regimes of detention and is despite the apparent rigidity of Article 5 of the ECHR which restricts the contexts in which detention is capable of being authorised. This reductive approach has been achieved by a mixture of: limiting what factual contexts are understood to fall within the purview of detention under Article 5, inventing new bases of lawful detention not contemplated by the Convention, employing the language of exception to give states the widest possible margin of appreciation to determine what measures (including detention) to employ to meet their objectives, and interpreting certain components of Article 5 as requiring only a limited proportionality analysis or none whatsoever to justify detention. These various approaches have served to undermine the general principle that all detention must be exceptional because the ECtHR has not explicitly required that detention be exceptional; all the Court requires is that detention is not arbitrary, which as explained, it has narrowly construed.

The European Court is by no means the only culprit of reductivism. Human rights courts and treaty bodies have had only limited success in clawing back against the tendencies of discrimination, securitisation, and criminalisation that frequently foster arbitrary detention, particularly in those areas of detention perceived to raise the greatest concerns about sovereignty, national identity, and national security. This is because for the most part they perceive their role as procedural and have shied away from clarifying the content of positive obligations in the area of liberty and security of the person. Where the problems lie, however, is mainly in the substance, not in the procedure. Consequently, cases continue to be adjudicated but they are having an increasingly marginal impact on stemming the tide of arbitrary detention. They just assuage the symptoms as opposed to identifying and addressing the why and the how. For the most contentious issues, human rights law risks becoming the apologist, the language and procedure of denial.

Where does this leave us? Having conceptualised arbitrary detention and analysed how the concept is construed, applied and at times, manipulated, the task ahead is to avoid becoming discouraged or destroyed by the weight of the manipulations and to continue to press against the conditions for the emergence of the resort to detention in the first place. As Guenther explains:

> one must not only grasp how it is "wrong" and try to make it "right", one must trace the contingent, yet constitutive structures that normalize the conflation of accountability with punishment – and in order to do this, one must situate oneself in relation to networks of carceral power that promise security and prosperity to some, while exposing others to containment, control, and state violence.[1]

---

[1] Lisa Guenther, 'Six Senses of Critique for Critical Phenomenology' (2021) 4.2 *Puncta: J Crit Phenomenology* 5, 1.6.

Index

References to notes show the page number and the note number (231n3).

A

ACHPR *See* African Charter on Human and Peoples' Rights (ACHPR)
ACHR *See* American Convention on Human Rights (ACHR)
ACommHPR *See* African Commission on Human and Peoples' Rights (ACommHPR)
Acosta Martínez v Argentina 112, 117
ACtHPR *See* African Court on Human and Peoples' Rights (ACtHPR)
Afghanistan 180, 183, 183n49, 190, 198, 202
Afkari, Elham 147
Afkari, Navid 147
African Americans 21, 116
African Charter on Human and Peoples' Rights (ACHPR) 31, 41, 105, 117
African Commission on Human and Peoples' Rights (ACommHPR) 38, 102, 117, 178
African Court on Human and Peoples' Rights (ACtHPR) 24, 104–105, 149
Agamben, Giorgio 86–87, 127, 182–183
Aguilar-Rodríguez, Marcos Antonio 92
Aishan, Yidiresi 171
Aksoy v Turkey 65
Alexander, George 153
Al-Hela v Trump 186
Ali, Ahmed Jaafar Mohamed 171
Al-Jedda v United Kingdom 176n14, 198–199, 200
Al Saadoon v United Kingdom 202
American Convention on Human Rights (ACHR) 27, 31, 41, 176n15
Ameziane, Djamel 76, 206
Angelou, Maya 52
annulment of citizenship 209–210
Anthony, Thalia 89
Arbel, Efrat 123
arbitrariness
 about 10–11, 10n1, 14, 17–18, 35
 of detention 2–3, 34–35, 37–39
 harm caused by 51–55

human rights and 17–19, 25, 28–29, 224–225
 interference (*See* interference, arbitrary)
 and law 14, 50
 moral 15–16, 20
 of power 11, 12–13
 See also detention; non-arbitrariness
arbitrary detention *See* arbitrariness; detention
Arendt, Hannah 67n86, 87, 87n7
Argentina, Acosta Martínez v 112, 117
armed conflict *See* international armed conflicts (IACs); non-international armed conflicts (NIACs)
armed forces *See* forces, multinational
Ashoori, Anooshe 240n150
Ashym, Ardak 152
Assadi, Assadolah 220–221, 243
Assange, Julian 47–48
Assanidze, Tengiz 159
Assanidze v Georgia 235n129
asylum seekers
 arbitrary detention of 39, 72, 73, 133–134
 criminalisation of 127–128
 discrimination against 92
 harms caused by detention 56–57, 59
 mandatory detention of 97
 positive obligations towards 43
Aust, Anthony 227
Austin v United Kingdom 165–166
Australia 53, 54n15, 56–57, 97, 121–122
Australia, A v 40, 42
Australia, Leo v 108–109, 110
Australia, Toonen v 28–29, 124, 124n207
A v Australia 40, 42
A v United Kingdom 37, 177n18, 178n27

B

Bae, Kenneth 216
balancing (of rights) 26–28, 26n96, 27n97, 29–30, 245

banal acts 67, 67n86, 78n141, 80
El-Baqer, Mohammed 144
Basu v Germany 118–119
Bauer, Michael 61
Begum, Shamima 209–210
behaviour
  criminalisation of 88–89, 142
  detention to control / punish 85, 101, 103, 123–125, 153–154
  pathologisation of 93–94, 135, 153
Belgium 220–221, 242–243
Belgium, Bouyid v 69
Bianku (Judge) 134
Bigo, Didier 143
biopolitics 86, 87
Blagg, Harry 89
Bonnie, Richard 151
Boochani, Behrouz 52
borders 20, 55, 87, 96–97, 126–127, 133–134, 135, 170–171
Bourdieu, Pierre 12, 23, 28, 50
Bout, Viktor 220
Bouyid v Belgium 69
Brigade *See* United Nations Stabilization Mission in the Democratic Republic of Congo (MONUSCO)
Brinkmann, Svend 93
Brunson, Andrew 216, 217, 221n43
Bull, Melissa 57
Burgers, Herman 69–70
Burkina Faso, Lohé Issa Konaté v 149
Bush (President) 183
Bush, Rasul v 181, 181n43
Butler, Judith 56, 86–87, 183, 249, 254

C

Cacho Ribeiro, Lydia 150–151
Cakal, Ergün 75
Çalı, Başak 27–28, 27n97, 48, 166, 170
Cameroon, Mukong v 37n156, 168
Canada 57, 122–123, 122n201, 219n30, 232, 242–243
CAT *See* United Nations Committee Against Torture (CAT)
CERD *See* Committee on the Elimination of Racial Discrimination (CERD Committee)
CESCR *See* United Nations (UN) Committee on Economic, Social and Cultural Rights (CESCR)
cessation, obligation of 235–236
Chahal v United Kingdom 133
children
  corporal punishment 77
  COVID-19 pandemic and 255n49, 263, 270, 271
  detention of 208
  harms caused by detention 59–60, 69
  violence against, state responsibility for 75
Chile 141n20, 161
Chile, Norín Catrimán v 121
China
  arbitrary detention by 212, 216, 219n30, 239, 242
  behaviour modification 153
  counter-terrorism legislation 143, 206
Christine Goodwin v United Kingdom 29
citizenship 209–210
class 16, 20, 21, 85
Cleveland, Janet 56, 59, 68
Coffey, Guy 57, 60
Cole, Phillip 20
colonialism 101–102, 119–123, 136, 213n3
Committee on the Elimination of Racial Discrimination (CERD Committee) 115, 120, 120n185
Committee on the Protection of the Rights of All Migrant Workers and Members of Their Families (CPRMW) 36, 36n153, 37n156, 38, 40
'in order to compel' 230–231
concentration camps 87, 97, 179
confinement
  about 9
  consent to 47
  COVID-19 pandemic and 258–259
  forced 125–126
  See also detention
conflicts *See* international armed conflicts (IACs); non-international armed conflicts (NIACs)
conformity 2, 85, 94, 124–125, 152, 278
consent to confinement 47
constitutional law 17, 181
Convention of Belem do Para 30n115
Convention on the Rights of Persons with Disabilities (CRPD) 102, 106, 107, 109–110, 277
Copenhagen Process 202
corporal punishment 77
Costello, Cathryn 131
Coulter, Jeff 93
counter-terrorism
  indefinite detention and 204–207
  legislation 143–144
  transfers of detainees and 201
courts
  African Court on Human and Peoples' Rights (ACtHPR) 24, 104–105, 149
  European Court of Human Rights (*See* European Court of Human Rights (ECtHR))
  Georgian Supreme Court 159
  Inter-American Court of Human Rights (IACtHR) 24, 38, 42, 112, 117, 120–121, 124, 130, 149, 155, 156
  Supreme Court of Canada 122
  UK Supreme Court 198, 199–200

INDEX

United States (US) Supreme Court 21, 158, 181n43
COVID-19 pandemic
  detention during 247–251, 262–265, 274–275
  duty of care during 258–262
  early release during 268–274, 272n140
  lockdowns 1, 245–246, 250
  proportionality test 251–254, 269
  quarantines 253, 254–255, 257–258, 264, 265
  Red List 257–258, 257n63
  rights enforcement during 248–249
  vaccines / treatment access 265–268
CPRMW *See* Committee on the Protection of the Rights of All Migrant Workers and Members of Their Families (CPRMW)
crimes against humanity 45, 45n198, 219, 273–274
criminalisation
  of asylum seekers 127–128
  detention as 88–93
  of dissent 142–150
  otherness and 2, 3, 34
  of people who use drugs 112, 112n140
  of poverty 89, 101–102, 102–105, 104n97
criminal law
  arbitrariness in 17, 17n51, 36
  on arbitrary detention 45, 45n197, 229–230
  behaviours, criminalisation of 89, 142
  detainees 263, 267, 270, 272n140
  detention as deterrence 95–96
  on torture 74n124
CRPD *See* Convention on the Rights of Persons with Disabilities (CRPD)
CRPD Committee *See* United Nations Committee on the Rights of Persons with Disabilities (CRPD Committee)
Cunneen, Chris 122, 123

D

Daes, Erica-Irene 151–152
Da'esh 196, 207–208
Danelius, Hans 70
death penalty 21, 30–31, 77, 202
Declaration Against Arbitrary Detention in State-to-State Relations 232, 243
Declaration on Friendly Relations 233, 234
Demirtaş, Selahattin 159
Demirtaş v Turkey 169, 219–220
derogation 176–178, 176n14–15, 177n18–19, 182, 185, 252
detainees
  COVID-19 pandemic (*See* COVID-19 pandemic)
  experiences of 51–55
  harms caused by detention 56–62
  hopelessness 51, 80, 277
  leverage, used for 212–215
  nationals, foreign and/or dual 212–215, 215–221, 222–223, 224–226, 231–233
  powerlessness 53, 59, 68–69, 70, 87, 260, 277
  release of, negotiating 236–241
  transfer of 200–203
detention
  about 9, 45–49
  arbitrary (*See* arbitrariness)
  behaviour, to control / punish 85, 101, 103, 123–125, 153–154
  confinement 9, 47, 125–126
  COVID-19 pandemic (*See* COVID-19 pandemic)
  as criminalisation 88–93
  Detention Guidelines (UNHCR) 44–45, 128, 128n227, 131
  as deterrence 95–98, 126–134
  discriminatory 39, 72–73, 99–100, 113–126
  dissent and (*See* dissent; dissenters)
  harms caused by 56–62
  house arrest 46, 48–49, 154–155, 182–183, 239, 273–274, 279
  indefinite 53–54, 58n40, 61, 204–207
  for leverage 212–215, 213n3, 222, 228, 229, 232, 236, 239
  non-arbitrariness and 40, 42–44, 175–176
  as pathologisation 93–95
  pre-trial (*See* pre-trial detention)
  purpose of 70–73
  and/as torture 44, 52–55, 64, 110
  See also the "reviled and resented"; the "undeserving"; the "unseen"
Detention Guidelines (UNHCR) 44–45, 128, 128n227, 131
deterrence, detention as 95–98, 126–134
Dicey, AV 13
Diderot, Denis 10
difference principle (Rawls) 15–16, 15n39
disabilities *See* persons with disabilities
discrimination
  COVID-19 pandemic, during 248–251
  detention based on 39, 72–73, 99–100, 113–126
  gender 123–126
  See also the "reviled and resented"; the "undeserving"; the "unseen"
dissent / dissenters
  criminalisation of 142–150
  cross-border persecution of 170–171
  environmental activists 159–163
  isolation of to prevent 154–155
  mass protest movements 163–167
  opposition politicians as 155–159
  pathologisation of 151–154
  targeting of 138–141, 138n8
  tolerance of 137–138

283

Djalali, Ahmad Reza 216
domination, arbitrariness of 12–13
drugs *See* people who use drugs
Dugard, John 240

E

East Germany 61–62
ECHR *See* European Convention on Human Rights (ECHR)
ECtHR *See* European Court of Human Rights (ECtHR)
Ecuador 162
Egypt 143–144
Endicott, Timothy 14
environmental activists 159–163
European Commission on Human Rights 67, 76
European Convention on Human Rights (ECHR)
 on arbitrary deprivation of life 30–31
 on citizenship annulment 209
 derogation clauses 176n15
 on detention 45–46, 131–132, 165, 176, 189, 198–199, 280
 on liberty, right to 129
 on proportionality test 32n126
 on torture 76
 on transfers of detainees 202
European Court of Human Rights (ECtHR)
 on arbitrary detention 37, 41–42, 71n109, 279–280
 on asylum 127
 on citizenship annulment 209
 on derogations 176n14, 178
 on detention 45, 46–47, 132–134, 169–170, 189, 198–200, 220
 on ethnic profiling 117–118
 on qualified rights 33
 on releases 270
 on restricting rights 28
 on right to liberty 159, 165, 260–261
 on right to life 247–248
 on right to privacy and family life 29, 33
 on torture 67–68
 on transfers of detainees 202
 on use of force 30–31
Evans, Malcolm 65
exception
 exigent 175–179
 of law 184–186
 person as 182–184
 of place 179–182
 zones of 3, 86, 87
exclusion, zones of 86, 87, 96, 207–210
expression, freedom of *See* freedom of expression

F

Fahmy, Mohamed 216
fairness, justice as 15

fair trial, right to 39, 44, 100, 217–218, 222, 224–225, 263
family life, right to 28, 29, 33, 208–209, 257
El Fattah, Alaa Abd 144
Fekete, Liz 97
Fernando Principles 121–122
Finland, Hämäläinen v 33n128
force
 excessive 31, 143, 164
 lethal 30–31, 41
forces, multinational 189–197
 See also international armed conflicts (IACs); non-international armed conflicts (NIACs)
Foucault, Michel 85, 87
France 116, 195, 242–243
France, Selmouni v 66
freedom 13
freedom of expression, right to 26, 27, 32, 42, 148–151, 150n73, 159, 163
freedom of movement *See* movement
Friendly Relations Declaration 233, 234
Furman v Georgia 21

G

Gambia, Purohit and Moore v 102
gender
 discrimination 123–126
 rights access / enforcement and 21
 See also women
Geneva Conventions 44, 176n14, 183–184, 184n52, 186–188, 189, 200
Georgia, Assanidze v 235n129
Georgia, Furman v 21
Gerlach, Alice 52, 57
Germany, Basu v 118–119
Gershkovich, Evan 216
Ghaderi, Kamran 224n56
Gilbert, Danielle 219n30, 238n142
Gladkiy v Russia 248
Gladue, Jamie Tanis 122
Gladue, R v 122–123, 122n201
Gopalanachari v State of Kerala 104n96
Gorobet v Moldova 95n55
Greece 67, 76, 91–92
Greek Case 67, 76
Greste, Peter 216
Grey, Anthony 239
Griner, Brittney 220
Grounds, Adrian 61
groups *See* marginalised groups; *specific groups (e.g., asylum seekers, people who use drugs)*
Guantánamo Bay, Cuba 53–54, 54n13, 58n40, 76, 95, 181, 183, 186, 204, 205–206
Guatemala 162
Guenther, Lisa 280
Guiffard, Jonathan 195
Guzzardi v Italy 48

INDEX

H

habeas corpus 177, 181, 205
Habré, Hissène 273
Hämäläinen v Finland 33n128
Hammond (Lord) 240n150
Hammouri, Salah 144
Harper, Phil 214
Hassan v United Kingdom 176n14, 198, 199–200
health, right to 247, 251, 259–260, 261, 265–266
healthcare 22, 208, 209, 260, 261
Hedges, Matthew 216
Hill-Cawthorne, Lawrence 186, 204
homelessness *See* persons who are homeless; the "unseen"
homo sacer 86, 87, 127, 179, 182
Hong Kong 166, 239
Hoodfar, Homa 216
hopelessness 51, 80, 277
Hostages case 37
Hostages Convention 226–228, 230, 231–233, 234, 235
hostage-taking 45, 61, 213, 220–221, 223, 226–233
Hostage-Taking Accountability Act (US) 228–229
house arrest 46, 48–49, 154–155, 182–183, 239, 273–274, 279
Howard League for Penal Reform 269–270
Howell, Alison 95, 95n52
HRW *See* Human Rights Watch (HRW)
human rights
  about 246
  absolute 25n89
  arbitrariness and 17–19, 25, 28–29, 224–225
  asylum, right to seek 127–128
  balancing of 26–28, 26n96, 27n97, 29–30, 245
  defenders 138–139, 138n8, 144–145
  limited 29–31, 41, 50
  obligations (*See* obligations)
  qualified 26–29, 29–30, 32–33, 42n184, 50, 149
  social conception of 21–24
  treaties 25–26, 30–31, 41, 120, 176–177, 201
  violations 21, 23, 44–45
  See also specific rights (e.g., privacy, freedom of expression)
Human Rights Committee (UN) *See* United Nations Human Rights Committee
human rights law
  about 3
  arbitrariness in 17–18
  non-arbitrariness and 25, 29–30, 31, 32, 34
Human Rights Watch (HRW) 113, 272n145
Hungary, Ilias and Ahmed v 132n250, 133–134

I

IACommHR *See* Inter-American Commission on Human Rights (IACommHR)
IACPPT *See* Inter-American Convention to Prevent and Punish Torture (IACPPT)
IACs *See* international armed conflicts (IACs)
IACtHR *See* Inter-American Court of Human Rights (IACtHR)
IASC 259
ICCPR *See* International Covenant on Civil and Political Rights (ICCPR)
ICESCR *See* International Covenant on Economic, Social and Cultural Rights (ICESCR)
ICJ *See* International Court of Justice (ICJ)
ICRC *See* International Committee of the Red Cross (ICRC)
ICTY *See* International Criminal Tribunal for the former Yugoslavia (ICTY)
IHL *See* international humanitarian law (IHL)
ILC 197, 240
Ilias and Ahmed v Hungary 132n250, 133–134
ill-treatment 44, 52, 62–64, 65, 68, 78–79, 110, 150, 191, 201, 247–248, 256
immigrants 39, 73
  See also migrants
indefinite detention *See* detention
indigenous peoples
  criminalisation of 89, 91, 162
  detention of 119–123, 162
  discrimination against 113, 114
  Mapuche people 121, 141n20, 161
'in order to compel' 230–231
Inter-Agency Standing Committee (IASC) 259
Inter-American Commission on Human Rights (IACommHR) 27, 38, 43–44, 53, 76, 106n110, 150n73, 250n30, 260
Inter-American Convention on the Prevention, Punishment and Eradication of Violence against Women 30n115
Inter-American Convention to Prevent and Punish Torture (IACPPT) 64n71, 70, 74n124
Inter-American Court of Human Rights (IACtHR) 24, 38, 42, 112, 117, 120–121, 124, 130, 149, 155, 156
interests, balance of qualified 13, 26–28, 26n96, 27n97, 32, 251, 265
interference, arbitrary 13–14, 18, 25–29, 30n115, 40, 176n15, 209
international armed conflicts (IACs) 174n16, 176, 183, 183n49, 186–187, 189, 190, 200, 204
International Commission of Jurists 125–126
International Committee of the Red Cross (ICRC) 188–189, 198
International Convention Against the Taking of Hostages *See* Hostages Convention

285

International Court of Justice (ICJ) 14, 36–37, 234, 235, 236
International Covenant on Civil and Political Rights (ICCPR)
  on deprivation of liberty 39, 260
  on deprivation of life, arbitrary 17n53, 30n115, 31–32
  derogations 176n15, 178
  on interference, arbitrary 18, 25–26
  prohibition on arbitrary detention 17n54, 40
  on protected grounds 100
  on right to freedom of expression 149
  on right to privacy 124
International Covenant on Economic, Social and Cultural Rights (ICESCR) 26, 247, 253
International Criminal Tribunal for the former Yugoslavia (ICTY) 54, 66, 187n69
International Criminal Tribunal for Rwanda 48–49
International Guidelines on Human Rights and Drugs Policy 111–112
international humanitarian law (IHL) 31–32, 44, 176, 183, 184, 187–188, 191, 194, 198
international law
  on arbitrariness 17
  on arbitrary detention 36n153, 39, 50, 189, 243, 277
  on immigration detention 128–129
  on non-intervention 213–214, 233–236
  on power of detention 199–200
  on protests 164
  on torture 74, 77
International Security Assistance Force (ISAF) 190
Interpol 170–171, 171n212
intersectionality
  of discrimination 72–73, 100
  of injustice 16, 21
Iran 146–147, 153–154, 160, 212, 214–215, 216, 220–221, 221n42, 242n154, 273
Iran Hostages Case 236
Iraq 166, 176n14, 180, 190–191, 199, 202
Ireland 94, 125
Ireland, Johnston et al v 33n128
Ireland v United Kingdom 67, 78n141
Irish Republican Army 30
ISAF 190
Ismail, Nasrul 266–267
isolation 153–154, 237, 242, 249–250, 255, 263, 265
Israel 67n88, 144, 272–273
Italy, Guzzardi v 48

J

Jarrar, Khalida 144
Jensen, Steven 20

Johnston et al v Ireland 33n128
justice
  as fairness 15
  intersectionality of 16, 21

K

Kavala, Osman 145, 145n46
Kavala v Turkey 71n109, 145n46, 169
Këllezi, Blerina 56
Kendall, Sara 24
Kenya 24
kettling 47, 165
KFOR 192–193
Klatt, Matthias 32n126
Korematsu v United States 178–179
Korur Fincanci, Şebnem 145n45
Kosovo 192–193
Kovrig, Michael 216, 219n30, 220, 242
Kozenko, Mikhail 152

L

labels 46–47, 85, 86–87, 104n97, 109, 113, 155, 182–184, 215
Lambert, Christine 98
Lambert, Joseph 227, 230, 232
Lau, Beatrice 238n141
law
  administrative 10n1, 17
  as arbitrary 3, 14
  constitutional 17, 181
  of contracts 17
  criminal (*See* criminal law)
  decolonisation of 122–123
  exception of 184–186
  human rights law (*See* human rights law)
  IHL (*See* international humanitarian law (IHL))
  international (*See* international law)
  rule of law (*See* rule of law)
  vagrancy laws 101–102, 104–105
lawful sanctions 77–78
Lawrence, Stephen 91
Leo v Australia 108–109, 110
Le Rond d'Alembert, Jean 10
lethal force 30–31, 41
leverage, detention for 212–215, 213n3, 222, 228, 229, 232, 236, 239
Levinson, Robert 228
liberty and security of the person, right to 35, 40, 42, 45, 95, 107, 129, 176n14, 189, 225–226, 251–254, 278–280
Libya 194–195
Liebrenz, Michael 267
life, right to 29–31, 30n115, 34, 41, 246, 247–248, 251, 265–266
limited rights 29–31, 41, 50
  See also human rights
Linconao Huircapán, Francisca 161
lockdowns *See* COVID-19 pandemic
Locke, John 13

Lohé Issa Konaté v Burkina Faso 149
Lovett, Frank 13, 14

M

Madrigal-Borloz, Victor 124–125
Maduro (President) 158
Mahsa Amini, Jina 125, 153–154, 166
Mali 195
Malta, Ramadan v 209
Mandela, Nelson 156
Mandela Rules 259, 261, 267
Mansour, Ahmed 171
Mapuche people 121, 141n20, 161
marginalised groups
 criminalisation of 89–91
 human rights and 17–19
 pre-trial detention and 43–44, 100, 104, 111–112, 115, 116–117, 121
 See also the "reviled and resented"; the "undeserving"; the "unseen"
Mark, Chi-Kwan 239
mass protests *See* protests
Mavronicola, Natasa 68–69
Maya Evans v Secretary of State for Defence 202
Mayr, Lotta 91–92
McCann, Farrell, and Savage v United Kingdom 30
Melzer, Nils 51, 53
men 125
Méndez, Juan 53–54, 54n13, 110
Meng, Wanzhou 219n30, 220
mental health
 facilities, involuntary commitment to 106–110
 harms caused by detention 56–62
 pathologisation of 93–95
migrants
 arbitrary detention of 40, 53, 98n70, 195
 consent to confinement 47
 COVID-19 and 256, 267–268, 271
 criminalisation of 90
 deterrence, detention as 96–97, 126–134
 prohibition of arbitrary detention 36–38, 36n153
 smugglers / smuggling 91, 92, 97–98, 126, 128n224
 women 52
Mingazov, Ravil 190
Ministry of Defence, Mohammed v 198–199
Minkowitz, Tina 109
MINUSMA 195
Mohammed v Ministry of Defence 198–199
Moldova, Gorobet v 95n55
Moncrieff, Joanna 93
MONUSCO 193–194
Moore-Gilbert, Kylie 216
motives 167–170
Mouffe, Chantal 16
movement
 freedom of 9, 117–118

restriction of 45–46, 49, 126, 126n220, 140–141, 155, 253–254
Muhammad v Spain 118, 119
Mukong v Cameroon 37n156, 168

N

nationals (foreign / dual) 212–215, 215–221, 222–223, 224–226, 231–233
NATO (North Atlantic Treaty Organization) 180, 192–193
Nauru detention facility 54n15, 59
Neal, Andrew 173–174
necessity ("absolutely necessary") 30–31, 41–42, 176, 176n15, 187, 187n69, 200, 205
negative obligations *See* obligations
NIACs *See* non-international armed conflicts (NIACs)
Ní Aoláin, Fionnuala 201, 207, 208
Nicaragua, Zelaya Blanco v 167–168
Nicaragua v USA 234
Niger 48–49, 279
Nigeria, Njemanze v 104n97
Njemanze v Nigeria 104n97
non-arbitrariness
 detention and 40, 42–44, 175–176
 human rights and 25, 29–30, 31, 32, 34
 rule of law and 13–14, 14n32, 185
 See also arbitrariness
non-domination 13
 See also domination
non-international armed conflicts (NIACs) 174–175, 176n14, 180, 183n49, 184, 186–188, 189–190, 197–198, 200, 201–202, 208
non-intervention 213, 233–236, 237–238
non-refoulement 79, 200–201, 200n149, 202, 203n166, 205n178
Nordgren, Loran 64n70, 66
Norín Catrimán v Chile 121
normalisation
 of arbitrary detention 2–3, 50, 78, 210, 226, 277, 279–280
 social 78
North Atlantic Treaty Organization (NATO) 180, 192–193
Nottebohm Case 231
Nowak, Manfred 68, 69

O

obligations
 negative 32, 33
 positive 32–34, 32n126, 42–44, 102, 118–119, 246–250, 258–262, 274–276, 279–280
Office of the United Nations High Commissioner of Human Rights (OHCHR) 249, 266
Ogiek community 24

Oman 221, 243
opposition politicians 155–159
otherness / othering
  arbitrariness and 2, 3, 34, 99, 132
  fear, based on 127
  human rights and 19
  labels and 85, 182–184
  pain and, infliction of 114
  targeting of 2
Otto, Dianne 174

P

PACE 116
Pakistan 144, 190
Palestine 144, 273
Palestinian hanging 65n77
Panama, Vélez Loor v 128n225, 130
pandemic *See* COVID-19 pandemic
Parliamentary Assembly of the Council of Europe (PACE) 116
Pasko, Grigory 145
Passeron, Jean-Claude 12, 23, 50
pathologisation 93–95, 135, 151–154
Pavlensky, Pyotr 152
Pavli (Judge) 119
peaceful assembly, right to 33, 162, 164
peace operations (UN) 191–192, 193, 195
Penal Reform International 265
people who use drugs 72–73, 90, 94, 111–113, 112n140, 135, 278
Pérez-Sales, Pau 62–63
Persian World Heritage Foundation 160
'any person' 227
persons who are homeless 102–105, 256
persons with disabilities 91, 255n49
persons with mental health disabilities 105–110
Peru 121
Pettit, Phillip 13
Pickering, Sharon 98
place, exception of 179–182
Pogge, Thomas 20
political prisoners 62, 156, 273
Pollard, Matt 74
Polubinskaya, Svetlana 151
positive obligations *See* obligations
poverty, criminalisation of 89, 101–102, 102–105, 104n97
power
  abuses of 2
  arbitrary exercise of 11, 12–13, 14, 19
powerlessness 53, 59, 68–69, 70, 87, 260, 277
pre-trial detention
  COVID-19 pandemic, during 269–270, 277
  as deterrence 95
  of dissenters 146, 157
  of marginalized groups 43–44, 100, 104, 111–112, 115, 116–117, 121

obligations, states' positive 43–44
  of smugglers 91–92
Principles of Medical Ethics, United Nations 259
prisoners of war 62, 187, 188–189, 204, 208
privacy, right to 18, 26, 28–29, 32, 33, 42, 104n97, 124, 124n207
profiling (ethnic, racial) 71, 116, 117–118
prohibition
  of arbitrary detention 36–38, 36n153, 40, 50, 167
  of refoulement 79, 200–202, 200n149, 208
  of torture 25n89
proportionality analysis (test) 30, 32, 32n126, 34, 40, 46–47, 50, 251–254, 269, 280
protests 163–167
psychiatry 151–154
PTSD (post-traumatic stress disorder) 56, 58, 59, 60, 62, 68
Pūras, Dainius 109
Purohit and Moore v Gambia 102
purpose of torture 69–73
Pussy Riot 152

Q

qualified rights 26–29, 29–30, 32–33, 42n184, 50, 149
  See also human rights
quarantines 253, 254–255, 257–258, 264, 265
  See also COVID-19 pandemic

R

race
  profiling 71, 116, 117–118
  rights access / enforcement and 21
racism 87, 99–100, 113–119, 127
Radwan, Mohammed Ibrahim 144
Ramadan v Malta 209
randomness 2, 11–12, 72, 278
rape 66, 124, 138n6
Rasul v Bush 181, 181n43
Ratcliffe, Richard 215, 240n150
Rawls, John 15–16, 15n39, 20, 22
Red List 257–258, 257n63
REDRESS xiii, 1
re-education 111, 153–154, 206–207
refoulement *See* non-refoulement
Refugee Convention 44, 73n116, 127–128
refugees
  arbitrary detention of 39, 44–45, 53, 73n116, 98n70
  consent to confinement 47
  criminalisation of 90
  deterrence, detention as 96–97, 126–134
  harms caused by detention 60
Registrar of the International Residual Mechanism for Criminal Tribunals 48–49

INDEX

release
  early 268–274, 272n140
  negotiations 236–241
religion 114–119
Requesens, Juan 158–159
Residual Mechanism 48–49
the "reviled and resented"
  about 3, 99, 113
  advocates for, targeting of 139
  gender or gender roles 123–126
  identity, racial, ethnic, or religious 114–119
  See also indigenous peoples
Rezaian, Jason 216, 220, 221n41, 222
rights
  absolute 25n89
  procedural 23, 236
  See also human rights
Ringelheim, Julie 119
Rivas, Lorena 57
Robben Island 156
Robert Levinson Hostage Recovery and Hostage-Taking Accountability Act 222, 228
Rodley, Nigel 74, 77–78
Rojas Marín, Azul 124
rule of law, non-arbitrariness and 13–14, 14n32, 185
Russia 144–145, 152, 195, 212, 216
Russia, Gladkiy v 248
Russia, Usmanov v 209
R v Gladue 122–123, 122n201
R v Sharma 122n201
Rwanda 48–49, 196–197, 279

S

Saadi v United Kingdom 73, 132, 134
SAGE values framework (WHO) 266
sanitisation 102, 114
Saro-Wiwa, Ken 159–160
Saucier, Roxanne 111
Scarry, Elaine 113–114
Schmidtz, David 11
SDF *See* Syrian Defence Forces (SDF)
Secretary of State for Defence, Maya Evans v 202
securitisation
  of detention 174, 175–176
  of dissent 142–147
  otherness and 2, 3, 34
Security Council *See* United Nations Security Council (UNSC)
self-harm 59, 263
Selmouni v France 66
sentencing
  Fernando Principles 121–122
  nationals (foreign / dual) 217, 221n39
  options 122–123
Sepúlveda Carmona, Magdalena 103
severity 64–69
sexual orientation 123–126

Seyed-Emami, Kavous 160
Sharma, R v 122n201
Silove, Derrick 56–57
SLAPPs 140
smugglers / smuggling 91, 92, 97–98, 126, 128n224
Snell, James 61, 214–215
social conception of rights 21–24
Sombatpoonsiri, Janjira 147
South Africa 22, 156, 179, 267n114
Spain, Muhammad v 118, 119
Spavor, Michael 216, 219n30, 220, 242
Special Envoy for Hostage Affairs (SPEHA) 222, 230, 241
Special Rapporteur *See* United Nations (UN) Special Rapporteur
special stigma (of torture) 65, 78–79, 78n141
SPEHA *See* Special Envoy for Hostage Affairs (SPEHA)
Standard Minimum Rules for the Treatment of Prisoners 77
Standard Operating Procedure (UN peace operations) 191–192
states
  arbitrariness and 17
  nationals, detention of foreign / dual 212–215, 215–221, 222–223, 231–233
  non-intervention 233–236, 237–238
  obligations of 32–34, 32n126, 42–44, 102, 118–119, 246–250, 258–262, 274–276, 279–280
  release of detainees, negotiating 236–241
  torture, involvement in 74–76
Stoyanova, Vladislava 33
strategic lawsuits against public participation (SLAPPs) 140
subjecthood 19–20, 113
Sudan 166–167
suicide 59, 95, 95n52, 160, 256, 263
Sultan, Aamer 58
Sumption (Lord) 199
suppression 113
surveillance 46, 140
Switzerland 237n140
Syria 196, 207, 208
Syrian Defence Forces (SDF) 196, 207, 208

T

Taner Kiliç v Turkey 145
Tauri, Juan 122, 123
Tejada, Daniela 240n150
terrorism
  about 143–144
  counter-terrorism 201, 204–207
  dissent as 145–147
  terrorist as label 182–184
Thailand 147
Thành, Bui Kim 152
Theu, Can Thi 164–165

289

Tình, Nguyên Năng 163
Toonen v Australia 28–29, 124, 124n207
torture
  about 62–63, 65n77
  arbitrary detention and / as 44, 52–55, 64, 110
  lawful sanctions and 77–78
  non-refoulement to 200–203, 205n178
  prohibition of 25n89
  purpose of 69–73
  severity and 64–69
  special stigma 65, 78–79, 78n141
  state involvement 74–76
  survivors of 1
torturing environments 62–63
transfer of detainees 200–203
treaties
  arbitrariness in 10, 17–18, 30–32, 176n15
  human rights 25–26, 41, 120, 176–177, 201
troops See forces, multinational
Trump, Al-Hela v 186
Tsampi, Aikaterini 170
Turgunov, Akzam 168
Turkey 145, 147, 159, 169, 196, 216, 221n43, 272
Turkey, Aksoy v 65
Turkey, Demirtaş v 169, 219–220
Turkey, Kavala v 71n109, 145n46, 169
Turkey, Taner Kiliç v 145

U

UDHR See Universal Declaration of Human Rights (UDHR)
Uganda 163
Ukraine 177n19, 179
Umerov, Ilmi 152
UNCAT See United Nations Convention Against Torture (UNCAT)
uncertainty 51, 58, 58n40, 63
the "undeserving"
  about 3, 99
  administrative detention of 126–134
  advocates for, targeting of 139
  See also asylum seekers; migrants; refugees
UNHCR See United Nations High Commissioner for Refugees (UNHCR)
United Kingdom, Al-Jedda v 176n14, 198–199, 200
United Kingdom, Al Saadoon v 202
United Kingdom, Austin v 165–166
United Kingdom, A v 37, 177n18, 178n27
United Kingdom, Chahal v 133
United Kingdom, Christine Goodwin v 29
United Kingdom, Hassan v 176n14, 198, 199–200
United Kingdom, Ireland v 67, 78n141
United Kingdom, McCann, Farrell, and Savage v 30
United Kingdom, Saadi v 73, 132, 134
United Kingdom Supreme Court 198, 199–200
United Nations Body of Principles for the Protection of All Persons under Any Form of Detention or Imprisonment 36
United Nations Commission on Human Rights 35–36
United Nations Committee Against Torture (CAT) 67n88, 68, 75, 77, 79, 144
United Nations Committee on Economic, Social and Cultural Rights (CESCR) 26, 253–254, 259–260, 262
United Nations Committee on the Rights of Persons with Disabilities (CRPD Committee) 72, 107–108, 110
United Nations Convention Against Torture (UNCAT) 53, 63, 64, 64n71, 69–70, 74, 77–79
United Nations High Commissioner for Refugees (UNHCR) 44–45, 128
United Nations Human Rights Committee
  on arbitrariness 129–130, 167–168
  on deprivation of life, arbitrary 21, 31, 34
  on derogations 177
  on detention, arbitrary 37–38, 40, 130–131, 176, 193
  on interference, arbitrary 25–26
  on principle of necessity 42
  prohibition on arbitrary detention 36
  on racial profiling 117
  on right to freedom of expression 150–151
  on right to liberty 260
  on right to life 247, 248
  on right to privacy 28–29, 124, 124n207
  on security detention 200
United Nations Interim Administration Mission in Kosovo (UNMIK) 192–193, 192n106
United Nations Multidimensional Integrated Stabilization Mission in Mali (MINUSMA) 195
United Nations Office on Drugs and Crime (UNODC) 97–98
United Nations peace operations 191–192
United Nations Principles of Medical Ethics 259
United Nations Security Council (UNSC) 49, 188, 191, 192, 194, 197–200
United Nations Special Rapporteur
  on the Human Rights Situation in Iran 273
  on Migrants 41, 90, 256, 267–268
  on the Promotion and Protection of Human Rights 201, 206–207, 208
  on the Promotion of Truth, Reparation and Guarantees of Non-Recurrence 274
  on the Rights of Indigenous Persons 120
  on the Right to Health 109–110, 112n140

INDEX

on the Situation of Human Rights
  Defenders 161–162
on Torture 51, 53, 68, 77–78, 110, 138n6
of UN Sub-Commission 151
United Nations Stabilization Mission in
  the Democratic Republic of Congo
  (MONUSCO) 193–194
United Nations Working Group on Arbitrary
  Detention (WGAD)
  on arbitrary detention 39, 41–42, 72–73,
    92, 100, 115–116, 120, 124, 125, 168
  cessation, on obligation of 235–236
  on detention 45–46, 47–48, 78
  on dissent 138–139, 144–145, 148, 150,
    164–165
  on drug treatment 94
  on indefinite detention 204–205
  nationals (foreign / dual), on detention
    of 217, 218–219, 242n154
  prohibition on arbitrary
    detention 36, 108n17
  on releases 270, 271
  on right to liberty 255, 263, 264
  on torture, detention as 54
United States (US)
  asylum seekers 92
  death penalty 21
  and Guantánamo Bay 95, 204–206
  on hostage-taking 228–230
  racial disparities in 116
  Supreme Court 21, 158, 181n43
  war on terror 66, 179, 180, 183–184, 186
United States, Korematsu v 178–179
Universal Declaration of Human Rights
  (UDHR) 25, 35, 37, 39, 78
UNMIK 192–193, 192n106
UNODC *See* United Nations Office on
  Drugs and Crime (UNODC)
UNSC *See* United Nations Security Council
  (UNSC)
the "unseen"
  about 2–3, 99, 101–102
  advocates for, targeting of 139
  arbitrary detention of 135, 278
  COVID-19 and 246, 256, 275
  people who use drugs 72–73, 90, 94,
    111–113, 112n140, 135, 278
  persons who are homeless 102–105, 256
  persons with mental health
    disabilities 105–110
Upper Silesia 15, 20
Urlaeva, Elena 152
USA, Nicaragua v 234
Usmanov v Russia 209
Usón Ramírez v Venezuela 149

V

vaccines 265–268
  See also COVID-19 pandemic

vagrancy laws 101–102, 104–105
Vandecasteele, Olivier 216, 221, 221n39,
  242–243
Vargas, Manuel Cepeda 155–156
VCCR *See* Vienna Convention on Consular
  Relations (VCCR)
Vélez Loor v Panama 128n225, 130
Venezuela 158
Venezuela, Usón Ramírez v 149
Verdirame, Guglielmo 29–30
victimhood 23–24
Vienna Convention on Consular Relations
  (VCCR) 234, 236
Vietnam 152, 163, 164–165
violations of human rights 21, 23, 44–45
Virchow, Rudolf 15–16, 20
von Werthern, Martha 60
vulnerable persons 43, 127, 245–246

W

Waldron, Jeremy 14
Wang, Xiyue 216
Warmbier, Otto 216
war on terror (US) 66, 179, 180, 183–184, 186
Waxman, Matthew 190
WGAD *See* United Nations (UN)
  Working Group on Arbitrary
  Detention (WGAD)
WHO 266, 268
Willis, Stacey 62
Winkler, Julia 91–92
Wohlfahrt, Stéphane 193
Wolfe, Daniel 111
women
  detainees 57, 273
  detention of 208
  gender discrimination 123–126
  human rights defenders 138–139, 138n8
  migrants 52
  pathologisation of 94
  violence against, state responsibility
    for 74n124, 75
World Conference against Racism, Racial
  Discrimination, Xenophobia and Related
  Intolerance 114
World Health Organization
  (WHO) 266, 268
World Organization Against Torture
  (OMCT) 270, 274
Wright, R. George 10n1

X

xenophobia 73, 85, 99–100, 113–119, 127

Y

Yamin, Alicia Ely 22
Yogyakarta Principles 124, 124n207
Yorm Bopha Case 168
Young, Iris Marion 99, 136

Z

Zach, Gerrit 70
Zaghari-Ratcliffe, Nazanin 61, 214–215, 216, 228, 240n150
Zelaya Blanco, Robert 168
Zelaya Blanco v Nicaragua 167–168
zones
 of exception 3, 86, 87
 of exclusion 86, 87, 96, 207–210
Zubaydah, Abu 204–205

Printed and bound by CPI Group (UK) Ltd, Croydon, CR0 4YY
18/06/2024